HOSPITALITY MANAGEMENT

An Introduction
2nd edition

TIM KNOWLES

Senior Lecturer in Hospitality Management
Department of Tourism and Leisure
Luton Business School

 LONGMAN

Pearson Education Limited
Edinburgh Gate
Harlow
Essex CM20 2JE
United Kingdom
and Associated Companies throughout the world

Published in the United States of America
by Addison Wesley Longman, New York

501 199851 ,

First edition published 1994
Reprinted 1996
This edition 1998
Reprinted 1998, 2001

ISBN 0 582 31271 X

British Library Cataloguing-in-Publication Data
A catalogue record for this book is available from the British Library

Library of Congress Cataloging-in-Publication Data
A catalog record for this book is available from the Library of Congress

Set by 3 in 9½/12pt Garamond
Produced by Pearson Education Asia Pte Ltd
Printed in Singapore (COS)

Contents

CHAPTER SEVEN *Legislation* 169

CHAPTER EIGHT *Restaurant and fast food industry* 194

Foreword

The UK hospitality industry's leading trade association the British Hospitality Association (BHA) has always recognised the wide diversity of sector groups within the industry. For the first time this broad church of sector interests is considered within one introductory book.

Along with a detailed analysis of the hotel industry, the book's consideration of the accommodation industry is expanded to cover other sectors such as timeshare, and camping and caravanning.

The brewing industry's links with the hotel, catering and leisure markets have been established since the 1960s, a point explored in Chapter 10. Many of the BHA's members work within the contract catering industry, now more commonly referred to as food service management, a sector which is also discussed.

This text is based on the author's wide experience of the hospitality industry and his lectureship experience at both undergraduate and postgraduate level will provide a good introduction to students of the industry. Equally managers already pursuing their career will find this book a useful reminder of the industry's structure and trends in the late 1990s.

The hospitality industry should be regarded as the core to the success of the UK economy. This comprehensive and cohesive book should make a positive contribution to the knowledge of both managers and potential managers in the industry.

Jeremy Logie FHCIMA
Chief Executive
British Hospitality Association

Preface

The hospitality industry is both national and international in nature, and in terms of accommodation it ranges from luxury hotels to budget guest houses, from city centre business properties to tourism resorts, and from motels to health spas. In the wider context timeshare, caravanning and camping should be considered a part of the industry.

The provision of accommodation, food and beverage services away from home form a substantial part of the activities of the hotel and catering industry. Such services vary in both size and diversity.

Looking to the wider picture, a large proportion of the hospitality industry can be set within the context of tourism. The tourism industry contains numerous subsets; many such as tour operators, travel agents, airlines and the wider leisure industry will be referred to within this book. It is these subsets and many more that make up the tourism industry, and provide an important link with accommodation and catering services. Allied to the tourism industry are a number of organisations that influence its running. Within the UK, some organisations are government linked such as the British Tourist Authority, responsible for marketing the UK as a tourist destination abroad.

The objective of this book is to draw all elements of the hospitality industry into one text, with an introductory chapter that discusses the tourism industry. In addition, it devotes chapters to the contract catering industry, the brewing industry and the leisure industry. For the first time these subjects are made readily accessible to the student.

It is hoped that the late 1990s will see a widening of hospitality courses, beyond just hotel and catering, and therefore demonstrate the diversity of the hospitality industry as illustrated by the numerous international case studies contained within this book.

This text is aimed principally at undergraduate degree students and while it is most appropriate to UK courses, it will also have direct relevance to English-speaking European hotels schools. Managers in the hospitality industry will find this book a useful addition to their personal library as it will give them an appreciation of the wider industry in which they work.

At the beginning of each chapter clear objectives are set for the reader and the chapters end with a summary of key points. As this is an introductory text, the reader is encouraged to follow up the extensive further reading at the end of each chapter. It is in this sense that the book should be regarded as a springboard for the student or manager to read the many excellent specialist textbooks available. This introduction to the hospitality industry concludes with a chapter on trends and developments, expected through to the year 2010.

Structure

This book aims to fill a gap in the range of academic textbooks available for the student. While there are numerous specialist textbooks and research papers on the hospitality industry, some are not readily accessible in most libraries and others are very expensive to purchase. The book draws on internal industry data in order to give an insight into some of the actual practices by including a number of detailed case studies, drawn from international sources.

This book is presented in twelve chapters and covers all elements of the industry from tourism and travel, through accommodation and hotel management, to the restaurant and fast food industry. It should be regarded as a first point of reference to students taking a degree in hotel and catering administration or a related subject within the wider tourism field.

Timothy Knowles
October 1997

Acknowledgements

A considerable amount of assistance was given to me in the preparation of this book. I would like to express my appreciation to all my colleagues within the Department of Tourism and Leisure, Luton Business School, University of Luton, and my friends at the International Centre for Tourism and Hospitality Research, University of Bournemouth. In addition I would like to extend my thanks to Dr Dimitrios Buhalis, Prof Chris Cooper, Simon Curtis, Patricia Daniels, Prof Graham Dann, Prof John Fletcher, Melvyn Gold, Peter Grabowski, Jonathon Langston, Jeremy Logie, Sebastian Macmillan, Stuart May, Enzo Paci, Jason Palmer, Dr Steven Pettitt, Paul Slattery, Leonor Stanton, Tim Steel, Judi Waldman, Graham Wason, John Westlake.

From industry I would like to acknowledge the support of Arthur Andersen Consulting, BDO Hospitality Consulting, British Hospitality Association, British Tourist Authority, Deloitte and Touche Management Consultants, Eclipse Research Consultants, Economist Intelligence Unit, Holiday Inn, Horwath International, Hotel and Catering International Management Association, Klienwort Benson Securities, Pannell Kerr Forster Associates, Resorts Condominium International, Travel and Tourism Analyst, World Tourism Organisation, World Travel and Tourism Council.

The case study on Spanish resorts in Chapter 1 was jointly written with Simon Curtis, Tourism Development Manager, East Kent Initiative. The case study in Chapter 12 on environmental initiatives in London Hotels was jointly written with Sebastian Macmillan, University of Cambridge, and Jason Palmer, Eclipse Research Consultants. The case study in Chapter 12 on THISCO was written with the assistance of Dr Dimitrios Buhalis, University of Westminster.

The figures and tables and some adapted commentary contained within Chapter 9 are reproduced from the British Hospitality Association's *Contract Catering Survey 1997* with kind permission of the Association.

Chapter One

The Hospitality Industry: its Links with Tourism, Travel and Leisure

Objectives

After reading this chapter you should be able to

- Relate the hospitality industry to the larger market of tourism, travel and leisure.
- Recognise the integral part that hospitality plays in the provision of services.
- Consider the national and international political, economic, social and technological factors influencing the hospitality industry
- Identify different markets by size and structure, and recognise common factors.

Tourism and hospitality

Definition of tourism

The boundaries between tourism, travel, leisure and accommodation are not easy to define since they blend into or overlap with each other.

A general definition of tourism, adapted from the United Nation's tourism policy-making body the World Tourism Organisation (WTO), should include these four points:

- Tourism involves the movement of people from one location to another outside their own community.
- Tourism destinations provide a range of activities, experiences and facilities.
- The different needs and motivations of the tourist require satisfying and these in turn create a social impact.
- The tourism industry includes a number of subsets which as a whole generate income within the economy.

From the perspective of the hospitality industry the key issue within this definition is that people at tourist destinations demand a range of activities, experiences and facilities. The provision of accommodation, food and drink is a key ingredient within the tourism industry. Equally the desired transport mode plays a central part in travelling to the tourist destination; indeed with cruise liners for instance, transportation, accommodation, food and drink are combined. Tourism is, in addition, defined to include travel on business as well as for leisure purposes, along with another category known as visiting friends and relatives (VFR).

Figure 1.1 relates two fundamental aspects of supply and demand, inasmuch as it identifies

Figure 1.1
Accommodation,
food and drink:
links with tourism

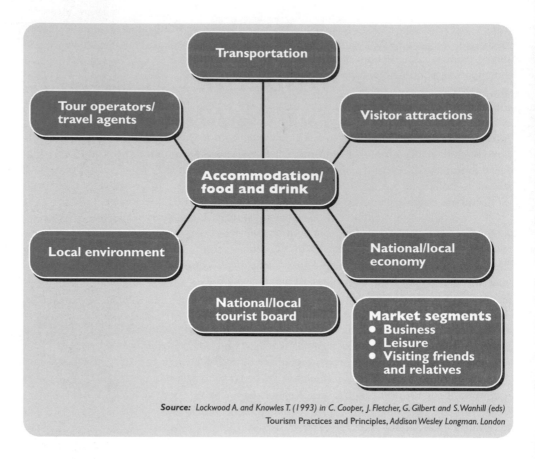

Source: Lockwood A. and Knowles T. (1993) in C. Cooper, J. Fletcher, G. Gilbert and S. Wanhill (eds)
Tourism Practices and Principles, Addison Wesley Longman. London

the supply sectors of the tourism industry and relates them to demand for those facilities and services. The term used in Figure 1.1 is accommodation, which reflects that in the hospitality industry a number of categories can be identified such as hotels, timeshare, caravanning and camping, cruise liners, etc. This figure also introduces the concept of market segmentation, with the three main ones being business, leisure and VFR. Further divisions can be made within these three categories such as conferences and incentive travel.

On arrival at the destination, demand for accommodation is made up from two areas:

● residents of the country travelling within it (domestic tourism)
● visitors to the country (foreign tourism).

This general definition can be followed up with a number of more specific market definitions. Two such market definitions are tourists and excursionists. **Tourists** are defined as visitors who spend at least one night in the country visited or (in the case of those taking domestic trips) those who spend at least one night away from home. **Excursionists** consist of day visitors and cruise visitors who return to their home or other location, such as ship or train to sleep. In terms of categories of tourism the WTO uses the term **leisure tourism** to include the taking of holidays, visiting friends and relatives and visiting for the purposes of engaging in sporting or cultural activities. **Professional tourism** includes visits made for the purpose of attending a meeting, conference or exhibition or for any other business purpose. **Other tourism** not classified as either leisure or business tourism includes visits made for such purposes as education or medical treatment.

Link between tourism and the hospitality industry

While the term **hospitality** is a frequently used title for different sectors of the hotel and catering industry, the term can also be expanded to cover all products and services offered to the consumer away from home including travel, lodging, eating, entertainment, recreation and gaming. Such an expansion of the term hospitality provides the link with tourism in so far as it provides a range of activities, facilities and experiences. However, the hospitality industry can include not only the commercial or profit sectors where payment is made directly by the customer but also the cost or non-profit sector where payment is made indirectly (an example outside the tourism industry but part of hospitality is contract catering). While there is a clear overlap with tourism, the hospitality industry consists of all those business operations which provide for their customers any combination of the three core services of food, drink and accommodation. This means that there are a number of elements of the hospitality industry that are quite separate from tourism, examples being restaurants and public houses that principally attract the local community. These sectors of the hospitality industry are considered in Chapters 8 and 10. All the sectors of the hospitality industry are illustrated in Figure 1.2.

Difference between products and services

Hospitality consists of a complex blend of tangible and intangible elements of both products – food, drink and accommodation – and the service, atmosphere and image that surrounds them. While it is quite common to talk in terms of the hotel product, Figure 1.3 illustrates that hospitality is actually a combination of both product and service that is tangible and intangible.

Services can be described as deeds, processes and performances, and the implication

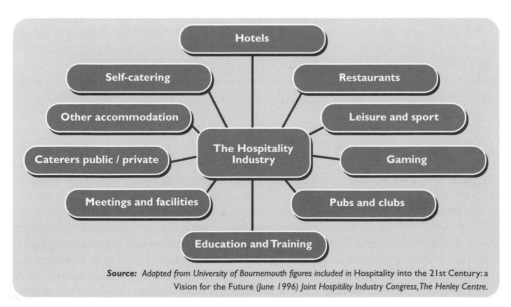

Figure 1.2 The hospitality industry

Source: *Adapted from University of Bournemouth figures included in* Hospitality into the 21st Century: a Vision for the Future *(June 1996) Joint Hospitility Industry Congress, The Henley Centre.*

Figure 1.3 The
hospitality product /
service mix

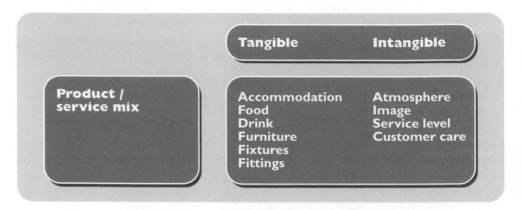

from Figure 1.3 is that services not only are produced by service businesses but also are integral to many manufactured goods producers. Figure 1.3 shows how the hospitality industry can be set within a tangibility spectrum. The term **services** implies intangibility and **product** implies tangibility; however there are no pure products or services but a spectrum reflected within Figure 1.3. It is important to recognise that there are differences between the management of services and products and this is reflected within the hospitality industry. The result of these differences is that

- services cannot be inventorised
- services cannot be readily displayed or communicated
- pricing is difficult and complex
- customer satisfaction depends on employee action
- difficulties arise in synchronising supply and demand of services.

The hospitality industry displays many of the characteristics of service industries in general but with the added complication of a production element, and it is this production side of hospitality that is far from straightforward. The need to provide the appropriate environment within which hospitality can be delivered means that most hospitality businesses need a substantial investment in premises and plant. This creates a high fixed-cost /low variable-cost structure. The variable cost in servicing a room is minimal although the hotel itself, particularly in the luxury market, has a high fixed cost. In general the financial break-even point for hospitality businesses will be quite high. Exceeding this level will result in high profits, but low volumes will result in substantial losses. This cost structure has implications for decisions on pricing, an issue that will be discussed in Chapter 5. Hospitality services suffer from fluctuations in demand. Demand will fluctuate over time, by departmental function, and by type of customer. The result is a mixture of patterns which makes forecasting and the unit's subsequent resource scheduling (both staff and stock) very difficult.

Hospitality cannot be delivered without the presence of the customer, who is directly involved in many aspects of the delivery of the hospitality service, and their combination determines the demand pattern for the operation. The customer is the final arbiter of satisfaction with both the service and product elements and therefore the judge of the quality of hospitality provided. Such comments inevitably place a focus on quality assurance and total quality management, matters considered in Chapter 12.

Achieving a satisfactory balance between demand patterns, resource scheduling and operational capacity is one of the most difficult tasks facing hospitality managers.

Managing customer demand to result in the optimum volume at maximum value is extremely complex. Too few customers overall and the cost structure of the business ensures financial ruin. Too many customers without the required capacity or resources and the quality of the experience suffers leaving customers dissatisfied.

Scheduling of resources is also critical. Too many staff on duty to cover anticipated demand and productivity, and profitability suffers. Too few staff on duty and service levels fall, along with staff morale. The key here would seem to be effective forecasting of demand levels.

To consistently deliver an appropriate level of product and service to each individual customer requires the efforts of many different teams of staff (both operational and back of house) who must be co-ordinated to deliver an acceptable standard every time. Catering for the needs of a single customer may be difficult enough but catering to the needs of many different groups of customers all with slightly different requirements multiplies the complexity of the problem. The importance of a co-ordinated team effort between the different functional groups of employees is self-evident.

In the final analysis the success of any customer experience will be determined by the interaction between the customer and the service provider. The point of contact between the customer and service provider is also an opportunity for the operation to sell its service and to generate additional revenue. From this analysis, it is possible to identify four characteristics which guide any discussion of the hospitality industry.

First, hospitality cannot be delivered without the presence of the customer, who also provides the source of revenue for the continued financial success of the operation. The customer is directly involved in many aspects of the delivery of the hospitality service, and is therefore the judge of the quality of hospitality provided.

Second, achieving a satisfactory balance between demand patterns, resource scheduling and operational capacity is one of the most difficult tasks facing hospitality managers.

Third, all hospitality operations require a combination of manufacturing expertise and service skill in a business which operates around the clock, 365 days a year, and is busiest when most other businesses are not. To consistently deliver an appropriate level of product and service to each individual customer requires the efforts of many different teams of staff who must be co-ordinated to deliver a consistent standard every time.

Fourth, however well planned and designed the hospitality operation is, however well scheduled the resources, the success of any customer experience will be determined at the interaction between the customer and the service provider. A highly skilled chef can spend many hours preparing the finest dishes and yet they can be ruined by the lack of care of the waiter. The point of contact between the customer and service provider is also an opportunity for the operation to sell its service and to generate additional revenue. A hotel receptionist can significantly increase the profitability of a hotel, for instance, by encouraging customers to trade up to more luxurious and more expensive accommodation. Referral of business from one operation in a chain to another can also provide added revenue. It is all the more surprising then that given the key role a service provider has in ensuring customer satisfaction and in improving revenue and profit levels that they still remain some of the least well paid and least respected members of staff.

Historical development of hospitality

The historical development of the hospitality industry, particularly the profit sector, is inexorably linked with the development of transportation, economic growth and in turn the tourism product. Throughout history, the industry has existed to serve the traveller with the provision of food, drink and shelter away from home.

The beginnings of the hospitality industry were established over 2,000 years ago with farmers in the Middle East travelling and trading their excess grain and other products. It follows that with such travel came the requirement for food, drink and shelter. While a number of civilisations thrived in the region of the Persian Gulf, such as the Egyptian and Roman empires, so did travel, trade and the requirement for hospitality services. The development of these empires was also fuelled by economic prosperity.

The decline of the Roman empire ushered in the establishment of Christianity with the holy lands attracting travellers, and was followed by a period known as the Dark Ages where it seems only the Roman Catholic Church thrived and took over the job of feeding travellers, though not commercially. The Renaissance period (AD 1350–1600) saw a renewal of travel and trade; although the church continued providing shelter, there was also the emergence of commercial accommodation for travellers.

The period AD 1600–1800 saw the beginnings of an activity known as the Grand Tour. Wealthy English people would send their sons to tour Europe to finish their education and immerse themselves in the arts and culture of countries such as Italy and France. The development of coaching inns and post houses during this period was an important element in the development of hospitality services and these were located along transport routes to serve the mail carriers of the day.

The Industrial Revolution, which began in the mid-eighteenth century, in England, led to changes in the methods of work; it was an age of invention with the development of the steam engine. The Industrial Revolution also ushered in an age of increased economic prosperity.

The emergence of the UK's railway network in the mid-nineteenth century resulted in a need for accommodation and the building of terminal railway hotels. Increased travel by the upper classes, both in the UK and abroad, stimulated the building of luxury hotels. A strong impetus was also provided by the great international fairs and exhibitions. The building of the railways had a profound development on seaside resorts and led to an expansion of hotels in those resorts to accommodate the increasing number of visitors. This growth continued up until the First World War; the industry did not recover its growth until after the Second World War.

During the late 1950s and early 1960s the hospitality industry grew because of such factors as an increase in real income, living standards, leisure time and car ownership. Another influence was the development of air transport during the 1960s which played a significant role in the accessibility of resorts (particularly in Spain) and the location of hotels. The location of industry and trade and the expansion of the motorway network created a demand for accommodation, food and drink, mainly servicing business travellers. Finally the growth in the number of package holidays since their inception in the 1960s has meant that many more people have stayed in hotels.

Accommodation supply and demand

An important influence on the tourism industry is the type of customer and the type of accommodation that customer demands. This section of the chapter will discuss the supply and demand factors contained within the accommodation industry.

Supply of accommodation

The world-wide accommodation industry is both large and varied. It consists of hotels and similar establishments ranging in size from as few as ten rooms up to usually several hundred rooms, but in some cases in the USA as many as 5,000 rooms. The vast majority of properties are independent small family-run properties. Only 21% of all accommodation properties fall outside this category of small capacity i.e. more than fifty rooms. Nevertheless, the larger properties account for the majority of all hotel revenue generated. The market for accommodation is not solely confined to hotels. It can include

- camping and caravanning
- timeshare
- people who visit friends and relatives
- self-catering in rented accommodation.

The international accommodation industry is a market concentrated in Europe with 47% of the world's hotel room supply. North America accounts for 29%, the Asia Pacific region 13%, with the balance spread over Africa, Caribbean and South America.

The WTO defines hotels and other similar establishments. These

are typified as being arranged in rooms, in number exceeding a specified minimum; as coming under a common management; as providing certain services, including room service, daily bed making and cleaning of sanitary facilities; as grouped in classes and categories according to the facilities and services provided; and not falling in the category of specialised establishments.

However, this interpretation and the analysis of industry structure can vary considerably. Indeed, in many countries no systems are in place which could even attempt to fulfil the provision of such data definitions.

These limitations mean that comparisons of the hotel profile in different European destinations must be regarded with extreme caution. The problem is at its greatest in Europe, partly because it has the longest heritage of hotel development, and thus a large variety of types of property, which, in different countries may or may not fall under the broad hotel categorisation. For example Italy's hotel capacity shows a room total of 942,000 although its definition is wide, including a broad spread of properties, such as small guest houses. In the UK by comparison it seems that the interpretation is far more conservative, and that rooms in the country's large number of smaller establishments are not included.

Given the link between tourism, travel and the demand for accommodation, the compact geographical nature of Europe prevents the accommodation industry from expanding to a level commensurate with the pace of tourist and business demand. Europe dominates the travel market: between European countries 77% of travellers are European, while less than 10% are from the United States. As intra-European travel may be accomplished in one day, this means that the actual accommodation demand from people travelling to a European destination could be relatively small. It can be estimated that the actual accommodation demand generated from total European Union (EU) arrivals is only 66% of their potential. In France 50% of visitors stay in hotels or similar accommodation. Contrast this position with the United States where popular travel routes often involve an overnight stay.

Comprehensive data on Europe's hotel sector are not readily available since some countries do not collect detailed information, but it can be estimated that hotel capacity in Europe amounts to 47% (5.08 million rooms) of world-wide capacity. Since the mid-1980s there has been a steady increase in the number of rooms available in Europe's hotels and similar establishments, and also a trend towards concentration in the hands of the major hotel chains. This rate of growth in capacity has been low, suggesting market

Table 1.1: Rooms
in hotels and similar
establishments in
selected European
countries 1993

UK	500,000
France	589,200
Italy	942,000
Germany	744,000
Switzerland	144,100
Austria	314,400
Belgium	54,100

Source: *Economist Intelligence Unit, national tourist offices, World Tourism Organisation, and author's estimates*

maturity in many parts of Europe. The relative share of total European capacity for each of its four sub-regions has consequently remained largely unchanged. Excluding the UK (for which aggregate data on the accommodation sector are not readily available), five countries in western Europe have almost 80% of the available hotel room capacity. These countries are Germany, Italy, Spain, France and Austria.

The UK (for which only partial information is collected) has approximately 500,000 rooms; the countries with the largest hotel capacity are Italy (942,000 rooms), Germany (744,000 rooms) and France (589,000 rooms): see Table 1.1.

In the USA, the accommodation market is predominantly domestic, whereas, in Europe the market is much more international. In seven out of the fourteen European countries, foreign visitors account for over 50% of all overnight stays in hotels and similar establishments. In key tourist destinations such as Austria and Portugal, the figure exceeds 70%. Since the 1980s the strongest growth in capacity has been achieved in Finland, Italy, Sweden and Germany, the latter because of the reunification of East and West Germany in 1989.

Demand for accommodation

In terms of demand for accommodation it is possible to distinguish between business demand and leisure demand. Some units will cater almost exclusively for one source of business but others will have a balance of sources that may vary according to the location and time of year. A large hotel may cater for both business and leisure guests, business guests staying Monday to Thursday and short break holiday guests from Friday to Sunday.

Clearly investment in and expansion of the hotel sector in any given country is the result of

- an expanding economy stimulating both domestic travel (for both business and leisure purposes) and international business traffic
- a growing tourism industry attracting international leisure visitors.

In Europe only 46% is domestic, reflecting the proximity of 'abroad' for most European citizens. In Germany only 16% of hotel guests are from overseas, while in Austria, the country with the highest foreign share, this reaches almost 80%. Sources of business for hotels and the composition of the market are identified in Table 1.2.

A survey by the management consultants, *Pannell Kerr Forster Associates Eurocity Survey 1997* (see Table 1.3), reveals that there are wide discrepancies across European cities in the proportion of hotel business accounted for by the domestic market. Although caution should be exercised in terms of the nature and size of this survey's

Europe	%
Domestic	45.6
Foreign	54.4
Government officials	1.5
Business travellers	37.8
Tourists (individuals)	21.8
Tour groups	16.2
Conference participants	10.5
Other	12.2
Total	100.0

Source: Horwath International

Table 1.3 Sources of business in selected European cities 1996 (% of total)

City	Domestic	Europe	USA Canada	Japan	Middle East	Aust-ralasia	South America	Far East	Other
Amsterdam	11.0	41.3	19.8	6.7	2.4	1.0	1.8	6.5	9.5
Athens	27.8	28.3	25.7	6.1	1.6	1.0	1.2	1.4	6.9
Barcelona	49.3	26.6	9.5	5.1	1.9	0.5	2.7	0.5	3.9
Berlin	62.6	22.3	6.1	2.8	0.7	1.3	0.9	1.9	1.4
Birmingham	81.1	8.8	4.6	1.0	0.4	0.2	1.0	0.6	2.3
Brussels	6.5	61.9	15.3	4.7	1.3	0.6	0.9	2.7	6.1
Budapest	2.5	66.7	18.9	4.6	4.4	0.4	0.6	1.1	0.8
Copenhagen	15.2	37.0	13.2	6.1	0.3	0.0	1.4	3.5	23.3
Edinburgh	62.2	13.4	17.0	2.9	0.3	0.5	0.4	0.4	2.9
Frankfurt	31.5	21.2	15.9	5.8	2.7	2.1	2.2	6.3	12.3
Geneva	10.4	43.7	13.4	8.5	11.4	1.5	1.6	1.8	7.7
Helsinki	28.8	43.5	10.6	7.4	1.1	0.6	0.7	2.9	4.4
Istanbul	18.1	38.8	12.5	6.0	12.5	0.8	1.1	4.4	5.8
Lisbon	19.2	56.7	9.7	4.4	2.8	0.5	1.9	2.2	2.6
London 1	29.9	18.3	17.4	8.4	5.6	1.4	0.9	4.3	13.8
London 2	23.9	16.2	34.6	7.4	6.8	2.3	1.4	4.3	3.1
London 3	19.1	17.9	39.0	3.5	7.4	1.9	1.6	5.5	4.1
London	26.6	17.7	25.5	7.3	6.2	1.7	1.2	4.5	9.3
Madrid	43.3	26.1	11.8	4.1	0.8	1.2	5.0	1.1	6.6
Manchester	74.2	11.8	6.9	2.0	0.6	0.9	0.2	1.4	2.0
Milan	31.9	23.8	14.5	21.2	2.1	0.9	1.9	1.8	1.9
Moscow	14.0	44.9	23.8	2.1	2.4	1.4	0.9	1.5	9.0
Munich	55.0	21.5	10.8	6.1	1.8	0.5	0.3	1.0	3.0
Oslo	51.1	31.2	7.9	3.4	0.0	0.2	0.5	1.5	4.2
Paris 1	12.7	29.5	14.9	23.2	5.1	0.9	2.0	7.2	4.5
Paris 2	6.7	28.1	34.0	11.8	7.8	2.3	4.1	1.7	3.5
Paris	11.0	29.1	20.2	20.0	5.9	1.3	2.6	5.6	4.3
Prague	7.3	51.3	20.7	6.6	2.3	1.9	1.4	0.5	8.0
Rome	22.9	22.4	22.2	14.4	1.3	2.3	2.8	5.1	6.6
Stockholm	47.4	30.2	8.0	4.2	0.4	0.4	0.9	1.9	6.6
St Petersburg	9.7	46.2	20.2	2.5	0.5	0.6	1.1	0.9	18.3
Vienna	14.9	50.8	13.9	9.8	2.0	0.6	0.8	2.1	5.1
Warsaw	25.5	43.2	14.3	2.7	3.2	1.4	0.5	2.3	6.9
Zurich	15.5	38.2	17.3	6.7	2.4	3.6	2.1	10.0	4.2
Average/Total	28.7	32.2	16.3	7.0	3.3	1.1	1.4	3.2	6.8

Source: Pannell Kerr Forster Associates, EuroCity Survey 1997
Note: 'Other' includes figures for Africa

sample it does give an indication of demand within a section of the European hotel industry.

BDO Hospitality Consulting, a London-based consultancy group, have calculated that for their sample of the UK hotel sector 1997, 19.5% of demand came from leisure breaks while 34.1% came from corporate business. Conference delegates accounted for 10.8%, tour groups 12.0%, rack (i.e. people paying full published price) 14.7% and other categories 9.0%.

Different types of accommodation will have a different balance of demand and this will vary according to location and the time of year. At the beginning of the summer holiday season a holiday village may cater mainly for large groups from a particular area of the country or a social organisation. In the middle of the season most bookings may be for individuals. However, a hotel in York, for example, may cater for group tour bookings during the peak summer and individuals for the rest of the year. Group bookings also occur for business travel but usually in the form of meetings, conferences or conventions.

A further distinction can be made between domestic demand and international demand. Some areas of a country will see very few international tourists whereas others on the main tourist routes or key destinations will be inundated at certain times of the year. In addition an accommodation unit will get a certain amount of its demand from the local community. This may be in the form of meals in the restaurant, use of the public bar, or its leisure facilities but could occasionally extend to accommodation.

Development of the accommodation industry

The history of the development of the accommodation industry shows how important location is to the success of an accommodation unit; that is, being in the most prominent or best location for a particular type of customer, and this may change over time.

The heavy reliance on space and building needed for most accommodation types means that its cost structure is heavily biased towards high fixed costs and low variable costs. In order to break even, an accommodation unit must achieve a relatively high level of occupancy. Any room, flat or placement unlet means a loss of potential revenue. In order to help to cover fixed costs at times of low demand many units will sell their accommodation at reduced rates; this will allow them to cover their variable costs and make a contribution to fixed overheads. These factors combine to make all accommodation units highly dependent on customer demand. Unless there is the right type of demand for the product provided, at the right price, in the right location, the business will not be able to survive. Indeed, when carrying out a feasibility study to look at the viability of developing accommodation in an area, the first subject for study should always be an assessment of demand.

A consequence of the fixity of premises is that all customers must be brought to the accommodation. This stresses the importance of raising customer awareness of the availability of the product and making it as easy as possible for customers to find the premises. This raises the issues of accessibility and transport networks.

Most accommodation units provide a range of extra services that can vary from television and video in the ròoms, to a resident disco or entertainer or more frequently a swimming pool and fitness centre. In most cases, the largest of these services is the provision of food and beverage. The importance of these extra facilities will vary depending on the particular market the unit wishes to attract. It will also depend on the gender and age of the client. Videos are most likely to appeal to those under 35, disco dancing to younger age groups and line dancing to older ones. The importance of these extra

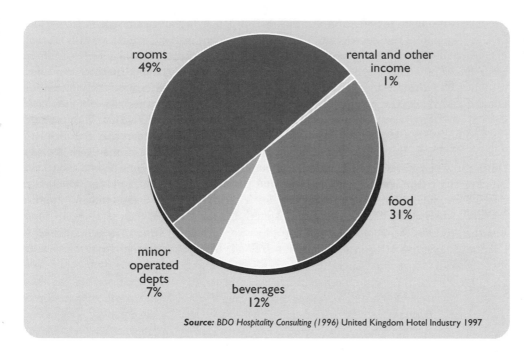

Figure 1.4
Percentage
distribution of
revenue

Source: BDO Hospitality Consulting (1996) United Kingdom Hotel Industry 1997

services can also be considered by type of travel: business travellers tend to stay in hotels on their own and so tend to prefer activities that can be done as individuals on their own. An indication of distribution of revenue from the average hotel in the UK is included in Figure 1.4.

The tourism industry

Several factors affect the tourism industry and its links with hospitality. Past and current influences are described as the general environment and include political, economic, social and technological factors (sometimes referred to as a PEST analysis). In applying such an analysis to the tourism industry the objective is to answer the following two questions:

- What environmental factors affect the tourism industry?
- Which of these were the most important in the past, the present and the future?

Having established the extent of the link between tourism and hospitality, this section will now consider the environmental factors affecting the tourism industry before appraising the constituent elements of the tourism product (apart from food, drink and accommodation).

Political factors

After the economic downturn of the early 1980s, the mid-1980s showed evidence of a complete recovery in world tourism; 1984 and 1985 were record years. However, the international tourism movement in 1986 was disrupted by the combined effects of the disaster at Chernobyl, the fall in the US dollar, the Libyan bombing incident and an increase in terrorist activity. The result was a shift in world tourism flows away from Europe and

North America, with tourists from North America perceiving European destinations to be unsafe. The end of the decade saw a return to normality with substantial growth. Further disruption to tourism flows was soon to come in the form of the Gulf War and the recession, illustrating that issues outside the tourism and hospitality industry can affect its general well-being. In 1990 the build-up towards the Gulf War affected both tourism volume and value. The war in early 1991 led to the virtual cessation of travel to the Gulf, Eastern Mediterranean and North Africa. The war in the former Yugoslavia throughout the first half of the 1990s destroyed a popular tourist destination for many Europeans; it will be well into the next millennium before the new countries in that area recover. During this period militant Islamic fundamentalists disrupted tourism in both Egypt and Turkey. The continued division of Cyprus into separate Greek and Turkish communities proved an intermittent flash point creating a negative image and affecting tourism arrivals to that island. The communist-inspired Shining Path movement in Peru, South America, terrorised potential tourists and the Irish Republican Army (IRA) continued to threaten tourism in London and Northern Ireland, despite occasional cease-fires in the mid-1990s.

Economic factors

By the year 2000, the largest industry in the world is likely to be tourism. Total world arrivals since the mid-1970s have expanded by an average growth rate of 5.1% per year. Receipts from tourism world-wide for the same period rose by a similar rate.

According to the World Travel and Tourism Council (WTTC), travel and tourism accounts for some 4.8% of direct and 5.4% of indirect gross domestic product (GDP) and its share of total capital investment is 10.7%. World-wide employment in the industry provides 204 million jobs, or one in nine of all workers.

Figure 1.5
International tourist arrivals (millions) market trends 1970–1996

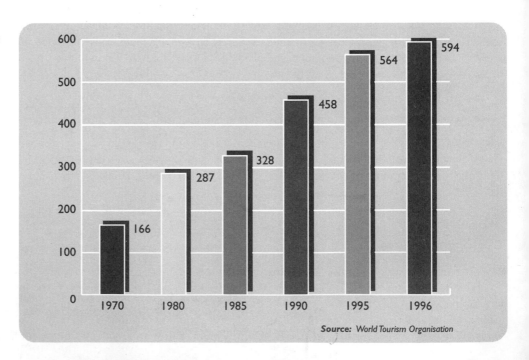

Source: World Tourism Organisation

Trends in international tourist arrivals for the period 1970–95 (Figure 1.5) show that tourism has grown at a remarkable rate; the figure for 1950 was just over 25 million.

Growth has not been evenly spread across countries or across regions. Europe can be considered the axis of world travel with an average growth rate of approximately 3.7% since the mid-1980s. It is by far the largest area in terms of tourist arrivals (60–70%), which has implications for the size and diversity of the accommodation industry in Europe. The EU alone accounts for nearly 40% of both arrivals and receipts.

The primacy of Europe in terms of tourism and accommodation will be a theme that runs throughout this book. Regional share of international tourist arrivals has changed over the period 1970 to 1995 with reductions in Europe and significant increases in the Asia Pacific region:

- Europe   1970   70.5%
- Europe   1995   59.4%
- Asia Pacific   1970   3.6%
- Asia Pacific   1995   15.6%

The 1980s saw a slowing of growth rates in international tourism illustrating the industry's direct links with economic factors. The decade opened with economic recession, falling disposable incomes and increased costs of travel which had a negative impact on travel. Length of stay fell, cheaper forms of accommodation were sought and the consumer switched to cheaper or neighbouring destinations, or travelled domestically.

The recession of 1990–92 experienced by the majority of industrialised countries exacerbated by the Gulf War also took its toll on the tourism industry.

The overall percentage of international tourist arrivals between 1990 and 1991 rose by about 1.5%, though this change does hide extreme variations for the regions. Arrivals in countries of East Asia and the Pacific, Americas and Europe rose while arrivals in the countries of South Asia, Africa and the Middle East decreased.

These figures are expected to change even more with the figures listed below projected to 2010.

- Europe   1970   70.5%
- Europe   2010   51.6%
- Asia Pacific   1970   3.6%
- Asia Pacific   2010   23.5%

Again, if one considers average annual tourist growth forecasts for the period 1990–2010, the world average is projected at 4.1% although differences can be seen within the regions (Table 1.4).

The main generating markets for inbound tourism to the Americas are other countries

Table 1.4 Average annual tourist growth forecasts 1990–2010

East Asia and Pacific	7.6%
South Asia	6.7%
Middle East	4.9%
Africa	4.6%
Americas	3.7%
Europe	3.1%

Source: World Tourism Organisation

in North America, Europe and Japan. However, there has been a marked growth in the number of arrivals from non-traditional markets. This incoming tourism flow is a result of

- offering competitive prices
- reducing air fares
- packaging Florida in tour operator brochures

The main destinations remain the USA and Canada with substantial movements between the two.

European countries as destinations now account for approximately 60% of all international arrivals, a share that has decreased since the mid-1960s for three possible reasons:

- It is easier and cheaper to engage in long haul travel.
- The market within Europe has reached maturity.
- There are problems in measurement and in the statistics produced which may underestimate growth.

However, Europe's share of international tourism receipts has been remarkably stable over the same period. Many western European countries are also major generators of international tourism. With the exception of the USA and Japan, the top six countries for international tourism generators in 1995 are to be found in western Europe. Indeed this ranking has changed since 1970 (Table 1.5).

Patterns are also changing with respect to the percentage of total international tourism expenditure by the top fifteen generators; in 1970 the figure was 89%, in 1995 it was 67%.

Western Europeans, particularly from Germany, the UK and France, also engage in long haul travel and are regarded as important markets to attract. This continued dominance of Europe can be explained in terms of a high disposable income within large segments of the population, the wealth of attractions, a large tourist industry and the necessary infrastructure. Europe consists of many small countries and so international travel need not entail great distances. This contrasts with the size of the USA and Canada resulting in most North Americans taking holiday trips in their own country. The easing of border controls in Europe since 1992 and the opening of the Channel Tunnel in the mid-1990s have consolidated European dominance in statistical terms.

When one associates tourism and the European economy, it can be seen that it is a vital industry for Europe, with the region continuing to generate a positive tourism balance of payments. In terms of employment in major destination countries tourism

Table 1.5 Top six international tourism generators

1970	Rank	1995
USA	1	Germany
Germany	2	USA
Canada	3	Japan
France	4	UK
UK	5	France
Italy	6	Italy

Source: World Tourism Organisation

accounts for nearly 10% of the workforce including those working in restaurants and cafés, hotels, restaurants and bars.

Levels of reliance on tourism in individual countries also vary considerably in comparing receipts with gross domestic product. With over 50 million tourists, France is the world's most visited country. The opening of Disneyland Paris and the Channel Tunnel is likely to see France continue in its leading position throughout the 1990s and into the next millennium. The main source market of outgoing tourism, by a large margin is Germany.

Domestic tourism is still more popular among Europeans than travelling abroad for a holiday, although growth in the domestic holiday market is less swift. However, levels of domestic holiday taking do vary considerably across Europe according the level of tourist attractions and climatic factors within the country concerned.

The political and economic changes that have characterised central and eastern Europe since 1989 exerted a number of influences on patterns of international tourism too, within and from the region. Just as the economic restructuring and social changes have yet to establish a settled and coherent pattern, so too patterns of tourism development appear far from stabilised.

In summary, central and eastern Europe experienced an increase in international tourist arrivals during the second half of the 1980s, and particular growth over the 1988–9 watershed, revealing a slight increase in its share of Europe arrivals. Eastern Europe returned the fastest average annual rate of increase in arrivals of the four WTO European regions. However, if one excludes the former Yugoslavia, the region's share of total world arrivals in late 1980s was only half that for the regions of western and southern Europe. Although large increases in receipts were recorded for the region in the second half of the 1980s, when excluding Yugoslavia, the increase for the 1988–9 period appears relatively low.

The quality of tourism in central and eastern Europe has often been low by accepted western standards. Accommodation, catering, utilities, transport and telecommunications have suffered from being regarded a low priority in these former eastern bloc countries. With respect to accommodation, for example, the newly developing private sector will need to generate more medium grade accommodation, and joint ventures for future investment in top quality accommodation will be necessary to develop and consolidate high spending conference and business tourism. There will also be a requirement for staff training at all levels of the tourism industry, not least in hotel management, catering, travel agencies and in such areas as computing, telecommunications and foreign languages to cater for new growth markets. There is also a lack of incentives and business philosophy, along with competition for resources. For some time, however, there will continue to exist much uncertainty over the future organisation of the tourism industry as decentralisation of state controlled systems gives way to privatisation. Legislative and regulatory frameworks appropriate for a restructured industry may be slow in coming about, particularly for potential foreign investors.

Within the UK, the tourism industry has grown strongly since the mid-1980s. Tourist spending, including domestic tourism, accounts for close to 4% of GDP.

Tourism is one of the UK's largest industries, employing 1.6 million people, including self-employed people. With the addition of the hotel and catering industry that figure rises to 2.4 million people. Tourism is also one of the fastest growing industries.

Large increases in 1995 for the second year running were seen in the total number of overnight tourism trips taken by the British within the UK and in the total number of nights spent away from home on those trips. These year-on-year increases in the volume of trips and nights away extended in 1995 to all four countries of the UK. Spending in the UK on tourism nevertheless amounted in total to less in 1995 than in 1994 even at current prices – the decrease was mainly caused within England. Holidays were the most important cause of the volume of trips or nights and value of tourism expenditure in the UK. Visits to friends and relatives were the cause of more than a quarter of all UK trips (29%, a little more than the 27% measured in 1994), one-fifth (20%) of the nights in the UK, and a tenth of the spending in the UK. Business tourism was only the third biggest reason for domestic trips accounting for one-eighth of trips in the UK (12%) and one-twelfth of UK nights (8%), but as business tourism is relatively expensive per night and per trip, it became the second most valuable cause of tourism expenditure in the UK after holidays. Stays in commercial accommodation were relatively long compared to those with friends and relatives or in other non-commercial accommodation types. The commercial sector comes close to a half (46%) of all nights in the UK and accounts for two-thirds (67%) of tourism spending in the UK.

The vast majority of trips away from home are to destinations within the UK. However, the minority of trips which spent any nights outside the UK lasted more than twice as long as trips within the UK and cost over five times more. This is a function of both distance that has to be travelled and types of trips taken abroad. Consequently, UK destinations account for 64% of tourism nights away from home and 46% of all tourism expenditure. Of all the trips taken by Britons, 66% are for what would be described as a holiday. After holidays, the next most important types of trips were visits to friends or relatives (19% of all tourism). Business and work-related tourism to all destinations and in all accommodation types is of relatively little importance (11% of all tourism).

Overseas business demand recorded through visitor arrivals is sensitive to exchange rates with an obvious time lag. There is a reasonable correlation between overseas business arrivals and the movement in exchange rates with the time lag seemingly shorter in the US market than in the European market. This time lag is significant since North Americans typically account for approximately 20% of UK visitor arrivals and a rapid pick up in demand from this market will be significant for overall demand. In Europe demand from continental business people, while encouraged by sterling's exit from the exchange rate mechanism (ERM) devaluation in 1992, will be tempered by the domestic economic situation in the two critical economies of France and Germany throughout the late 1990s.

In terms of the leisure sector, a weak sterling may act as a stimulus to demand, as it will give a relative price advantage to the UK industry, in respect of both overseas and domestic customers.

The trend in consumer confidence is critical in determining the likely direction of consumer spending and domestic tourism leisure demand. Confidence in the business sector closely correlates with interest rates which continued to remain relatively low in the second half of the 1990s.

Social/cultural factors

Social factors continue to affect the development of the tourism industry. As consumers from the mature northern European markets become more sophisticated and adventurous in their holiday habits and new technologies supersede traditional ways of distributing the holiday product, there is every reason for concern over the long-term future of some of the original mass tourist resorts established in the 1960s and 1970s. Key social factors since the mid-1980s include the following.

- A growing preference for long haul holidays which are becoming more affordable and offer a higher degree of exoticism. The proportion of the UK air holiday market attributable to long haul rose from 8% to 16% between 1986 and 1996. Summer 1996 in the UK saw a fall in the sale of short haul packages by 14% over summer 1995 and an increase in long haul sales by 21%.

- An ageing and more sophisticated market increasingly interested in new holiday experiences rather than the sun and beach product. A growing movement of beach boredom is now taking hold.

- A shift away from the traditional package holiday as technology allows tour operators to reach the consumer directly, thus saving the commission costs of travel agents. Travel agents' share of the UK package market has fallen from 87% to 74% between 1986 and 1996. Tour operators can use savings to improve the quality of the product, increase profitability or reduce prices.

- A market shift towards independently arranged holidays as consumers become increasingly aware of booking techniques and seek a higher degree of control and flexibility over their holidays. Growth of 22% in the UK independent market has been forecast between 1996 and 2000 against 13% growth in the air inclusive package market. The growth of tailor made holidays is further testament to this trend.

- Legislative changes e.g. the ongoing deregulation of the airline industry are likely to reduce the price of independent holidays and increase the relative price of the traditional Mediterranean holidays.

In taking these social factors into account there is a new tourism developing, the notion that mass production in tourism is rapidly being replaced by a more flexible form of production characterised by quality, innovation and market segmentation. Some have described this as a post-fordist consumption stage. Here, the suggestion is that there is a move towards new tourism stimulated by a more quality conscious and independently minded consumer and by new technologies now being used to maximise yield rather than volume. As the mature northern European markets begin to desert the older mass tourist resorts, there will undoubtedly be new markets from which to draw volume, such as the emerging economies of eastern Europe. However the purchasing power of these people will remain relatively low for a decade or more. Even when they do mature, the rapidity at which the new and more environmentally appealing destinations are now emerging will attract these markets.

Technological factors: computer reservation systems

A fourth group of factors affecting the tourism industry is technology. It is widely held that the travel and tourism industry owes its phenomenal expansion to the computer reservation systems which have become a critical marketing tool. One of the critical competitive issues confronting the international travel industry is the emergence of a few dominant airline computer reservation systems (CRS) that control the sale and distribution of a wide array of travel services. It is important to make the distinction between CRS (which are owned by a small number of airlines) and airlines' internal computerised reservations systems (which virtually all airlines have). Indeed, reservations systems were originally developed by carriers in the USA to enhance their own internal ticketing process. However, they have emerged to become one of the most powerful strategic tools of the travel industry, with an almost unlimited potential for future travel and tourism sales and distribution applications. A few giant computer reservations systems developed by major air carriers currently dominate the CRS industry, giving the airline owners a tremendous competitive advantage over their 'have not' competitors. In the mid-1990s the penetration of CRS in the US and European travel agencies was virtually complete, while the battle for global CRS markets was just beginning. The future role of CRS will determine which carriers will dominate the global airline market; it is sure to accelerate as airlines throughout the US and Western Europe continue to form international alliances.

The purpose of this section is two-fold. The first is to examine the increasing importance of the CRS to major airlines both in the US and elsewhere in their struggle for world market position. The second purpose is to discuss some critical issues inherent in CRS applications, using the experience of the USA and Europe since the mid-1980s as a model, in order to identify the strategies that are likely to occur as a result of increasing sophistication of CRS in the travel and tourism industry.

In the early years of aviation, with the limited number of carriers and available flights, airlines simply presented their scheduling and pricing information to consumers by distributing timetables and advertising in newspapers. As more carriers entered the industry and the existing airlines expanded their route structures, the practice of interlining became commonplace. Interlining made it mandatory for the industry to create a comprehensive, multi-carrier guide which would provide passengers with the detailed information necessary for them to make an informed purchase decision.

Concurrent with the publication of the multi-carrier guides was the emergence of the travel agent, who facilitated the sales and distribution of airline tickets by providing consumers with expert guidance in selecting from among the increasingly complex number of options available. As world-wide growth in passenger aviation progressed, ticket sales through travel agencies became an important component of the channel of distribution.

By the 1960s, the airline industry had grown to the extent that computers were needed in order to keep track of the massive inventory of available seats. Computerised reservations and ticketing procedures offered airlines significant improvements in productivity over the cumbersome and time-consuming manual process involving telephones and telexes. The powerful CRS of the 1990s, were originally developed by the major US airlines, not as a competitive weapon, but rather to improve the efficiency of their own internal reservations systems. The simple, relatively inexpensive internal system first developed in 1962 by American Airlines helped it to obtain a dominant position in the market. CRS were a natural progression of this early internal technology and American Airlines was the first to realise the benefits of expanding its computer systems to include on-line terminals with direct reservation capabilities located in travel agencies.

American Airlines first began marketing its CRS extensively in this way immediately following the deregulation of the airline industry in 1982. Its CRS named Sabre has assisted American Airlines in capturing a large market share and has been an integral key to the competitive advantage the company has secured. The deregulation of the airline industry fuelled the rapid development and expansion of CRS world-wide, and has led to the many dynamic sophisticated systems currently in existence.

Shortly after deregulation the remaining airlines realised that they could no longer compete with those utilising CRS technology. The major airlines either began development of their own systems or merged with other firms that already possessed the technology. The reservation systems are usually on-line, so all information provided about seat availability and cost tends to be accurate and current. The travel agents know exactly how many seats and what class of seat are available, making the service they provide appear more valuable to a consumer.

CRS have diversified into many other reservation functions such as car rentals, hotel reservations, train reservations and other tourism and hospitality sectors. Product diversification is making the airline systems appear more attractive to travel agents as such systems would not only improve their competitive advantage but also increase their profitability.

In Europe similar development took place but the highly regulated European environment of the early 1980s, which posted co-operation rather than competition between European airlines, led to significant differences in the way the European systems were built and operated.

The American CRS systems were constructed as a single central database. Airlines supplied inventory and price data to them for their own systems. In contrast, the European systems such as British Airways Travicom were 'multi-access' systems. Users had to choose to which airline they wished to connect. The system then routed users directly through to the individual reservation system of that airline. Although these systems were simpler and cheaper to construct and maintain, the data and functionality that they provided to travel agents was very limited in comparison with the US systems.

Such a situation did not remain unnoticed by Sabre and the other US majors, who started to export their services to Europe and other continents. By the mid-1980s the major European airlines were nervous that the superior functionality of the US systems would shortly begin to attract agents away from using their own systems, and that they would thus lose control of their own ticket distribution within their home markets. In mid-1987 therefore, two European airline consortia announced the formation of the Galileo and Amadeus CRS systems. British Airways (BA) is a major shareholder in Galileo. The objective of these two consortia was not only to protect their home markets, but also to develop additional revenue streams. Both consortia entered into technical partnerships with existing US system operators. Their objective was to shorten development time-scales and to reduce the total level of investment required. In practice neither Galileo nor Amadeus has achieved anything like its originally announced timetables. None the less, the vital need for this investment by the two European airline consortia has been emphasised by the increasingly successful US penetration of the European agency markets.

These two European systems have made substantial investments since 1987. Galileo saw in the mid-1990s the launch of international and domestic air fare capabilities and now offers several tourism services such as hotel and car rental bookings.

The system, presently based in Madrid, Spain, is accessed by about 17,500 agencies in nine countries through their national CRS connection to System One's core in Miami, Florida.

Four main trends can now be discerned in the multinational CRS world:

- regulatory pressures
- globalisation
- an application explosion at the point-of-sale
- expansion of travel-related sales.

Regulatory pressures

In the USA, as a response to a long history of anti-competitive behaviour by the CRS systems, and in Europe resulting from an EU determination to operate an open skies policy in reservation systems rather than among the airlines themselves, regulating activity has had and will continue to have an increasing impact on the CRS chains.

Globalisation

This is seen in various ways. Even the name Global Distribution Systems (GDS) is increasingly being used by the CRS companies to describe themselves. There are several inter-CRS marketing agreements. Galileo has been prominent in developing these, and now has partners in North America, Japan, the Middle East and Australasia. In the UK there are now effectively only three multinational CRS systems: Galileo, 27% owned by BA; Worldspan, owned by TWA and Delta; and Sabre/Amadeus combine. All three systems are developing leisure-related databases or products, either alone or in conjunction with other parties.

An application explosion at the point-of-sale

In the UK the largest travel agent, Lunn Poly, has operated its network of over 500 agencies on Viewdata systems. Viewdata offers telephone-based access to travel databases; it does not offer interactive capabilities for the user and therefore it is effectively an electronic booking service. However, the long-term trends favour greater CRS usage and take-up as leisure becomes increasingly 'de-packaged' and the CRS vendors' strategy towards European travel agents changes. Worldspan has offered European agents the lowest cost entry option into the CRS market, an option taken up by many of the smaller agencies in the UK, the Netherlands and Switzerland. By contrast Sabre has competed head-on with Amadeus and Galileo for the larger business travel agents in the major business travel generating markets.

Expansion of travel-related sales

Coupled with this trend towards the provision of leisure products is the delivery of additional services, at the point-of-sale, by or through the major CRS systems. This trend is particularly noticeable in the USA and is certainly being seen elsewhere. At the most basic level, this means personal computer (PC)-based terminals with vastly superior functionality to the old 'dump' terminals, which required highly trained operators. However, the PC environment is only a platform to build on. Apart from the CRSs themselves, other service providers as well as third party software suppliers are rushing to develop applications of all kinds. Pre-trip audit software, which continually checks already booked airline segments for cheaper fares available under the various airlines' yield management systems, is an interesting example. More significant is the development of integrated multimedia databases by major publisher or tour operators, in co-operation with the CRS companies. One example of this is the Reed-developed Jaguar system, now branded Sabrevision in its guise as a joint venture with Sabre. Jaguar seeks to function as a highly specific marketing tool, for example delivering pictures of hotels or cruise ships and their facilities at the point-of-sale at the same time as price and availability data are displayed.

Tourism supply

A description of the UK travel industry is normally applied to those elements with a role in the marketing of travel to UK residents within the UK or on an international basis. It is therefore normally defined to include:

- UK based retail travel agents
- UK based outgoing tour operators
- domestic tour operators
- transport principals providing services within the UK, between the UK and overseas, such as airlines, coach operators and car ferries

● foreign based principals are also sometimes included within the UK travel industry, for example multinational companies in this sector.

Travel agents and tour operators

In the mind of the travelling public, travel agents are not always clearly distinguished
from tour operators. They do perform distinct and separate roles even though some
companies operate in both sectors. Travel agents are retailers while tour operators are
wholesalers responsible for assembling and wrapping the various parts of the travel package. These parts normally consist of transportation, accommodation and related services
in varying proportions. Despite this logical distinction, they will be considered together
because of their close relationship and because they face many common issues, not least
the issue which concerns the distribution channels between customer and principal.

The main trade association of the industry in the UK is the Association of British Travel
Agents (ABTA) founded in 1950. ABTA represents both retail travel agents and tour operating sectors of the travel industry. It operates through a tour agents' council and a tour
operators' council representing the sometimes different interests of the two sides. Each
council operates through a system of assembling committees and regional committees.
One of its key roles is a public relations one, whereby ABTA seeks to create a favourable
business environment for its members. As part of this activity, it attempts to generate
media coverage at regional and national level in order to encourage early bookings. At
the present time, ABTA acts as a self-regulatory trade association, a situation brought
about by the introduction in 1965 of the so called **stabiliser closed shop agreement**
between tour operators and travel agents. This means that ABTA tour operators who wish
to sell foreign inclusive tour holidays or other travel arrangements through a third party
can do so only through ABTA travel agents, or such agents as they choose to appoint as
their agents and vice versa. This provides a strong incentive for both tour operators and
retail travel agents who belong to ABTA. However, the association is now reviewing its
structure following the publication of the European Commission's **Directive on Package
Travel**. Some in the industry are assuming that this directive, which provides for the government licensing of tour operators, would see the end of the stabiliser rules.

The tour operating industry is highly competitive and its instability is illustrated with
the collapse of a number of companies in recent years. In terms of industry supply in the
late 1990s the three main tour operators are Thomson, Owners Abroad, and Airtours.

Thomson is by far the largest UK tour operator with an estimated 35% of the market,
as much as the next two operators in the league table combined. Owners Abroad is now
the number two tour operator in the UK. Travel agents can be divided between leisure
and business agencies. Apart from the multiples, the travel agency sector is fragmented
with half of the market shared between 5,000 or so firms.

In terms of the future, the most important issue for the industry is perhaps the
European Union *Directive on Package Travel*. The basis of the directive is that under its
terms all operators would be required to offer financial protection to the public.

Air transport

The air transport industry is a global one and even the sectors of it which serve the UK
tourism industry include foreign as well as UK based airlines. In addition, the commercial
behaviour of UK airlines is influenced by UK and European regulatory bodies, specifically

concerned with aviation matters and for administering government policies towards monopolies and mergers. Foreign governments and the regulatory bodies, not least those in the USA, also have an influence. The industry also includes organisations concerned with providing the supporting infrastructure of airports and air traffic control systems.

In 1944 the International Civil Aviation Organisation (ICAO) was established as a specialised agency of the United Nations to foster the development of international air transport. While ICAO provides the framework for intergovernmental co-operation on technical matters in the civil aviation field, the International Air Transport Association (IATA) facilitates commercial co-operation between airlines and provides a forum in which they can decide matters of common interest. The market for passenger transport by air is split into many segments. The basic division is into international and domestic travel. Within each of these market segments, sub-segments may be identified, i.e. business, inclusive tour, visits to friends and relatives. The most significant contribution of air travel to the development of UK travel and tourism is the international package tour, the core of which has already been seen as traditionally the charter airline.

The UK airline industry consists of large carriers who set out to satisfy all markets, as well as smaller niche airlines specialising in serving particular market segments, i.e. charter airlines serving the package tour market. In the context of the UK travel and tourism industry there is also a particularly important place occupied by the charter carriers, who have traditionally served the UK inclusive tour market and cover a high percentage of trips. In terms of annual total operating revenue the two largest companies are British Airways and Britannia.

British Airways is the dominant UK-based supplier of scheduled services from Heathrow, although taken together, foreign airlines also have a significant presence there. Formerly the state owned flag carrier until its privatisation in 1987 it is still by far the largest UK airline. The main strategic issue facing the airline is how to achieve sufficient size and collaboration to qualify as a global carrier able to survive in the US-dominated big league of mega carriers.

UK ferries

Some 30 million sea journeys are made each year between the UK and other countries compared with a corresponding figure for air-travel of around 78 million journeys. The sea journeys cover much shorter average distances than the air journeys and are almost entirely between Britain and Ireland or mainland Europe. Most services are provided by vehicle carrying ferries using conventional ships, while passenger transportation use is also provided by hovercrafts, hydrofoils and high speed catamarans.

The vehicle ferries which operate across the English Channel as well as the North Sea and Irish Sea seek to serve the needs of several distinct markets, with the main market being the carriage of driver accompanied vehicles, both commercial and private. Although there are roll-on, roll-off ferries on a number of routes including the North Sea, many of these cater primarily for commercial traffic. The bulk of the tourist traffic by sea uses the short sea routes linking Dover and Folkestone (on the English side) with Calais and Boulogne (on the French side). In terms of market share i.e. sea ferry services used by UK resident holiday makers, the three largest companies are Sealink, P&O Ferries and Brittany Ferries.

Channel Tunnel

Many of the recent changes to the pattern of services offered by the cross Channel ferry operators can be attributed to the opening of the Channel Tunnel. Although Eurotunnel, operator of the Channel Tunnel, and the ferry companies have different views as to the extent of any likely diversion of business from ferry to tunnel, both sides agree that such diversion would be substantial, amounting to between 80 and 90% of foot passengers, 50% to 70% of accompanied car traffic and between 25% and 40% of commercial road vehicle traffic.

Clearly the service nearest to the tunnel's alignment, Folkestone–Calais, are placed under the greatest competitive threat and hence are most at risk. On the other hand there is commercial logic in attempting to concentrate services on the busiest route, which is perhaps Dover to Calais. Such a service would probably operate as a thirty minute shuttle, matching the rail shuttle system proposed by Eurotunnel. This would mean combining the services of several operators and would require the approval of the UK's Monopolies & Mergers Commission. However, other routes are probably far enough away from the tunnel to be able to look forward to the prospect of a profitable operation based on serving the growing car holiday and road haulage markets.

A historical perspective on the tourism industry and one of its component parts (hotels) will now be considered with reference to British and Spanish mass tourist destinations.

> ### Case Study: History and development of British and Spanish mass tourist destinations: future problems ahead?

Introduction

The Tourist Area Life Cycle (TALC) is a concept developed by Richard Butler (see further reading), whereby resorts are viewed as 'products' which experience a series of evolutionary stages in consumer demand. The cycle is summarised as birth, growth, stabilisation, maturity, stagnation and decline/rejuvenation. It is, however, difficult to use the concept to contrast a UK inland resort such as Bath with a coastal resort such as Brighton or indeed French historic resorts such as Deauville with modern resorts such as Canet-Plage.

Among the first generation of mass tourist resorts (such as Brighton) which have stemmed decline, most have relied heavily on their nineteenth-century built heritage and on a reorientation of product towards the day rather than overnight visitor. The second generation of mass tourist resort, e.g. Benidorm, generally lack an attractive built legacy and are frequently located in areas without a large regional catchment population. Most tellingly, these resorts are struggling to overcome the confinement caused by overly rapid and uncontrolled development.

The first generation resorts: the British experience

The British seaside resort (to adopt Butler's TALC) experienced a pre-stagnation life cycle of around 150 years and has been coping with life in the post-stagnation phase for some 30 years. The British resorts generally responded slowly to market decline. The more resilient resorts have accepted the shrinking of their accommodation bases as they

case study continues ▶

case study continues

reorientate themselves to the day visitor market where appropriate and invest in new facilities to attract family holidays. In addition, efforts have been made to tap into growth markets such as conferences and domestic short breaks, which help to extend the season, through product development initiatives.

The British resorts which have proved most resilient have four main advantages over second generation mass resorts of Spain:

- Their development was over a sufficiently long period of time such that tourism was not the only component of the economy.
- They were not dependent on tour operators to provide visitors since the domestic UK market has traditionally bypassed the middle man.
- They are, in most cases, within one hour's drive of vast metropolitan catchment areas, the source of day visitors.
- They were designed and planned in the heyday of the British empire, an affluent period when great delight was taken in public architecture and facilities.

Resort survival in Britain has been achieved by a diversification of the economic base, a contraction of the accommodation base, and a reorientation to new consumer markets. A level of post-stagnation stabilisation has been achieved by the survivors after three decades.

The issue for Spain's leading mass tourist resorts is whether it will reach a similar stabilisation phase and how long will it take?

Mass tourism: the second generation

Mass tourism, as personified by the second generation resorts of Spain, has been defined by some as

> a phenomenon of large scale packaging of standardised leisure services at fixed prices for sale to a mass clientele.

It requires the shifting of large volumes in order to work, with quality and differentiation being sacrificed for low prices.

Second generation mass tourism in Europe emerged in the 1960s as cheaper air travel brought warm Mediterranean destinations within holiday range of an increasingly affluent north European market. The domestically orientated holiday markets of the UK, Germany and Benelux were enticed on their first foreign holidays by the promise of uninterrupted sunshine and by tour operators able to package the holiday product in an attractive format.

For the consumer, the package deal removed the uncertainty of foreign travel; for the producer, conscious that demand would be price dependent, it was necessary to build high volume so as to maximise economies of scale in purchases from its sub-contractors. This relationship evolved over the 1970s and 1980s, with tour operators becoming more efficient in consolidating the product and seeking market growth in volume rather than value. In order to achieve ambitious volume targets, tour operators relied heavily on price in developing the market. In Spain, where the cost of living was well below the European average until the 1980s, very economical packages were offered and visitors' purchasing power was high.

case study continues ▶

case study continues

Through such competitive pricing, more latterly accentuated by early booking and late season discounts, price has always been the dominant feature of the tour operator commercial marketing mix. The increasingly competitive nature of tour operating has reinforced the role of price in driving volume in their economic equation.

The rapidity of demand growth and the volume ambitions of the leading tour operators were reflected in the emergence of a new type of holiday resort, based on high accommodation density and a remarkable pandering to the tastes of the northern European 'invaders'. The philosophy demanded that large numbers of visitors should be sought and all should be accommodated as closely as possible to the beach. Spain, with its amenable summer climate, plethora of golden beaches and the encouragement of its national government, became the host to a succession of mass tourist resorts which subsequently attracted a degree of notoriety. Benidorm, Torremolinos, Lloret de Mar and Magaluf in Mallorca were all transformed from fishing villages into high rise urban resorts in fifteen years of intense development between 1960 and 1975.

From the resort perspective, mass tourism engendered an unhealthy dependency relationship. The original entrepreneurs who built hotels and developed attractions in the resorts were frequently financed in part by the foreign tour operators who were then guaranteed future volume or 'bed quotas' at preferential rates.

By the mid-1980s, signs of fatigue in the physical fabric of these resorts were already apparent, barely two decades after the first package tourists had arrived. Weaknesses were revealed in the resort infrastructure while the errant disregard for the region's natural ecology was increasingly being questioned by a segment of the consumer base.

The market has shown some resilience after the recessionary doldrums of 1990–91 but the high volumes of 1994 and particularly 1995 required a major stimulation of the market by the tour operators through price discounting.

The susceptibility of operators to fluctuations in the general economic environment are heightened by the long lead times required to assemble a holiday programme (around eighteen months). Tour operators are required to make strategic forecasts of likely demand levels and hope that their judgement proves accurate. When it invariably does not, they revert to tactical price-based marketing in order to sell surplus supply. The top five tour operators now control over 65% of the total UK package tour market. Vertical integration has enabled major tour operators to fully harness new developments in information technology and to extend efficiencies in aircraft load factors and distribution through tied agents.

Consumer pressures

As consumers from the mature northern European markets become more sophisticated and adventurous in their holiday habits and new technologies supersede traditional ways of distributing the holiday product (e.g. teletext, Internet, direct booking) there is every reason for concern over the long-term future of the original breed of mass tourist resort. There have been four key consumer and facilitating trends in recent years.

- A growing preference for long haul holidays, which are becoming more affordable and offer a higher degree of exoticism. The proportion of the UK air holiday market attributable to long haul rose from 8% to 16% between 1986 and 1996. Summer

case study continues ▶

case study continues

1996 in the UK saw a fall in the sale of short haul packages by 14% over summer 1995 and an increase in long haul sales by 21%.

● An ageing and more sophisticated market increasingly interested in new holiday experiences rather than the sun and beach product of the Mediterranean mass tourist resorts. A growing movement of 'beach boredom' is now taking hold.

● A shift away from the traditional package holiday as technology allows tour operators to reach the consumer directly, thus saving the commission costs of travel agents. Travel agents' share of the UK package market fell from 87% to 74% between 1986 and 1996. Such a scenario will allow the operator to feed distribution savings into improving the quality of the holiday product;

● A market shift towards independently arranged holidays as consumers become increasingly aware of booking techniques and seek a higher degree of control and flexibility over their holidays. Growth of 22% in the UK independent market has been forecast between 1996 and 2000 against 13% growth in the air inclusive (package) market. The growth of tailor-made holidays is further testament to this trend.

The applicability of the TALC

It is perhaps surprising that only meagre research has to date been carried out on the post-stagnation phase of resort evolution. The second generation of mass tourist resorts are generally a good fit to the TALC but are showing signs of worryingly short life cycles. A period of discovery was typically followed by rapid development during which outside interests (foreign tour operators) took control. Consolidation was generally reached in the late 1970s and stagnation set in during the late 1980s as first environmental concerns and then prolonged recession in the northern European markets took effect. In the post-stagnation era of the 1990s, a limited number of resorts are struggling to offset decline (Lloret-de-Mar may be cited as an example) but most reacted quickly to implement rejuvenation measures. The scale and exposure of mass tourist resorts is such that local governments in Spain were generally alert to the downturn in demand.

The survival of these resorts is likely to depend upon their inherent strengths and on the strategic choices which they make regarding rejuvenation and perhaps more specifically repositioning. At present, many resorts claim to be investing heavily in their product but are actually only tinkering while others have concentrated resources into marketing at the peril of new product investment initiatives. Ultimately, as new competition emerges throughout the world, only the fittest and most enlightened will survive in the longer term.

Of most concern is the inherent vulnerability of resorts which continue to function at the whim of their 'masters', the foreign tour operators. Where supply is so concentrated and diversity of markets limited, vulnerability is most apparent.

The TALC is a valuable conceptual framework in which to place the evolution and current status of Spanish mass tourist resorts. While resorts will follow a different life cycle evolution, which may evolve over a century or just a few decades, they ultimately reach the critical stagnation phase. For decline to be offset, it would appear that the resort reaction should consist of the following:

case study continues ▶

case study continues

- gradual usurping of control from outsiders and encouragement of greater local involvement and power
- swift formulation of a rejuvenation strategy
- implementation of radical rejuvenation measures aimed at re-structuring the resort rather than temporary and arbitrary face lifts.

Resort practice in Spain

Three examples of resort rejuvenation, typifying the new spirit of improvement and investment in Spanish coastal resorts, are briefly described.

Mallorca

Mallorca is the largest of the Balearic Islands to the east of the Spanish mainland; it has, in many ways, set the agenda for other mass market resorts to follow, combining legislative and investment initiatives to control future development and reorientate the island's image. Around 30% of the island has now been set aside as a natural preservation area. Development controls were introduced in the late 1980s to limit building densities and heights and to restrict new hotel development to four star standard or above. Such measures persuaded Thomson, the UK tour operator, to invest £10 million in upgrading a series of three star hotels on the island with which it had a longstanding contractual relationship. Maximum publicity has also been achieved by the authorities who have introduced schemes to improve the aesthetic qualities of the main resorts which have included new beach esplanades and, most radically, the beginnings of a 'desaturation' project. This has involved the dynamiting of several of the island's more unsightly old promenade hotels.

Benidorm

Benidorm, the largest mass tourist resort in the Mediterranean in accommodation capacity terms, responded quickly to the first signs of structural weakness and major market decline. Its product renewal strategy has combined asset protection of its beaches with innovative development of new attractions and public amenities. These initiatives are enabling a gradual repositioning of its resort product, without the loss of the dynamism and sense of fun for which it is famous.

Gran Canaria

Gran Canaria is one of the Canary Islands in the Atlantic Ocean; its principal resorts are of a recent vintage, the development boom having taken place in the mid-1970s to early 1980s. The complex of mass market resorts on the southern tip of the island (San Agustin, Playa des Ingles and Maspalomas), with some 200,000 bedspaces, in fact represent the second highest concentration of tourist beds in Spain, after Benidorm. Much of the development comprises apartments, second homes and timeshare. The lack of a real seasonality

case study continues ▶

case study continues

problem and the relative youth of the tourist plant shielded the Canaries from the market downturn which affected the mainland and the Balearics. However, many of the resorts have exceeded the natural capacity of their beaches (Puerto Rico in particular) and the first signs of waning interest from the UK market have been evident since the mid-1990s. Recognition of the need for resort renewal is now beginning to take hold and new quality parameters have been set in recent legislation. Future development will focus on up-market and exclusive marina-based resorts typified by Puerto de Mogan and Pasito Blanco.

The travel industry

UK leisure travel

To interpret the domestic market it is more realistic to look at the trends over several years because holiday taking is subject to gradual shifts in demand and significant changes from one year to the next are very much the exception.

Nearly two-thirds of the adult UK population take a holiday away from home each year and so inevitably take part in one or more elements of the hospitality industry. Of those taking holidays, just over half take one holiday while the rest take two or more. August is the most popular month to start a holiday followed by July, September and June in that order. The winter period from November to February is the least popular, with under 10% of holidays starting during that time.

The major mode of transport used by UK resident holiday travellers in getting to their destination both in Britain and abroad is the private car, even where business car use is excluded. The use of scheduled air services for holiday travel is greater than the use of chartered service. It is likely that several factors are at work here. As well as a trend towards travellers making their own independent travel arrangements using scheduled services, fly-drive arrangements are particularly popular in the growing North Atlantic market. Furthermore, inclusive tours frequently use the services of scheduled as well as chartered airlines.

Domestic holidays have not performed well over recent years and the overall number of UK holidays taken by UK residents has fallen by 1% since 1990 to reach 57.7 million (see Table 1.6). The big dip in the figures occurred in 1993. Despite the downward trend in volume, total spending has risen by 25% over the period. In a falling market, this highlights one of the major disadvantages of a UK holiday – the price of accommodation which can push up costs to be more expensive than a holiday overseas.

Table 1.6 Volume and value of UK holidays taken by UK residents 1990–5

	Million	*Index*	*% Change*	*£ million*	*Index*	*% Change*
1990	58.4	100	–	7,350	100	–
1991	58.3	100	–	7,750	105	+5
1992	59.9	103	+3	8,085	110	+4
1993	54.9	94	−8	8,425	115	+4
1994	56.0	96	+2	8,762	119	+4
1995 (est)	57.7	99	+3	9,200	125	+5

Source: *United Kingdom Tourism Survey (English Tourist Board, Northern Ireland Tourist Board, Scottish Tourist Board, Wales Tourist Board)*

In contrast, the number of overseas holidays taken by UK residents has risen by 16% to reach 24.7 million (see Table 1.7). This growth has not been consistent and the numbers fell by 2% in 1991, owing to the effects of the Gulf War and by a further decline in 1993 due to the effects of the recession. In terms of value, the overseas market has grown by 30% up to 1995. The growth has not been steady and was static during 1991 and 1993 when volume dropped slightly. Despite this growth, the cost of holidaying overseas has fallen in real terms, another advantage that this market has is over the relatively expensive domestic market.

In terms of choice of holiday, weather is the most important consideration when choosing a holiday, for all segments of the market irrespective of gender, age, class or region of residence. One method used to segment the market is socio-economic groups as recommended by the Institute of Practitioners of Advertising.

The choice of destination as an issue varies widely between both age and class, along with the decision maker within the family group.

Times of economic recession may affect patterns of holiday choice in terms of age, class and region within the UK, but many people see a holiday as a necessity. The options may be to take fewer holidays, stay in the UK rather than go abroad, book late to get a bargain, take a shorter holiday or choose a cheaper form of accommodation.

Another sector is the visiting friends and relatives (VFR) group, where spending is lower than other leisure spending. This is not just because VFR trips are shorter but because spending per night is less as travellers do not pay for accommodation and pay a reduced amount for catering. At around 4 million visits per year, the VFR segment is an important component of the UK market. One other UK domestic market of significance is the growing short break sector, both for holidays in the UK and abroad.

Overall, inclusive tour travel has fallen significantly since the peak reached in 1988, a trend which it was feared could have been much worse, given the impact of the Gulf War in January and February 1991 and the Civil War in former Yugoslavia.

As illustrated in Table 1.8, in terms of volume the UK market has an estimated 70% share in 1995, with the overseas market taking the remaining 30%. However the UK has been falling consistently down from 73% in 1990. Yet as consumer confidence has returned the multi-holiday pattern has become established and UK volume share will stabilise as holidaymakers supplement their overseas holidays with shorter UK based breaks.

In terms of value market share, holidays taken in the UK and those overseas are more evenly matched with UK holidays taking an estimated 51% of the market and overseas holidays 49% (see Table 1.9).

Table 1.10 shows that the short break holidays are a buoyant sector of domestic tourism; many holidaymakers are supplementing an annual long holiday overseas, with

	Million	Index	% Change	£ million	Index	% Change
1990	21.3	100	–	6,817	100	–
1991	20.8	98	– 2	6,849	100	–
1992	23.2	109	+12	7,987	117	+17
1993	22.9	108	– 1	7,969	117	–
1994	23.1	108	+ 1	8,131	119	+ 2
1995 (est)	24.7	116	+ 7	8,842	130	+ 9

Table 1.7 Volume and value of overseas holidays taken by UK residents 1990–5

Source: United Kingdom Tourism Survey (English Tourist Board, Northern Ireland Tourist Board, Scottish Tourist Board, Wales Tourist Board)

one or even two short holidays at home. Although the number of short holidays have not increased consistently with the decline in long holidays in the UK, the gap between short and long holidays is closing and short holidays are becoming more important to the industry. The volume share of the long holiday market has fallen from 54% to an estimated 52% over a six-year period, while short holidays have risen by two percentage points to 48%. Long holidays have fallen by 6% over the period to 29.8 million. In contrast to this the short holiday market has performed well, showing an estimated growth of over 4% over the period to reach 27.9 million.

Despite all this, what appears to have happened is that many potential holidaymakers are determined to get away even if it means economising at their destination. Looking to

Table 1.8 Volume market share of UK and overseas holidays taken by UK residents, 1990–5

	UK holidays			Overseas holidays			Total holiday	
	Million	*Index*	*%*	*Million*	*Index*	*%*	*Million*	*Index*
1990	58.4	100	73	21.3	100	27	79.7	100
1991	58.3	100	74	20.8	98	26	79.1	99
1992	59.9	103	72	23.2	109	28	83.1	104
1993	54.9	94	71	22.9	108	29	77.8	98
1994	56.0	96	71	23.1	108	29	79.1	99
1995	57.7	99	70	24.7	116	30	82.4	103

Source: United Kingdom Tourism Survey (English Tourist Board, Northern Ireland Tourist Board, Scottish Tourist Board, Wales Tourist Board)

Table 1.9 Value market share of UK and overseas holidays taken by UK residents 1990–5

	UK holidays			Overseas holidays			Total holiday	
	Million	*Index*	*%*	*Million*	*Index*	*%*	*Million*	*Index*
1990	7,350	100	52	6,817	100	48	14,167	100
1991	7,750	105	53	6,849	100	47	14,599	103
1992	8,085	110	50	7,987	117	50	16,072	113
1993	8,425	115	51	7,969	117	49	16,394	116
1994	8,762	119	52	8,131	119	48	16,893	119
1995	9,200	125	51	8,842	130	49	18,042	127

Source: United Kingdom Tourism Survey (English Tourist Board, Northern Ireland Tourist Board, Scottish Tourist Board, Wales Tourist Board)

Table 1.10 Volume market share of UK long and short holidays 1990–5

	Long holidays			Short holidays			Total holiday	
	Million	*Index*	*%*	*Million*	*Index*	*%*	*Million*	*Index*
1990	31.7	100	54	26.7	100	46	58.4	100
1991	32.2	102	55	26.1	98	45	58.3	100
1992	32.5	103	54	27.4	103	46	59.9	103
1993	30.3	96	55	24.6	92	45	54.9	94
1994	29.5	93	53	26.5	99	47	56.0	96
1995	29.8	94	52	27.9	104	48	57.7	99

Source: United Kingdom Tourism Survey (English Tourist Board, Northern Ireland Tourist Board, Scottish Tourist Board, Wales Tourist Board)

the future, there is some evidence that holidays, particularly holidays abroad, are becoming considered as necessities by an increasing proportion of the population. This means that at least for those in work, holidays are still taken even if times are hard, but length of stay and expenditure may be curtailed.

Another hopeful indicator is that the level of foreign holidays is now significantly below its 1988 peak, providing considerable scope for renewed growth as demand and the economy recover after the mid-1990s. Holiday expenditure is normally among the first sectors to recover from a downturn. Longer term, some see a fundamental change in the nature of the package holiday customer, accompanied by demands for a guaranteed minimum quality standard.

UK business travel

In addition to leisure travel, a second major demand segment of the hospitality industry is business travel.

The business travel market is made up of many sub-sectors, the major segment being the business traveller. One important component is the conference and exhibition market, and another is the incentive travel market where holidays are awarded as prizes for sales performance. The UK incentive travel market is estimated to be worth over £300 million, part of a much larger incentive industry. The interesting issue here is that incentive travel spans the border between leisure and business.

The holiday travel market dominates the market for UK domestic tourism whatever basis the measurement, be it trips made, nights spent or expenditure. However, although domestic business tourism produces relatively few trips and relatively fewer nights, it creates 15% of total domestic tourism spending. The comparison is 12% business trips out of a total of 121 million trips for all purposes. Domestic tourists use a wide variety of accommodation, particularly hospitality provided by friends and relatives. It is perhaps surprising to note that such accommodation is used even by domestic business travellers. Nevertheless by far the largest share of accommodation used by business travellers is taken by hotels with an even higher share of spending accounted for by them i.e. 66% of trips, only 57% of nights but 81% of spending.

In terms of the dominance of the private car in total domestic tourism, 72% of trips for all purposes use this mode of transport including business and the picture looks much the same if only business travel is considered. British Tourist Authority figures suggest 67% use the private car, the main difference from the overall picture being that on average the domestic business traveller uses the private car somewhat less but other modes more. The average expenditure per domestic trip is somewhat higher for business travellers. It has been shown that since business trips are in general shorter than leisure trips the discrepancy in average expenditure per night is even more marked.

Looking to the future, UK domestic tourism for business purposes was affected in the early 1990s but has been well placed to benefit from the economic recovery post-1994.

One feature of business travel demand that is likely to change between 1996 and 2006 is the proportion of women business travellers. For instance the proportion of women customers using the US-based hotel chain Radisson rose from 1% in 1970 to 30% in 1990 and 44% in 1991. This proportion will probably have reached 50% by the year 2000. Such a trend will have implications for accommodation provision. However, perhaps the most immediate concern of the hospitality industry at present relates to the prospects for growth in international travel demand by UK business people. This sector of the market has shown that it has been able to weather some of the economic storms of the past. The rationale for this is quite often it is when times are bad, a foreign export trip becomes even more urgent. This suggests that prospects for this sector are probably quite reasonable with recovery in the sector likely to lead rather than lag a more general economic UK recovery.

Summary

This chapter has given an overview of the tourism and travel industry and has shown that the hospitality industry is one element of the wider tourism picture. This chapter commenced with a definition of tourism and through it, the link between the provision of services and the hospitality industry. Economic significance was also considered. It went on to discuss elements such as tour operators, travel agents, airlines, UK ferry market and the wider European picture. A brief comment was made on tourism within central and eastern Europe, along with an analysis of common accommodation characteristics.

Further reading

- Albert-Pinole I. (1993) 'Tourism in Spain: evolution and factors of Spanish tourist development', in W. Pompl and P. Lavery (eds) *Tourism in Europe: Structures and Developments*, Wallingford: CAB International, pp. 242–61.
- Bray R. (1996) 'The package holiday market in Europe', *Travel and Tourism Analyst* 4: 51–71.
- Butler R. (1980) 'The concept of a tourist area cycle of evolution', *Canadian Geographer* 24: 5–12.
- Cooper C.P. (ed.) (1989–91) *Progress in Tourism Recreation and Hospitality Management*, vols 1–3, London: Belhaven Press.
- Cooper C.P. (1990) 'Resorts in decline: the management response', *Tourism Management* 11(1): 63–7.
- Cooper C.P., Fletcher J., Gilbert D., Wanhill S. and Shephard R. (eds) (1998) *Tourism Principles and Practice*, 2nd edition, London: Longman.
- Cooper C.P. and Lockwood A. (eds) (1992) *Progress in Tourism Recreation and Hospitality Management*, vol. 4, London: Belhaven Press.
- Cooper C.P. and Lockwood A. (eds) (1993–4) *Progress in Tourism Recreation and Hospitality Management*, vols 5–6, London: John Wiley.
- English Tourist Board (1991–1996) *The UK Tourist Statistics 1990–1995*, London: ETB.
- Howitt S. (1996) *Travel Agents and Overseas Tour Operators*, 12th edn, London: Key Note.
- Medlik S. (1991) *Managing Tourism*, London: Butterworth Heinemann.
- Middleton V. (1994) *Marketing in Travel and Tourism*, 2nd edn, Oxford: Butterworth Heinemann.
- NEDC (1992) *UK Tourism Competing for Growth*, London: National Economic Development Office.
- Pearce D. (1995) *Tourism Today: A Geographical Analysis*, London: Longman.
- Plog S. (1974) 'Why destination areas rise and fall in popularity', *Cornell Hotel and Restaurant Association Quarterly* 14(4): 55–8.
- Poon A. (1993) *Tourism, Technology and Competitive Strategies*, Wallingford: CAB International.
- Williams A. (1996) 'Mass tourism and international tour companies', in M. Barke, J. Towner and M. Newton (eds) *Tourism in Spain: Critical Issues*, Wallingford: CAB International, pp. 119–36.
- Williams A.M. and Shaw G. (eds) (1991) *Tourism and Economic Development: Western European Experiences* (2nd edn) London: Belhaven Press.

Chapter Two

Profile of the Accommodation Industry

Objectives

After reading this chapter you should be able to

■ Understand emerging trends, ideas and issues that drive the hotel industry and set them within the context of the accommodation industry.

■ Comment on the recent history of the hotel industry and consider possible future developments.

■ Appreciate that timeshare and camping and caravanning represent sectors within the accommodation industry.

Accommodation provision in the UK

History

In the late 1940s the UK hotel industry looked very different from the late 1990s for it was still living in a pre-war atmosphere. Traditional family holidays were usually spent at either Blackpool or Brighton. Managers in the four or five star hotels were usually trained at Lausanne Hotel School, Switzerland or possibly Cornell University in the USA. British hotel training was still thought to be slightly inferior even though courses were being set up at places such as Westminster College and Battersea College (later to be known as Surrey University).

By the 1960s, however, business people who travelled around the country and the growing number of overseas visitors expected a standard of service and a range of amenities comparable to hotels on the international circuit. During the 1960s, there came a series of dramatic changes, mostly imposed rather than initiated, such as the first transatlantic flight; Pan Am's 707 brought North America so much nearer to the UK. The phenomenal growth in flying opportunities and the resultant competition heralded by the introduction of these planes gave a new impetus to flying to and from North America. The arrival of the statutory Hotel and Catering Industrial Training Board (now known as the Hospitality Training Foundation), the Development of Tourism Act 1969 and the Fire Precautions Act 1971 all added pressure to change by improving standards, controls and sales potential. These external pressures were complemented, almost simultaneously, by a reorganisation of the industry's two major representative voices within the UK. The British Hotel Restaurant Caterers' Association (now known as the British Hospitality Association) as the trade association for the industry, and the Hotel and Catering Institutional Management Association (HCIMA) as the professional body (now known as the Hotel and Catering International Management Association).

Accommodation types

There are a wide range of accommodation types available in the UK and a number of distinctions can be identified. An important distinction in accommodation is the split between serviced and non-serviced types.

Staying in serviced accommodation, the customer would expect things to be done for them. Serviced means that staff are available on the premises to provide some services such as cleaning, meals, bars and room service. The availability of such services even if in fact they are not used, are included (explicitly or implicitly) in the price charged. Non serviced means that the sleeping accommodation is provided furnished on a rental basis, normally for a unit comprising several beds. While services for the provision of meals, bars, shops and cleaning may be available on a separate commercial basis, as in a holiday centre, they are not included in the price charged for the accommodation.

One main problem in reporting on the accommodation industry is that there is no generally accepted definition of a hotel, although in Chapter 1 the WTO definition was quoted (p. 7). The serviced sector in the UK ranges from first class and luxury hotels, which provide full service on a 24 hours a day basis at a relatively high cost, all the way down to homely bed and breakfast establishments. The non-serviced sector, known in Britain as self-catering accommodation, comprises a wide range of different units including villas, apartments, timeshare, chalets, cottages, caravans and camping, the bulk of which are rented equipped but with no personal services included in the published price. The bulk of self-catering units still cater for a budget priced market and the cost per person per night is very much less than could be obtained in the serviced sector.

In the late 1990s there are so many variations of serviced and non-serviced accommodation products that the distinction is often blurred in practice, although this difference remains useful for the purpose of analysis. Moreover there is no simple way of differentiating between accommodation units of different types and standards. For instance, the process of classification of the hotel industry has been attempted at various times in the UK. However, these attempts have concentrated largely on distinguishing hotels and other residential establishments, and they tend to rely on a system of voluntary registration. To add to the difficulties of measuring the industry, the national tourist boards (England, Wales and Scotland) define hotels in different ways. In addition to the various tourist board registration schemes, the Automobile Association (AA) and Royal Automobile Club (RAC) produce the best known of the private classification schemes. These schemes give some indication of quality of the approximately 27,000 hotels in the UK (although not all commentators are agreed on that figure).

Table 2.1 illustrates the type of accommodation for UK holidays by *volume* in the period between 1993 and 1995. Commercial self-catering accommodation is more popular on British holidays than serviced accommodation. The single most popular option is staying with friends and relatives.

In contrast Table 2.2 illustrates the type of accommodation for UK holidays by *value* for the period 1993 to 1995. Commercial self-catering accommodation takes a larger proportion of holiday spending than serviced accommodation.

Of over 27,000 hotels within the UK, 83% are within England, a high proportion of which are bed and breakfast establishments. This latter point can be estimated by analysing the distribution of hotels by size. The largest number of hotels are in the 4–10 room category. In Scotland and Wales, larger hotels are concentrated in the main centres of population such as Edinburgh, Glasgow and Cardiff. London has the largest concentration of hotels (both large and small) reflecting its importance as a business and leisure tourist destination.

Table 2.1 Types of accommodation for UK holidays by nights 1993–5 (%)

	1993	1994	1995
Friends and relatives	39	40	42
Hotel/motel/guest house	17	16	18
Rented self-catering	13	12	11
Caravan	17	15	16
Camping	4	4	4
Bed and breakfast	2	2	2
Holiday centre/village	4	3	3
Boat	1	1	1
Timeshare/second home	1	1	2
Other/transit	2	3	3
Total commercial accommodation	51	48	46
Of which serviced	19	20	20
Of which self-catering	31	28	26
Total non-commercial accommodation	49	52	54

Source: United Kingdom Tourism Survey (English Tourist Board, Northern Ireland Tourist Board, Scottish Tourist Board, Wales Tourist Board)

Note: Columns may add to more than 100% because more than one type of accommodation may be used on some holidays

Table 2.2 Types of accommodation for UK holidays by value 1993–5 (%)

	1993	1994	1995
Hotel/motel/guest house	32	32	35
Rented self-catering	14	12	12
Friends and relatives	28	29	24
Caravan	12	11	13
Holiday centre/village	4	4	5
Camping	3	3	3
Bed and breakfast	2	3	4
Boat	1	1	1
Timeshare/second home	1	1	1
Other/transit	2	3	3
Total commercial accommodation	64	62	67
Of which serviced	36	36	41
Of which self-catering	29	25	27
Total non-commercial accommodation	36	38	33

Source: United Kingdom Tourism Survey (English Tourist Board, Northern Ireland Tourist Board, Scottish Tourist Board, Wales Tourist Board)

Note: Columns may add to more than 100% because more than one type of accommodation may be used on some holidays

The various regions have many hotels with a small number of bedrooms, most of which are bed and breakfast establishments. Outside London, the largest number of hotels are in tourist regions such as the West Country, Lake District and Blackpool. Many hotels are also found in areas that have a high population and business concentration, namely Southern England and the South East. The West Country tends to have smaller hotels, catering for leisure travellers. A similar pattern can be seen in Scotland.

If one strips out the figure for bed and breakfast establishments (4–10 room category) the total number of hotels in the UK is estimated to be 20,600. The number of hotels by type and category can be estimated using data from the tourist boards, the RAC and AA. The value of the hotel market, broken down by type, can also be estimated.

Industry supply

In addition to the classification schemes another source of information on the UK's hotel industry is the Government's Central Statistical Office; of the hotels included, only 4.8% have a turnover of over £1 million pounds. Since 1987 there has been little change in this statistic, although the number of hotels in the lowest bracket, turnover under £50,000, has declined reflecting, to some extent, a concentration of ownership.

The major hotel companies own approximately 6% of all hotels in the UK. The top ten hotel groups in the UK own nearly 800 hotels with a combined turnover of approximately £4 billion. Since 1989, four out of the top ten hotel companies have been taken over. Crest was taken over by Forte in May 1990; Mecca Leisure was acquired by the Rank Organisation in 1990; Jarvis Hotels acquired Embassy in 1990; Forte was taken over by Granada plc in 1996. The background to some of these major companies will now be discussed. Only three hotel companies in the UK, Granada, Whitbread and Thistle, have over 100 hotels.

Forte

Forte (a division of Granada plc) operates 506 hotels world-wide of which 384 are in the UK, making it the largest UK hotelier. The company's UK exposure to London is high. The company's major restructuring operation in May 1991 launched its new branding of existing products and was subsequently modified in January 1996 after Granada's £3.9 billion takeover (see case study on p. 66). The history of Forte can be traced back to 1934 when Charles Forte (now Lord Forte) opened a milk bar in central London. During the

Figure 2.1 *History of Forte 1992–6*

The name of Trust House Forte Hotels was changed to Forte plc in a £16 million marketing campaign (1992). Development of six brands/collections to fit each of the hotels.

Focusing management and financial resources on the core hotel and restaurant activities.

Reorganising the firm to create a sharper and more focused company with shorter lines of communication, lower cost base and a stronger customer orientation.

Strengthening the management team through the recruitment of a substantial number of new executives.

Reducing the firm's overall debt with disposing the stake in Kentucky Fried Chicken and Gardner Merchant as well as reducing the share in Alpha Airports Group.

Investment in existing assets: hotels, restaurants, Little Chefs, Travelodges, and motorway service areas.

Creation of the Forte/Agip chain of hotels in Italy.

Greater emphasis on sales and marketing, quality, service standards and the control of costs.

Purchase of the Meridien chain of hotels from Air France.

Long-term incentive plan for most senior executives.

Sale of the Harvester chain of restaurants to Bass plc. Sale of Lillywhites, Griesons, Travelodge USA and White Hart Hotels.

next 25 years Lord Forte transformed this small food service operation into the largest hotel chain in the UK, as well as developing a presence in other continents. Its assets encompassed the full breadth of the hospitality business from a stake in the Savoy Group, the George V in Paris to the Little Chefs that serve Britain's road network. Sir Rocco Forte took over as chairman in 1992 and Figure 2.1 illustrates the changes he implemented up until the bid in November 1995.

Since Granada's takeover of Forte hotels at the beginning of 1996 the victors' booty included a dazzling portfolio of over 100 Forte Exclusive and Meridien properties worldwide; among Granada's self-imposed deadlines was a commitment to sell off the Exclusive properties by early 1997. Selling the crown jewels has proved harder than imagined. One of the most prominent hotel sales in the London market during 1996 was Granada's disposal of the Hyde Park Hotel for £86 million. The property was acquired by Hong Kong based Mandarin Oriental Hotel Group, thus making a return to the London hotel scene after ending their involvement with the Ritz the previous year. Another disposal was the sale of the Westbury in New York City, which was bought by Chelsfield in February 1997. This was packaged with the Forte Grand Westbury in London for a total of £90 million. Two other London Exclusive properties, Brown's and the Grosvenor House, remain unsold at the time of writing. The Grosvenor House, possessor of one of the largest banqueting venues in Europe, with a likely value somewhere between £300 million and £400 million, has been illustrative of the difficulties surrounding the piecemeal sale of these assets. Reports circulated that extensive repair work was required on the building on Park Lane and the names of possible buyers bandied around have included Saudi Prince Al-Waleed, who has already bought another exclusive gem, the George V in Paris. Granada turned down an offer from Sir Rocco Forte to buy back the properties as an entity thus committing themselves to a piecemeal sale.

Thistle Hotels plc (formerly Mount Charlotte Thistle Investments Ltd)

This group was purchased by Brierley Investments Ltd (BIL) in October 1990. In May 1991, BIL sold 30% of its stake in Mount Charlotte to two Singapore government agencies. The company was floated on the UK stock market during 1996 raising over £350 million in a share flotation. Thistle is London's largest hotel operator with 24 properties and 6,557 rooms.

Mount Charlotte acquired the Thistle group of hotels in 1989, with Thistle accounting for about 4% of the group's turnover. In 1996 the group had approximately 106 hotels mostly in the three and four star category, biased to the London market. The company's two main core products are Highlife Value Breaks and Conference Plan. Highlife was formed to meet the demand of shorter stay visits and the latter the conference market. In 1990 the company moved to create a more integrated and international system. This enabled it to sell a variety of rates world-wide and to connect directly to the major airline reservation systems.

Queens Moat plc

The company was formed in 1967 when its founder John Bairstow converted his home into a hotel. In 1972, Queens Modern Hotels Ltd was purchased and in 1982 it acquired 25 hotels in Grand Metropolitan's Country Hotel range, doubling the size of the company. The company moved into continental Europe in 1986. The company is predominantly a mid-market group with 79% of its rooms at the three star level and low exposure to the UK economy, a total of 86 hotels.

The company's strategy has been to develop critical mass in a country and then to develop a brand with a national identity rather than to have one international brand. It has extended its portfolio by the acquisition and development of hotels franchised to Holiday Inns. Queens Moat now owns and operates 25% of the Holiday Inns in Europe. An advantage of this, is that it has access to the Holidex reservations service, and the identity of the world's major mid-market hotel.

Because of the company's financial problems in 1993, the company was suspended from the London Stock Exchange pending clarification of its accounts. Its founder John Bairstow resigned in August 1993; the company was subsequently relisted under new management, with a substantial reduction in room stock.

Jarvis Hotels

Jarvis took over the Allied Lyons chain of Embassy hotels in July 1990 and operates approximately 62 hotels throughout the UK. The early 1990s saw the company's three and four star hotels refurbished as Summit Hotels with an emphasis on conference facilities, and health and fitness centres.

Whitbread plc

This British brewer has a considerable interest in the hospitality industry. In addition to its brewing, pub retailing and restaurant interests, it also has the Whitbread Hotel Company (WHC). The hotel section has a number of brands, perhaps the most visible being its budget hotel Travel Inn with over 110 sites. With its link up with Marriott, twenty-two hotels are trading under the Marriott flag, a further six former Lansbury hotels have been converted to the 'Courtyard by Marriott' brand, while fourteen will for the present remain unbranded.

Ladbroke plc

Ladbroke is one of the largest companies quoted on the London Stock Exchange with its largest core business being hotels. In terms of size it took a quantum leap forward in 1987 with the purchase of the International Hilton chain. Ladbroke own the Hilton operations outside the USA although it announced a joint marketing agreement with its US counterpart in 1997. By owning a hotel chain across forty-six countries the risk is lessened of national recession affecting the company. Within Hilton's room stock, 92% trade at the higher levels of the market. Hilton in the UK is London dominated where 50% of its rooms are located, although only ten of its forty-two UK hotels are in the capital. Throughout Europe as a whole, 80% of the company's hotels are in gateway cities.

Hilton specialises in marketing its single brand to a range of the world's hotel demand categories, hence the importance of world-wide brand advertising. Moreover, the company's central reservations system linked to the main airline booking systems becomes crucial in providing ease of access for potential customers around the world.

Bass plc

Founded in 1946 by Pan American World Airlines, Inter-Continental's early development was along the airline's routes. Under Pan Am's ownership the company was almost entirely a hotel management company. In 1981 Inter-Continental was bought by the UK's Grand Metropolitan, which sold it in 1988 to the Saison Group. In 1989 Saison sold a 40% interest in the company to SAS but bought back that share in 1991. Restructuring of the company took place in 1994 when the real estate side of the company and the hotel management operations were separated. The company is primarily a hotel management company although it also owns, leases and has joint venture and franchise arrangements on its hotels. The company has three distinct types of hotels within its operations:

Inter-Continental Hotels and Resorts, Forum Hotels International and Global Partner Hotels and Resorts. The company has a total of 143 hotels in 55 countries. During 1998 the company was purchased by the British company Bass plc.

Organisations

Both the hotel and catering industry and the wider tourism industry contain a number of industry related organisations, some on a purely UK basis and others with a world-wide membership. These organisations can be considered under three broad groups:

- educational and professional bodies
- trade associations
- government related authorities.

Educational and professional bodies

The development of catering education has been very closely linked with the development and growth of the two professional bodies which formed the Hotel Catering and Institutional Management Association (HCIMA) in 1971: the Institutional Management Association (IMA) and the Hotel and Catering Institute (HCI), now known as the Hotel and Catering International Management Association.

The Institutional Management Association had been operating in its particular field of activity since its formation in May 1938. A committee of representatives made up of employers, employees and educationalists with the support of government was responsible for educational developments in institutional management and the introduction of a Certificate of Institutional Management in 1944.

The Hotel and Catering Institute was established as a professional body in 1949. The forerunner was the Catering Trades Education Committee, an advisory body created at national level for the purposes of studying the educational needs of the industry and encouraging the provision of adequate training facilities. Until 1943, technical education in the catering industry on the hotel side was available only at Westminster Technical College.

The HCIMA is a professional body for managers within the food and accommodation service industries. Its objective is to set and maintain standards of management, education, experience and practice for the benefit of its members, the industry and the general public. Membership is open only to those who meet the strict education and industrial experience standards required and who accept the code of conduct and disciplinary procedures of the HCIMA. The Association has some 22,000 members of which approximately 20,000 are resident in the UK. The other 2,000 are spread throughout 90 countries in the world.

One of the areas in which the HCIMA is involved is the provision of qualifications for the hospitality industry. This brings it into contact with a number of other organisations. The Hospitality Training Foundation (HTF), formerly known as the Hotel Catering Training Company (HCTC) and also the Hotel and Catering Training Board (HCTB), owes its origin to the Industrial Training Act 1964. Each Board comprised representatives of employers, employees and educationalists. The HCTB was established in 1966 and covers nearly all aspects of the hotel and catering industry. It advises employers and assists them in the training of their staff. This includes the provision of schemes of training from which both employers and employees can benefit. The HTF sees its training policies and priorities as focusing on a number of issues ranging from management development and management training to issues such as industrial release, the craft side of the industry and training for unemployed people.

The HCTC was set up in November 1989. This was as a direct result of the government's decision set out in its White Paper Employment for the 1990s. That decision stated that the remaining statutory training bodies, of which the HCTB was one, should move as quickly as possible to becoming an independent non-statutory training organisation. With more than 350 professional staff in over 60 training centres, the HTF is the largest training organisation within the UK industry. Any profits generated from the training division's commercial activities are used to help the HTF board of trustees maintain the real value of their assets and reserves. The HTF is financially supported by the profits from its three new trading divisions; The Stonelow Group, The Hospitality Awarding Body and The Hotel and Catering Training Company. These fund and promote essential core work in areas such as human resources information and research, occupational standards and careers work.

Trade associations

The British Hospitality Association (BHA), formerly known as the British Hotel Restaurant Caterers' Association (BHRCA), is the industry's trade association.

The BHA is a trade association that represents companies, not individuals unlike the HCIMA. More than 12,500 hotels, restaurants and catering operators are members of the BHA and a further 7,000 hotels are affiliated through local hotel associations. Almost every major hotel restaurant and catering company, as well as the majority of independent hoteliers, are members. The BHA provides a direct service to members through its publications and purchasing schemes. The association is a powerful voice to government, civil servants and to other related organisations.

Government related authorities

The task to be completed by a national tourist office is the effective and efficient defence of the country's stake in the tourism market with its massive implications for foreign currency earnings and employment. Britain's national tourist office, the British Tourist Authority (BTA), is an agency of government responsible for discharging the tourism function in overseas markets as far as marketing is concerned. The BTA is the agency with the unique role of a destination marketing authority. It has an advisory role to government and key interests in providing options for development based on market research and intelligence. It also liaises with government and key interests in the development of the government's tourism policies. The BTA has the responsibility for preparing the marketing strategy which will implement agreed government policy in consultation with the industry. Most importantly it provides a co-operative marketing base, a focal point for consultation and co-operation.

It is pertinent at this point to look at the origins of the BTA. It was set up in 1929 as the Travel Association of Great Britain and Ireland, surviving in various forms of voluntary membership for the next forty years. The Development of Tourism Act 1969 established the BTA alongside the English Tourist Board, Northern Ireland Tourist Board, Scottish Tourist Board and Wales Tourist Board. These national boards are responsible for marketing in the domestic UK market. Subsequent to this, the Scottish Tourist Board was given statutory powers to market Scotland overseas so long as its policies were complementary with the BTA. In addition regional tourist boards enable the development of tourism locally. They use funds, when available, as a lever to achieve private sector funding.

Employment

About 2.5 million people are directly employed in the UK hospitality industry with 66% of these jobs in the commercial sector. Forecasts indicate that employment could increase by 400,000 to the year 2010 with some 130,000 of these jobs created by 1999. These are direct jobs and do not include any new employment created by support industries. When the effects of turnover are included in the employment forecasts, the industry will need to fill 590,000 vacancies a year of which some will be craft and the rest managerial. In discussing employment levels within the UK's hotel industry many people refer to the Department of Employment's *Employment Gazette*.

Of these 2.5 million people approximately

- 24% work in hotels
- 22% in restaurants
- 27% work in pubs
- 13% work in contract catering
- 14% work in clubs.

In years to come, it is clear from demographic trends that there will be a reduction in the supply of school leavers for this expanding industry. This implies a need to refine recruitment, training and employment practices for adults coming into the industry, either for the first time or returning after a period of absence.

Hotel grading schemes

Hotel grading schemes are a method of categorising hotels according to their facilities. Most schemes have five category ratings, from a single hotel or inn at the bottom category to a luxury hotel at the top. In the UK there are several schemes operating such as the AA, RAC, English Tourist Board (ETB), Michelin and Egon Ronay.

The AA operates a five star rating scheme and has introduced a percentage quality rating. Star classification is essentially a guide to the type of hotel, indicating the character of the accommodation and service it sets out to provide. It is based on a minimum requirement for each star rating level.

Following an application for grading, the hotel receives an unannounced visit from an inspector who stays overnight and takes every opportunity to test as many of the services as possible. Having settled the bill the following morning, the inspector arranges a thorough inspection of the entire premises.

The resulting classification indicates the following:

- **One star** hotels and inns generally of small scale with acceptable facilities and furnishings. All bedrooms with hot and cold water, adequate bath and lavatory arrangements, meals provided for residents, but their availability for non-residents may be limited.
- **Two star** hotels offering a higher standard of accommodation and some private bathrooms and showers. A wider choice of food is provided but the availability of meals to non-residents may be limited.
- **Three star** well-appointed hotels with more spacious accommodation, a large number of bedrooms with private bathrooms and showers. Fuller meal facilities are provided, but luncheon and weekend meal services to non-residents may be restricted.
- **Four star** exceptionally well appointed hotels offering a high standard of comfort and service with a majority of bedrooms with private bathrooms and showers.
- **Five star** luxury hotels offering the highest international standards.

From the AA's point of view, the classification scheme provides a service to its 5 million members, public relations for the company and an important source of revenue. The company has introduced a quality assurance scheme which involves five key concepts:

- cleanliness
- quality of food
- staff efficiency and service
- hospitality
- bedrooms.

This measure will appear as a percentage and will mean that the public will have a more thorough evaluation of the hotel, if, of course, the hotel chooses to enter the quality assurance scheme. Unlike stars which are open to discussion, the percentage score is not negotiable and is reviewed twice a year. It includes marks given to reflect the inspector's personal opinion of the services offered. The AA has changed its standards since before the First World War, when it began operating. An example is the bathroom ensuite; the AA decided it should be standard in all four and five star hotels and should be in a number of lower category rooms, which has meant that private bathrooms are the norm in the 1990s. Decisions are based on the reports of inspectors, their instinctive feelings, what the public is beginning to demand, and therefore what the hotel industry should supply. This is backed up by the AA's market research. The AA places importance on ensuring that the standards are in response to public demand. By laying down widely publicised criteria required before different stars can be awarded, the AA is effectively telling a hotelier: if you do this, you stand a chance of getting an AA appointment; if you don't, there is no chance. This is an example of how the AA, along with other organisations such as the RAC and the ETB are influencing the hotel industry.

The importance of classification to the potential hotel guest is that it can be used as a fast selection criterion. It is a source of comparison between hotels. For the hotel it can be a valuable marketing tool if the information is known to the customer.

However, the classification schemes have been criticised for being misleading, inconsistent and confusing. A hotel having five crowns issued by the English Tourist Board, four stars by the AA and not being listed by Egon Ronay does not assist either the potential customer or the hotelier. The associations in question are not independently financed, with each scheme charging for inspection. Classification on quality is subjective, reflecting the inspector's personal opinion of the services offered and providing a snapshot picture taken at one point in time. The star rating system is an increasingly inaccurate guideline for selecting a hotel for either business or holiday accommodation because of massive price differentials. Hotel grading schemes are clearly here to stay, but there are a number of arguments for and against their use and effectiveness.

Demand for hotel accommodation

Looking to the longer term, three key factors will influence the pattern of demand for UK hotel accommodation:

- rising affluence
- freetime
- demography.

Rising affluence

Rising affluence in the late 1980s accelerated the demand for relatively high cost leisure pursuits, such as holidays and weekend breaks. It needs to be remembered that a projected rise in real disposable income of say 2.5% would translate into a 3.5% rise in spending on leisure services of which demand for accommodation is one component. This relationship is explained by the economic term **elasticity of demand**. Looking to the medium term, future growth in the UK economy is expected to the year 1999 which will be translated into a high level of demand for hotel accommodation. Economic growth leads to increases in disposable income. Increases in trade and commerce derived from economic growth similarly fuels demand for business travel. Demand for accommodation is closely linked to demand for travel which in turn is sensitive to economic cycles in the main originating countries and in the international economies of the world.

Freetime

Freetime not only affects the time available for leisure and specifically demand for hotel accommodation but also affects the customer mix. The amount of available leisure time will contract over the next few years for significant groups of people. This will be due to a wide range of factors, the key ones being changing work structures and mounting pressures at work, growing female participation in the workforce, increasing mobility and the rising need for continuous education. These factors will increase the value of time and money allocated during free hours and will lead to expectations of the quality of services and products to rise. In addition to the obvious price and income factors influencing travel demand, social, work patterns and consumer tastes also have an impact within the overall growth of the tourism industry. Consumer tastes and preferences also change. This changing mix has boosted demand for relatively time intensive leisure activities such as weekend and holiday breaks.

Demography

Demography will also affect the mix of demand for hotel accommodation. There will, for instance, be a very substantial projected decline in the 25–34 age group over the next few years (see Figure 2.2). Conversely there will be a growing demand for accommodation suitable for families in the 35–44 age group. The population of the western world is ageing, changing several segments of the population significantly in terms of relative

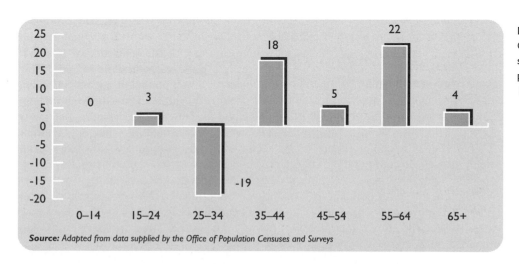

Figure 2.2
Changing age structure of the UK population, 1995–2005 (%)

Source: Adapted from data supplied by the Office of Population Censuses and Surveys

importance. Age has become a more important factor in determining consumer behaviour as various age groups develop different interests and consumer patterns. Young professionals constitute a major travel market in developed countries. The 25–44 age group tends to be better educated and more widely travelled than previous generations. The growing older segment (55–64) of the population includes a significant segment with retirement savings and relatively higher disposable incomes for leisure travel. With time and income available, this segment is more inclined to travel and also tends to stay in better class accommodation when they do so.

Market segments

Some better defined market segments are emerging:

- single and female travellers
- short breaks
- green tourism.

It is these three key factors which will have a significant influence on the UK hotel industry between 1997 and 2007.

Single and female travellers
Single and female travellers are significant factors, both on business travel in markets such as Europe and North America and on holiday travel for markets such as Japan. Since the early 1970s female employment has risen by one-fifth, while male employment has fallen. Women increasingly take part in many areas and activities previously dominated by men; their buying power will grow and this will be translated into a demand for hospitality services.

Short breaks
Short breaks are increasing their share of the travel market: city centre holidays, island and mountain destinations are increasingly popular.

Green tourism
As some coastal environments suffer from congestion and pollution, green tourism in general is likely to become a key issue from the late 1990s on. For the hotelier there is a constant need to adapt to changing market characteristics and demand patterns.

Accommodation provision in Europe

There is an overwhelming concentration of hotel rooms in western Europe accounting for approximately 41% of the world-wide total. If central and eastern Europe is included, this figure rises to over 44%. A number of countries within Europe feature high in size ranking with Italy, Spain, France, UK, Austria and Greece amounting to about 33% of the total. The hotel industry comprises the largest sector of the overall tourism industry, with accommodation accounting for 32% of total receipts. The accommodation market in Europe remains highly fragmented, with most companies independent and family owned, and publicly quoted hotel companies consisting of an estimated 20% of the European accommodation stock. Within Europe, most hotel chains remain rooted on their home turf. Accor is primarily French orientated and Forte/Granada, UK. In recent years many have branched outside their sphere of influence.

France

France, Europe's number one tourist destination, provides a wide range of accommodation types that can be split into three main sectors. First, hotels are graded from one to four star luxury. In addition to the hotel groups, there are collections of private hotels such as the Logis de France and the Relais Château. Second, camping and caravan sites have four grades from one to four star. Third, the Gîtes de France provide reasonably priced self-catering accommodation in or near small country villages. The gîte itself may be a small cottage, village house or flat in the owner's house.

France has over 50% of its capacity in the two star category and 39% of its guests are from overseas. The French hotel market is the most advanced in Europe in terms of product segmentation. Accor dominates the French market and along with Société de Louvre accounts for 87% of quoted hotels in France. The dominance of these two companies act as a barrier to the development of other hotel brands. A characteristic feature of quoted companies in the French market is the 57% exposure to the economy lodging segment. This is a major difference from the UK and most other countries where this segment accounts for a much lower proportion of quoted room stock.

Accor is now a world-wide chain with its centre of gravity in France, where it has 34% of the group's total room stock. It is the largest hotel company in western Europe and the world's largest operator of owned hotels with 2,313 properties and 261,380 rooms in some 65 different countries. The present day Groupe Accor has grown very rapidly from its foundation in 1967, making it one of the younger companies to have risen to prominence in the international hotel industry. Its origins lie in the opening of the first Novotel hotel in Lille in 1967. Under the corporate name of Novotel SIEH this gave rise to the development of a chain of hotels under Novotel and also Ibis in 1974 and Mercure in 1975, mainly throughout Europe and Africa. By the end of the 1970s the company had 210 hotels and had begun its diversification into the restaurant business. In 1980 the company bought an interest in Jacques Borel International (JBI), a move which among other developments brought with it the Sofitel hotel chain. Full control of JBI was achieved in 1982 and in 1983 the company changed its name to Accor. In 1985 Accor developed its new Formule 1 budget hotel concept and in 1990 it acquired the Motel 6 chain in the USA.

Italy

Italy has 42% of its capacity in the three star category and 25% in the two star sector. The Italian hotel market is highly fragmented with a few chains having little market share. Out of the country's 975,000 rooms less than 10% are operated by stock exchange quoted companies. These include Accor, Ciga/ITT Sheraton, Jolly (the only quoted Italian hotel company) and Forte/Agip (Granada). The major cities in Italy are Bologna, Rome, Milan, Venice, Florence and Naples and represent 55% of the quoted rooms stock. Overall 57% of demand is generated from within Italy. The market for hotel accommodation is dominated by the holiday market as the country is a major holiday destination. Because of the business base in Italy, there is limited exposure to foreign business travellers which explains a lack of interest by the hotel chains in expanding within the country.

Spain

Spain has 45.6% in the three star sector and 21.7% in the four star sector. The country attracts some 60% of its guests from overseas. Spain's largest hotel operator, Cofir, is in-digenous and controls 55 hotels. Other companies, such as Accor, Holiday Inn, Hilton and Forte/Granada, have begun to establish a presence in the country. These companies have concentrated their interests around Madrid, Barcelona and Seville. Because of its re-liance on foreign and domestic holidaymakers for more than three-quarters of its demand, this limits its attraction to the major companies. Until the market has an all-year-round de-mand, rather than a dependence on the spring or the summer, it is unlikely that major companies will show much interest.

Germany

In Germany, only 16% of hotel guests are from overseas. The first hotel groups to move into Germany did so in the early 1960s. These were chains such as Inter-Continental, Hilton and Sheraton. Domestic chains, such as Steigenberger AG and Maritim, were either non-existent at this time or very restricted in operations. The focus of the international hotel groups was to develop city centre locations targeted at a high market level and were mostly operated under management contracts. The chains who followed them were Ramada, Novotel and Holiday Inn; as a result, the boom in hotel construction was from 1963 to 1973. However, it was not until the mid-1970s that German hotel companies had a major impact on the market. At present, there is a combination of German and International Groups operating within the country. Although hotel chains aimed for pri-mary locations, the hotel market is still largely fragmented, due to the dominance of the small family-run hotel within the hotel market. The Hotel Garni, serving breakfast only, features strongly within the German hotel industry. German hotel facilities are mainly di-rected at the business traveller and an increasingly important sector of the industry lies in conferences. Following this, the German hotel product changed over the years to reflect this significant sector of the market. Most of the hotels built recently have a special em-phasis on this sector. Germany operates no standard classification scheme within its hotel industry. However, the German Hotel Association (DEHOGA) provides a grading system within its annual *German Hotel Guide*. This grading system operates by the attributes and facilities of the hotel (such as restaurants, bars, room service, and mini-bars). The sum of these values results in a classification; much of the process of classification is left to the discretion of the hotel proprietor. Nevertheless, it should be an aim for the future to in-troduce a nationally acknowledged classification scheme. A majority of the major hotel companies have their room stock located in the primary cities and a relatively low ex-posure to secondary and tertiary locations.

Germany in the 1990s still has an industry structure where most properties are family owned, although the dynamics of the German market are changing as the country has been earmarked as a strategic opportunity for many hotel chains. Accor (137 hotels), Queens Moat Houses (under the Queens Hotel brand, 36 hotels), Manor Care (33 hotels) and Holiday Inn (46 hotels) have expanded rapidly into this market. In Germany the major hotel companies have a high exposure to the upscale market; while there are no major hotel cities, the primary cities include Munich, Frankfurt, Bonn, Berlin and Hamburg.

Switzerland

The Swiss Hotel Association lists around 2,600 hotels and pensions that are members of the Association. In addition there are 450 camping and caravan sites and youth hostels primarily for the under 25s. Switzerland is able to offer a wide range of health spas, clinics, climatic health resorts and convalescent homes.

The Netherlands

All Dutch hotels are classified according to the Benelux Hotel classification which beside awarding one to five stars for facilities consists of the following types:

- Hotel/café/restaurant   an establishment built and fitted out to provide accommodation and in which a café and a restaurant or a café/restaurant are also operated.
- Motel   a hotel/café/restaurant integrated with a motorway or trunk road and adapted to the special needs of road users.
- Hotel/restaurant   an establishment fitted out to provide accommodation in which a restaurant is also operated.
- Hotel Garni   an establishment providing accommodation in which only bed and breakfast are provided.
- Apartment Hotel   an establishment providing accommodation in flats, studio flats or the like, let out by the day.

The relative importance of these different types of accommodation is difficult to assess but they can be considered under a number of headings such as nights per trip, spend per trip, spend per night, purpose of visit. This analysis of the European hotel industry will now be extended to a case study on one former eastern European bloc country, Hungary, with special attention to its capital Budapest.

Case Study: Hungarian tourism and the up-market hotel industry in Budapest: a country in transition

Background

Hungarian tourism and hotel industry needs to be set within the context of the political and economic environment. Despite signs of political liberalisation appearing in the 1980s in 1989 90–95% of the country's properties were still in state ownership. Thus the first task of the new democratically elected government was to manage the transition to a market economy. In terms of economic transition the new government inherited $20 billion of foreign debt, a collapse of the traditional industries, unemployment at over 12% in 1995, GDP decreasing by 25% between 1989 and 1994 and inflation at over 22% in 1995. Tourism in Hungary is characterised by large tourist traffic but relatively modest economic yield. In terms of international arrivals in 1995, the country occupied fourth place in Europe. However, on the basis of centrally registered hard currency income, it does not even appear ranked in the top twenty European countries; daily expenditure of foreign visitors is around $40, equivalent to one-third of the western European average.

The composition of international travellers differs from other European countries: two-thirds originate from other east European countries, with many excursionists coming from neighbouring countries. The average length of stay of foreign tourists is also lower than

case study continues ▶

the European average due to the high proportion of former communist bloc travellers, whose buying power is far weaker than that of the western European visitors.

Budapest hotel market

The Budapest hotel market is characterised by the fact that the higher the category of the hotel, the higher the occupancy rate. Although room occupancy in the higher category of hotels has shown slight improvements since 1995, it is still below the rate of the early 1990s when it reached 77%. In 1994, the average occupancy of high category (four and five star) hotels was 65.2%. In 1994, the total number of up-market hotels was twenty-three units, situated mainly in the capital. There are four five star hotels, all in Budapest, and thirteen of the nineteen four star properties are also located in the capital.

Budapest received 35% of the total tourist turnover in 1994, which was 7% higher than 1993. The majority of international tourism in Hungary is concentrated in Budapest and its surrounding areas. Over three-quarters of the incoming foreign tourists visit Budapest, which often means overcrowding and high occupancy (76%) during the summer months. In contrast the winter months see occupancy rates in these hotels below 50%. Hotels therefore suffer from fluctuating demand levels. The shortcomings of the market may be due to a lack of experienced and properly qualified personnel, who grew up under more than forty years of a centrally directed, inward looking and east concentrated economy. Looking to the future, with proper marketing initiatives and qualified personnel, demand for hotel accommodation in Budapest is expected to grow. An increase in quality and standards from the hotel supply side will, it is hoped, facilitate an influx of more international tourist arrivals to the capital. International hotel chains are moving into Budapest, and the city is amongst other European capitals, which offers accommodation from Marriott, Hyatt, Hilton, Kempinski, Ramada, Novotel and other Accor properties. Two out of the three major, previously state-owned hotel companies are privatised which gives an indication by the present government to move further towards a market economy and away from its former communist history.

Accommodation provision in North America

The US hotel industry is vast with 47,350 units and 3.45 million rooms. It is one of the nation's largest employers with 1.527 million workers, 32 people for every property that is open. The USA is by far the largest hotel country in the world and is efficient in so far as only 19 quoted companies account for nearly 11,000 hotels, an average of over 550 hotels per company. In the UK the average number of hotels by quoted company is only 27. Three companies, Hospitality Franchise Systems (HFS), Manor Care and Bass account for 77% of the quoted hotels in the USA. By room ranking these three companies plus Marriott account for more than 78% of total rooms. There are ten major hotel cities in the USA – Atlanta, Boston, Chicago, Dallas, Houston, Los Angeles, New York, Orlando, San Francisco and Washington DC. The only other major hotel cities in the world are London, Paris and Toronto. The main development over the past few years in the USA has been economy lodging which now accounts for more than 26% of the quoted room stock and continues to be the fastest growing sector. In terms of hotel size there are 44 hotels in the US (out of a total of 58 in the world) with 1,000 rooms or more. The country therefore benefits more than any other from the economies of scale inherent in these hotels.

Another characteristic feature of the US market is the 62% of rooms which are franchised hotels with an affiliation to Bass, HFS and Manor Care. More than 27% of the rooms in terms of affiliation are in management contract hotels and these are operated by the main native US chains – Marriott, Hilton Hotels Corporation and ITT Sheraton. In the USA, the 370,000 quoted company rooms under management contract is equivalent to all the quoted hotel rooms in the UK, illustrating the extent to which this approach to hotel investment and management differs between the USA and Europe.

While the industry's growth rate was impressive during the 1980s, it was very slow in the early 1990s and with growth in full service properties stalled, construction tended to be biased towards cheaper and smaller economy hotels, and consequently average hotel size fell. This trend was also reflected in lower staffing levels of these properties as the number of employees per hotel drifted lower.

The US hotel industry is affected by economic factors just like other regions of the world such as the UK or mainland Europe. In this respect the early 1990s saw a fall off in demand with a reduction in average achieved room rates; however, such a trend only partly explained problems within the US hotel industry. Between 1982 and 1992 the industry added over 1 million rooms, a 42.8% rise and enjoyed compound annual growth of 4.1%. Travel demand grew at 3.1% during the same period resulting in the industry adding rooms into a steadily more saturated market with the excess supply affecting results. Within the US hotel industry, business travel is the most important sector. This sector represents one-third of overall hotel demand with conference and convention business playing a key role as well, with another 20%. Almost half of demand comes from the business sector. The link therefore between the economic health of the USA as a whole and success within the hotel industry is therefore very clear. On a regional basis, the fastest growing hotel market will correlate with the best local economies. Job generation means more business for hotel companies, thus, markets like San Diego and Minneapolis, home to an increasing number of businesses, eclipse a slower growth market such as Vermont.

The largest hotel markets reflect more than the presence of industry and jobs. California and Florida, the market leaders, display strong employment, and appeal as leisure and tourist destinations.

Despite perceptions to the contrary, large hotel chains do not control the industry. The ten largest chains who actually own, manage or franchise hotels, control only 25% of the market. Marketing consortia like Best Western simply link independent properties to a reservation system; there is no common ownership. As pricing and demand pressures have intensified, independent hotels have been among the most vulnerable and cannot compete easily without access to the marketing and reservations systems of the major chains. To avoid financial problems, many hotels have affiliated themselves with chains, largely through franchise agreements in which ownership management is maintained.

Industry supply

A number of companies dominate the US hotel market: Hospitality Franchise Systems (HFS), Manor Care, Marriott Corporation, Hilton Hotels Corporation, ITT Sheraton, Bass plc and Promus Companies.

Hospitality Franchise Systems
HFS is a public company trading on the New York Stock Exchange which has a short history having been founded in June 1990. It is a pure franchise company owning no equity

in any of its properties and has a mission in life to service and support its franchisees. The brands that now form the company's portfolio have a much longer history than HFS. Howard Johnson was founded in 1925, Ramada in 1954, Days Inn in 1970, Super 8 Motels in 1973 and Park Inns in 1986. Villager Lodges is a recent acquisition based in south-eastern USA. On July 2 1990, a leveraged buy out group Blackstone Capital Partners acquired through its wholly owned subsidiary HFS, the Ramada and Howard Johnson Chains. The purchase brought HFS a franchising operation without any real estate ownership and was the foundation of a period of rapid growth which catapulted the company into the world's largest hotel firm in just a few years. In January 1992, HFS acquired Days Inn and one year later it acquired Super 8 Motels. Finally in 1993 HFS bought Park Inn International. During 1993, Blackstone sold its entire shareholding in HFS and left the board, leaving HFS as a public company.

Manor Care

Choice Hotel International inc is a subsidiary company of Manor Care which owns 90% of the company's stock. Choice Hotel International is one of the world's largest hotel chains with 3,431 hotels and 296,623 rooms. Very few of these properties are owned, managed or leased; the balance are under franchise to the company's seven major brands – Friendship Inns, Quality Inns, Roadway Inns, Sleep Inns, Comfort Inn, Clarion, and Econo Lodge brands. The company concentrates on franchise systems and now covers all the moderate and economy limited service price segments. While the company is represented in nearly forty countries, over 80% of its portfolio is based in the USA.

Marriott Corporation

Marriott Corporation retains one of the hotel industry's most respected brand names, with several brands consistently topping the travel surveys. About half of the company's operating revenue and earnings is generated by hotel services. The balance is provided by contract food services including the Travel Plazas and Host International Services. Marriott's growth in the 1970s and 1980s was fuelled, in part, by aggressive development and sales of hotels. The company was particularly adept at marketing a package of properties to partnerships and foreign buyers. Despite discounting affecting the company's full service hotels, its newer brands orientated to lower price points such as Courtyard, Fairfield and Residence Inns, have outpaced industry averages and continue to perform well. On the food service side results have been mixed with low travel demand contributing to problems at Host International. However, a major part of the company's earnings still come from the hotels sector.

Hilton Hotels Corporation

Hilton Hotels Corporation has been a public company since 1946 and maintains one of the industry's best known brand names recognised virtually throughout the world. This world-wide recognition is not the result of hotels operated by this company. Hilton International was spun off from the corporation as long ago as 1964 and in 1967 TWA acquired the company as well as the rights to use the Hilton name overseas. Hilton Hotels Corporation retained the right to use the name in the USA. Hilton International is owned by Ladbroke plc. The US company boasts a striking array of major hotels with strong market image, reputation and location in such key business markets as New York (New York Hilton, Waldorf Astoria), Chicago (Palmer House, Conrad Hilton), San Francisco (San Francisco Hilton) and Hawaii (Hawaiian Village). Hilton owns, leases or manages 92,000 rooms. At the same time the company operates 10,000 hotel rooms in Nevada with 7,000 in Las Vegas alone in the Flamingo and Las Vegas Hiltons. The company has indicated that it will spend $100 million to refurbish the Flamingo Hilton. The company's most recent development, the 2,000 room Flamingo Hilton in Laughlin, Nevada, has been exceptionally successful. Hilton purchased a hotel casino from Bally's Grand located in Reno, Nevada. The company has gaming exposure in Australia and has announced intentions to develop a casino hotel in Chicago in tandem with projects launched by Caesar's World and Circus, but Hilton Hotels Corporation can hardly be regarded as a global company. Of its 223 hotels over 97% are to be found in the USA with only 6 hotels abroad owned by its subsidiary Conrad Hotels International.

ITT Sheraton

ITT Sheraton is a wholly owned subsidiary of ITT corporation and is one of the few hotel chains that can described as truly global. Beginning operations in the 1930s in the USA the company opened its first hotel outside the country in 1949. It now has 177 non-US properties out of a total of 419 hotels. In 1994 Sheraton purchased 35% of the luxury Italian chain, Ciga hotel group, adding to the stake the company had already acquired on the stock market and bringing its total holding to just over 70%. The company's operations include owned and managed hotels, management contracts, franchises and joint ventures. Early company growth in North America was through ownership but internationally through the various forms of management agreements. Sheraton has basically three levels of quality among its hotel brands: these are the top of the range Luxury Collection, the up-scale Sheraton hotels, the mid-scale Sheraton and the Four Points Hotels. During 1997, Sheraton was the subject of a hostile takeover bid from Hilton Hotels Corporation. The company was finally purchased by the American Real Estate Investment Trust (REIT), Starwood.

Bass plc

Holiday Inn International was purchased by Bass, the UK based brewer, during the period 1988–90 and is one of the largest hotel brands with over 2,000 hotels, of which 65 are in the UK. Holiday Inn is the world's largest single hotel brand. The company has grown from a US domestic chain, which began operations in 1952 – mid-market hotels which developed along the interstate highways, then airport sites, city centres and suburban office locations to a world-wide chain operating or franchising hotels in over 62 different countries. Of the over 2,000 hotels, just 92 are company owned or leased by Holiday Inn world-wide. There are also some joint venture agreements. The remainder of the hotels are owned and managed by independent franchise operators. Holiday Inn's portfolio is dominated by the USA which contains 87.4% of the room stock. In Europe most of the hotels are owned and operated by Queens Moat House. In the UK, the withdrawal of Scotts Hospitality from the Holiday Inn network in 1992 reduced the company's room stock in the UK by 40.1%.

Promus Companies

Promus Companies is dominated by Gaming with its Harara brand among the most visible in the industry. However, 20% of earnings are divided by three hotel brands, Hampton Inns, Embassy Suites, and Homeward Suites. The company is relatively new, having been spun off in 1990 from the Holiday Corporation, when that company sold the Holiday Inn's business to Bass plc. In the hotel sector the company operates as a mixture of owner operator, manager and franchisor, with franchising being the best description of the bulk of the hotel business. Of the 586 hotels in the company, 98% are located in the USA. The company has been specially successful at marketing brand value with all three brands ranking extremely high in customer satisfaction and emphasising value for money with 100% satisfaction guarantee.

Future

Looking to the future a number of themes can be identified within the US hotel industry. The industry's operating pressures have quickened the pace of consolidation. As a result, many independents have been forced to affiliate with larger chains either through outright sale, management agreement or franchise operations. This has allowed chains to expand their market share with minimal capital outlay. Most hotels have opted for management or franchise agreements rather than purchase. Such arrangements are generally quite profitable with few inherent risks. Franchisees incur modest investment and operating fees in exchange for access to a large reservations and marketing system. The franchisor realises an initial fee plus a percentage of gross revenues. The incremental costs of adding new units is very low with concomitantly higher margins. In times of economic difficulty, it has always been the chains that weather the storms of economic problems. The size, market breadth and marketing clout of larger chains, stand them in good stead. On average, major chains produce occupancy levels 10 percentage points above the industry average. Also, it is going to be value-pricing, particularly within the economy hotels sector that will see growth in the 1990s and beyond. Such hotels offer reasonable rates to an increasingly cost-conscious customer base; they offer good value for money and should continue to attract demand. In summary it can be seen that brand name affiliation will become a critical element of success within the US hotel industry. Independent properties will require some marketing links to survive, also international markets will claim a larger role in hotel expansion. American companies have relatively little exposure overseas, indeed quite the opposite has occurred, a number of foreign interests now control large domestic chains, namely Accor, which owns Motel 6 and Bass plc which owns Holiday Inns.

Timeshare

The accommodation industry extends wider than just hotels and important sectors that will be considered are timeshare and other related products, and camping and caravanning.

History

The beginnings of timeshare lie in Switzerland, where in the early 1960s the German Alexander Nette developed the concept at a hotel he managed in Ticino. His initial idea developed into a company called Hapimag. Hapimag is a co-operative holiday club whose purpose is to purchase holiday apartments and then apportion holiday time to its owner members. So, as a business, it serves its owners' and customers' interests simultaneously. Today, Hapimag is a successful company with more than 900,000 shareholders and 45 vacation properties throughout Europe.

The beginning of timeshare as a commercial activity with real estate promoters seeking customers was Superdevoly, a ski resort development in the French Alps, which was marketed in 1965 with the immortal slogan '*Don't rent the room, buy the hotel: it's a lot less bother* '. Here, the philosophy was based on selling the right to use for vacation purposes, fixed weeks at the hotel.

The bulk of growth in timeshare subsequently took place in the USA and may be partly attributed to a collapse in the Florida property market in the mid-1970s which forced developers to seek new ways to dispose of condominiums. In this sense, timeshare was

Table 2.3 Trends in world-wide resort timeshare industry 1980–94

Year	No timeshare projects	No owners	Intervals sold	Sales volume $ million
1980	506	155,000	100,000	490
1985	1,774	805,000	245,000	1,580
1990	2,357	1,800,000	405,000	3,240
1992	3,050	2,363,000	500,000	4,250
1994	4,145	3,144,000	560,000	4,760

Source: World Tourism Organisation (1996) Timeshare: The New Force in Tourism

godsend: it enabled the developers to sell off property at a multiple of its real estate value, achieved mainly through a marketing effort confined to the local vacation area. Florida real estate salesmen knew that the best way to sell the space was to use intensive hard sell techniques to persuade the customer to part with an affordable sum of money to secure their place in the sun once a week a year. As this sales formula was put into practice, it was soon discovered that the primary drawback of such a formula was the lack of flexibility requiring buyers to vacation in the same place at the same time each year. The solution came with the development of the exchange system in the mid-1970s; this will be discussed later in this section.

Although some authorities pointed to the USA as a maturing market in timeshare as a reason for the move to the UK, it was a British businessman, Frank Chapman, who developed the first such scheme at Loch Rannoch in Perthshire in 1975. The first timeshare scheme in England was the refurbishment of the Osborne Hotel in Torquay in 1979. After these developments much of the growth in timeshare sales to the UK market can be attributed to timeshare projects in Spain and Portugal, primarily the Canaries, Costa Del Sol and the Algarve. Indeed it could be suggested that the European timeshare boom of the 1980s is the story of the British buying timeshares in Spain and Portugal while on holiday there. The growth of the world-wide timeshare industry is illustrated in Table 2.3.

Market size and type

The USA is the leader in the world-wide timeshare market, containing 37% of resorts, 49% of the owners owning in the area and 52% of the owners residing in the area. People owning in the area represents owners who have actually purchased a timeshare interval in the area in question, regardless of where they live. The owners residing in the area represent owners who live in the area in question, regardless as to where they own. This distinction arises because significant timeshare development markets such as Spain are not the same as important timeshare markets such as the UK. Collectively, the USA and Europe contain 66% of the resorts, 70% of the owners owning in the area, and 74% of the owners residing in the area.

In the USA, the predominant timeshare market, the entrepreneurial beginnings of timeshare are being followed by the entry into the business of operators with a more established profile. Some of the well-known names within the hospitality industry are the major chains such as Marriott, Hilton, Sheraton, Hyatt and Radisson who have entered the market along with the Walt Disney Corporation.

European timeshare is the second largest regional market area in the world and it has its roots in Britain since the English-speaking entrepreneurs who started the boom sold mostly to British holiday makers in the Canary Islands and the south of Spain. Accordingly, the largest number of timeshare owners are British, but other markets are growing rapidly. Germany is Europe's second largest market. The size of the population and its propensity to travel and holidays make this still a high potential marketplace, though growth has been slow in recent years owing to economic and political circumstances.

Consumer profile

As would be expected with the purchase of any expensive consumer good, timeshare buyers have been those people with reasonable disposable incomes. They tend to be aged between 35 and 55, married but without dependent children. Their most frequent purchase (80%) is of time in a one or two bedroom apartment, with a trend towards one bedroom apartments.

In North America over 50% of the heads of households of timeshare owners are between 35 and 55 years of age. Another 22% are between 55 and 65. The average age is from 49 years in Canada to 53 in California and Hawaii. The vast majority (85%) of owners represent married households, but this is not surprising as the marketing is usually geared to couples. Since most timeshare owners are over 45 years of age, only 33% have dependent children living at home. When compared to all US households, timeshare owners

- have higher incomes: 62% have incomes over $50,000 compared to only 25% of all households
- are more in the middle age category: 74% of the household heads are between 35 and 65 compared to only 52% of all household heads
- are more highly educated: 54% of heads of households have graduated from college/university compared to only 24% overall
- are usually married: 85% compared to 58% in the population overall.

Based on other studies in Europe, Asia and Australia, this US profile holds true around the world.

Consumer motivation

The motivations of people making timeshare purchases are often identified as

- **Economic**   purchasing tomorrow's holiday at today's prices
- **Quality**   having units built and furnished to a high specification maintained to high standards
- **Flexibility**   exchanging units through the resort exchange companies.

Of these three motivating factors, the one which has been used most often in the past to persuade potential customers to purchase has been the first, while the third represents the strongest factor once purchase has been completed. The second factor is important, but as in most things you get what you pay for.

Consumer finance

The proposition that a timeshare purchase saves money over the cost of buying self-catering holidays on a rental basis is open to doubt. However, in one form or another this claim is repeated with astonishing regularity even by supposedly impartial and well-informed commentators. Some 56% of purchasers in North America gave the purchasing decision of saving money on future vacation costs. People buy timeshare for a variety of reasons, and 72% of owners in North America gave the exchange companies as the most important reason for purchase.

Most developers recognise that the extra quality features of marble ensuite bathrooms, quality fitted kitchens and integral sports and leisure facilities help sell the units for little extra cost when apportioned over all 50 intervals of the year. One frequently stated reason in North America is that 62% regard the purchase as giving a quality vacation accommodation. Of course, the cost of maintenance can be high and the high service charges that owners have to pay are a common complaint. In recent years the full impact of this has been reflected in caution on the part of the buyer.

Exchange companies

One of the main disadvantages of timeshare has been that it locked the customer into spending their holidays at the same time each year and in the same place. Although exchange arrangements are now sophisticated it remains true that not everybody succeeds in getting the exchange they want or on the terms they think are fair. There are two big companies in this market, Resort Condominium International (RCI) founded in 1974 and Interval International (II) founded in 1976, which are becoming akin to tour operators in providing or arranging extra services, flights and car hire. This is in addition to the exchange service for which they charge a fee.

Over 70% regard the facility to exchange as a reason for purchase. The developer knows that increasingly customers buy into whichever development offers them the most cost-effective route to exchanging elsewhere, in this respect it is a case of the tail wagging the dog rather than facilitating timeshare operation. The exchange system increasingly determines what will be developed. There is nothing wrong in this *per se* except that the exchange system is a duopoly so RCI in particular have a great deal of control over the value of a timeshare development. The relative size of the two main exchange companies is illustrated in Table 2.4.

Office of Fair Trading Report

An authoritative analysis, at least in respect of timeshare overseas, was provided by the Office of Fair Trading (OFT), whose Report on Timeshare was published by HMSO in

Table 2.4 Major exchange companies key operating statistics 1994

	No of timeshare owners registered as active members		No of exchanges confirmed in the year		No of timeshare resorts available in system	
	(000)s	*(%)*	*(000s)*	*(%)*	*(000s)*	*(%)*
RCI	1,894	81	1,397	83	2,853	72
II	436	19	283	17	1,127	28
Total	2,330	100	1,680	100	3,980	100

Source: *World Tourism Organisation (1996) Timeshare: The New Force in Tourism*

1990. It shows that the claims of timeshare developers that their product is an investment or will save money are misleading and that they frequently ignore the cost of interest forgone on capital.

On a simplistic level, what timeshare offers is use of a villa for one week every year for an annual charge, with service charges and travel costs extra. Such extra charges are not controllable. This assumes the value of the purchase does not rise through time and there is plenty of evidence to suggest that values have actually eroded. It is no exaggeration to say that the majority of timeshare products can be offered by a tour operator as a self-catering rental unit on a more cost-effective basis.

However, the counter-argument from the timeshare industry is that the report did not compare like with like. Many timeshare purchasers focus on the flexibility provided by the exchange process and the quality of the product and, perhaps through their higher than average incomes these purchasers are less interested in cost and investment *per se*.

In February 1991, the Secretary of State for Trade and Industry published a response to the OFT report. One element subsequently introduced into law was the Timeshare Act 1992, giving purchasers in the UK a fourteen day period to change their mind. At that time Portugal had a fourteen day cooling off period and France seven days. The EU Timeshare directive of 1994 will mean that from 1998 all member states of the EU must introduce a minimum ten day cooling off period, during which potential timeshare purchasers are entitled to a full refund of their deposits.

Holiday property bond

There have been other innovations in shared use holiday club products, one of which is worthy of mention. The holiday property bond (HPB) appears to offer greater flexibility in more respects than timeshare. Based in the UK, HPB sells exclusively to the British market and the value of the units (bonds) is quoted daily. The system works in purchasing units to be used at different times of the year and in different resorts. The purchaser is not tied to the fortunes of any particular resort. In order to replace the security of investing in a property, the holiday property bond has a system of investing in fixed interest securities. The interest from these securities helps pay for the operating costs of the development. Thus investors in holiday property bonds generally get less holiday time per £1,000 than in timeshare but their service charges are much lower. By the end of 1994, HPB had nearly 20,000 owners and over twenty properties in eight countries.

Camping and caravanning

Caravan and camping holidays may be defined as a trip away from home and making use of a pitch. Accommodation within this market can be a touring caravan, static caravan, chalet, pitched tent or trailer tent.

Fixed pitch sites are usually in commercially managed parks which range in size from 5 to over 500 units. Holidays are typically of one week's duration, but are increasingly marketed on a two, three or four night basis, especially in weeks outside school holidays. Reflecting both planning requirements and the economics of operation, most holiday parks are open for business only between March and October. Some caravans and chalets are used as second homes and may be let to friends and relatives on an informal basis. This sector therefore has both commercial and non-commercial elements. The commercial life of a holiday caravan is often as short as five or six years before they are sold on to private owners, while chalets may be expected to last twenty years or more before replacement.

History

Holiday caravans and chalets constitute a large and historically important sector of the domestic tourism industry. The origins of caravanning can be traced back to 1907 when the Caravan Club was formed in response to the Edwardian upper classes' demand for open air recreation. It was not until the 1950s and 1960s that static caravanning emerged as an inexpensive means of holidaying for everyone. The popularity of a caravan as an alternative to other forms of holiday accommodation was mainly due to the success of park operators in providing value for money holidays which better catered for the needs of the baby boom generation than the traditional serviced accommodation sector. After two decades of almost continuous growth, the demand for caravan holidays halted and in many areas declined from a peak achieved in around 1977. The early 1980s witnessed a radical change in the pattern of domestic holiday taking brought about by the sudden affordability of sunshine holidays abroad. These market trends called for significant changes in the operation and management of holiday parks, requiring the site operators to reappraise their market position and strategies for the future. However, the industry has generally responded to these challenges with substantial investment in both products and promotion. Market prospects for the 1990s appear more positive than during the 1980s.

Market size

Camping and caravanning is much more than just a minority interest: it is a significant and sizeable sector of the UK holiday market. There are 330,000 caravan holiday homes and 560,000 touring caravans currently in use in the UK. Approximately 7% of the British population are engaged in caravan and camping each year. The Caravan and Camping Club and the Caravan Club have 189,000 and 275,000 members respectively. The average length of a stay is around 6 nights for rented caravans and slightly less at 5.5 nights for chalets. Since the mid-1980s the volume of the holiday caravan and chalets market in England has varied between 8 million and 10 million trips. The number of nights in the holiday rented sector has fallen by around a quarter. There has been a change in demand for the different types of static units. Demand for privately owned units has grown while demand for rented units has declined.

Visitors staying in these forms of accommodation spend rather less per night than holiday visitors in general, reflecting the low cost of the accommodation element of this type of tourism.

Market type

There is a wide range of sites available for caravanning and camping. Often a single site will offer accommodation in static units (caravan and chalets) and will also hire out pitches for touring vans and tents. Some offer a single form of accommodation. The size of the site varies too. Certain sites are allowed to offer pitches only to five touring caravans while sites with up to 200 static units are not uncommon. The majority of commercial sites in the UK are licensed caravan parks, are commercially operated and most offer accommodation in static units and hire out pitches for touring vans and tents. The English Tourist Board's statistics show that of the 1,600 parks offering static caravans and chalets, 30% offered only static units but the remaining 70% also accommodate touring vans. The Caravan Club and the Camping and Caravan Club operate sites solely for touring vans.

Many of these sites are open to non-members. Certified sites are sites for up to five caravans plus tents and are open only to members of these organisations. Unlicensed sites are sites of no more than four acres of pitches for up to three touring caravans for a maximum of twenty-eight days. Finally, rally sites are sites on which one of the two clubs may hold a rally lasting up to five days without obtaining formal planning permission or a licence. On-site facilities may include retail outlets, catering facilities, car parking and leisure facilities.

Despite improvement to equipment and levels of comfort, camping and caravanning is still a very seasonal activity compared to self-catering or holidays as a whole. For example 61% of all caravan and camping trips take place in the three summer months and 92% take place between April and September. Reflecting this seasonality, most caravan parks are closed during the winter.

Grading

The 1980s was the decade when the official grading of holiday parks and caravans became essential to the objectives of the national tourist boards as they sought to improve and promote this sector of the tourist industry.

Official grading not only acts as a summary statement of the quality of facilities, but also stimulates improvements in facilities as park operators seek to attain higher grading. The British Graded Holiday Park Scheme, derived jointly between the industry's trade associations and the national tourist boards, was introduced in 1985 to enhance marketing, demonstrate to the public the high standards available in parts of the industry and assist people in choosing a holiday park with confidence.

The grading is presented in the form of bands derived from a scoring scheme which awards marks for facilities and requires minimum standards of attainment. The grades are indicated as ticks; those sites attaining four or five ticks are eligible to have their caravan or holiday homes for hire assessed under separate grading schemes operated by the national tourist boards. These are the Rose Award scheme in England, the Dragon Award scheme in Wales and the Thistle Commendation scheme in Scotland.

In 1988 the British Holidays Home Parks Association (BHHPA) agreed that after an introductory period all member parks should be graded. Since 1991, only graded parks are allowed to remain within the BHHPA and promote themselves in its publication. If grading is to expand, the industry's customers must display an awareness of the system, otherwise grading cannot be shown to be instrumental in holiday park selection and thus important for park managers to attain.

Legislation

The development or extension of a caravan site require planning permission just as with any other development. Caravan sites also require a site licence under the Caravan Sites and Control of Development Act 1966. Site licences are issued by the local authority and only after planning permission is granted. Tents are not covered by the 1960 Act but by the Public Health Act 1936, together with subsequent town and county planning legislation.

Summary

This chapter has profiled the accommodation industry and has indicated a wide range of subsectors. Within the hotels sector and the timeshare sector comparisons were made within the UK, with mainland Europe and North America along with industry structure, market dimensions, customer profile and the major companies involved in the industry. The UK market for camping and caravanning was also considered.

Further reading

- Arthur Andersen (1996) *London Five star Hotels Performance Survey*, published quarterly, London: Arthur Andersen.
- Barclays de Zoete Wedd (1993) *Hotels and Leisure Review*, London: BZW.
- BDO Consulting (1996) *United Kingdom Hotel Industry 1995*, London: BDO Consulting.
- BDO Consulting (1997) *United Kingdom Hotel Industry 1996*, London: BDO Consulting.
- Economist Intelligence Unit (1995) *The International Hotel Industry: Corporate Strategies and Global Opportunities*, London: EIU.
- Henley Centre (1996) *Hospitality into the 21st Century: A Vision for the Future*, London: Joint Hospitality Industry Congress.
- Key Note (1993) *Camping and Caravanning*, 8th edn, London: Key Note.
- Key Note (1994) *Market Reviews: Tourism and Travel*, 4th edn, London: Key Note.
- Kleinwort Benson Securities (1991) *Quoted Hotel Companies: The World Markets*, London: KB.
- Kleinwort Benson Securities (1992) *Quoted Hotel Companies: The European Markets*, London: KB.
- Kleinwort Benson Securities (1993) *Quoted Hotel Companies: The European Markets*, London: KB.
- Kleinwort Benson Securities (1994) *Quoted Hotel Companies: The World Markets*, London: KB.
- Kleinwort Benson Securities (1995) *Quoted Hotel Companies: The European Markets*, London: KB.
- Kleinwort Benson Securities (1996) *Quoted Hotel Companies: The World Markets*, London: KB.
- Kleinwort Benson Securities (1997) *Quoted Hotel Companies: The World Markets*, London: KB.
- Knowles T. and Lockwood A. (1993). Accommodation Industry in Tourism, Principles and Practice, Editors, Cooper C., Fletcher J. and Gilbert D. First Edition, Addison Wesley Longman.
- Krutick J.S. (1991) *The European Hotel Industry: The Race is On*, London: Salomon.
- Krutick J.S. and Halstead J.C. (1990) *The European Hotel Industry: Dawn of a New Era*, London: Salomon.
- Krutick J.S. and Vignola M.L. (1991) *US Lodging Industry on the Rebound*, New York: Salomon.
- Marsh J. (1987) 'Caravan parks: a £780 million industry', *Leisure Management* 7(2): 30–1.
- Mintel (1992) *Hotels 1992 Special Report*, London: Mintel International.
- Mintel (1993a) 'Special report: holidays 1993', *Leisure Intelligence* pp. 8–11, 40–51.
- Mintel (1993b) Camping and Caravanning, *Leisure Intelligence* 1: 1–29.
- Pannell Kerr Forster Associates (1995a) *Eurocity Survey 1995*, London: PKF.
- Pannell Kerr Forster Associates (1995b) *Middle East and Africa Survey 1995*, London: PKF.
- Pannell Kerr Forster Associates (1996a) *Eurocity Survey 1996*, London: PKF.

- Pannell Kerr Forster Associates (1996b) *Middle East and Africa Survey 1996*, London: PKF.
- Pannell Kerr Forster Associates (1997a) *Eurocity Survey 1997*, London: PKF.
- Pannell Kerr Forster Associates (1997b) *Middle East and Africa Survey 1997*, London: PKF.
- Pannell Kerr Forster Associates (1997c) *London Trends Survey 1997*, London: PKF.
- Pannell Kerr Forster Associates (1997d) *UK Trends Survey 1997*, London: PKF.
- Smith New Court (1995) *Some Way Up Already: Leisure and Hotel Research*, London: Smith New Court.
- Touche Ross Greene Belfield Smith Division (1990) *The European Incentive Travel Survey 1990*, London: Touche Ross.
- Touche Ross Greene Belfield Smith Division (1991) *European Golf Facilities 1991*, London: Touche Ross.
- UK Tourist Boards (1997) *The UK Tourist Statistics 1996*, published annually, London: BTA.
- Ventures Consultancy Ltd (1989) *The Self-Catering Market for Holiday Caravans and Chalets*, London: BTA/ETB.
- World Tourism Organisation (1996) *Timeshare: The New Force in Tourism*, Spain: WTO.

Chapter Three

Internationalisation and Growth

Corporate strategy

In considering the internationalisation and growth of the hospitality industry, much of the discussion in this chapter will be set within the context of corporate strategy. The literature on strategy suggests that a hospitality organisation will make decisions about resource allocation according to some predetermined plan of action. It is also suggested here, that if an organisation is to be successful, then there must be a co-alignment between the wider environment in which it functions day-to-day, the methods it employs to take advantage of the threats and opportunities in the competitive environment and the way it is organised internally. Without this match it is difficult to achieve long-term success. The important questions in relating these issues to hospitality firms is whether they will be able to achieve the necessary match, whether the general and competitive environment will support planned growth, and whether the methods chosen to fuel growth and control quality will be successful. Both the reasons and methods for growth within the hotel industry will be discussed in this chapter.

Growth of hotel groups

The growth of hotel groups in this section will be considered under three headings:

● theoretical background

● motivations

● determinants.

Theoretical background

From a theoretical perspective the growth of hotel groups can be explained by the potential advantages of size. An economist would use the term *economies of scale* in identifying these advantages which take several different forms. Financial economies enable the group to raise finance internally and borrow on better terms. Managerial economies derive from the fact that administration costs do not necessarily increase in line with the volume of business, e.g. centralised room bookings. Technical economies are also associated with the benefits of centralisation, for example the provision of services such as laundry and maintenance from the centre to individual units. Such economies of scale allow the firm to spread the risk and enable it to offset losses in some areas against profits in another. Economies of scale coupled with the need to expand into key markets around the world have been, in part, the cause of recent mergers and acquisitions of hotel companies. As a result of that trend, the international hotel sector is evolving towards a new pattern of industrial concentration in which the global market is dominated by a small group of large hotel companies. The choice of region to expand into reflects the individual objectives of the company, by either: locating to a region with an established demand, or by locating in an area which will in the future experience growth in demand.

Motivations

The central motivation for the major hotel corporations to expand is one of profitability. Europe and North America, which between them receive three-quarters of all international tourist arrivals, are areas for firms to consider. The Asia Pacific region where the size of the tourism market is increasing at a very high growth rate is another region where the chains have sought to expand and in doing so maintain profit growth. In recent years changes have occurred. European (especially British and French) hotel interests have been playing an ever more important part, and now control some of the best known chains and brands in the world. The emergent economic power of the Asia Pacific region is beginning to influence the international hotel scene.

Determinants

In analysing the determinants of growth, hotel companies have traditionally been keen to expand overseas for a number of reasons. In addition to the obvious search for new markets as a prime route for growth, there is a need to expand profitability in areas that promise high revenue, and the perceived need to exploit differences in the economic cycle in different areas of the world as an insurance policy against recession in the major markets. At present, the prevailing attitude among international hotel companies is that in order to become successful a hotel company has three basic options:

- to become global through greater market coverage both geographically and by segment
- to create a focused approach to a particular national or regional market
- to fill a well-defined niche in the marketplace.

Growing importance of hotel chains

Since the mid-1980s there has been a significant change in the ownership of hotels worldwide, with the tendency to construct and operate larger properties, which require larger investments. The hotel owner is usually a financial institution, insurance company or a number of joint equity owning companies, which typically employ an industry expert to help control and monitor their hotel investment.

Independent hotels tend to be smaller in size, and are increasingly surviving mainly in niche market segments of the hotel industry. Although these may seem difficult times for independents, a select number will continue to have a privileged place in the market because they can make decisions on their own without recourse to institutional investors, be flexible and offer personalised services to a specific market segment. With this exception, however, the hotel industry is experiencing a gradual but steady switch from independently owned and operated hotels, to hotel chain affiliation. In the late 1940s, fewer than one hotel in ten had any chain affiliation. In the late 1990s, more than 60% of all hotels in the USA belong to chains. This rapid growth of hotel chains can be attributed to three factors:

- emergence of franchising systems
- hotel management contracts
- need for corporate growth.

The expansion of hotel chain companies has already been explained by the desire for and availability of economies of scale. It is through this that the advantages provided by national and international reservation networks, staff training and marketing programmes can be recognised. In the USA, Canada and Europe combined, there are an estimated 3,000 hotel groups with more than 10 hotels each. The 200 largest companies account for the operation of at least 20% of all bedrooms.

Geographical trends

A number of geographical trends among the world's hotel chains can be identified. In North America, hotel companies have a continuing interest in Mexico, the Caribbean and Europe, and in particular the growth of the budget hotel sector. Mexico continues to draw interest from international and domestic companies. US company Hotel Franchise Systems (HFS) has opened hotels in Monterrey, Mexico. Spain's Sol group has significant interests in the Caribbean as does France's Accor. In South America Hyatt International has opened hotels in Buenos Aires, Argentina and Santiago, Chile and is looking at more suitable locations in South American cities.

In the UK, the recession in the hotel industry ended in 1994. According to London based Arthur Andersen Hospitality Consulting, the up-market London hotels reported an increase in occupancy and average rate in 1996 compared with the previous year. However, on the European mainland, economic conditions worsened during 1995–6 in France and Germany, unaccustomed to a recessionary climate.

In Asia, Japan's corporate, economic and political problems have influenced not only the Japanese economy but also the regional economy. Hong Kong continues to be an economic focal point for the region. Mainland China has drawn interest because of its economic swing toward a free market economy, the easing of political tensions, plus the sheer size (and buying potential) of its population.

The strategy of being geographically diverse in terms of guest mix and location seems ever more beneficial. As economists worried about the mainland European recession in the period 1994–7 and analysts warned of an impeding overbuilt Asian market, the USA was just starting to see its hotel supply and demand equation swing back into balance.

The evidence from this discussion is that the advice to keep a balanced portfolio and look beyond domestic markets holds true for hotel companies as well as for individual investors.

Strategies in the expansion of hotel businesses

The hotel industry has traditionally adhered to the true entrepreneurial spirit of profit making in a flexible, unrestricted business environment, seizing each opportunity as it comes, without considering its long term impact. The fiercely competitive environment of the mid-1990s, due to a maturing industry and declining growth rate, has shifted competition toward a battle for market share.

The large number of competitors, difficulty in establishing differentiation, cost in new build hotels, renovation of physical structures, plus high fixed costs, will continue to intensify competition within the industry. Adapting to the new rules of the global marketplace, hotel operators are developing new growth strategies for success. Some of these growth strategies include the following:

- **New product development** Technology offers the means to construct new accommodation concepts, one of which comes close to resembling the automated hotel.

- **Diversification of products offered through multi-tier marketing** Hotel chains began to diversify into markets below and above their usual focus some years ago as a response to intensifying competition. In the early 1980s, the US based hotel company, Choice International, began a multi-tier strategy by introducing Comfort Inns and Quality Royale. This diversification trend has been followed by most leading chains and has continued in the 1990s, as most companies wish to expand into secondary markets which usually prelude the establishment of up-market hotels.

- **Conversion of older-service hotels into economy properties** that have the brand name of a well-known chain, to adapt to shifting demand in markets where primary sites are hard to find.

- **Embracing the product substitute** Many of the larger hotel chains have linked technological and marketing resources with scheduled airlines, who offer frequent flyer programmes aimed at the regular business traveller.

- **Entry into related markets** The Marriott Corporation and Accor have penetrated the market for Continuing-care Retirement Communities (CCRC), offering housing, meals and health care for elderly people.

- **Creative marketing programmes to trigger latent hotel demand** The greatest single challenge for the international hotel industry is to achieve greater market penetration by being more resourceful and expanding from the main industry into that of non-traditional competitors, such as the information and recreation industries.

- **Penetration of international travel and tourism markets that show potential for hotel growth** For example, the Japanese government introduced a programme intended to double the number of Japanese overseas travellers from about 5 million in 1986 to 10 million in 1991. A similar increase is expected to the year 2000.

- **Delegation of authority and decision making down the line in order to keep close to the customer** A growing number of companies in the hotel sector are committed to excellence and are paying more attention to the human resource elements in their operation.

- **Management contracting for non-traditional hotel owners** For example, hotel development, particularly in Hong Kong and Singapore, has been characterised by multi-facility real estate developments. This trend is spreading to Western Europe, particularly to major city locations.

- **Increase of franchising as an option to expand** with the reduction or elimination of direct monetary investment by hotel chains as a major advantage. Franchising in the international hotel market is becoming more significant as large corporations move towards offering less capital intensive, economy properties, which become fundable by proprietor operators.

- **Targeting the growing leisure market for business expansion** has become a practice for several airlines and hotel chains.

- **Providing new self-service computer terminals in existing hotels to enable hotel guests to check in and out** One of the most frequent complaints of travellers is waiting in long lines to check in and out of hotels. The front desk/reservations department can also be troublesome and inefficient for the hotel operator.

- **Development of expertise in the main-line industry** A growing number of hotel management companies concentrate their efforts on opening and operating hotels, by providing a complete and totally integrated service package leading a property to growth and bottom line profitability.

Patterns of growth

It has already been established that for many hotel companies the key to prosperity in the current industry environment is growth. With the location-specific nature of the hotel industry, growth translates into greater market coverage, increased visibility, and greater opportunities for cross destination marketing in addition to the benefits of economies of scale and scope. Therefore, hotel companies continue to seek new ways to increase their market share. The pattern of growth of hotel groups is a major determinant, both of chain size, and, of prospects for further expansion. There are three basic forms through which a hotel company can develop:

- acquisition
- management contracts
- franchising.

Acquisition

As groups expand, so the patterns of growth become more complex causing the emergence of combinations of the above forms as well as new ones such as sale and leaseback, joint ventures and strategic alliances. The first method of growth, acquisition, is illustrated in a case study on the takeover of Forte by Granada. The second and third methods of growth, management contracts and franchising, will also be discussed in detail within this chapter.

Case Study: Forte/Granada hostile takeover bid

Granada Group plc, a television and leisure conglomerate launched a £3.3 billion hostile takeover bid for Forte plc on 22 November 1995. The final result of this bid led to the end of the Forte family involvement in the group created by Lord Forte in the 1930s.

Background to Forte

The history of Forte began in 1934, when Charles Forte (now Lord Forte) opened a milk-bar in Upper Regent Street, London. This was the start of the Forte empire, and within five years Charles had established a profitable milk-bar chain.

During the next twenty-five years Lord Forte transformed this small food-service operation into the largest hotel chain in the UK, as well as developing a presence in other continents of the world. Its assets encompassed the full breadth of the hospitality business from a stake in the Savoy Group, the George V in Paris to the Little Chefs that serve Britain's road network.

Lord Forte's son, Rocco, finally moved into the family business, after qualifying as an accountant. Over his fifteen-year period with Forte, Rocco gradually worked his way through the managerial hierarchy, to become chief executive in 1982. In 1992 when Lord Forte stepped aside to become president, Rocco became both chairman and chief executive.

Managerial changes and improvements

When Rocco was appointed as chief executive in 1982, many people presumed that he would have adopted his father's autocratic approach to management, where in reality the opposite happened. Over the years that Sir Rocco held such a position, he increasingly asserted his own authority, first by replacing his father's old friends and colleagues on the board with younger men who had established track records in business and commerce. Second, he tried to run the firm as a multinational company, noting:

> This company is no longer a family business. It is a major public company with public shareholders. We have an international dimension which we never had before, and it is a thoroughly professional business in the modern sense.

Sir Rocco had become 'his own man', but during the takeover period he finally conceded to pressures from the business media and the city by splitting his roles, choosing to remain as chief executive, and appointing Sir Anthony Tennent (previously deputy chairman) to the role of chairman.

It can be noted following his appointment as chairman in 1992, Sir Rocco restructured his senior management team, evidenced by the fact that 70 of his 100 senior managers had been at Forte for only two years or less, and set about restructuring the company through the disposal of peripheral businesses. This included a reduction in the stake of Alpha Airports, the sale of Gardner Merchant as well as the disposal of Harvester to Bass plc. One of the problems that Sir Rocco never resolved, according to many investors in the city, was that of hanging on to their Savoy stake. A 69% stake in this exclusive hotel business gave Forte less than a quarter of the voting rights. This in fact was a major element in the actual outcome of the bid, and was picked up strongly by Gerry Robinson,

case study continues ▶

chairman of Granada. His vision of Forte's management philosophy was somewhat different from that of Sir Rocco's, accusing the firm of operating without serious managerial control as well as being slow in the rebranding of their hotels portfolio. Rocco attacked this suggestion when the bid was put forward, arguing that the group had no experience in the running of an international hotels and restaurant business. Robinson replied: *'running hotels is the same as any business'*, where the most important and simple principle is choosing the right staff, usually from within the company, getting a clear idea of what the company is trying to achieve and most important of all *'letting management get on with it'*.

Through all this change in Forte's management, many investors have been rather apprehensive about the firm's new ideas, culminating in a fall in the Forte share price in London. Since 1992 the shares have under-performed by more than 30% on the all-share FT index. In defence of his company's recent failings, Rocco defends both his and the firm's record, noting: 'which hotel company has performed well over the last five years, when the whole industry was first devastated by the Gulf War, and then secondly the world-wide recession?'

Strategic growth

Throughout its sixty year-long history the company grew from a small scale hotel operation, to a totally global hotel and restaurant firm. Due to this status, Forte was represented by the following share composition:

- 80% of shares owned by city fund managers, mostly on behalf of ordinary pension fund investors, significantly the largest being Mercury Asset Management (MAM), with a share of nearly 14% of the total share stock
- 12% by private investors
- 8% by the Forte family

In its 1995 report, Kleinwort Benson Securities note that the most positive profile for any hotel company in 1995 is to sell obsolete hotels, and increase a London exposure. Further, there is the requirement to develop budget lodges as well as expand with an international presence. In essence all of these actions had been pursued by Forte. Forte's 1995 profile was as follows:

- 888 hotels
- 95,965 rooms
- presence in 37 countries

These figures represent a 12.4% increase in room stock since 1994, mainly through the addition of 54 hotels acquired in the Meridien chain buy-out from Air France. In terms of their 888 hotels, 74 are situated in major locations (i.e. city centres, airports, etc.) and a further 248 hotels are situated in secondary locations.

In the UK, Forte is by far the largest hotel operator, with 346 hotels. This figure represents 24.4% of the total UK roomstock of publicly quoted hotels. Forte was also the largest hotel operator in London.

case study continues

Forte introduced brands and collections in 1992, when they became Forte plc. Brands refer to those hotels that are similar throughout the portfolio, while collections are a culmination of their individual properties, which are seen as either exclusive in status, or representing British heritage.

The London hotel market is forecast to increase by 5% between 1997 and 2000, requiring hotel companies to have a major presence there.

Reviewing Forte's presence in foreign markets, statistics show that 13.1% of their hotel profits for 1994 came from their international hotel presence, where investors predicted an increase to 16.4% in the year to January 1997. Forte's addition of the Meridien chain was such a way to help them reach this position. This acquisition was seen as being extremely important for Forte, given their target of attaining international hotel player status. Further, this acquisition was seen as beneficial as the economies of continental Europe had started to recover from recession, and were seeing an increase in business demand for hotels in Germany, France, Italy and Spain, heavily represented by Meridien. Within continental Europe, Forte had a total of 67 hotels, accounting for 12,870 rooms. Further afield, in particular in the USA, Forte's presence was fairly weak with insufficient exposure to be a threat to their competitors in either the budget sector (Travelodge) or the upscale market (Exclusive/Meridien). It can be noted that before the Meridien acquisition, Forte was mostly represented in the Middle East through their Grand collection of hotels, mostly run as management contracts.

The Granada bid

During the morning of 22 November, Granada plc, a diversified leisure group with interests ranging from contract catering to television programmes, launched a hostile bid for Forte plc valued at £3.2 billion. The Granada attack came on the back of an announcement of an increase in pre-tax profits by 32% to £351 million, with a turnover of £2.38 billion, a 14% rise in the year to September 1995. The offer to investors was made on the basis of four new Granada shares and £23.25 cash payment for every fifteen Forte shares. On the day of the offer, the bid of £3.2 billion valued Forte shares at 326p. Granada's offer therefore represented a 23% premium on Forte's share price, even though Forte's five year summary (compared with 1990–1) showed that operating profits were down 11%, earnings per share down 41% and dividends down a further 24%. The offer price was therefore seen as high for a company that had recently been suffering sluggish growth.

The bid took Forte by surprise: it appeared to be unprepared to defend an overture of this magnitude. This could be seen clearly in the timing of Granada's announcement as that morning Rocco was out of his High Holborn office, travelling up to the Yorkshire moors to engage in country pursuits. As the day progressed Sir Rocco travelled to London, meeting his father and senior directors to discuss how they would challenge the bid. Forte therefore had until 23 January, the final closing date for shareholder acceptance.

This proposal by Granada was from the outset a hostile takeover, and focused on which of the company chairmen had the will-to-win. Announcing the bid, Gerry Robinson noted that the problem with Forte is their *sluggish response to market opportunities*, pointing to the failure of Forte to capitalise on its market-leading position in the

case study continues ▶

lodge sector (Travelodge), '*thus allowing Whitbread with their Travel Inn brand to catch up*'. During the first week of the offer (22–29 November), Sir Rocco led his company's defence well, showing 'imagination and vision' in commenting on his rival's offer. During these early stages Forte's competitors actually spoke out in favour of its defence, where Gavin Simonds, joint managing director of the Inter-Continental hotel group noted that he '*was both surprised and impressed with the strength and speed of Forte's response*'.

During the Christmas holiday period both parties went away to determine their best defence, in an attempt to win over the shareholders. Sir Rocco wrote an internal memo to all members of staff, pointing out the proposals of the offer, and the implications of a Granada takeover. This document noted:

> *First let me say a little about our aggressor. As you may know, Granada is a mixed collection of businesses, including TV and computer rental, contract catering, TV broadcasting, motorway service stations, travel and textile rental. On paper, Granada has grown in recent years, but mainly by buying companies. There is no clear logic about how these businesses benefit from being looped together.*

The implication from this was that Granada knew little about hotel and restaurant businesses, as all it owned were twenty-seven motorway service areas and two hotels, both situated in the UK. Forte had hotels in fifty countries as well as management relationships with around 150 business partnerships. Prior to the bid, Forte had spent time strengthening its international management team, making progress in reshaping and focusing the business. The brand position had also been reviewed since it was first implemented in 1992, investing in key market areas and disposing of businesses which were not central to its expertise.

On 9 January 1996 Granada raised its bid for Forte, the final day for such a measure under the takeover regulations from £3.3 billion to £3.9 billion, an offer that many outsiders could not afford to turn down. Analysts were now predicting that Granada's extra move into Forte showed its utmost determination to win, where investors commented: '*they have gone now and put their money where their mouth is*'. Forte knew that the latest offer was going to be hard to beat, but both the company and investment team tried their utmost attempting to sell businesses that account for almost half total turnover. This included a buy-back of 20% of their share capital and a distribution to shareholders of their 68% stake in the Savoy hotel group.

On 18 January Granada raised its own personal stake in the Forte group, moving from a 9.2% share to just under 10%. The purchase of a further 8.3 million shares at 384p followed the £336 million market raid on 16 January. One of the main sellers of Forte's shares was the Post Office pension fund, referred to as the Hermes fund. Their sale was not due to incumbent management, rather a concern that Forte shares may not rise much further. In the same week, the largest city fund investors in Forte, Mercury Asset Management sold 9 million shares, cutting their Forte holding to 14%. In the first of week of January though, MAM had actually bought 13 million Forte shares, at a price between 360 and 362p. By such a large holder dealing in Forte shares, many financial personnel envisaged problems, with MAM thus playing a pivotal role in the later stages of the final outcome.

One of the ways that Forte hoped to win the battle, especially after the latest proposed bid from Granada, was through the selling of parts of its business. In the heat of the battle Forte proposed to sell its roadside restaurant and part of its hotel business to Whitbread,

case study continues

for a price of £1.05 billion. This disposal was on the assumption that Forte would defend the offer, and would include 430 Little Chef and Happy Eater restaurants, 26 Welcome Break motorway service stations as well as 127 UK Forte Travelodges. The response to such a sale in the middle of a takeover bid astonished many investors, referring to Forte as a firm running scared whose only option of survival was through a demerger. In the eyes of the directors of Granada this was seen as a cheap sale, well below the equivalent figure contained in its own offer for the whole company. According to Gerry Robinson, *'Forte's break-up plan is an admission of the management's failure to obtain a reasonable return on assets'*.

Continuing further in its sell-off of different businesses, in January Forte also concluded the sale of its US Travelodge business for $160 million (£103 million) to HFS, a US franchise group who also own Ramada, Howard Johnson Hotels and Days Inn. This part of the business represented almost 40% of Forte's total roomstock, but the properties, a mix of owned, leased and franchised businesses, were tired and required a significant amount of investment. Also Forte offered a £500 million share buy-back scheme, as well as a further dividend hike in an attempt to win over their investors. To bolster their international presence, Forte proposed to strengthen their fifty-eight-strong Meridien chain through the opening of a further twenty-six hotels via management contracts.

As 23 January (final offer day) came ever closer the camps continued to battle hard. Forte's break-up proposals were referred to as lacking both commercial and financial sense, and its forecast of profits for the year end January 1996 being £135 million showed a return on assets of only 7.2%. A spokesman for Granada dismissed these profit figures as inadequate, claiming to be able to trim off more than £100 million a year from Forte's costs through a mixture of combined purchasing and by cutting back head office and staff. In essence Granada was concerned with Forte's disposals, in which it was allowed to sell up to 10% of its asset value.

Charles Allen, chief operating officer at Granada, said these moves were clearly an admission of defeat. *'It looks like something that has hastily been put together. It's clearly not part of a long-term strategy.'* He also commented on the 'blindness' of Forte's management in terms of its 'trophy hotels' and the battle for control of the Savoy Group. Focusing on five star hotels meant cost-generating businesses such as contract catering had been both neglected and sold off. In his eyes, *'rather than sell Gardner Merchant, which was a strong performing and resilient business, Forte should have sold its stake in the Savoy Group'*. Forte accused Granada of being a mixed conglomerate, *'that was achieving growth through acquisition'*. Sir Rocco also commented that Granada's intention to sell off Forte's Exclusive hotels (according to Granada as 'trophy hotels'), would be seen as a way of making a fairly fast buck, and did not make commercial sense.

Outcome

It was late afternoon on Tuesday 23 January 1996 that Rocco and the Forte group, after two months of battling with Granada, finally heard the outcome from their shareholders' vote. The decision had gone in favour of Granada: around 65% of the shareholders had backed the proposed offer, resulting in the takeover of one of the largest hotel operators in the UK. In this long-running battle Sir Rocco did not anticipate that his shareholders

case study continues ▶

would consign the company, in his words, '*to destruction*'. The 8% personal stake that Sir Rocco had in Forte plc was worth around £300 million, but in his eyes and his father's this is little compensation for the humiliation of defeat. In his speech to the press prior to the final outcome, Sir Rocco noted:

> *The saddest thing of all to me if we do not succeed is that it will all be wasted. The potential of the business will never be realised. That is the regret I would have more than any other.*

It can be noted that Forte did not fail in its attempt to win the vote, rather Granada had to fight hard to win. Until a few days before the vote, most people thought that Forte would win, re-entering the marketplace as a much more focused and well-managed business. In the last few days the pendulum swung in favour of Granada, mainly due to the raise in its bid-offer, and probably more important the last minute decision by MAM to back Granada's cause. In essence being the largest individual city fund holder (14% stake) in Forte the company had decided that Granada's proposal was too good an incentive to miss.

Analysis and conclusion

This case of Forte and Granada has many lessons for large multinational businesses. At no time before 22 November 1995 did Forte think that it was about to be involved in a takeover bid; indeed, Sir Rocco was out of the office on the morning when the bid was launched. Complacency is therefore a word that many investors, as well as senior personnel within the industry, used to describe Forte, in that no company when operating in the fast paced 1990s is safe from takeover. Sitting in a position where it was the largest hotel operator in the UK, Forte should have realised that it posed great opportunities for its competitors.

During the battle period, both chairmen were seen to be aggressive in their attempts to win. Comments made about Forte were obviously taken on-board by shareholders, as Gerry Robinson continually denigrated senior management. As the final voting day approached, other senior figures in the industry started to question Forte's managerial approach, mainly in its stance to implement changes into its international business. In essence this has been one of the major faults with Forte – lack of competitiveness in the international market, instead of depending too much on the UK accounting for 80% of total profits. The acquisition of Meridien could have been used to enter such markets, but Forte was not aggressive enough in expanding the product abroad.

In winning the battle, Granada announced what it intended to do with Forte:

- Reduce Forte's brands to three: to make Meridien the main international brand, keep the mid-price Posthouse brand (but increase prices) and retain Travelodge. (One might be surprised to hear that the Meridien chain may be sold. In earlier defences of this brand, Gerry Robinson noted that it was essential if Granada were to become an international hotel player, but are now prepared to sell the brand as part of a £2.1 billion disposal. This would leave Granada consisting mainly of roadside restaurants and middle-market British hotels.)
- Merge Forte's Little Chef and Happy Eater roadside eateries.

● Sell Welcome Break, Forte's motorway services stations, as otherwise there would be too large a monopoly as it already runs Granada services.

These decisions fit in well with Gerry Robinson's earlier proposals, as Granada's bid-document led on the belief that Europe and the rest of the world needed to see more of a push from the Meridien brand, as well as the continuation of the roadside lodge. Forte had let Whitbread take too much market share through their Travel Inn brand, which needed to be won back in the face of such a lucrative hotel market. In further explanations concerning Forte, Mr Robinson also picked up on the firm's failure to deliver adequate value to its shareholders, partly because of its retention of 'trophy assets' (Savoy stake and Exclusive hotels) that did not produce good returns. Granada will attempt to sell-off its stake in the Savoy Group and its remaining share in Alpha Airports, which is expected to raise in excess of £500 million for the group.

Granada is not going to focus all operations on hotels, in fact only 24% of its business will be accounted for by this sector. Rather, the benefit from the Forte buy-out is the share that Granada receive in the roadside eateries market. Through Little Chef and Happy Eater, Granada is able to raise its leisure portfolio, to account for 29% of its business operation, thus becoming the largest player in what can be described as a fairly lucrative market. The Exclusive portfolio of hotels does not really fit Granada's image, and therefore may be sold. In reviewing this whole takeover many people are now referring to Granada's buy-out as an asset-stripping affair, which enables it to keep parts of the business that can be incorporated easily into its existing operation, while selling those businesses that are of no use to the group. In essence the whole affair can be referred to as a case of 'synergy', in that the sum of the parts is greater than the sum of the whole, i.e. selling the Forte parts separately to different companies will enable Granada to make profit on such disposals.

There have been press reports of Sir Rocco and his senior partners attempting to buy back the London hotels portfolio, as well as the stake in the Savoy Group from Granada. The problem with such an approach is that it is not entirely in his own hands to carry out such a manoeuvre, as presently Granada is happy with its acquisition and is in no rush to dispose of Forte's operations. In many investors' eyes Granada may lose face if it were to quickly sell back some of its operations, especially to the company it had just bought them from. Granada has the time to wait; Sir Rocco has in the meantime fulfilled his intention to get back into the hotel business with the creation of Rocco Forte and Associates and R.F. Hotels. The industry has lost one of the most successful hotel companies in the world, where the name Forte was represented throughout the major continents. One must now hope that Granada keeps the success of Forte alive, enabling the business to remain successful as well as to continually challenge the dominance of European and American multinational firms.

Management contracts

Background

The management contract has become a popular approach to growth in the hotel industry because, just like franchising (discussed later in this chapter), little capital is required compared with an asset acquisition growth strategy. It is usual in the 1990s that the management contracting firm will be expected to provide some equity and will have to share some of the decision making with the actual owners of the property – an aspect that distinguishes it from franchising. Equally performance expectations will be greater in a management contract than franchising.

In order to realise these expectations, this type of strategy (management contracting) will also require a strong list of competitive capabilities if a company is able to sustain growth. Specifically, management firms will have to demonstrate effectively that they can generate a certain number of room nights as a result of their competitive strengths. This drive for growth will require the management contracting firms to develop more sophisticated global pricing and marketing efforts.

For this strategy to work there has to be a large number of clients wishing to obtain managers for their hotels. In recessionary times this is common as there are a large number of hotels in receivership. However, these properties in receivership may not conform to the firm's normal portfolio standards, thus there is a danger that the concept will be compromised. Success through expansion by management contracts will be largely determined by the ability of the company to attract properties that conform to its portfolio requirements.

Definition

A management contract can be defined as a written agreement between the owner and the operator of a hotel or motor inn, by which the owner employs the operator as an agent to assume full responsibility for operating and managing the property. As an agent, the operator pays in the name of the owner, all operating expenses from the cash flow generated from the property, retains management fees and remits the remaining cash flow, if any, to the owner. The owner supplies the hotel property including any land, building, furniture, fixtures, equipment and working capital and assumes full legal and financial responsibility for the project.

History

The first hotel property that was operated under a hotel management contract was the 300-roomed Hilton in San Juan, Puerto Rico. It opened on 9 December 1949 and was run through a profit sharing lease arrangement: it can be seen as a combination of a lease and a management contract. It was the Puerto Rican government that built, furnished and equipped the hotel, providing all needed capital. The government then leased the hotel to Hilton in return for two-thirds of the gross operating profit. Hilton had to provide only expenses and working capital. This kind of arrangement was adapted for other Hiltons in Istanbul, Mexico and Cuba. With the Cuban revolution in the late 1950s and the loss of the Hilton in Havana it became clear to Hilton that political developments outside the control of hotel management companies could cause the company to lose a considerable amount of money. Therefore it developed future arrangements in what has become known as a management contract.

Under these arrangements, the property owners take the full risk of operating losses and have the ongoing responsibility of supplying working capital. Before the Second World War it was the norm to operate and at the same time own hotel properties. Within developed countries and in the colonies of the major European powers, the economic and political situation was generally stable and suitable for real estate investments. The economic depression of the 1930s, however, caused a change in the willingness of banks and investors to invest in hotels, since many hotel owners defaulted on their mortgages. As a result, emerging hotel chains like Hilton had to invest their own equity in their developments. Rather than building expensive new hotels, Hilton mostly acquired and rebuilt older hotels like Stephens in Chicago or the Plaza in New York.

After the Second World War, world trade started to develop. Hilton International and Inter-Continental competed to provide hotel accommodation of North American standard for US travellers who went abroad. Both hotel chains had close links to the dominating airlines, TWA and Pan-American Airlines, that encouraged them to provide accommodation at foreign locations. Overseas expansion was not very attractive for hotel companies, however, since political and financial instability made capital investment a risky venture. In addition the big chains were not able to provide enough capital themselves to cope with the fast growth of the travel market.

Leasing arrangements were difficult to establish since English law did not apply in most locations, and many leasing arrangements were a complicated and costly process. In addition overseas owners and developers were reluctant to commit themselves to long term leases with untested operators. Management contracts as they were applied by Hilton accounted for these difficulties: they provided owner and operator with adequate returns for a suitable duration. However, other US chains did not follow the example of Hilton and very few management contracts were signed during the 1950s and 1960s. Companies in the US and European markets relied on ownership, leasing and franchising.

In 1970 the ten major US chains had twenty-two management contracts; by 1975 they listed 182. The economic recession at the beginning of the 1970s forced many hotels to revert to institutional lenders and real estate investment trusts were keen to sell their properties that had proven to offer little or no appropriate return on investment. These companies either formed their own management division or looked out for hotel management companies that could turn their operations around in time before the operations were sold. Apart from their expertise in operating and marketing, big chains could provide the sophisticated reservation networks (marketing and technical economies of scale) which were a key factor for success. As a result, lenders invested in hotel projects only if they were managed by a well known company. During this time a wide number of US hotel companies diversified into management contracting. Simultaneously, new independent management contracting companies were formed to participate in new developments. By 1975, some 60 independent contractors held more than 500 management contracts.

The expansion continued until the beginning of the 1980s, when the recession forced smaller, less prudent management contractors out of the market. Until then, the management contracts of these independent contractors were almost solely found within domestic US markets.

Outside the USA the development of management contracts during the 1950s and 1960s was a slow process with European companies operating only a few of them. European contracts were more of an *ad-hoc* nature than a systematic policy of diversification and expansion. Hallway Hotels Overseas (established in 1966) was the first big British company to develop and manage a number of hotels under management contracts in African countries. In 1969 the hotel development incentive scheme launched by the British government supported investments in hotel projects by giving financial incentives. As a result, an overcapacity of hotel rooms emerged in certain parts of Britain in the early 1970s; at the same time the economy went into recession. Short term management contracts with experienced hotel contractors allowed some hotel owners to turn their initially weak investment into a profitable one. After the end of the incentive scheme in 1974, suitable hotel sites at a financially feasible price were rare and the money market tight. In order to be able to expand, some UK hotel companies turned to management contracts as a fast and profitable method of enlarging their hotel group.

The world-wide travel market continued to expand during the 1970s and created a need for hotel developments in many parts of the world. While demand in Africa and the Far East grew steadily the oil boom in the Middle East required a substantial amount of new hotel developments to cover the fast growing demand. The economic and political situations in these countries were unstable, and legal restrictions prevented the free movement of capital. The management contract was perceived as a sound way for hotel companies to gain market share within these countries. The urgency of development also grew due to the impact of the toughening of competition amongst hotel companies. Apart from Hilton International and Inter-Continental, Sheraton, Hyatt and Marriott have been competing in the five star market. Holiday Inn and Ramada have been competing on the four star market segment. Forte (now Granada plc) and Grand Metropolitan at that time both entered the management contract market successfully from the UK, together with Meridien, a French company and subsidiary of Air France until 1994.

A legislative factor in the USA which affected the development of management contracts was the Economic Recovery Tax Act 1981 which provided financial incentives for real estate investors in hotels. Many new products were designed for specific market needs and many new brands were launched on the market. Despite this development, competition for management contract arrangements was getting tougher since many investing companies (owners) gained valuable experience about the hotel industry, and used their knowledge to negotiate contracts in their favour. Due to the rising negotiating power of hotel owners, hotel operating companies were forced into arrangements that included a partial equity stake of the operator. As domestic areas became more and more saturated, hotel corporations increased their activities abroad. Major international hotel chains sought to expand to gateway cities of Europe, the Far East and Australia. In addition, the changes in eastern Europe, the former Soviet Union and China are likely to open the doors to foreign investors and entrepreneurs. Such countries offer sound possibilities for expanding hotel companies, and the use of management contracts will generate the appropriate business affiliation.

However, terms of expansion are becoming more difficult for hotel companies as international investors are becoming more knowledgeable and tougher negotiators. The market conditions in the 1990s are to owners' favour. The world-wide recession in the beginning of the 1990s left most of the hotel industry in a poor condition. Most independent chains as well as many major hotel chains suffered a lack of capital for necessary expansion plans. Banks and lenders hesitated to invest in hotel projects that were seen as offering a less than attractive return on investment. Hotel investors can now choose their operating partners out of a wide range of reputable names that compete for profitable and strategically well-placed locations. This forces the operators to invest part of their capital and share some of the risk involved in decreasing amounts of remuneration. An example is now given of a management contract proposal for a hotel in Germany.

Case Study: Holiday Inn, Stuttgart, Germany: management contract proposal

Background

The Holiday Inn in Stuttgart has 325 rooms with minibars, pay-TV, satellite TV, hairdryers and trouser press. The public areas consist of two restaurants, one bar, conference area for up to 600 people, a gift shop, a leisure centre with solarium, fitness and sauna. An underground parking facility provides space for 120 cars. In order to achieve a commercially justifiable average room rate for the hotel and to provide potential customers with an adequate idea of the value proposition of the hotel, the suggestion is that it should be branded as a Holiday Inn and not as a Holiday Inn Garden Court.

The central proposition for Holiday Inn to decide was if a fifteen year management contract should be granted. The hotel was currently trading as a Holiday Inn Garden Court Brand and the thinking was for Holiday Inn to contribute $130,000 towards the costs of converting the hotel to its core brand. The owning company wanted Holiday Inn to take over the management during May 1996.

Growth strategy

The key strategic issue for Holiday Inn is that in Germany it enjoys a high level of distribution (fifty-seven hotels in 1996) and Stuttgart is a strong location in which it needs to have representation. The benefit for both parties is that the value proposition Holiday Inn offers is that it would be able to improve the delivery of business to the hotel. In addition with a German private investor as the owner, this proposal could be used to further underline the value of a Holiday Inn management contract and therefore have a spin-off effect for further management contracts in Germany where currently a number of private investors and funds have problems with their lessees.

Market

An important element for Holiday Inn when considering this proposal was a market analysis. Stuttgart is one of the main cities in the south of Germany with a high level of corporate business. It is also the gateway to the famous Black Forest which attracts many leisure travellers. The market in 1996 was depressed and suffering from an oversupply in hotel rooms, leading to a price war which resulted in lower average room rates. However, in the longer term every economy has its cycles and therefore it could be suggested that the hotel has a hidden future profit opportunity when the economy of Germany improves. The hotel is located in a business park with a monopoly position on the north-east side of Stuttgart. In terms of visibility and accessibility it is approximately 1 km from the motorway exit and the Daimler-Benz factory and head office are only 3 km away.

Owner of hotel

The hotel is owned by Deschler Beteiligungs GbR and was operated by Senator Hotel GmbH under a franchise licence. In March 1996 the owner terminated the lease contract with Senator Hotel GmbH and founded a new management company,

case study continues ▶

Poss-Hotelverwaltungs-GmbH, which is fully controlled by the owners. This new company entered into a new lease agreement. Upon termination of the lease contract in March between the owner and Senator, the owner and his son-in-law, Mr Poss (who plans to take over control of the entire business as of 1997) together founded a new company, Poss Hotelverwaltungs-GmbH. This is a limited company with share capital of DM 100,000. The purpose of this company is to control the administrative management of the hotel.

A new lease contract has been made between the owner and this administrative management company. The intention is that Holiday Inn Hotel GmbH would enter into a management contract with Poss Hotelverwaltungs-GmbH.

Management contract proposal

The proposal was for Holiday Inn to enter into a fifteen-year management contract with Poss Hotelverwaltungs-GmbH in respect of a 325 room core brand hotel (post-conversion). Effective from May 1996, the contract would allow for renewal options of five-yearly periods by mutual agreement of both parties. Holiday Inn would make a contribution towards conversion costs of $130,000 and would not make any other direct investment, guarantee or grant of exclusivity.

A complex system of management fees due to Holiday Inn was included in the proposal, with a basic fee 2% of gross operating profit and a graduated incentive fee dependent on performance. In terms of gross operating profit (GOP), this financial term includes the base management fee, sales and marketing assessments, Holidex and accounting services *before* the GOP is calculated.

Over a three year period Holiday Inn believed the following key ratios of occupancy and average daily rate (ADR) would grow in real terms thus:

	Yr 1	Yr 2	Yr 3
Occupancy (%)	65	69	73
ADR	DM 85	DM 93	DM 97

From a financial sensitivity perspective it would be only if occupancy dropped by 10% points and rate fell overall by DM 14 that Holiday Inn would receive only the base fee of 2%.

Franchising

With tourism in Europe expected to grow rapidly between 1997 and 2012, there is a greater need to raise customer awareness of the hotel brand through increased presence and marketing activity. Surveys of the European hotel industry show that the top ten chains operating in Europe provide as much capacity as the next forty chains combined. The pressure for increased size in order to gain marketing economies of scale, both from unaffiliated and chain hotels, has never been greater.

Franchising has increased enormously since the mid-1970s within the hospitality industry, spreading the market and giving new opportunities for the hotel business. In the USA it has been continuously growing; in Europe it is also starting to be important, especially within fast food restaurants such as Pizza Hut, Pizza Express, McDonalds and Burger King. It is in these kinds of restaurants where franchising began and since then, this type of business has been expanded towards other areas of the hospitality industry such as hotels.

Definition

Franchising literally means '*to be free*'. In its basic form, it is a method of doing business in which the parent company (the franchisor) sells to another party (the franchisee) the right to distribute its products or services. The type of franchise system used in the hospitality industry is business format franchising. Under business format franchising a well-known product or service owner allows another party to market its products or services using the parent company's name, trade mark and its business format, i.e. production and marketing techniques. In return, the franchisee pays the franchisor an initial franchise fee and an ongoing royalty, usually 2–8% of gross sales. In the hotel industry, the franchise pays an average fee of around 5% of the room's turnover for the right to brand the hotel. Holiday Inn is an example of business format franchising.

Franchising has been called the last and the best hope for independent business in an era of growing vertical integration within the hospitality industry. It helps small businesses compete with the big ones; it also offers a unique opportunity to people with limited capital and experience.

Many definitions of franchising have been offered over the years, because franchising covers a very broad range of business. Some definitions are very general and try to include all possible types of franchise, while others are more specific to a particular type of franchise but will not necessarily be broad enough to cover all aspects of the franchise industry. All agree that franchising is a method of distribution, and it is perhaps easiest to view the great variety of distribution arrangements as a continuum with at one end of the spectrum, a simple agreement between two parties for the distribution of a product or services; and at the other end of the spectrum, a complicated and comprehensively defined two-party relationship. The British Franchise Association (BFA), the UK trade organisation, has proposed the following definition of franchising:

> *A franchise is a contractual licence granted by one person (the franchisor) to another (the franchisee) which*

- permits or requires the franchisee to carry on, during the period of the franchise, a particular business under or using a specific name belonging to or associated with the franchisor, and
- entitles the franchisor to exercise continuing control during the period of the franchise over the manner in which the franchisee carries on the business which is the subject of the franchise, and
- obliges the franchisor to provide the franchisee with assistance in carrying on the business which is the subject of the franchise (in relation to the organisation of the franchisee's business, the training of staff, merchandising, management or otherwise), and
- requires the franchisee to pay to the franchisor sums of money in consideration for the franchise, or for goods or services provided by the franchisor to the franchisee, and
- which is not a transaction between subsidiaries of the same holding company, or between an individual and company controlled by the franchisee.

This definition does not mention any requirement for a franchisee to invest in the franchised outlet. Another franchising definition appears in the by-laws of the International Franchise Association (IFA), the US trade organisation.

> *A franchise operation is a contractual relationship between the franchisor and the*

franchisee in which the franchisor offers or is obligated to maintain a continuing interest in the business of the franchisee in such areas as know-how and training; wherein the franchisee operates under a common trade name, format and/or procedure owned or controlled by the franchisor, and in which the franchisee has or will make a substantial capital investment in his [sic] business from his own resources.

This definition is concise and quite comprehensive, yet begs a number of questions in addition to providing answers. This definition will be far better understood by those who already have a working knowledge of franchising and the type of transaction.

These two definitions have basic features which must be present in every business format franchise:

- There must be a contract containing all the terms agreed.
- The franchisor must initiate and train the franchisee in all aspects of the business prior to the opening of the business and assist in the opening.
- After the business is opened, the franchisor must maintain a continuing interest in providing the franchisee with support in all aspects of the operation of the business.
- The franchisee is permitted under the control of the franchisor to operate under a trade name, format and/or procedure, and with the benefit of goodwill owned by the franchisor.
- The franchisee must make a substantial capital investment from his or her own resources.
- The franchisee must own the business.
- The franchisee will pay the franchisor for the rights which are acquired in one way or other and for the continuing services which will be provided.
- The franchisee will be given some territory within which to operate.

Historical development

Contrary to popular belief, franchising is not an American invention, but first emerged in Britain during the Middle Ages when certain powerful nobles would pay a lump sum to the government and agree to provide continuing personal support and services in return for the right to collect local taxes. The nature of franchising has of course evolved over the centuries.

Monopolies

Franchising resurfaced in the eighteenth and nineteenth centuries when the long-term right to a monopoly in some form of trade or commerce would be granted either by a legislative body or by royalty to a franchisee. As consideration for the granting of this right, the franchisee would make an initial cash payment and would also have certain continuing obligations to the franchisor.

Tied houses

The next major step in the history, development and evolution of franchising came with the tied house agreements between UK breweries and landlords which became established during the eighteenth century and which still exists in the 1990s. During the 1700s there was a period of growing concern over the increasing social problems resulting from the widespread availability of alcohol. Legislation was therefore introduced in order to regulate the sale of beer and spirits. Public houses were required to hold a liquor licence in order to be allowed to sell alcohol. Since only a restricted number of licences were granted, the value of those inns which were successful in obtaining these licences rapidly rose. Many prospective landlords found they could not afford to purchase hostelries. The breweries therefore stepped in and started buying the licensed premises themselves and leasing them to the publicans. As part of the agreement, the publican would undertake to sell exclusively beer made by the brewery. The legislation also required that the standard of many existing inns be improved, so the breweries offered to finance the required improvements in many hostelries in return for which the landlords would agree to a tie arrangement.

Franchising in the hotel industry: a growth strategy

This discussion of franchising can be set within the wider context of a growth strategy, specifically as a way to expand the market easily, and as a way to reach the market quickly. This approach reduces risks and as a consequence strengthens the product's positioning as well as the brand name – so important to increasing sales. Franchising has implications within corporate strategy in respect of many factors such as finance, the franchisor–franchisee relationship, marketing, consumers, branding, and so on. All these points will be expanded within this section.

Global expansion of hotels through franchising is very popular, especially with established franchisors in the USA. Franchising is one means of providing the capital needed for global expansion of hotel chains when the domestic economy is in recession and loan capital is scarce. It can be regarded as the primary engine for driving business growth as firms do not have to, or cannot obtain, the large amounts of capital needed to acquire assets in the context of an aggressive growth strategy. The high risk associated with expansion by acquisition in recession is the central reason why franchising has become so popular in the USA where franchising as a whole grew by 114% during the 1980s. This is simply because it diversifies risk away from the franchisor and on to the franchisee.

Reasons for growth

Four general reasons can be identified for the growth in franchising since the mid-1970s.

Role of service activities
This is possibly the most important environmental factor responsible for the rapid growth of the franchising industry in recent years. Many service industries are personnel-intensive and they often rely on a distribution network consisting of a large number of outlets dispersed over a relatively large geographical area. The franchising technique is particular suitable for this type of operation as it offers considerable advantages in terms of staff motivation, and may also reduce some of the problems associated with controlling local management from a remote head office. Changing lifestyles, such as the increasing number of women going out to work, and the greater leisure time and affluence enjoyed in the west, have resulted in a growing demand for services. In short, the social and economic environment has become increasingly conducive to the emergence of a great variety of franchises.

Value placed on self-employment

The increasing value that society places on self-employment has also encouraged the growth of franchising. Entrepreneurialism is viewed in a favourable light, and a high level of self-esteem and social acknowledgement can be gained through self-employment. As a result, an increasing number of people are experiencing the desire to escape the bureaucratic environment of the large organisation and to go it alone by starting their own small business. Many studies have shown that there is indeed a widespread desire among ordinary workers to run their own business. Unfortunately, most of these would-be entrepreneurs lack either the necessary skills or the confidence to set up a totally independent business. However, the franchising system overcomes many of the problems commonly associated with starting a business, and thereby provides a much easier route to self-employment and the social esteem that goes with it. The extent of the social value that is placed on entrepreneurialism can be seen in many of the adverts that are often used to sell franchises. These adverts tend to emphasise the social and psychological benefits of 'being your own boss', just as much as the potential financial rewards. So long as society continues to place a value on being self-employed, then franchising can be expected to grow.

Unemployment

While many people are attracted to self-employment as a means of escaping the frustrations of employee status, other individuals are forced to consider starting their own business because there seems to be little prospect of securing any other form of employment. During the economic recession of the early 1990s many people turned to self-employment, sometimes using their redundancy payment as capital. Franchising may be an alternative for many of these people as they may lack necessary human capital (i.e. the skills and knowledge) to start a totally independent venture, although there are also doubts as to whether they make the best franchisees.

Availability of finance

The growth of franchising has also been helped by the increase in recent years of the availability of finance on more attractive terms than are usually offered to independent small businesses. Banks have developed special arrangements specifically designed to provide suitable funding for franchisees. Furthermore, the financial institutions have warmed to franchising and a number of franchisor companies have been successfully floated on the stock market. The growing involvement of the banks and financial institutions has proved to be the key element in the expansion of franchising, and has generally helped to increase the profile and respectability of the industry as a whole.

Business format franchising

One main approach to franchising in the hospitality industry is through business format franchising (see p. 78). Business format franchising is characterised by an ongoing business relationship between franchisor and franchisee that includes not only the product, service, and trademark, but the entire business format itself, a marketing strategy and plan, operating manuals and standards, quality control, and continuing two-way communications.

Franchising as a legal or marketing concept is not new. There has been a surge of interest since the early 1970s resulting in the rapidly expanding use of this marketing method. First generation franchises are undoubtedly an important means of product distribution. Nevertheless, when writers use the term franchise they are more often referring to what has become known as the business format or second generation franchises. Business format franchises fall into three broad categories mainly distinguished by the level of investment needed from the franchisee:

- *Job* franchises
- *Business* franchises
- *Investment* franchises

Job franchises

These require a minimal financial investment by the franchisee, and can usually be operated from the franchisee's home. The largest part of the total investment may be, say, the purchase price of a van. The term *job* franchise derives from the fact that the franchisee is in effect buying a job. One-person operations which do not require business premises, such as domestic maintenance services and mobile vehicle servicing, are ideal for job franchising.

Business franchises

These require a much larger investment in stock, equipment and business premises. Because the scale of operation is much larger than that of a job franchise, the franchisee will normally be unable to run the business single-handedly and will usually have to employ additional staff in order to operate effectively. The range of business franchises is vast, and includes photocopying and printing services, picture framing, business services (such as accounting, security or contract catering), dry-cleaning and take-away fast food operations.

Investment franchises

These require a relatively large investment by the franchisee, often in excess of £250,000. Franchisees who undertake investment franchises are concerned primarily with earning a return on their capital investment rather than with providing themselves with employment. One example of an investment franchise is a franchised hotel.

Relationship between the franchisor and franchisee

Franchising is a system of distribution whereby one party (the franchisor) grants to a second party (the franchisee) the right to distribute products, or perform services, and to operate a business in accordance with an established marketing system. The franchisor provides the franchisee with expertise, trade marks, the corporate image, and both initial and ongoing support, in return for which the franchisee pays to the franchisor certain fees. The objective is that both parties benefit from each other.

The relationship between the two parties could, by virtue of the controls exercised by the franchisor over the franchisees, be held to be that of master and servant. A successful franchise relationship relies heavily on mutual trust between the two parties. The franchisor has to trust the franchisee to make appropriate operating decisions concerning the daily operation of the outlet, and similarly the franchisee has to feel confident that assistance is available from the franchisor should it be needed. The relationship will turn sour as soon as either party begins to mistrust the other. This is one of the reasons why the operating manual and the franchise contract should be as comprehensive as possible so that both parties know from the outset exactly what their rights and obligations are.

Methods of global franchising

Many of the established global franchisers originate in the USA; their expansion is accounted for by the relative hostility and saturation of their US competitive environment as compared to other regions of the world.

In the USA, franchise growth takes place through the sale of one or multiple franchises, most often with territorial and time restrictions. A common method is through the installation of a master franchisee who may be an individual or a business. The master franchisee assumes virtually all roles of the franchisor by selling and administering sub-franchises. While the use of hotel franchising through the master franchise arrangement approach has advantages of greater regional integration and even less risk to the original franchisor, there can also be some serious problems. If a franchisor is in conflict with a single site franchisee their problems are less serious than a conflict with a master franchisee; a disagreement with the master franchisee can totally disrupt a firm's expansion strategy. In 1992 Scotts Hotels (UK) Ltd resigned its master franchisee arrangement with Holiday Inn in the UK and switched to an arrangement with Marriott. The result was that Holiday Inn's representation in Britain was dramatically reduced and its flagship hotel at Marble Arch, London, had also gone. The dispute originated from contractual differences but inevitably resulted in the redesign and rescheduling of the expansion strategy of Holiday Inn in the UK. This example of Scotts emphasises that it is essential for there to be a good relationship between the partners in a franchise relationship. If this relationship fails, the consequences are greater than if there was conflict between manager and head office relating to an internally funded expansion strategy.

The franchisor is faced with a problem when expanding globally to destinations thousands of miles apart. There has to be control over the franchisees to ensure brand uniformity; however, franchisors also have to promote innovation if they are to keep the business proactive and ahead of the competition.

Franchisors therefore have to select a control system suitable to their objectives, which should include flexibility for new product development, a symbiotic relationship with the franchisees and the extension of brand uniformity to geographically dispersed hotels.

Franchisees need advertising to encourage international business travellers and generally heighten awareness of the hotel in the eyes of the public. The franchisor needs to provide advertising because it is part of the contractual agreement, but more importantly because it is necessary to exercise control. To combine all the objectives, the franchisor advertises the brand standards, which generates demand and also motivates the franchisee to reach and maintain those standards.

Success in expansion through franchising is primarily dependent on maintaining a good franchisor–franchisee relationship, and exerting control to ensure the brand is standardised. The results of not achieving this could be portfolio quality disparities, which diminish regular customer demand, or the strategic problems associated with losing a master franchisee.

Competitive methods used by franchisors

New technologies, selling strategies and marketing concepts are also presenting a competitive advantage to hotel franchisors. These new methods are being implemented not only to attract new customers, but also to gain more franchisees within the right market segment. The implementation of new competitive methods is essential to keep a clear and privileged position for the franchisor and only the most innovative methods could help to keep that position in the future. The purpose of this section of the chapter is to introduce several of these methods that are being implemented in the hotel industry by the franchisors.

Technology-based systems

Technology is used to take advantage of slower moving competition by providing better service, improved decision making and increasing revenue. Hotel operators now realise that a brand in itself is not enough. Owners and management companies are demanding that franchisors also provide powerful reservation networks.

The link to a centralised reservation system (CRS) is considered one of the most important benefits of joining any hotel franchise. With a sophisticated CRS, a hotel chain provides individual property owners and managers with a tool to increase reservations, maximise sales, implement yield management, enhance market capabilities and improve guest services. Faced with unprecedented operational and guest service challenges, a CRS may be essential to survival.

The way hotel companies sell to consumers has changed dramatically over the past few years. Many US hotel chains have or are in the process of implementing new reservations systems that utilise yield management to allow better control of their rooms inventory. They are using the latest technology to provide hotels with a wealth of information that can help forecast demand and increase occupancy and revenue. The systems are also linked to airline CRSs in order to allow travel agents to make direct bookings.

Technological development had certainly made a great impact on front office activities over the years, and is likely to continue to do so in the future. Software packages cover virtually every front office function from reservations, room allocation, guest history, billing and accounting to the production of management information. Even though its introduction within the hotel industry is slow, big international hotel chains have created their own systems; some hotels are pooling their resources in powerful consortia and others are buying or renting the technology. Six examples are given below.

1. Holiday Inn

The Holidex system is the largest hotel reservation network in the world and is owned by Holiday Inn. It services Residence Inns, Embassy Suites and Hampton Inns, in addition to Holiday Inn. This investment in technology is felt to be one of the company's key competitive methods in its approach to franchising.

2. Best Western International

The STAR system is Best Western International's global reservation system. It enables property-to-property and world-wide reservations in 30 seconds; this on-line system has real-time inventory so that when a room is sold, it is immediately depleted from the inventory.

3. Choice Hotels International

Sunburst 2001 is Choice Hotels International's new reservation system, which will give travel agents easier access to the firm's inventory and comprehensive information on each of its hotels. It is also making use of additional technology, such as automated self check-in/out machines in public areas, together with in-room video systems.

4. ITT Sheraton
Like the other hotel firms examined, ITT Sheraton has expended funds to develop an improved on-line reservations system; this has real-time inventories, provides complete information on rack rates and packages as well as a guest history. It maintains a free phone number linked to its seventeen reservation centres around the world, offering services to forty-four countries.

5. Hilton Hotels
The computer reservation centre, Compass Computer, is jointly owned by Hilton and Budget Car Rental, with both vendors operating in separate parts of the same system. Although among the first hotel central reservation projects, Hilton's system has been enhanced consistently over the years and is among the most functionally rich and successful of systems.

6. Marriott Corporation
The Marsha system employs several advanced reservation techniques, such as on-line property access to the central database, that are not found elsewhere. Marriott is planning to expand further the capabilities of the system, particularly in such areas as Management Information Systems (MIS) and statistical reporting.

Although considerable investment will be required to upgrade existing in-house reservation systems and link them with several selected mega CRSs, the major hotel groups stand to benefit above all others in the short term and gain a competitive edge.

Hotel product branding: segmenting the marketplace

Explicit within this discussion of hotel franchising and the companies involved is the topic of hotel product branding and segmentation of the marketplace. Product branding is generating increased interest in hotel groups throughout the world. As competition increases and operating costs escalate, the multipurpose hotel offering a variety of costly facilities is finding it harder to operate profitability and serve diverse groups such as convention delegates, leisure travellers and air crews.

The branding of hotels to identify particular properties with specific market segments is not a new concept, but the idea is generating increased interest among hotel chains with franchise outlets throughout the world. No longer can hotel groups profitably serve and satisfy within one establishment the requirements of groups as diverse as business travellers, conference delegates, holidaymakers, air crews and tour parties. Holiday Inn continues to lead the way among the more recent and active advocates of branding.

For many chains, product branding has been forced upon them. The lack of new sites for hotel building in many cities has meant acquisition has been the only way to expand. However, many hotels also acknowledge that product branding is a necessary step in a highly competitive international market environment in which the products on offer had become almost indistinguishable from one chain to another.

The principal market sectors that the international hotel chains seek to attract are varied, according to the location of individual hotels and the type and standard of hotel, but generally can be categorised. Thus, branding has come about for three principal reasons:

- In response to the need to tailor the hotel product to the specific needs of the user.
- As hotel groups sought expansion through acquisition during the 1970s and 1980s, many chains found themselves purchasing a disparate group of properties often of widely different star ratings. In this case it was a logical step to categorise the re-

sultant hotel portfolio into different hotel types or brands as a more cost-effective and timely approach than seeking to bring all the hotels up to a common standard.

● Hotel classification and star-rating systems adopted in many countries lack consistency and do not provide the hotel user with sufficiently clear indication of the style of hotel or level of service available. Branding within hotel chains can provide a more accurate indication to the consumer as to the standard of hotel product and level of service expected.

Holiday Inn, like many other hotel chains, is developing a portfolio of hotel brands. Although hotel chains have different ways to approach branding, they have a common aim of attracting a wide range of market sectors and developing brand loyalty. This is being achieved not through the development of multi-role and multi-market hotels, but through carefully planned hotel brands and sub-brands designed, developed, operated and marketed to satisfy the needs, expectations and budgets of clearly defined market sectors.

The USA is the home of hotel brands. Branding is more developed there than in most other hotel markets and, if branding theory is correct, harder brand hotel chains should have exhibited distinct success. The USA during the 1980s saw the emergence of a proliferation of hotel brands and this has resulted in deteriorating performance and in changes in ownership of many of the major hotel chains. It is too early to judge the success of all these acquisitions, although the case of Ladbroke's purchase of Hilton International is generally regarded as one of the best hotel transactions of the 1980s. Ladbroke has almost tripled profits since the acquisition and enhanced the status and value of the Hilton International brand in the process. From this example it is also clear that the quality of hotel brand management is important to the success of the brand.

A specific feature of the US hotel chains is that most are involved in franchising hotels rather than in ownership and management. Franchising is responsible for the major expansion of branded hotels in the USA. It has been less popular internationally and rare in the UK. Among the reasons for the popularity of franchised hotels is that most chain expansion since the mid-1950s has been by new builds, and franchisors have been able to provide a formula for hotel owners and operators to ease and reduce the development costs. One of the reasons why hotel franchising is rare in the UK is that expansion has been by acquisition and most older hotels cannot conform to the brand specifications of many franchisors.

The use of marketing and advertising

The operating environment of the hospitality industry is becoming increasingly volatile, uncertain and complex in the late 1990s, and the assistance that franchisors can bring to franchisees is beyond doubt. There can be little doubt that the level of competitive intensity is rising to heights never before experienced by industry owners and operators.

In the hospitality industry, for instance, hotel marketers no longer rely on broadly defined market segments (e.g. corporate travellers, tourists, convention business). Marketing experts are pinpointing a select group of potential customers and learning everything about their location, habits, attitudes, friends, travel companions, priorities, and pleasure points. In the 1990s hoteliers are looking at the client instead of the type of product they can offer: market segmentation is considered one of the most important factors for hotel marketers.

The role of marketing in the commercial hotel sector strives to increase room-occupancy by devising improved products which appeal to customers. It is notable that the role of marketing in business varies between types of economy. Marketing as applied to capitalist businesses aims to produce satisfied customers for a satisfactory return to the business proprietors.

The growing strength of hotel groups within the international hotel industry gave rise to common standards, operations and marketing communications among their individual units. There is little doubt that the hotel business is an international business and is globally focused. Hotel organisations in recent years are increasing their international operations world-wide.

A major advantage for a franchisee upon joining a franchise system is the immediate access to a marketing concept which has been tried and proven successful in a specific environment. Thus the franchisee achieves very substantial benefits from a saving in time and expenditure that would be required to plan and implement a marketing system.

The advantages of joining a franchise have already been pointed out; one of these advantages is the direct link to a marketing concept, and through this marketing concept, the franchisee can gain an easy market penetration. With the help of the franchisor, franchisees can obtain a greater market exposure than they could have gained on their own. Another major advantage is the acquisition of considerable expertise and experience in marketing, advertising and promotional activities organised by the franchisor prior to, during or after their unit's opening. For these reasons franchisors are continuously developing new marketing concepts to attract new franchisees and also to be able to compete in the marketplace.

Marketing includes a whole collection of activities which the company performs in relating to its market. Many of these activities are combined in the marketing mix, which is made up of the four Ps – Product, Price, Promotion and Place. Each component of the marketing mix can be manipulated in order to influence demand in the marketplace.

Promotion is communication by the firm with its various audiences with a view to informing them and influencing their attitudes and behaviour in a way favourable to the firm. It is aimed at enhancing the image and position of the company and its products. The promotion mix includes advertising, selling, sales promotion, public relations, sponsorship and direct mail. Therefore, it must be stressed that advertising is simply one element in the promotion component of the marketing mix. For hotels, advertising is used to enhance the brand name; it is a way of communication between the clients and the hotel owners. A proper marketing campaign can help to increase the number of clients and therefore hotel profits.

Summary

Throughout this chapter the theme has been the internationalisation and growth of the world-wide hotel industry. Contrasting the major chain hotels with the smaller independents, the chapter has shown that the structure of the industry is changing, with the hotel chains highlighting a number of reasons for this desire for growth. All this discussion was set within the context of corporate strategy. Three main methods of growth were identified: acquisition, management contracts and franchising. The relevance and importance of the latter two methods of growth were discussed in depth.

Further reading

- Bell C.A. (1993) 'Agreements with chain-hotel companies', *Cornell Hotel and Restaurant Association Quarterly* 34(1): 27–33.
- Connell J. (1992) 'Branding hotel portfolios', *International Journal of Contemporary Hospitality Management* 4(1): 26–32.
- Crawford-Welch S. and Tse E. (1990) 'Mergers, acquisitions and alliances in the European

hospitality industry', *International Journal of Contemporary Hospitality Management* 2(1): 10–16.

● Cullen T.P. and Rogers J.L. (1995) 'Quality and price perceptions', *International Journal of Contemporary Hospitality Management* 7(2): 151–60.

● Dawson S. and Go F.M. (1995) 'Expanding in a barrier free Europe', in F.M. Go and R. Pine (eds) *Globalisation Strategy in the Hotel Industry*, London: Routledge, pp. 129–67.

● Eyster J. (1980) 'How to negotiate a contract, Part I and II', *Cornell Hotel and Restaurant Association Quarterly* February: 75–82; May: 49–60.

● Eyster J. (1988a) 'Terms and termination', *Cornell Hotel and Restaurant Association Quarterly* August: 81–90.

● Eyster J. (1980b) 'Management contracts', *Cornell Hotel and Restaurant Association Quarterly* May: 42–55.

● Eyster J. (1993) 'The revolution in domestic hotel management contracts', *Cornell Hotel and Restaurant Association Quarterly* February: 16–26.

● Go F. (1989) 'International hotel industry: capitalising on change', *Tourism Management* 10(3): 195–200.

● Hotels (1991) 'What's ahead in reservations technology?', *Hotels* 25(10): 93–4.

● Hotels (1992) 'Is your CRS working hard enough?', *Hotels* 26(8): 71–2.

● Hotels (1993) 'The ABCs of yield management', *Hotels* 27(4): 55–6.

● HOTREC (1995) *The HORECA Sector and the European Union*, Brussels: HOTREC.

● Housden J. (1984) *Franchising and Other Business Relationships in Hotel and Catering Services*, London: Heinemann.

● Knowles T., Teare R., Eccles G. and Costa J. (1996) Managerial Implications Within a Hostile Takeover: a case of Forte Plc, The European Case Clearing House, Bedford, UK.

● Knowles T., Teare R., Eccles G. and Costa J. (1996) Granada Group: a successful story of mergers and aquisitions, The European Case Clearing House, Bedford, UK.

● Lodging Hospitality (1989) 'Futures trends in chain franchising', *Lodging Hospitality* 45(5): Supplement 22, 24, 26.

● Lydecker T. (1987) 'Franchising: who swings the most chain?' *Restaurant Institute* 97(8): 30–5, 46.

● Messenger S.Y. and Lin S.M. (1991) 'International hotel advertising', *International Journal of Contemporary Hospitality Management* 3(3): 28–32.

● Morgan M.S. (1991) 'Traveller's choice: the effects of advertising and prior stay', *Cornell Hotels and Restaurant Association Quarterly* 32(4): 40–9.

● Olsen M.D. (1993) 'International growth strategies of major US hotel companies' *Travel and Tourism Analyst* 3.

● Reid R.D. and Sandler M. (1992) 'The use of technology to improve service quality', *Cornell Hotels and Restaurant Association Quarterly* 33(3): 68–73.

● Rounce J. (1987) 'International hotel product branding: segmenting the market place', *Travel and Tourism Analyst* pp. 13–22.

● Slattery P. (1991) 'Hotel branding in the 1990s', *Travel and Tourism Analyst* 1: 23–5.

● Slattery P. (1994) 'The structural theory of business demand: a reply to Hughes', *International Journal of Contemporary Hospitality Management* 13(2): 173–6.

● Slattery P. and Johnson S. (1993) 'Hotel chains in Europe', *Travel and Tourism Analyst* 1: 65–80.

● Stoner C. (1988) 'Own or manage? European–Asia–US chains disagree', *Hotels and Restaurant International* January: 24–30.

● Tarrant C. (1989) 'UK hotel industry: market restructuring and the need to respond to customer demands', *Tourism Management* 10: 187–91.

● Warnick R. (1987) 'Management companies: a new perspective', *Lodging* February: 36–54.

Chapter Four

Hotel Management: Dimensions and Structure

Objectives

After reading this chapter you should be able to

■ Identify a range of hotel product types and the team that manage them.

■ Understand the relevance of planning regulations.

■ Consider the stages of a feasibility study.

■ Identify the elements within commissioning the property.

Hotel product type

The issue of product type can be linked to the subject of hotel product segmentation. Product segmentation can be defined as

> *The development by hotel companies of accommodation concepts designed to meet the needs of specific target markets.*

While the available supply of accommodation in the UK is reasonably well spread over all categories, the chains predominate in the middle and upper markets of the hotel industry. The lower category and economy segments remain largely in the hands of the independent operator although this aspect has been changing over the past few years.

The 1980s resulted in a widening of the market gap between the upper-middle/first-class markets and the economy market, the latter traditionally epitomised by small independent hotels. Opportunities offered by this widening gap have been recognised by a number of hotel operators. At the forefront have been new-build establishments providing a good standard of accommodation with en suite facilities in the economy market segment and associated with existing catering outlets, commercially justified in their own right. Companies in this field have been Travelodge, Travel Inns, Accor and Campanile.

Within the middle and first-class markets, hotels have traditionally been service driven. However, new concepts are emerging which respond to those consumers who are more rooms orientated.

In France, by contrast, the majority of establishments are small and around half are ungraded. Of the graded hotels over 80% are in the two star or lower categories. Prior to the 1960s there were no French national chains and there were no foreign groups operating hotels in the country. In the 1990s there are about thirty hotel chains. These chains in the 1970s developed in the middle and upper tiers of the market. Since 1978 the expansion shifted towards the economy sector.

Branding

The hotel industry has sought to benefit from branding as well. Hotel brands first emerged in the USA. The influence of Holiday Inn was central to this development because it started with Kermons Wilson's idea of what facilities a Holiday Inn should include, and quickly became the USA's largest hotel chain. Holiday Inn was a new-build chain which facilitated easy and inexpensive expansion, and franchising allowed the company to have its name on hotels owned and managed by others, thus accelerating its penetration of the market. The Holiday Inn's success has been taken up by most hotel chains world-wide to the extent that in less than four decades branding has, for many operators and commentators, become synonymous with the very idea of hotel chain.

Branding is the single most successful marketing initiative of the twentieth century. Its heritage is solidly rooted in consumer products which, through branding, have sustained growth and longevity.

Hotel facilities

A business hotel, a tourist hotel or a resort hotel each demands its own particular package of facilities. The modern hotel guest expects to find many auxiliary facilities in addition to the basic ones of accommodation, food and drink. A guest may expect to find a telephone, radio and television in the room, or be able to telex and fax messages. The guest may wish to purchase newspapers and magazines, have suits dry cleaned, or shirts and socks laundered. Many hotels provide a hairdressing establishment where a guest can get a shave or a haircut, a gift shop to buy presents and souvenirs. The hotel may provide a service for reserving tickets for the theatre or making travel arrangements, and sports facilities such as a squash court or swimming pool, and an opportunity to relax with a sauna and massage. A wide range of banquet or conference facilities may also be provided. All or some of these auxiliary facilities and also the restaurants and bars may be available to non-residents. Many of these facilities may not be run by the hotel itself but be leased to independent operators, thus the gift shop in the hotel foyer could well be run by a local trader as could the newspaper, magazine and bookshop.

Organisational structure

The hotel's organisational structure is concerned with such matters as the division of tasks within the firm, positions of responsibility and authority and relationships between them. It introduces such concepts as the span of control (the number of subordinates supervised directly by an individual), the levels of management (the numbers of tiers through which management operate) and delegation (the allocation of responsibility and authority to designated individuals in the line of command).

All these activities must be co-ordinated to ensure that they contribute to the overall needs of the guest and to the net profitability of the hotel. Since they are so different from one another and many lend themselves to being run independently, hotels tend to be divided for operational purposes into departments composed of like activities. There are two main departmental classifications, the first of which encompasses the revenue earning or operated departments such as accommodation, food and beverages and auxiliary services. There is also the service or overhead departments such as accounting and marketing. The latter form the other main classification. Departmentalisation not only helps to establish the organisational and administrative structures and procedures in a hotel, but also lays down the foundation for the accounting structure.

The operating departments are split into two further sub-classifications – major and minor. The major operating departments consist of the primary activities of the hotel (those dealing with the provision of accommodation, food and drink), while the minor operating departments consist of the subsidiary revenue earning activities such as telephone and telex, guest laundry and valet, secretarial services, equipment hire, hotel shops and leisure complexes.

All those activities concerned with the reception of the guests, allocation of their room, cleaning and servicing of it and ensuring that charges relating to it are actually recorded and notified to the accounts department are traditionally part of the rooms department. A traditional division often exists between the reception of the guest and the servicing of the rooms, thus the rooms department may be subdivided into reception or front office and housekeeping. In some instances, these activities may be controlled by two separate departmental managers but in others they be integrated under a rooms manager or more typically a front office manager.

The food and beverage department contains all those activities concerned with supply, provision, preparation and service of food and drink in the hotel. Typically this department is headed by a food and beverage manager who leads a team consisting of head chef, banqueting manager, restaurant manager, head barman, room service, supervisor and chief steward or back of house supervisor. The last is responsible for such matters as glassware, crockery and cutlery, its cleaning and maintenance and cleanliness of all back of house areas. The number of restaurant and other managers will be related to the number of food and beverage centres in the hotel.

Administration of the hotel is typically concerned with accounting, human resource management, security and safety functions including contracted out security services. Property operation, maintenance and energy, cover activities such as engineering (both mechanical and electrical), heating, ventilation and refrigeration activities. This area also extends to ground maintenance, responsibility for contracted out building and plant repairs and redecoration work. The marketing department includes sales, advertising, public relations and other promotional activities.

The most efficient organisation structure has usually been found to be one that follows the pattern of the operated and serviced departments and provides for profit centre responsibility.

The number of staff employed in any one department will depend on the volume of business, the range of facilities provided and the demand pattern. Larger units could employ a purchasing officer or materials manager, painters, decorators, carpenters, upholsterers, etc., while smaller units would amalgamate several functions into one. In practice there may be a number of traditional variations particularly in relation to the rooms department.

The rooms department is likely to be split into two sections with the head receptionist responsible for reception and advance bookings, and the head housekeeper for housekeeping, linen rooms, laundry, guest laundry and valet. The former would report to the front office manager and the latter usually reports to the general manager.

In some cases the sales and marketing function takes on the responsibility for advance bookings in addition to the normal spheres of operation such as banquet and conference sales and restaurant promotions.

The accountant may take responsibility for the routines of purchasing and stores and also for food and beverage cashiering.

The function of the food and beverage manager, personnel manager and sales and marketing manager may be held by assistant managers who will also organise a rota system with the general manager to become a duty manager and accept responsibility for the overall running of the hotel during various times of the day or night.

Income control, more commonly known as the night audit, is generally carried out after the food and beverage services have been closed down by the night auditor. A night manager and night porters may be employed if business warrants it. Many hotels may prefer to limit guest services and use either vending or self-catering facilities for night service. But night services such as night porters and room service staff are usual in four and five star establishments.

Management team

The management team consists of the hotel general manager, one or more deputy or assistant managers and the heads of departments. A discussion of the management structure is concerned with these posts and the relationships between them. According to the size of the hotel and the particular arrangement in operation, the hotel's chief executive may be variously designated as managing director, general manager or simply hotel manager. This individual may, to a greater or lesser extent, participate in the formulation of hotel policies and strategies and be responsible for their implementation and for the hotel's performance. In larger hotels, this level may be subdivided between a managing director or general manager and the hotel manager or resident manager. The former then reports to the board and normally co-ordinates the work of the specialist departments and of the hotel or resident manager, who is in turn responsible for the day-to-day management of the hotel's activities. The complexity and continuity of the hotel's activities usually gives rise to the need for one or more deputy or assistant managers. A deputy hotel manager normally has authority over the heads of departments, but there is much variation in the role, in terms of authority and responsibilities. In some instances they are the hotel manager's deputies in all but name in respect of the whole operation or some parts of it. In other cases they have specific responsibilities in addition to their general role as the manager's deputy. But many assistant managers perform roles which are more appropriately described as those of general assistants or personal assistants to the manager. Yet in other cases, their main role is guest contact. All these roles may be appropriate in particular circumstances but effective hotel management calls for a clear definition of responsibility and authority. The relationships with heads of departments are especially important in this context. Titles which describe the particular roles can be helpful. In order to provide clear-cut lines of responsibility and authority and an effective co-ordination of related activities, some hotels function without assistant managers as such. Those who would normally be in such positions are allocated to specific responsibilities and appropriate titles to describe them.

Heads of department fall into two distinct categories. Heads of operated departments are known as line managers with direct lines of responsibility and authority to their superiors and to their subordinates in respect of each operated department. Heads of service departments are specialists who provide advice and service to line management. They relieve them of such tasks that are more effectively discharged through the appointment of specialists. They have no direct authority over employees other than those of their own department. Line management includes head receptionists, head housekeepers, head chefs and restaurant managers. Specialists includes marketers, accountants, buyers, personnel and purchasing officers and similar posts.

Feasibility studies

Having appraised in the wider context the subject of corporate strategy in Chapter 3 and the internal structure of a typical hotel in this chapter, we shall now consider feasibility studies and place them initially within the framework of planning and development.

Planning and development

The subject of feasibility studies needs to be set within the context of the planning system as this can be a key determinant of success. The legal framework will be considered in Chapter 7.

In the UK, the planning system is designed to regulate the development and use of land in the public interest. Responsibility for the day-to-day operation of the system is given to local authorities using two main instruments or methods:

● The development plan provides the main framework of policies and proposals, comprising a structure plan prepared by the county council and local plans which are usually prepared by district councils.

● Development control is the process through which applications for planning permission for development are determined.

In principle the planning system interacts with proposals for a hotel development in the development process, chiefly through the operation of development control. This planning and development process is illustrated in Figure 4.1.

Exploratory stage

The exploratory stage at which a potential developer is carrying out an investigation about possible sites for a development may involve visits to a large number of different areas and planning authorities. This is partly to review the suitability of the site in terms of market conditions and other factors, and partly to test the likely reactions of the local community and the planning authority. Such a stage is closely related to a market feasibility study.

The second stage is when the developer makes a formal approach to a local planning authority with a reasonably firm proposal, although, even at this stage it may still be exploratory. These are serious inquiries at which the developer may be willing to go to appeal if unsuccessful in obtaining planning permission. This is the stage at which the time taken to obtain planning permission may be crucial to the developer. Throughout this process a knowledge of planning policies and attitudes by the council to the proposed development should be considered vital. As the process continues and a site has been chosen, a more detailed knowledge of local authority policy aims is required prior to a formal planning application.

Objectives of feasibility studies

The objectives of a feasibility report are numerous but should generally accomplish the following five purposes:

Figure 4.1
Planning and
development
process

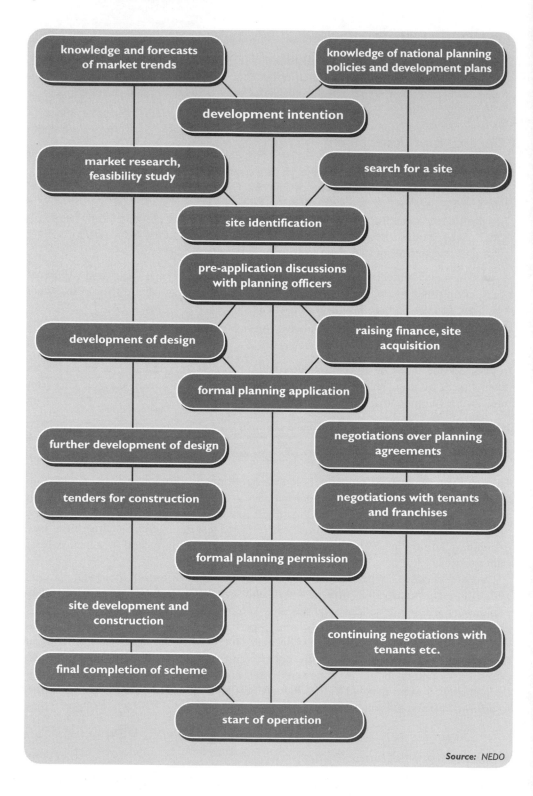

knowledge and forecasts
of market trends

knowledge of national planning
policies and development plans

development intention

market research,
feasibility study

search for a site

site identification

pre-application discussions
with planning officers

development of design

raising finance, site
acquisition

formal planning application

further development of design

negotiations over planning
agreements

tenders for construction

negotiations with tenants
and franchises

formal planning permission

site development and
construction

continuing negotiations with
tenants etc.

final completion of scheme

start of operation

Source: NEDO

- assist in obtaining financing
- assist in obtaining and negotiating contracts for a franchise, lease or management contract
- guide the planners and architects of the facility
- assist in formulating operating and marketing plans
- serve as a guide in preparing the initial capital and operations budget.

Proposal letter

Before a feasibility study is commissioned the consultant (if one is used) prepares a proposal for the client. The primary purpose of the proposal letter is to clearly define the scope and limitations of the study. As in any contract, the letter defines the obligations of both parties and outlines what the consultant will do in the performance of the study and what will be included in the final report. Those commissioning feasibility studies should carefully study the consultant's proposal letter and ensure that the final feasibility report will address their unique concerns, goals and needs. The consultant's proposal letter should also define the limitations of the feasibility study. Those commissioning the study should take care that the limitations proposed by the consultant do not undermine their own objectives and goals. Finally a fee and payment schedule should be included in the proposal.

Scope of feasibility studies

The scope of a feasibility study is defined by specifying the items to be analysed and the emphasis to be placed on each of them. Here is a list of items found in most feasibility studies:

- market area characteristics
- project site and area evaluation
- competition analysis
- demand analysis
- recommended facilities and services
- estimate of operating results.

The accomplishment of these issues and their interrelationship are identified in Figure 4.2.

The degree of emphasis that a feasibility study places on any one of these items will vary from one project to another. If those commissioning the feasibility study have already defined the hotel concept and the project's parameters, then the consultant's proposal letter should state that the feasibility study will analyse market demand, critique the proposed concept and project, and recommend appropriate changes.

Types of feasibility studies

The typical feasibility study for a proposed project has essentially two elements:

- market appraisal
- economic or financial feasibility.

Figure 4.2 Basic
approach to
feasibility studies

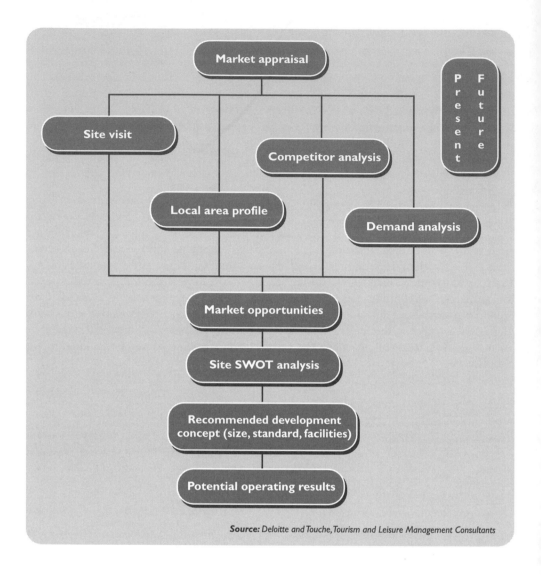

For a project to be pronounced economically feasible the analysis must be brought to the point where an estimate of the return on investment (ROI) can be made. In order to determine the ROI realistically, consideration must be given to the total project cost, the financial structure of the deal and the tax implications of the resulting profit or loss within the context of the owner's total portfolio. Much of that information will not be known at the time of the initial study. A final determination can not be made as to the project's economic feasibility until later in the overall development process.

Market appraisal with operating projections

Some feasibility studies are based on supply/demand studies and include financial projections made to point of income before service of any debt. Most firms that conduct these kinds of studies refer to them as market feasibility studies with operating projections. These reports identify and quantify potential markets for hotels and estimate revenues and expenses to the point of income.

A market feasibility study for a hotel project is typically (although not exclusively) conducted on a micro-level. This means that the market analysis is restricted to the area in which the project site is located. The market is analysed by establishing potential demand generators and the reasons for guest visitation, both current and future levels. This research should extend to such factors as

- type of demand
- spending potential
- seasonality/weekly patterns
- ancillary demand.

This aspect of the study, which is termed demand analysis, is illustrated in Figure 4.3.

The micro-level approach is successful for commercial hotels and for properties in destination areas but not for some resort hotels or conference centres. In these cases potential guests are usually far removed and the analyst must search for trends outside the area of the proposed site and within the areas from which the guests are expected to originate. This kind of market feasibility study is conducted on a macro-level. Both micro- and macro-approaches cover the same basic topics and require a similar methodology, but macro-analysis may require more time and cost more to complete.

For example, an airport hotel project may require a demand analysis that researches airline passenger traffic, more so than a city centre hotel project. The market for a hotel in London can be world-wide. Highway traffic patterns are important for many types of properties but they would become a central concern for a new roadside hotel project.

- Establish potential demand generators
- Research potential demand
  - current and future levels
  - type of demand
  - spending potential
  - seasonality/weekly patterns
  - ancillary facilities demand
  - current supply choices and why
  - market penetration analysis
  - build up and stabilised levels of demand
- Quantify demand for proposed development
  - current supply/demand scenario
  - future projections by sector
  - fair share analysis
  - would the new product be used, how much and how much would potential customers pay

Source: Deloitte and Touche, Tourism and Leisure Management Consultants

Figure 4.3
Demand analysis

Market area characteristics

The reason why both demographic and economic indicators should be assessed within the proposed property's market area is to determine the general prosperity of the area surrounding the proposed hotel, its buying power and its ability to attract visitors from outside the region. Both the present condition and if possible its condition in the recent past should be considered as a basis for future projections. Essentially what the consultant would be establishing is a local area profile. Most of the data studied in this section are directly related to other sections of the feasibility study, such as demand analysis and an estimate of operating results. Market area characteristics can be covered under eight points:

- population
- income
- employment
- retail sales
- commercial and industrial activities
- tourism
- transportation
- other characteristics.

Population
The study should carry out an analysis of the growth trends and shifts in population (both positive and negative) on the area of the proposed property, using the most up-to-date statistics available. The researcher in this instance would be looking for general trends in, for example, age groups. It could therefore be assessed whether the average age of the population is increasing as a result of a decline in younger groups. However, the importance of this information varies with the market that the property expects to attract. For example, if the market is expected to attract groups from outside the area of population then these trends will not be of any great significance. However, the success of the proposed property's food and beverage operation may depend very much upon the population trends in the area. It is often the case that future data projections are more informative than historical ones.

Income
The next step in the process is an analysis of the income (personal, disposable or discretionary) of the population within the chosen location. When this information is compared with population data, the relationship between the two can be examined. This should provide a useful potential market base for a property's facilities and services.

Employment
The employment statistics available for the area will help determine availability of staff for the hotel. Their structure and content will also affect the use of the facilities and services of the property.

Retail sales
The feasibility study will also look at the retail sales statistics for the area, because they describe consumer spending patterns and therefore eating and drinking out sales. They

will help indicate whether the area is a viable retail centre for the proposed property; this will influence the provision of food and beverage facilities. Retail sales also influence the overall market condition.

Commercial and industrial activities

All feasibility studies should stress the aspect of commercial and industrial activities. Such enterprises in the area should be examined for their economic stability, especially those enterprises that are usually important generators for the proposed property's business. Recent changes are particularly important when evaluating this factor rather than long-standing trends. As well as stability, the researcher should also be looking for diversification in the industrial base.

Tourism

Throughout the feasibility process it would seem that the main emphasis is upon industrial and commercial factors, but adequate attention should still be paid to the leisure market. This is because of its seasonality and ability to fill rooms which would otherwise be empty when the commercial market is slow. Tourist trends should be indicated in terms of their place of origin, spending patterns and their method of transportation. Typically, the research of the leisure market involves gathering attendance figures for the area's attractions, such as theme parks, golf courses, museums and leisure centres.

Transportation

The study should examine the general transportation trends in the area with relation to the proposed property. For example, the number of airline passengers, passing motorists or existing networks should be considered. At this stage, any proposed changes in nearby airports and roads should be assessed for their effect on the proposed hotel.

Other characteristics

If there are other characteristics of the area which may serve as a main reason for visiting the market area, they should be included, with their effect on the proposed property. For example, the area may include a university or a military base, which may be a potential source of business.

All these points can help determine the stability of the area's economic environment. An important point to note when considering these statistics is that an indication of the expanding or contracting nature of the local industrial base can be obtained by examining changes over several years rather than an absolute number in any one year. At this point it is useful to examine expected labour costs, especially if the data reveal that the property may have to compete for employees in a market paying higher wages because of the area.

Site Evaluation

The actual site upon which a hotel is built is one of the most important determinants in its ultimate success. It has been said many times that the three most important factors for a hotel's success are location, location and location.

The hotel should be in the most convenient location to attract the type of guest for which it was designed. Once the hotel is built, then it is impossible to move so this makes the correct choice of location vital in the process. Generally, the site is known and only its suitability for a particular type of development serving a particular market segment is in question. If a consultant has been commissioned to carry out the study and the site is known, then the issue will be whether the site is suitable for the type and class of property proposed. This analysis will consider factors affecting the convenience of the site for the expected demand: its size, shape, accessibility and visibility. The site could be one of three types:

● greenfield site – new build
● existing building – conversion/refurbishment
● existing operation – additional facilities.

Competition analysis

An analysis of the competition means that within a feasibility study there must be an inventory of all accommodation facilities in the proposed hotel's market area. Such a list of hotels and restaurants is useful not only for determining market feasibility but also for establishing marketing strategies. After a rooms inventory has been drawn up and the hotels have been segmented by class and sector, then there should be an analysis of these factors:

● demand volume for the facilities
● adequacy with which the competition satisfies the demand
● strengths and limitations of the competition
● points of difference between the proposed property and the competition.

These will help identify the new property's **unique selling point**. This information can be obtained from an on-site inspection, review of local directories and interviews with hotel managers. An examination should also be made of any other hotel projects which may be at various stages of development. In addition, an analysis of local restaurants should be made as these will present competition for the food and beverage operations of the hotel.

Quantify demand

Much of the information obtained is needed to quantify the demand for the proposed property. Such conclusions presented form the basis for recommendations regarding the proposed property's facilities and level of service. They also form the basis for the hotel's estimated operating results. The relationship between market appraisal and viability is shown in Figure 4.4.

Possible sources of information which could be used to establish demand are local chamber of commerce statistics, hotel sales figures (if they are available) and interviews with local hotel managers.

Demand generators such as local industries should be contacted in order to obtain information for room night estimates. Throughout these interviews such factors as the number of rooms needed, location and property preferred, seasonality of need and the length of stay can be determined. Eventually the study arrives at a detailed market segment profile. The characteristics of each segment are ascertained, such as length of stay, seasonality and price consciousness. As well as room night demand estimates, there must be

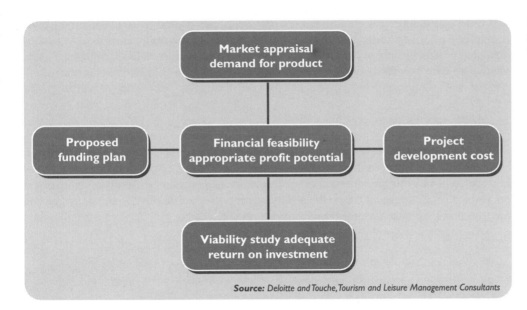

Figure 4.4 Market appraisal and viability

Source: Deloitte and Touche, Tourism and Leisure Management Consultants

food and beverage demand estimates. If only resident guests are expected to use the facilities, then the task is quite simple to estimate the percentage of guests who will use the facilities and services. However, this is often not the case, and a food and beverage demand analysis is required. This must begin with an analysis of the market area, its restaurant and bar sales, and interviews with managers, to estimate overall demand. Another important point to be considered throughout this process is that any other properties which are in the pipeline must be taken into account as they will have an effect on the property.

Recommended design, facilities and services

No cost estimates can be made until there is an idea of the property's size, quality and facilities. Recommendations on design and facilities must be made which will satisfy the market needs researched in the previous sections, keeping in mind the strengths and weaknesses of the competition. However, in many cases the researcher already knows from the developer the size and type of the property and its facilities; it is more a case of determining whether these facilities and design are suitable or not. If the person carrying out the feasibility study has architectural plans for the project, then these plans must be evaluated in terms of the rooms, facilities and public areas. However, if no plans are presented then recommendations should be made on the following:

- overall concept
- type and number of guest rooms
- type, number and capacity of food and beverage facilities.

In recommending the total number of guest rooms this is based on the expected level of demand and seasonality of demand levels. The type of guest room recommended is one which meets the needs of the demand profile, i.e. the mix of single, multiple occupancy and special features. Recommendations for food and beverage facilities are also made, based on information gathered on occupancy levels and competition. Recommendations concerning price structure, opening hours and themes are typically considered. It is the objective of this section of the study to ensure that the recommended facilities are commensurate with the needs of the major segments determined in the market appraisal.

Estimate of project cost

Having considered the revenue side of the project, it is necessary to estimate the cost as accurately as possible in order to compare it directly with the amount of profit which may be received from the investment. Forecasting this cost is often based on a series of experience based estimates. This viability analysis requires accurate cost estimates, an outline funding plan and net profit forecasts, which will

- provide cash-flow projections
- illustrate a break-even point
- establish a return on investment.

Estimate of revenue

This stage in the process can be seen as the ultimate test of feasibility of the proposed hotel and is illustrated in Figure 4.5.

The objective of this section is to project the operating results of the hotel given the expected occupancy and average rate. Generally the length of period covered can vary from between five and twenty years. In the majority of hotels in the UK, and indeed throughout the world, room sales represent a major proportion of the profit. Therefore, in most estimates of operating results this is the first factor to be dealt with. In order to carry out this calculation, the following information is needed:

- anticipated rate of occupancy (from the demand analysis)
- tariff structure
- anticipated ratio of single and double occupancy
- seasonality factor
- business mix.

Figure 4.5
Estimate of revenue

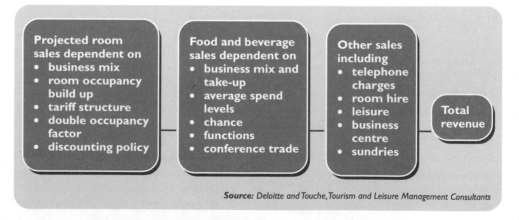

Source: Deloitte and Touche, Tourism and Leisure Management Consultants

The necessary calculations must then be executed taking into account that none of the above factors will remain constant over the given period and that fluctuations are considered when calculating for each year.

The next item to be assessed is the food and beverage sales. There are two accepted methods of calculating this factor:

- The assessor uses personal experience and expert judgement to estimate the income from each facility per day and this is multiplied by the number of days in the year.

- The assessor estimates food and beverage sales on the basis of a percentage of room sales or percentage of total sales and income of the hotel. This assumed percentage is based on the statistics of the relevant market. Generally this percentage falls between 60 and 90% of room sales depending on the character and facilities of the hotel.

Food and beverage revenue is dependent on

- business mix and take-up
- average spend levels
- chance business.

Finally, as far as operating expenses are concerned, both direct and indirect, the cost of payroll and other related expenses can be estimated only after expert examination of the entire operation. The operating statistics of similar hotels are generally followed in order to calculate all the items of expenditure.

The final result is then put together for assessment to conform with the UK's **Uniform System of Accounts**, which is used throughout the hotel industry. The Uniform System of Accounts will be discussed in Chapter 5. Conclusions are drawn as to whether the project is feasible or not, and also whether it would produce an adequate return on investment and therefore whether to continue with the project.

In summary it can be said that this approach to feasibility studies relies to a great extent on a systematic and logical sequence of events, and using as far as possible quantitative measures. However, it must be borne in mind that the scientific nature of the approach could be more true in appearance than reality. Given the cost of development, the increasing competitive environment and the volatility of the economy in the late 1990s, undertaking a new hotel project is a major investment. Such an undertaking requires thorough planning and finely tuned communication. A feasibility study is an indispensable analysis which can satisfy diverse interests while meeting the common need of all participants in a new hotel project.

Having considered the details of a feasibility study, the next stage in the hotel development process is commissioning the property.

Commissioning the property

Arising out of a hotel feasibility study, with its analysis of both the market and the investment, comes a draft policy for the project which is used to aid the design process. With the help of architectural and technical specialists the final design is arrived at and the construction phase can begin. Finally, near completion of the project an operating policy for the establishment is written. This relationship is illustrated in Figure 4.6.

Figure 4.6 The commissioning process

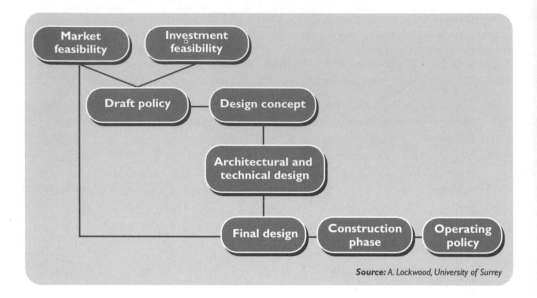

Source: A. Lockwood, University of Surrey

Management process

The commissioning process commences once the market and investment feasibility study has been completed. It is a process that at one level is a management process and needs to consider five points:

- Time to complete the project is limited so there is a need to assign priorities and at the same time to maximise productivity.
- A need to co-ordinate both the building of the physical property and the interaction between a range of specialist advisers.
- The cost of a hotel or resort complex can run into many millions of pounds and so the necessary financial systems need to be in place, budgets need to be established and the responsibility for those budgets needs to be allocated within the management team. As the project progresses, variances will emerge between the original budget and actual expenditure. Those variances should be monitored and explanations given for why they occurred.
- There is, throughout this management process, a considerable number of decisions that need to be made. In order to make the right decisions, an effective information system needs to be established. Such a system will need to recognise the interdependence of various parts of the project.
- Throughout the process there is the central issue of communication both internally and externally. Internally, there is communication between members of the management team. This aids both the decision making process and the co-ordination of the project. Members of the management team will communicate with the external specialists in order that the project can be designed and built within the agreed time scale.

The four main areas of consideration within the commissioning process are

- physical resources
- human resources

- marketing planning
- operational planning.

Physical resources

The physical resources of the project include both the construction of the unit and the equipment contained within it. Construction includes the structure, services and decor of the building. Equipment includes the schedule lists, product research and trials, quotations, ordering, delivery and receiving, storage and installation.

Human resources

Under the area of human resources, factors such as organisational structure, recruitment and training need to be considered. Subjects such as personnel planning, programme of appointments, advertising and selecting need to be completed. Once recruited, staff need to be inducted into the organisation and training programmes established. Decisions need to be taken as to who undertakes these training programmes.

Marketing planning

In order that the profitability of the unit is assured there is a requirement for pre-opening marketing planning. Staff will need to be allocated to the reservations and marketing departments and responsibilities need to be determined. The next stage in the process is a need to identify and research markets such as local business and societies, exhibitions and tour groups and incentive travel. Once this is completed a budget can be prepared and room prices can be determined at least twelve months in advance. Promotional material will be developed; in that process, special events may be created.

Operational planning

Managers can sit down at their computer terminals and answer many questions on stored data that were formerly inaccessible. Their computers store a bank of linked statistical techniques and decision models that make up a decision support system. In this way the operational planning of a project can be implemented. Such an approach will help managers make better decisions. A model can be defined as a set of variables and their interrelationship is designed to represent some real system or process. Models are built by managers who apply scientific methodology to achieve understanding and prediction of some management problems. Mathematical models represent a useful step in the process of symbolising a verbal model.

One such approach is **network analysis** (or **critical path analysis**) which portrays the events that need to occur to complete a project. The events usually shown as circles are connected by arrows indicating precedent relationships. In this respect, event six could not occur before events four and five are completed. By estimating the completion time of the task (sometimes the optimistic and pessimistic completion) the analyst can find the earliest date to completion of the entire project. The network will contain a critical path that defines the earliest possible completion time. Unless the critical path is shortened there is no way to complete the project earlier. This approach is the basis of planning, scheduling and controlling projects, such as the development of a new hotel. One distinction that can be drawn in this approach is between deterministic and stochastic models.

A deterministic model is one in which chance plays no role, the solution is determined by a set of exact relationships.

A linear programming model is deterministic because the relationships are exact and the costs of data are known (e.g. for every £100 increase in advertising expenditure, sales increase by £1,000).

A stochastic model is one where chance or random variables are introduced explicitly. An example is queuing models which are of interest to hotel and catering managers. Queuing models describe waiting time situations and answer two questions:

- What waiting time can be expected in a particular system?
- How will this waiting time change if the system is altered?

These questions are of interest to reception areas, restaurants and airline ticket offices. Wherever customers wait, there is the danger that waiting time will become excessive, leading some customers to switch to competitors. If the current system breeds long queues, the analyst can simulate the effects of different queue-handling arrangements. The purpose of these statistical procedures and decision models is that they will greatly enhance the managers skill in making better informed decisions.

Design criteria

The purpose of the market study is to ascertain the viability of the project by estimating room occupancies and average achieved room rates within a hotel. From information gathered during the study, recommendations can be made regarding the standard of hotel, plus the optimum size of the project in terms of bedrooms and support facilities including restaurants, bars, leisure and conference facilities. While the location of a hotel is certainly of prime importance, changing social, commercial and transportation patterns can make what was once an excellent location less desirable. For instance when the local naval base closes or when a new bypass takes traffic around the town instead of through it. Seven points can be identified as to what makes a good location:

- proximity to demand generators
- ease of access
- proximity to transportation systems
- accessibility from local roads
- attractive surroundings
- availability of primary infrastructure and good topography.

Design team

The traditional method of design and construction is for the client to appoint a core of professionals comprising

- architect
- structural engineer
- mechanical and electrical engineer
- quantity surveyor.

This group would usually expand to include an interior designer, a landscape architect and possibly a kitchen designer and specialists in conference audiovisual equipment and leisure facilities.

The mixed responsibilities and relationships within the design team are affected by the method chosen to contract the construction of the hotel and they may include the services of a professional project manager. The client or hotel operator is also an important member of the design team.

The process leading from design through to production of information required for competitive tendering would normally be the prime responsibility of the architect. It is also likely that a cost consultant, normally the quantity surveyor, would be involved from the early stages to advise on the projected costs and to assess viability, and later to prepare contract documentation for the construction process.

The architect's role is broadly defined by the Royal Institute of British Architects' *Plan of Work*, which details the services provided by architects and the fee scales. The initial activities carried out by the architect are to assess the proposed site and initially liaise with the appropriate local authority and advise on the preliminary feasibility of the project. If a development proposal is considered viable then the architect will liaise with the quantity surveyor to establish a budget cost. Based upon the preliminary design proposals, assuming that the project was well received, further liaison takes place with all members of the design team. This is in order to progress the architectural, structural and building service concepts to the detailed design stage which is cross checked against the budget. No project can be successfully designed without a clear understanding by the architect of the client's intentions and requirements.

Architects and interior designers with hotel design experience should assist the client with the development of the brief, based upon an outline proposal, but naturally the more precise the client's input, the quicker an acceptable design can be drawn up. While some clients are able to provide a detailed brief, it is more often the case that the brief develops as the architect's sketch plans evolve. It follows that as sketch designs are prepared, the impact of site restrictions, fire regulations, local authority requirements and other factors will affect the design concept and therefore the final design.

Design brief

Once the site of the proposed hotel has been selected, the outline design brief has to be prepared. The basic information required is as follows:

- grade of hotel
- number of bedrooms
- size and mix of bedrooms
- range of public rooms
- range of leisure facilities
- range of business meeting rooms,
- any special features e.g. nightclubs and car and coach parking.

As circulation requirements evolve, the design progresses, more specific information is required from the hotel operator to define bedroom furnishing standards, catering equipment, laundry methods, administrative offices, in-house maintenance facilities, etc. It is at this stage that the hotel company's technical manuals are of valuable assistance to the design team, ensuring that the required standards both in construction and in facilities provision are met.

A hotel project or refurbishment cannot be successfully designed without a clear understanding by the architect of the client's intentions and requirements. Many hotel companies have developed technical manuals, which cover their requirements for specific hotel brands. They detail bedroom sizes, layouts and equipment specifications. These manuals are a means of establishing quality control for a specific hotel product. While they provide general guidelines, it would be unusual for a comprehensive brief to be available for a given project, specifying precise schedules for accommodation areas, spatial relationships, organisation flows and environmental requirements. Technical manuals are useful in ensuring that company standards are maintained on an international level, but it should be recognised that national and local buildings regulations affect actual building proposals. Manuals of this nature should therefore concentrate on performance specifications, allowing the design team the necessary flexibility to satisfy local legislation and regulations.

An interior designer may be involved at an early stage in a development or refurbishment, and may participate in the space planning of the hotel. The designer may be presented with the architect's final design and take details of interior space from that point. In any event, it is wise to involve the interior designer at an early stage, since any decisions and proposals that are made will have an effect on the architect's decisions and vice versa. Both parties have to work closely together to ensure acceptable end results. With certain types of developments such as refurbishment, the interior designer may be the lead discipline instead of an architect or project manager. The interior designer can liaise with the local authority on some aspects of the project. Indeed with regulations regarding fireproofing of upholstered furniture for commercial use, the interior designer is probably the best person for the job. The interior designer can produce tender documentation for separate pricing of shop fitting sub-contract work, or this can be included as part of the overall main contractor's tender document. The interior designer can also provide information and obtain tendered prices, where appropriate, for furniture, fittings and equipment. All design disciplines will usually be involved at this stage to inspect work being carried out by the contractor.

Land purchase options

In terms of purchase options, the developer will invariably seek to acquire the site on a freehold basis as this will provide greater flexibility, and more importantly greater security when raising funds for development of the hotel. Alternatively the site may be sold on a leasehold basis with payment of a premium guaranteeing a long ground lease of 99 or 125 years at an annual peppercorn rent. If this route is followed, the freeholder will retain ownership of the site and secure no income during the term of the lease. Upon termination of the lease, the ownership of the land and buildings will pass to the freeholder. Sites can also be disposed of on a long ground lease basis of 99 or 125 years upon payment of an annual rent which is fixed for 5 or 7 years and reviewed or alternatively an annual review can be built into the lease terms. Such approaches will vary depending on the location, competition for the site and the economic climate.

Construction costs

There are many factors influencing the development costs of hotels, with probably the most variable price component being the land cost. In general, land costs can add anything from £1,000 per bedroom to £50,000 per bedroom, or even more. Generally, the higher the land cost per room, the greater the perceived 'trophy' value of the project. Variations in the groundwork costs depend partly upon the nature of the ground; for example it may be reclaimed land which is cheaper to buy but requires deep piling. While land prices in Paris and London are comparable, provincial land in France is 50% that of land in the UK, as France has fewer than half the number of people per square kilometres of land than does the UK. The cost of land cannot be divorced from planning permission (a point made at the beginning of this chapter).

In most continental countries, the use to which land is to be put is decided in advance of application. Many countries have similar systems under which a series of plans are drawn up, indicating areas already developed, or with development potential, with not only their projected use but also site densities, building heights and sometimes, depending on the country, the architectural character of the building required.

When these development plans are being drawn up, consultations take place with interested bodies such as the Chamber of Commerce. All this prepares the ground for future hotel development. Thus a developer knows if an application is likely to be acceptable and the parameters of the design requirement. All this takes some of the unpredictability out of the planning process. The time taken to get planning permission is for the most part briefer on the continent than in the UK.

Construction costs generally range between 50% and 80% of total development costs and include all building work from site preliminaries through the actual construction to the fitting of all mechanical, electrical and plumbing services and internal finishes. The prices of fixtures, fittings and equipment are highly sensitive to the type and category of hotel and can include special installations through to soft furnishings and furniture. Other costs include professional fees to designers, architects, consultants, along with the financing of the project, pre-opening expenses and hotel direct supplies. Taken together all these expenses represent the total development costs of a hotel project.

The building itself encompasses the second group of costs which are more predictable but more likely to be affected by planning requirements. Exterior appearance can add to costs. Other areas include internal finishing and services. When budget hotels were first built in the UK, the cost of services was up to double that of an equivalent hotel in France. Some of the extra cost (15–20%) could be put down to stricter regulations in the UK. For example, UK water authorities demand tank storage to offset possible mains failure, whereas any visitor to a similar hotel in Europe knows that when mains water runs out, so does the hotel's. Other areas include ventilation, the issue of legionnaires' disease and more extensive use of copper pipe against plastic. Additionally, hotels in France are likely to be all electric, and so have a lower capital cost than gas heating, which is cheaper to run. Other costs include complying with fire regulations. In the UK, interpretation is up to the fire officer while in France a detailed code is followed.

Unit costs per square metre are influenced by many factors, such as, building height and configuration, construction methods, site conditions, type of heating/cooling systems, and quality of finishes. The cost per bedroom, while being affected by all of the above, is also reliant on the proportion of building space per room, i.e. the extent of public areas and other facilities in relation to the bedrooms. In general, the ratio increases as the quality of the hotel rises. Construction costs by market sector break down into two sections:

- The first is those applicable to the lower cost hotels. Obviously, the cost factors and the requirement of repeatability lead to the adoption of system building techniques. Under these arrangements, large sections of the building are assembled off site. Systems building is more acceptable in France than in the UK. One hotelier has adopted the technique and can now construct a hotel in fifteen weeks.

● The second market sector consists of four and five star hotels which are usually bespoke for prestige reasons. The design is more complicated with more public rooms and facilities.

Construction methods

When one considers construction methods, a hotel may be divided into two zones:

● bedroom accommodation
● public service areas.

Each zone dictates a preferred construction method on the criteria that the bedroom block will be by its nature a modular compartmentalised space, and the public areas will require larger open environments and clear spaces free of columns and obstructions. In fact the arrangement of a hotel can take many forms and the relationship of bedroom accommodation to public service space will have an immediate effect on the construction and structural approach of the design. For public and related back of house facilities, it is advisable to create a framed structure giving unrestricted internal space for areas such as conference rooms, restaurants, swimming pools and kitchens.

Framed structure buildings allow greater choice when selecting finishes and designs. For internal and external walls frames may be constructed in steel or concrete and each material has specific advantages and disadvantages. In both steel and concrete framing, the internal walls can be constructed from a range of materials. Concrete blockwork is used only to ensure effective sound control and either timber stud or metal stud partitioning can be used to reduce weight for structural purposes. One approach in lieu of framing is to stack prefabricated modules either in skeletal form or a complete finished room unit. This approach is limited in its scope in terms of height and requires extreme care when co-ordinating the units with other elements which by their nature cannot be prefabricated. The concept of prefabricated en suite bathrooms has attracted much interest in recent years. It is now cost-effective to produce bathroom units made to the client's specifications and fully fitted and finished away from the site. Producing them in the factory means that full control over workmanship and materials can be exercised and that final on-site work is kept to a minimum.

Spatial planning

Any hotel should use its space well: those that do not, risk paying a cost penalty during construction and later when the hotel runs less efficiently than it could have done. The secret is to plan the interrelationships between the various functions within the hotel, ensuring that the correct space allocation has been made for specific areas. One of the prime requisites of hotel planning is to maintain a relationship between public and service circulation routes. The former must flow from the entrance lobby to reception, to bedrooms. Within the public front of house areas, such as the restaurant, bar and lounge, these must also be easily accessible from the reception foyer. If conference and leisure facilities are included within the development, these must be accessible from the hotel foyer. For developments with extensive banqueting facilities, it is often worth providing a separate entrance foyer. This avoids congestion in the main hotel lobby when major events attracting non-resident guests are being held. Back of house circulation should avoid intrusion into public areas. Kitchen facilities in particular must be correctly located to provide efficient service to all food service areas, including restaurants, conference rooms, bedrooms and staff restaurant. Ideally distances between food preparation service areas should be as short as possible and should negate the need for remote or secondary kitchen areas. Vertical circulation of guests and services is an extremely important aspect of hotel design. The selection of the correct type and location of lifts relative to the entry level design and bedroom block layout will greatly add to the efficiency of the hotel operation and to guest comfort. Bedroom block building has a number of elements which interact to achieve efficiency such as the construction and operational arrangement of bedroom units, number of escape stairs and the number of bedrooms serviced by each cleaner. Corridor length in excess of basic fire escape distances will incur the penalty of an additional escape staircase. Consideration of flow patterns and their impact on the relationship of areas within the hotel should be undertaken at an early stage of the design in order to optimise space usage and avoid unnecessary dedicated circulation space or duplication of space and equipment.

Local authorities will dictate a minimum number of car parking spaces required for hotel development. It is not unusual for 75% of a site to be designated for parking, roads and landscape with only 25% required for the footprint of the building. Meeting rooms and conference facilities require additional parking space although a proportion of designated bedroom related spaces would be used because these spaces will in fact cover for in-house conference use. In city centre locations it is unlikely that site areas will allow surface parking to the numbers required.

In terms of spatial guidelines, overall the area per bedroom is affected by the grade of hotel. The purpose of preparing an analysis of the hotel design based on the gross constructed area per bedroom is that it gives an indication of the efficiency of the design. When used as part of the design brief, it is a method of controlling costs by avoiding misuse of space and overspecification.

Procurement

Within the construction industry, there are a number of recognised routes for the placing or procurement of a building contract.

Choice of the appropriate route for a particular development will depend on a number of factors, such as, the time available, degree of certainty required in the final construction costs, quality and the degree of control desired over the final design. There are three main categories of contract or procurement method:

- traditional
- design and build
- management contract.

Traditional

The essence of traditional forms of contract is that there is a distinct separation between the design and construction roles. There are three basic types.

Lump sum is whereby the contract is let to a contractor based on a fully developed set of design drawings and specifications prepared by the architect and engineer.

Remeasurement contracts are whereby the contract is let on the basis of a preliminary set of drawings and specifications and a bill of approximate quantities or schedule of rates. Work is measured as it proceeds and valued in accordance with contract rates.

Cost reimbursement is a contract in which it is let on the understanding that the contractor will be paid for the actual cost of all materials, labour and plant, etc. used to construct a building, plus an agreed fee to cover management costs, overheads and profits.

Within each of the traditional procurement routes, the design role is carried by the clients design team, comprising architect, engineers and quantity surveyors, and is kept distinctly separate from the construction role carried out by the contractor.

Design and build

Under design and build contracts, the contract is tendered on the basis of a client's brief, to which the contractor adds and submits with the tender the proposed design solution to satisfy the client's brief. The brief must be a precise statement to ensure that the client gets what is required in terms of quality and facilities, and to allow the contractor to use all available skills, design specialities and expertise to satisfy the requirements. The term 'turnkey' is commonly applied to a development of design and build contracts whereby the client employs a single contractor or employs an organisation not only to design and construct a building, but also to administer other functions such as site finding, arranging finance and leasing details, obtaining planning permission, etc. Having appointed a briefed turnkey contractor, further direct involvement need only be minimal until such time as the client opens the door on the completed building, hence the name turnkey.

Management contract

Management contracts have become popular in recent years. These are applied to large or complex projects where the organisational planning and co-ordination skills, and experience of a large contractor are used to manage a large number of specialist sub-contractors involved in such a development. The management contractor does not carry out any construction work but manages and organises the work carried out by others. The contractor is usually appointed at the same time or soon after the design team and will be heavily involved with them in development and planning of that project.

Tendering process

Each of the routes just mentioned may under the right circumstances be used for a hotel development.

Because of the specialist and often prestigious nature of hotel construction, there is a need for contractors to have a demonstrable level of expertise and experience in building and fitting out hotels. It is therefore inadvisable to invite open tenders whereby any contractor may submit a tender bid for a hotel contract. Traditionally five or six suitable contractors are pre-selected, on the basis of a proven record. Traditionally most tender procedures have been single stage, whereby a complete package of final tender information is received by a contractor who then formulates a tender and submits it for acceptance by the client.

Two-stage tenders whereby a number of contractors are invited to submit a first-stage tender based on pricing documents related to the preliminary design information are now widely used. From the first-stage tenders submitted, one or more contractors are invited to participate in the second-stage tender whereby more detailed and complete pricing documents are submitted by the contractors. Within most standard forms of contract there is a provision for client-preferred specialist manufacturers and suppliers to be nominated or imposed upon the main contractor. This allows a client to maintain a degree of control on the specification.

Construction costs for a typical hotel will vary because of the different nature and influence of such factors as location, ground and site conditions and market forces on construction costs. The detailed costing of an individual hotel development cannot be determined by reference to typical costs. Each project must be treated on its merits and any developer wishing to build hotels would find it difficult to refer to industry norms. Across the UK there are marked differences in tender prices due to regional variations in the markets for locally available labour and materials.

It must be said that the commercial success of a hotel requires the right physical product. A product in terms of design and facilities should be market driven and its construction should be cost-efficient and offer value for money. If when the building has been constructed there is insufficient restaurant or storage space or administrative space for staff, this fault could not be attributable to the staff. It could however be the fault of the design team or the design brief.

Summary

This chapter introduced the concept of hotel product type and set it within the context of product segmentation. Comments were made about the range of facilities within hotels and the management team that supports them. A precursor to the subject of feasibility studies was shown to be the issue of planning and development. Detailed comments were then made on commissioning the property.

Further reading

- La Hue P.M. (1988) 'Accuracy of feasibility studies: cause for concern?', *Hotel and Motel Management* 13 June.
- Medlik S. (1989) *The Business of Hotels*, 2nd edn, London: Heinemann.
- NEDC (1991) *The Planning System and Large Scale Tourism and Leisure Developments*, London: National Economic Development Office.
- Overstreet G.A. (1989a) 'Profiles in hotel feasibility', *Cornell Hotel and Restaurant Association Quarterly* February.
- Overstreet G.A. (1989b) 'Profiles in hotel feasibility: the consequences of overbuilding', *Cornell Hotel and Restaurant Association Quarterly* May.
- Pannell Kerr Forster Associates (1990) *Hotel Product Segmentation in Europe*, London: PKF.
- Pannell Kerr Forster Associates (1992) *Hotel Design and Construction in the United Kingdom*, London: PKF.
- Rogers H.A. (1975) 'Pricing in the hotel industry', MPhil thesis, University of Surrey.
- Teare R. and Boer A. (1991) *Strategic Hospitality Management: Theory and Practice for the 1990s*, London: Cassell.
- Teare R. and Olsen M. (eds) (1992) *International Hospitality Management: Corporate Strategy in Practice*, London: Pitman.

● Ward T. (1989) in C.P. Cooper (ed.) *Progress in Tourism Recreation and Hospitality Management*, vol. 1, London: Belhaven Press.
● West A. and Purvis E. (1992) 'Hotel design: the need to develop a strategic approach', *International Journal of Contemporary Hospitality Management* 4(1).
● Zodrow G.A. (1989) 'A new look at feasibility study', *Lodging Hospitality* May.

Chapter Five

Aspects of Management

Objectives

After reading this chapter you should be able to

- Identify the key financial elements of revenue and costs within the hotel industry.
- Discuss the uniform system of accounts.
- Consider the importance of both price and yield management.
- Relate the principles of marketing to the hospitality industry.

Financial decisions

Any hotel organisation, be it small or large, uses money, and in most cases will not survive if it mishandles its finances. While the scale of operation may vary and the desired outcomes differ from hotel to hotel, the basic financial principles are universal. The first part of this chapter is concerned with some of these principles.

The primary purpose of learning about finance is to enable informed decisions to be made about the financial affairs of a business. These decisions can be extremely varied, and may include areas such as:

- catering equipment (a capital investment decision)
- pricing
- credit terms
- hotel capacity
- level of fixed overheads
- business efficiency
- cost control
- financial risks.

The objective of this section is to demonstrate some aspects of financial management, aimed at hotel management.

Sources of revenue and operating costs

Revenue

The full service hotel can be split into three major areas of operation: rooms, food and beverage, and other. Rooms revenue does not in a typical UK provincial hotel account for even half of total turnover while in London the figure is higher (see Figure 1.4 on p. 11 for an average UK breakdown).

The two key components of rooms revenue are the level of occupancy and the average achieved room rate. The latter represents only the price achieved on rooms sold, however, and bears little resemblance to the full price or 'rack rate'. Typically most rooms are sold at a discount to rack rates, and therefore the relationship between average achieved room rate and rack rates is an indication of the efficiency of an operator in terms of maximising yield on the available roomstock. The trade-off between occupancy and rate in maximising yields concerns the marginal cost of attempting to move one or the other upwards. A reduction in the discount at which a room is sold has a near enough zero marginal cost, whereas selling an extra room night will lead to increased costs in terms of cleaning, linen and other services. This puts a floor on the price at which a hotelier can afford to sell a room night and means that a reduction in discounting should have a greater impact on profitability than equivalent increases in occupancy. However, this assumes that such a reduction can be replicated for every room sold throughout the period, whereas it makes sense to sell an extra room for a night at any price above marginal cost to generate additional profits as the product on offer is perishable.

A further problem in this occupancy/rate trade-off is the intra-week trading cycle. There is a distinct difference in the demand patterns in business hotels at weekends, which is largely derived from leisure customers. The major hoteliers operate hotels largely aimed at business users. Given the fall off in demand at weekends in the primary locations, such hotels are run with greater business risk. As only small adjustments to staffing levels can be made at weekends and other aspects of the cost structure, the focus even more turns to occupancy and the yield it provides. However, while room occupancy declines at weekends, bed occupancy is much less affected. Such trends in city centre locations are reversed if one considers seaside locations.

Food and beverage operations along with other areas of income further distort the trade-off between occupancy and rate because selling an extra room will pull through additional business in other areas. The importance of such revenues is very high to provincial hotels. Over the past few years the percentage of total revenue derived from beverage sales has declined.

The gross margin on food and beverage sales is less than room sales, so the change in margin mix is altering in the hotelier's favour. However, this puts extra pressure on total hotel yields and places extra importance on increasing room yields.

According to the Uniform System of Accounts for Hotels (discussed later in this chapter), other operated departments consist of telephone services, laundry and valet services, leisure centre memberships and other departments. The latter could include concession fees, rental income from shops within the hotel and commissions from various sources. All these areas are becoming increasingly important especially for provincial hoteliers.

This ability to generate additional sources of revenue has seen the increasing prevalence of leisure facilities (discussed in Chapter 11) and allows hotels the option to market their facilities to local communities as well as hotel guests.

Operating costs

There is no standard cost structure for a average hotel but it is possible to consider a typical breakdown of costs. The most obvious feature of such an analysis is the proportion of labour costs and the size of these is coming under the most scrutiny by operators as they seek to reduce labour bills and achieve greater productivity.

The nature of fixed and variable costs in a hotel is illustrated by the fact that as revenue declines, labour and other costs increase proportionally (for an average in the UK hotel industry distribution of expenses see Figure 5.1).

Hotels have been taking steps to reduce staffing levels. The number of employees per room has fallen both in London and elsewhere in the UK. This trend has led to an increase in multi-skilling and the increased use of cheaper part-time labour. Some of these revenue and cost factors are illustrated in Table 5.1, where the performance of the Westbury Hotel, London, is compared with data from Arthur Andersen Consulting London.

This discussion of revenue and costs will now be set within the context of the Uniform System of Accounts for Hotels.

Uniform System of Accounts for Hotels

This system of accounting for hotels was developed in 1926 by the Hotel Association of New York City, and later adopted by the American Hotel Association of the United States and Canada. It has developed over the years and is now in its eighth edition. It was originally developed in response to two needs.

- In the hotel industry of the 1920s (and in many places during the 1990s) labour turnover rates were very high. It was not uncommon for hotels to spend longer training staff than those staff would work for them once they were trained. Frequently, however, these staff would move within the industry, and it was seen to be a great waste of resources for staff to be continually trained in different systems. If systems were standardised the amount of retraining needed when staff moved hotel but kept the same job title would be minimal.

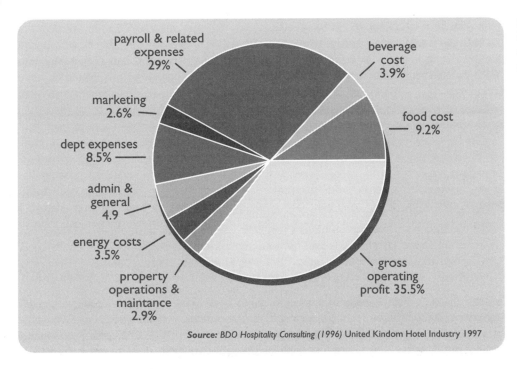

Figure 5.1
Percentage distribution of expenses

Source: BDO Hospitality Consulting (1996) United Kindom Hotel Industry 1997

Table 5.1 London five star hotel performance survey 1995: comparison with the Westbury Hotel, London

Key performance indicators	Westbury Hotel, London 1995	Arthur Andersen, 1995
ROOMS DEPARTMENT		
Number of rooms	244	256
Average room rate (net)	87.7	157.81
Occupancy (%)	85.6	83.2
Room yield	94.2	131.34
GEOGRAPHICAL ORIGIN OF GUESTS		
UK	24.7%	21.7%
Rest of Europe	26.2%	25.7%
USA/Canada	24.8%	31.2%
Japan	15.1%	6.2%
Other	9.2%	15.2%
TOTAL	100.00%	100.00%
Rooms payroll cost/rooms revenue (%)	10.8	12.2
F&B DEPARTMENT		
Food gross margin %	69.9	70.6
Beverage gross margin %	71.0	75.4
Beverage/food revenue %	26.6	54.1
SPEND PER COVER (£)		
Restaurants	22.30	23.80
Banqueting	25.68	36.54
Room service	16.98	14.08
Total F&B	21.65	26.43
COVERS PER EMPLOYEE PER DAY		
Total F&B covers/total F&B employees	6.45	4.83
PAYROLL STATISTICS		
Total F&B payroll/total F&B revenue	35.8	33.0
PAYROLL STATISTICS		
Total annual payroll cost per employee (£000)	14.89	14.79
PAYROLL COSTS/TOT REVENUE %		
Operating departments	16.0	19.6
Non-operating departments	4.0	5.3
TOTAL	20.0	24.9

Source: Arthur Andersen Consulting (1996)
Note: F&B = Food and beverage

● If informative comparisons are to be made between sets of accounts they need to be drawn up on the same basis (or to be recast on the same basis). The use of a uniform and detailed system of accounting allows standard operating and financial statistics (and other information) to be produced almost mechanically, thereby allowing meaningful comparisons to be made.

A further great advantage from the operating perspective is that a detailed allocation dictionary can be produced for the 'awkward' items, so that a uniform treatment can always be achieved. If something unusual comes up, such as supply of replacement coat-hangers for hotel rooms, the allocation dictionary will identify the department (in this case 'rooms') and the subclassification (operating supplies). The main argument here would be whether these were fixed assets or operating expenses; the allocation dictionary clearly settles it in favour of operating expenses.

It is not possible to produce a single system which will cater for all possibilities, of course. A very large hotel complex will need much more detail in the accounts than a small one; this system essentially analyses to the greatest degree which could be required and then expects the smaller organisations to amalgamate headings and departments as needed.

The system is an American one, and clearly the terminology and layouts used are the American ones. These are normally retained regardless of which country the system is being used in. This terminology is different in several places from the UK usage. The differences are usually obvious, but there is a need to careful in matters such as 'stock'. In the UK 'stock' or 'stock-in-trade' means goods held for resale (the equivalent US term is 'inventory'); in the USA 'stock' or 'common stock' is equivalent to UK share capital.

The complete set of financial statements includes a balance sheet, an income statement, a statement of owner's equity and a statement of changes in financial position (a cash flow statement).

The UK has available an alternative system known as the Standard System of Hotel Accounting. This differs only in detail from the Uniform System, and a knowledge of one will make the other relatively easy to follow. The Uniform System is the older and more widely accepted system internationally, and thus is the one considered in this section.

Both systems are based on a structured profit and loss account, or income statement. It is designed to present information in a style relevant to day-to-day management, and is in the form of a summary operating statement, supported by department schedules.

A balance sheet is normally accompanied by a series of computed financial ratios. These ratios are used to provide a measure of a hotel's financial strength and stability. These ratios are particularly useful to potential creditors (principally banks and other lending institutions) and investors. Following, are more detailed explanations of the various types of ratios that can be computed using balance sheet information.

The price decision

One key issue in the financial management of a hotel is the price decision, which requires the identification of the firm's overall objectives and required performance. This will vary from an individual proprietor to the professional entrepreneur, the latter aggressively searching for the highest return. The pricing objectives should be specific, quantified and operational.

In addition to the financial aspects of pricing there is great potential in the hotel industry to use price as an active element in the marketing of a property. However, pricing decisions are invariably complex and difficult requiring a combination of flair, judgement and technical expertise.

Evidence suggests that firms have evolved pricing procedures based on known cost considerations rather than elusive demand functions. Within the hotel industry five methods can be identified in establishing price:

- cost plus pricing
- rate of return pricing
- contribution pricing
- price discrimination
- backward pricing

Cost plus pricing

This starts from a cost calculation and adding a percentage mark-up to derive the selling price. Costs used may be current costs, expected costs or budgeted costs at a given output level. In the hotel industry the normal procedure for food and beverage pricing is to express the profit mark up in terms of gross profit margins; gross profit representing sales revenue less direct material input costs. Cost plus pricing is administratively easy to use and can by adjusted readily in an inflationary world. The greatest draw back of this method is that it ignores demand and the amount that consumers would be willing to pay for the product.

Rate of return pricing

The rate of return pricing method is based on the objective of obtaining a specific return from capital employed. An estimate of anticipated turnover is made and then allowing for the fixed costs that have been covered, an appropriate percentage addition to direct costs is calculated. However, no sales forecast can realistically hope to estimate demand without taking price into consideration yet this approach uses a sales forecast to determine price. This circular interdependence between sales forecasting, occupancy and price is a major defect of this method.

Contribution pricing

Contribution pricing requires an accurate delineation of the fixed and variable costs of the hotel. Break-even charts aid the understanding of this approach and illustrate the relationship between costs, capacity and profits. Traditionally, break-even charts are presented by drawing in fixed costs plus variable costs to arrive at total costs. The intersection of the total revenue function indicates the break-even point. The difference between total revenue and variable costs i.e. the contribution, has relevance for the hotel industry when low occupancy is a problem. It means that in flat periods, business should be accepted providing it covers variable costs, even if average costs are not covered. Variable costs become the floor for pricing decisions, but in many cases the price charged can be substantially above variable costs and relate to market demand.

Price discrimination

Price discrimination involves the sale of similar products/services at different prices. Different buyers have different price elasticities, i.e. you are charging what the market will bear. It must therefore be possible to separate buyers on a group, geographical or time basis, and as with train services there are peak and off peak periods.

Backward pricing

Backward pricing involves reversing the normal process of moving from cost to price and commences with an agreed or approved price. Marketing considerations usually dictate the price which will be decided on the basis of consumer profiles and competitors' policies. If the approved price does not permit satisfactory profit margins, adjustments are made to the product in order to facilitate satisfactory returns. The service element in hotels can be readily adjusted.

Selecting the pricing method

The pricing methods selected by business people will reflect their motivation, their individual expertise and the needs and characteristics in the industry in which they operate. The actual impact of price as a marketing device will depend on the image, quality, location and the age of the individual unit. The attitudes of the consumer will also be fundamentally important. In particular, the consumer's price awareness and price sensitivity will determine the limits within which price can be used as a promotional aid or a psychological tool. Price awareness will depend on the frequency of purchase and the consumer's ability to remember the price. Most consumers adopt a threshold type of approach, establishing an upper and lower price limit that delineates the boundary of anticipated expenditure. The ability to remember price will depend on the prominence that price is given in the transaction and the ease with which price can be identified. Many customers, particularly new customers, are reassured by an all-in price because it ensures that they remain within their threshold limits of expenditure. However, the extent of this influence will also depend on consumers' sensitivity to price.

Quality perception in any service industry is inevitably subjective. Value and quality can be assessed effectively only after the service has been sampled. The more differentiated the service available, the greater the uncertainty and difficulty selection and choice becomes. In these circumstances, consumers frequently resort to using price as an information cue or an indicator of quality. Expensive hotels may be regarded as a status symbol and so it is important not to underprice. Pricing to be the most expensive place in town may be an appropriate policy. Low price units must not fall below the consumers' floor price.

Pricing policy

In considering the pricing policy of a hotel, a range of options can be identified and their suitability investigated. The hotel can initially follow the market and become a price taker or be a price maker. It can price above or below the market level. The actual option will depend on the interrelationship between the internal and external environmental factors. The interdependency of hotel departments will require an integrated approach.

Analysis of the environment
The first stage in the pricing policy process requires an analysis of information such as past, present and anticipated market demand by market segments. Consumer profile and average spend, degree of competition and the internal cost structure of the hotel should also be considered. This first stage requires an analysis of the environment in which the hotel operates.

Accommodation
The high overhead costs and low variable costs involved in providing accommodation give the price maker a wide degree of discretion when deciding on price. In the short run, the floor for pricing will be variable costs and the ceiling is the amount that con-

sumers are willing to pay. In the long run, of course, price must cover all costs. Price concessions are used if they bring in extra business above the variable costs. There may be spillover from accommodation to demand for food and beverage. If demand is consistent, a uniform pricing policy may be adopted. If the market segment is price inelastic, especially if price is regarded as a quality indicator, then pricing above the market level can bring substantial rewards. The personal preferences and perceptions of customers will need careful monitoring. At the lower end of the market and to ensure high occupancy, pricing below the market level can bring substantial benefits. However, the threat of price wars may constrain price decreases as an active means to improve occupancy.

Location

A good location will mean much greater freedom regarding pricing policy. Features such as accessibility, proximity to scenic beaches or to the commercial or business activities of the area all contribute to good location. A poor location may mean that price is used as a marketing variable. Poor location may be compensated for by providing value for money. Emphasis may be given to regular customers and a lower mark-up will probably have to be accepted. The use of price as an informational device to attract customers is worth consideration.

New hotels

This is a situation where the degree of uncertainty will be at a maximum and historical factors cannot provide guidance. The degree of differentiation and the amount of competition will be the price variables affecting the degree of manoeuvrability open to the unit. The initial price charged in a new hotel will exert an influence on the future patterns of demand. A low price charged initially will attract customers especially if demand has a high elasticity, so that the market is captured and this will also forestall the entry of new firms. However, there will be difficulty in raising prices as this may alienate customers. This low initial price is referred to as price penetration policy. A high initial price may be more profitable if the demand is inelastic. This is feasible when the valuing of services is difficult especially where customers want something different. Also it is easier to lower prices if necessary. However, the site must be unique. The new unit pricing philosophy will be influenced by

- unsatisfied demand
- displacement demand
- created demand.

The type of demand will affect the pricing policy. Pricing policies will also be considered at the feasibility study stage (see Chapter 4).

Package tours

The wholesaler or industrial buyer will be much more informed than the normal individual consumer and will be capable of assessing competitive offerings, qualitative features and supply relative to demand. In these situations bargaining and negotiating skills are important, with variable cost the floor below which the price should not be dropped. The discounts given to these buyers are confidential and may vary from group to group. This discrimination is possible because of the market's segmentation and, if used on the basis of varying demand elasticities, can enhance profitability. Prices are fixed well in advance and should take into account inflation and exchange rates.

Conferences and special functions

In this respect both quality and quantity are important. If there is more than one hotel in the area then price comes into the equation. Direct bargaining and negotiation skills are also of relevance and bidding procedures may be adopted. If a conference is going to be held at a certain town and the accommodation is to be provided by numerous hotels, then reduced prices are rarely necessary unless demand is considerably less than the supply available.

Implementation of the pricing decision

The next step in the pricing process is to ensure that the policy is implemented as effectively as possible. With a small unit locally controlled there will be few problems. The large group will require administrative controls and checks to see that if decisions are centrally made, they will be implemented and fully appreciated by the local or branch manager.

As a final point, decisions should be monitored and compared with the expected or intended results, sometimes known as 'yield'. 'Yield management' will now be explored in a case study in four London hotels.

Case Study: Application of yield management in London hotels

Background

A survey on yield management practices was conducted on the basis of four in-depth interviews of key front office personnel at the Forum Hotel, the Mayfair Inter-Continental and the Hotel Meridien in London, and the Forte Crest, Heathrow Airport. Some of the results of the interviews will now be considered.

What is yield management and its objectives?

The Forum sees yield management as the process of managing the bedroom inventory to provide the optimum mix between occupancy and rate with a view to increasing the revenue. That can be done only within the supply and demand equation of what market conditions are providing at any one time.

While the Forte Crest did not make this link with supply and demand it does focus specifically on the yield per room. Like the Forum it makes the link between sales, managing bed stock, rate and length of stay. The interest at Crest is not only the room rate but also its total spend that is food and beverage.

The Mayfair confirmed these views and introduced the concept of differing market segments. One point stressed by the Mayfair is the need for information in the system – about how much the room cost to clean, how much food and beverage one person would consume, etc. Interestingly the Mayfair talked about 'gut feeling' in making yield management decisions which implies a judgemental element in the decision-making process.

case study continues ▶

case study continues

The Meridien concurred with the points already made, illustrating them by comparison with the airlines approach, the objective being to maximise revenue.

Six key points come out of these definitions of yield management:

- price
- length of stay
- market segments
- competitive situation
- need for information
- importance of management judgement

Developing a yield culture

In considering training about yield management, differences emerged between the hotels. While the concept is introduced to operative staff in the Forum, yield control is kept at the level of management, i.e. office manager, director of sales, reservations and travel trade sales manager. It is those four people who control the yield. At the operative level there is a seven stage traffic light colour scheme and that is transposed on to an availability board in the reservations office. Operative reservation staff work purely on that scheme. Decisions to override the colour scheme are made by management. The managers hold departmental meetings to present the figures and talk about decisions and how the hotels mix of business has been arrived at.

Crest take a more in-depth approach to training at various operational levels. Reception staff learn what the availability controls are and what they mean, so that when they see a marker by a particular date they are able to understand what that marker means. Within reservations the hotel spends time explaining the theory behind what the hotel is trying to achieve. The hotel accountant gets involved in the training process by looking at two scenarios of a booking: cheap group midweek business that blocks out corporate business for four nights thus identifying two profit scenarios.

The level of training in yield management at the Mayfair is similar in approach to that at the Forum. The only staff who are actually trained to use yield are in reservations or front office, i.e. the front office manager, the assistant front office manager, reservations manager and assistant; nobody else gets involved. The information on yield is then passed to all staff. Training of management is normally once a year.

The Meridien (at the time of the research) had recently been taken over by Forte (in turn taken over by Granada plc) and was in the process of switching from the Air France system to Fortress II. Training for management and operative staff took place both at the hotel and in the company's CRS centre at Aylesbury.

An appropriately designed and delivered product

Marketing

Each of the four hotels attracts a different market segmentation mix. At the Forum, busi-

case study continues ▶

ness is very broadly 30% aircrew, 30% group and leisure and 30% transient corporate high rated. Within these three broad categories a wide range of segments can be identified. In terms of discounts, the hotel offers 50% discount subject to availability to travel agents.

The Crest and the Meridien chains have throughout the company quite strictly defined market segment categories. Two segments which are very important at the Forte Crest are the airline crew business and airline passenger business. Within the leisure sector the hotel has several segments that look at the Leisure Break brochure and divide those up into bed and breakfast, dinner, bed and breakfast, one night packages, two night packages and touring holidays. The system is quite structured and therefore comparisons by regions and as a company can be made. At the weekends fairly low rated business is accepted in the struggle for occupancy.

At the Meridien on a daily basis it was suggested that possibly 60% or sometimes even higher is corporate business and the rest is leisure or groups. The quiet period is at the weekend where the weekend rate is probably quite low yielding group market. The hotel tries to encourage groups during the quiet parts of the year like January, February and August.

Operational tactics

An area discussed in the interviews was the relevance of yield management when there are extreme differences in demand levels. The relevance of computer systems was questioned by the Forum manager in the difficult trading days of 1991. When demand was extremely low (it was suggested) there was no need for a computer to instruct management to sell every room at the lowest rate available on the market. It would seem that computerised yield management systems are effective only when market conditions are buoyant. Another factor comes with a fixed price hotel room, a common element within the Forte brands. In those hotels the principle of 'yield' is based around length of stay and in the short term there is no opportunity to manipulate price. It is therefore being suggested that a yield management system can really be effective only when the hotel has a certain level of market demand, and when it has a range of rates available.

One can contrast this view with the Forte Crest where in times of low demand, yield management was regarded as even more important. The view expressed was that yield management not only is there for when business was booming but also applies when business is not booming. The emphasis here is perhaps on occupancy rather than rate with the objective to ensure that the hotel can maximise whatever market is out there and generate some revenue.

In considering these issues to do with price there is an inevitable link with perceptions of quality. Put simply, on an airplane you do not want a back-packer in T-shirt and jeans sitting in the first-class section at an Apex rate, because airlines wish to protect their rack rate in the first class section. However, there is within the airlines the process of upgrading of suitable clients when the economy section is full, the objective being to maximise yield. The same principle applies within a hotel company such as the Mayfair that does not want certain clients from the Forum (both hotels are owned by the same company). Both properties implicitly understand the link between price and quality.

One issue was that all four hotels were reluctant to specify a baseline price below which they would not go. From a yield management perspective £1 of profit is better than no profit at all from what may be an empty bedroom, the implication is that there is still an emotional element in setting price – what some might call a head vs heart decision.

Another aspect concerning yield management is the price sensitivity of the market segments attracted to each of the four hotels. The hotels were remarkably similar in relying on management judgement; they gauged people's reactions, used the skills of negotiation, skills of reading people, skills of reading body language, and many other things that come into the negotiation process.

At all four hotels it was clear that decisions on yield management involve a number of managers across a range of departments. For instance at the Crest the decision ultimately rests with the general manager. However, managing the day-to-day bed stock is the responsibility of the rooms division manager. The hotel's sales and marketing director also has a major input into the decision. In the latter's case the booking may not be good in the short term but it may be beneficial over the longer term. At the end of the day it is a judgemental decision as to whether a short-term or long-term view is taken.

All the four hotels operated a policy of overbooking in order to maximise yield; this sometimes means that if they are full, there are book outs to other hotels from time to time.

At the Forte Crest there is 'daylight business' for airline crews and passengers, sometimes boosting occupancy to over 100%. This is relatively cheap business because the hotel can turn the room round with fewer costs to cover. It costs approximately £5 to clean a room which may be sold for £30. Monitoring at the Crest is constant as its room availability, markers or constraints can change every five or ten minutes. Room availability needs monitoring because the firm's central reservations can go straight into the hotel's system.

Forecasting

The Forum forecasts by market segments using PCs. Initially when the hotel forecast three months ahead it would have been taking into account what happened the previous year, the price increases that have been secured over the year, any events that will be taking place this period that did not take place the previous year and vice versa. It is on this basis that the hotel may increase or decrease the forecast. The manager is then looking and changing that forecast on an almost daily basis so at any one point during the month occupancy and rate can be predicted. The Forum regards computers as sophisticated tools that will generate reports every day and on the basis of what is happening strategies are changed accordingly.

The Crest and the Meridien also forecast by market segment on a five-weekly basis. This is broken down and sent to head office. They also forecast the next six months on a weekly basis. The hotels have a provisional breakdown of what they expect the market breakdown to be by day, by month, and by segment.

Forecasting is with the use of historical data, trends and specific pieces of business that the hotel may have in the system for conferences or groups already on the books.

The importance for the Crest is in controlling airline crew and passenger business, which is fairly low rated. The hotel then looks at the higher rated business, determines where the levels are and where the management anticipate them moving. The hotel also maintains space for higher rated business so if an enquiry comes in, it can be considered.

Technological Support

The Inter-Continental group including the Forum and the Mayfair was in the process of changing to the German Fidelio computer system. At the Forum the system was first launched in the sales office. The Forum was at the time of the interview using HIS, and regarded it as old technology not suitable for a 900 bedroom property. The functionality of the system was questioned, for example the need to have two folios when splitting the bill thus doubling the work. The Forum was therefore working yield management manually, although the new system Fidelio will have the ability to interface with more up-to-date real time yield management systems. To go fully computerised there is a need for full integration, because the sales office, front office and accounts need to be integrated. This fully computerised approach means that the manager hands over the control of the inventory to the computer instead of using personal expertise, so a good quality yield management system will make experienced rooms division managers obsolete.

However, the disadvantage of a computerised system is that it requires a lot of attention and management, and it can not take what could be called emotional decisions into account. An emotional decision might mean taking a cheap group on a good night in September because they are going to produce business for the hotel in a quiet December period.

At the Mayfair, the yield system is linked into the hotel's property management system by the process of downloading data twice a day. There could be a problem if the hotel takes an amendment to a group booking over the telephone, and then the booking as it was originally put into yield stays the same until updating at the end of the day. This problem will be resolved as the system is updated.

Concluding remarks

The central purpose of this case study has been to identify the extent to which yield management systems, which has been discussed in great depth in the literature, have been implemented into the four London hotels. What has been noted through reviewing the available literature and research into yield management practices at the four hotels is that irrespective of progress, the theory is far in advance of the practical application of yield management. Clearly the efficacy of theory with respect to hotels has shown that implementing innovation is a complex venture.

Since its inception in the 1950s, progress has been endemic to yield management. When it was first implemented into the US airline industry, the results were record profits in an industry in recession. This effect in a parallel capacity constrained service, the hotel industry, was recognised and yield management, its strategies and systems were introduced in the 1980s. However, investment in yield management (YM) has not surprisingly been restricted to the large hotel groups and with a few exceptions has been concentrated in the USA. Similarly the key research projects on this subject have been virtually

case study continues ▶

confined to the USA. Caution, however, is important: virtually all YM users are US based as YM in Europe remains mostly at the conceptual level with minimum practical realisation.

Whereas the use of YM in the airline industry has resulted in increased revenue running into millions of dollars, the benefits for the hotel industry are seen as qualitative rather than objectively quantifiable, though increased revenue is often cited as the reason for implementing YM. The lack of data validating increased revenue claims has prompted scepticism regarding the US enthusiasm for YM. In this respect a clear difference was found between the literature on YM and the practices adopted for hotels which were researched.

A clear contrast was noted between the academic view of yield management and the views of the four managers interviewed. The literature focuses on occupancy and room rate in order to maximise yield, yet the views of the four managers extended this definition to a range of important issues. Occupancy and rate needs to be set within the context of market conditions and the London hotel market has seen supply and demand fluctuate considerably over the past few years. It was also noted that yield management in its theoretical sense is applied to the rooms division, yet management at the four hotels were interested in the total spend, for instance, in the hotels' food and beverage outlets.

The marketing concept

Definition

Having considered financial management within the hotel industry another important area which will now be discussed is marketing, which has been defined in various ways by different writers. The Institute of Marketing offers the following definition of marketing.

> *Marketing is the management process responsible for identifying, anticipating and satisfying customer requirements profitably.*

The marketing concept is a business philosophy that arose to challenge the previous concepts and was fully crystallised in the mid-1950s. It was a new idea in business which replaced a production-oriented way of thinking and can be described as

> *a philosophy of business which states that the customers want and need for satisfaction is the economic and social justification of a company's existence.*

It is the marketing concept that proposes the best way to achieve organisational objectives and consists of determining the needs and wants of target markets and delivering products and services to satisfy those needs and wants more effectively and efficiently than competitors.

Market focus

No hotel company can operate in every market and satisfy every need nor can it even do a good job within one broad market. It is important to point out that a hotel must classify and target the markets it wishes to serve. Companies do best when they define their target markets and prepare a tailored marketing programme for each segment.

Hotels should define customer needs from the customer point of view, not from the management perspective. Being customer-oriented, a company will not only retain its customers but also attract new customers. This market focus on customer satisfaction is the best indicator of the company's future profits. Thus it may be vital for a customer-oriented hotel to regularly measure its customer-satisfaction levels each period and set if necessary improvement objectives.

Co-ordination is important in marketing and means two things. First, it requires the various marketing functions, such as salesforce, advertising, product management, marketing research, and so on, to be well co-ordinated not only among themselves but also from the customer point of view. Second, marketing needs to be well co-ordinated with the other hotel departments. Marketing works only when all employees appreciate the effect they have on customer satisfaction. Therefore, a company, managed under the marketing concept, is required to organise, co-ordinate, and control its entire operations as one system directed towards achieving a single set of objectives applicable to the hotel. For this reason, the marketing concept requires the hotel to carry out internal marketing as well as external marketing.

Internal marketing involves applying the philosophies and practices of marketing to people who serve the external customers so that the best people can be employed and retained, and they will do the best possible work.

It is widely appreciated that the purpose of the hotel marketing concept is to help organisations achieve their objectives which are not only to satisfy customer needs but also to make profits. Hence, to achieve their objectives, they seek a profitable way to satisfy the target market's needs and wants. Companies from an external perspective can make profits by satisfying customer needs better than competitors can. Therefore, companies are highly involved in analysing the profit potential of different marketing opportunities.

Process of marketing planning

The success of marketing planning is dependent to a large part on the strength of a competitive analysis whatever the state of competition. The needs of such strategy and planning in relation to competition requires that first, market share must be increased or maintained to improve profitability. Second, the competitor's products are launched head-on against existing products. Third, the competition has advantages through such factors as environmental considerations, new technology, government regulation and customer attitudes. Finally, new opportunities develop when competition becomes vulnerable, e.g. in product shortages.

Strategic marketing planning can be seen as an advantageous tool which provides a systematic framework guiding all the elements of an organisation to the achievement of agreed objectives. Marketing, as one of the generational functions, plays a crucial role in the company's strategic planning by focusing exclusively on the formulation of the product.

Hotel marketing planning leads to the setting of long-term marketing objectives which are consistent with the company's overall objectives, and the formulation of strategies and specific plans for achieving them. A strategic marketing plan represents the guideline within which the short-run, detailed tactical or operational marketing plans must be developed concerning specific campaigns for target markets.

The precise steps in the process of strategic marketing planning are problematic due to various approaches by different writers. However, it is possible to envisage the marketing planning process as a staged sequence involving analysing marketing opportunities, researching and selecting target markets, designing marketing strategies, planning marketing programmes, and organising implementing controlling marketing effects.

Hotel marketing planning

Hotel marketing strategies can be seen as broad issues that are central to the utilisation of marketing planning. A hotel marketing strategy can be a basic statement about the desired impact to be achieved on demand in a given target market, but the stress in the planning process is on the selection of target markets and the development of marketing resources so that marketing objectives are achieved.

Various principles may be considered: the company profile, the prime prospects, the competitors, and company objectives. The detailed approaches for implementing these strategies are determined through specific marketing programmes, such as advertising, sales promotions product development programmes, and sales and distribution programmes. It is evident that a strategy isolated from the competitive environment would be ineffective and unrealistic. Therefore, it requires marketers to be able to use competitive strategy effectively in order to achieve their goals.

There is a problem in drawing a framework for marketing strategy because some authors claim that the marketing of services is different from the marketing of goods while others disagree. Despite confusion over the approaches in services marketing, most of the themes may be related to the characteristics of the service industry and, by implication, hotel marketing.

The characteristics of services present both challenges and opportunities to hotel marketers. To deal with these service characteristics, it is suggested that the right marketing mix should be developed and objectives represent the ends that management seek in implementing a marketing programme. Therefore, marketing strategy can be seen as the composite of many decisions made in the programme's design. To some extent, a firm's marketing strategy may be described as a combination of two basic elements:

● target marketing
● the marketing mix.

Target marketing

The concept of target marketing is a refinement of the basic philosophy of marketing. It is an attempt by hotel companies to relate the characteristics or attributes of the business that match most closely the customer requirements.

It may be that the total market is too large and consists of too many potential customers for the company to be able to deal with. The overall market may be geographically dispersed and the hotel company may lack the resources to serve it properly. The market for a particular product or service may be too heterogeneous, in terms of the purchasing requirements of individuals or organisations making up the market, for any one company to serve adequately.

By targeting specific groups of consumers or market segments instead of attempting to serve the demand requirements of an entire population for a particular product category, the hotel is able to develop more effective programmes and gain a competitive advantage by developing a more satisfying marketing mix which should also be more profitable for the company.

Market segmentation

Market segmentation is considered as the first essential step in the overall of target marketing and is the act of dividing a market into distinct groups of buyers who might require separate product and marketing mixes. Market segmentation can be defined as

pursuing a marketing strategy whereby the total potential market is divided into homogeneous subsets of customers each of which responds differently to the marketing mix of the organisation.

Market segmentation is used to identify those market segments that are likely to be heavy users of the hotel product. At the same time, segments that hold little potential receive minimal or no attention and scarce marketing resources are not used chasing after market segments with little sales potential. Therefore, after the segments are identified, the company can design a marketing mix to meet the needs of consumers in the segments which are attractive to the company. This can actually improve sales and profits as it allows the hotel to target specific market segments that are much more likely to patronise the organisation's facilities. A number of major variables that are used to segment markets are identified in Figure 5.2.

Traditionally, hotel marketers have preferred to use demographic and geographic data for segmentation because it is easier to define and measure. However, there is an increasing use of psychosocial criteria such as social class, lifestyle, and culture for segmentation.

Hotel product positioning

Following on from this discussion, a related subject, hotel product positioning, can be seen as the act of designing the company's product and marketing mix to fit a given place in the consumer's mind. Hotel product positioning can be defined as

a marketing strategy that chooses a package of benefits that is attractive to customers in the target market and distinguishes the product or company from its competitors.

Geographic segmentation

Region	Cities	Country	Neighbourhood

Demographic segmentation

Age	Income	Sex	Occupation
Family size	Education	Religion	Family life cycle
Race	Nationality		

Psychographic segmentation

Social class	Lifestyle	Personality

Behavioural segmentation

Occasion	Benefits	User status	Usage rate
Loyalty status	Readiness stage	Attitude towards product	

Figure 5.2 Major segmentation variables for consumer

Using marketing research the hotel should establish the position of competitors' products in any given market segment and then decide whether to offer a product very close to a competitor's offering or to attempt to fill a gap in the market. Once the hotel has established its product positioning strategy it is then in a position to go on to plan the details of its marketing mix.

The marketing mix

The nature of the service industry is different from that of manufacturing industry, therefore the traditional marketing mix – the 4Ps of Product, Price, Promotion and Place – are regarded as inappropriate in a service industry like hotels. One proposal is a modified framework, the 7Ps, with the addition of People, Physical Evidence, and Process. Another suggestion is that the service marketing mix consists not only of 4Ps, i.e. traditional *external marketing,* but also of two other marketing efforts, namely *internal marketing* and *interactive marketing.*

External marketing can be described as the normal work done by the hotel company to prepare prices, distribute and promote the service of the hotel company. Internal marketing can be described as the work done by the company to train and motivate its internal customer, its customer contact employees and supporting service personnel, to work as a team in order to provide customer satisfaction. Interactive marketing can be described as the employees' skill in handling customer contact.

Marketing mix for the hotel industry

Every hotel is likely to operate in a different environment with different priorities and limitations, and there is no single formula of deciding the marketing mix. Nevertheless, a guideline for marketing action is necessary and this will be centred around the four Ps.

Product
Product is the most fundamental element to satisfy the customer's needs and in the hotel industry it includes both goods and services. The hotel product is judged on the basis of 'performance' rather than the tangible goods itself. The manner and expertness factors, and quality of the goods or services are essential, but other experiential factors will enter into a guest's evaluation. The other guests are a part of the service experience as is every other factor that enters into the guest experience. Therefore, the '*total experience*' during the stay at the hotel rather than just the room and its facilities and services is what the guest buys and remembers. The product offered by the hotel comprises physical products such as food, beverages, and accommodation services as well as '*emotional satisfaction*'. Emotional satisfaction has two elements. First, there is the image of the way in which the hotel represents itself. Second, there is atmosphere which is to do with what people expect to take place in the hotel and what they think of these expectations. Neither image nor atmosphere can be separated from the physical aspects of the product or the service and changes in the physical or service environment will also lead to changes in the emotional environment.

Price
Price is regarded as a flexible and important variable in the marketing mix and has already

been considered in this chapter from a financial perspective. Too often hotel managers consider price from a financial perspective and ignore the marketing implications. Price is a powerful tool in increasing sales because it can be rapidly and frequently adjusted to bring supply and demand into balance, at a relatively low cost, whereas other elements of the mix can neither be moved nor easily be changed. Price considerations include levels of prices, discounts, allowances and commissions, terms of payment and credit. Price may also play a different level of significance from one service to another and therefore, customers' perceptions of value obtained from a service and the interaction of purchase *vis-à-vis* quality are important considerations in many price mixes. In the hotel industry, perishability of services has great impact on pricing consideration. The fluctuations in demand make it important to use the price mechanism to optimise and flatten out demand. Short-term price tactics such as discount pricing, differential pricing and promotional pricing are used to adjust to various market situations when necessary. Pricing can also be strategic in marketing because business objectives such as profitability, sales volume, growth and elimination of rivals can be pursued. In a hotel marketing context, demand-oriented pricing based on the price sensitivities of customers and intensity of demand should be generally used. However, due to the rising cost and growing competition, more and more companies will use cost-based pricing and competitive pricing.

Place

Place or location of the service provider and their accessibility are important factors in services marketing. Accessibility relates not only to physical accessibility but also to other means of communication and contact. Thus the types of distribution channels used and their coverage are linked to the crucial issue of service accessibility. For hotel marketers, location can be the strongest selling point if it is favourable. In contrast, price can be the main constraint as it cannot be moved to reach customers and may result in loss of business. Therefore, distribution channels play an important role in the delivery of services speedily and efficiently to the customers.

Promotion

Promotion is essential in order to communicate with targeted customers for effective selling through personal selling, advertising, public relations, sales promotion, packaging and merchandising. For long-term effect, advertising, personal selling and packaging can be used while sales promotion generates a short-term effect. In strategic hotel marketing, promotion helps to smooth variations in customer demand, counter seasonality pattern and resist competitor pressures. Owing to the high degree of similarity among hotels, communication with target customers is indispensable.

Personal selling is a two-way process while the remainder are one-way communications, going only from the marketer to customer. This approach is believed to be the most powerful tool in a high customer contact industry because face-to-face communication can enhance deep personal relationship with customers and generate a quicker response. Personal selling generally refers to sales calls made by a company representative on prospects or existing customers. In the hotel industry, personal selling also includes the work of personnel who give services, such as restaurant staff or desk clerk, in persuading guests to increase their level of expenditure.

Advertising is on the increase as competition in hotel intensifies. Some advertising is aimed at building a company's image (generic advertising) while other ads are promotional and seek immediate patronage.

Public relations uses newsworthy events related to an operation to gain news coverage. It includes speeches, charitable donations, and special events, which create publicity. Events are usually presented in a way that is of interest to readers.

As a short-term marketing tactic, sales promotion is very useful to iron out the seasonality of demand. It is often supported by promotional advertising which offers an incentive for customers to induce purchase. It includes premiums, coupons, and special packages.

In facing a rising sales labour and media cost, it is desirable that the expense should be kept down. Joint promotion may help to cut the cost. Hotels can get other organisations, such as tourist boards, shopping centres or theme parks, to contribute to their marketing effort, thus sharing the risk and cost as well as assisting in the implementation of the campaign.

Internal marketing

In a service business like hotels, people are a company's most important competitive asset, particularly when the performance is people-based rather than equipment-based and the quality of the service rendered is inseparable from the quality of the service provider. Therefore, in the hotel industry, there is no escaping the necessity to communicate, motivate, train and involve people as they represent the key to productivity and profits.

Internal marketing involves applying the philosophies and practices of marketing to people who serve the external customers so that not only will the best people be employed and retained but also they will do the best possible work. It is therefore important that the hospitality industry must furnish its employees with behavioural as opposed to solely technical skills. Training through internal marketing is a major issue that the hospitality industry needs to address.

It is especially true for the hotel industry that customer-contact personnel are a potentially important segment as a 'second audience' for advertising. When the performances of people are what the customers buy, the advertiser needs to be concerned not only with customers to buy but also with motivating employees to perform. When it is well conceived, advertising can have a positive effect on employees. It is therefore suggested that a hotel company needs to advertise to its employees as well as its customers. Moreover, it requires a hotel to satisfy employees as well as customers. Therefore, management should carry out internal marketing and create an environment of employee support and reward for good service performance.

Interactive marketing

Interactive marketing is seeking to protect the customer base and sees the customer as an asset with the management's function to attract, maintain, and enhance customer relationships. Interactive marketing begins once the customer is inside the establishment where it is possible to engage in direct face-to-face marketing. Therefore, any hotel that attempts to engage in interactive marketing must first have engaged in internal marketing to ensure that their employees have the ability to engage in an effective relationship with customers.

The purpose of this section has been to set the scene in terms of the marketing concept and relate that concept specifically to the hotel industry. At a practical level marketing inevitably revolves around the planning process and the four elements of product, price, promotion and place.

Both financial and marketing themes are explored in the following case study involving the management of a hotel in receivership. A number of other key issues are also highlighted.

> ## Case Study: Management of a hotel in receivership: key issues

This case study explores the challenges faced by receivers during the management of a hotel while in receivership. It is based largely on the receivership of the Royal Hotel, London, which had a turnover in the region of £1.5 million. The Royal has some fifty bedrooms and extensive conference and banqueting facilities.

The hotel was bought in the late 1980s, during the UK's economic boom, for over £4 million. It weathered the recession of the early 1990s, but towards the end of 1994, the directors were having difficulties in meeting their interest charges and capital repayments. In early 1995, receivers were appointed with the objective of maximising the pay-out to creditors.

The hotel would eventually have to be sold; the timing of such a sale was critical. If the overall health of the business could be improved under the management of receivers, then the achieved sales price might be higher, thus maximising the pay-out to creditors. An initial market analysis of the area and operational review identified that

- better focused sales and marketing efforts could result in an improvement in both rooms volume and rate
- operational efficiencies could be achieved through improved buying and better control
- staff morale and customer satisfaction could be enhanced through a substantial maintenance and cleaning programme.

Together with the bank, the decision was made to operate the hotel, improve profit levels and review the best time to sell within six months to one year.

Definitions

Who is an administrative receiver?

An administrative receiver is defined by the UK's Insolvency Act 1986 as

> *(a) a receiver or manager of the whole (or substantially the whole) of a company's property appointed by or on behalf of the holders of any debentures of the company secured by a charge which, as created, was a floating charge, or by such a charge and one or more other securities; or (b) a person who would be such a receiver or manager but for the appointment of some other person as the receiver of part of the company's property.*

When is a receiver appointed?

> *In general terms a receiver is appointed by a secured creditor, usually a bank, when its security is in jeopardy. A receiver's main function is to realise the assets for the benefit of the preferential and secured creditors. His primary duty is to the*

case study continues ▶

case study continues

debenture holder, but while he does not have any duty to agree the claims of the unsecured creditors, as agent of the company he does have a general duty of care towards them arising out of common law as opposed to statutes.

Challenges faced by the management team of a receiver

There are three groups, key to a hotel's success, whose concerns and motivations must be addressed with care by the receivers:

- existing and potential customers
- staff
- suppliers.

Also critical is the relationship between the receiver and

- the debenture holder
- planning authorities
- licensing authorities
- local residents
- the previous owners/directors of the hotel, among others.

The key issues surrounding these relationships are now explored.

Existing and potential customers

Initial period of receivership

When a hotel goes into receivership, customers are immediately worried:

- Will my deposits for future bookings be honoured/returned by the receiver?
- Will the receivers be able to service any of my future bookings?
- What standards will be delivered by the receivers?

Since receivership has a negative image, some customers will wish to take their bookings to a competitor. Potential customers who might have booked prior to receivership may never book because of the uncertainties inherent in receivership situations.

Those customers who maintain their bookings at the hotel usually want reassurance from the management at the hotel and from the receiver or the appointed agents that the booking can be serviced and of the standard that can be expected.

A receiver does not have to honour deposits paid to the company prior to receivership. Nevertheless, if the hotel is to continue trading, it is usual to honour deposits where bookings are maintained at the hotel. However, where clients cancel their bookings, the receiver cannot refund deposits which were paid to the previous company, and the depositor becomes another unsecured creditor.

Convincing existing customers that they should maintain their bookings with the hotel is an immediate challenge faced by the receivers. There is little that can be done, except

case study continues ▶

case study continues

reassure and, if appropriate, clarify areas where investment or maintenance is likely to be undertaken. A number of functions at the Royal were won back on the basis of promises to clean carpets and curtains, repair the air conditioning, clean and polish chandeliers, and ensure adequate supplies of equipment.

Maturity period of receivership

Following the initial period, the key issues to be addressed by a receiver are standards of product and delivery, the sales and marketing process, and pricing policy.

Standards of product and delivery The standards of delivery (both in terms of the product and service) must be superior to that expected by customers, to smooth the sales and marketing process of the hotel during receivership. If word of mouth is positive after the initial few bookings, this will assist in dispelling the negative image of receivership.

The sales and marketing process This is an area which is normally neglected prior to receivership and does not receive immediate attention at the outset of a receivership due to the many other urgent demands. In order to increase the overall 'health' of the business, it is an area that needs focus. The sales and marketing process has to overcome not only the continuing negative image of receivership, but also any previous bad experiences at the hotel. When a hotel goes into receivership, it is usual to find that the overall standards slipped many months ago, thus alienating many customers. The job of winning customers back after they have had a bad experience is difficult in any hotel; it is even more so in a receivership situation.

Assuming that the standards of the hotel are improved immediately after the hotel goes into receivership, it is only once customers have actually experienced the hotel under the new regime that they are convinced and the selling and marketing of the hotel becomes an easier task.

Pricing policy This is reviewed as part of the initial market appraisal. Prices may be altered as the positioning of the hotel is defined. This is established taking account of

- competitors' prices
- standard of the hotel *vis-à-vis* that of competitors
- definition of the market segments which are likely to generate demand for the hotel
- costs of providing the various services.

End of a receivership

Managing the hotel through the sales process presents many of the challenges faced in the initial period of receivership. Once customers know that the hotel is on the market, they question the security of their deposits, whether their bookings will be honoured and the standards that can be expected from the new owners.

This is again a period of reassurance. During receivership, all deposits are held in a trust account and released to the trading account only when a booking has taken place. If a booking is for a date after the sale of the hotel is completed, the deposit will be transferred to the new owners at the point of sale. The sale contract will always contain a

case study continues ▶

case study continues

clause requesting that the new owners honour any bookings undertaken by the receiver. It is however difficult to give reassurance as to the quality of service and product under a new owner, particularly when the owner is not yet known.

Staff

Initial period of receivership

When a financial institution appoints receivers to take over the affairs of a hotel, there are mixed emotions among the existing staff:

- **Anger** at being kept in the dark: quite often staff will have no idea as to the financial state of the hotel.
- **Uncertainty** about what the receivers will do. Will they honour my contract to date? Will I get paid for last week/last month/my holidays? The pattern of receiverships is one of peaks and troughs. The majority of businesses go into receivership at month or quarter end, when wages or rent payments are due and cannot be met.
- **Fear** about what will happen to jobs. Will they sell the hotel? When and who to?
- **Relief** that things could not continue as they were for much longer.
- **Betrayal** because the directors had promised a pay rise this month.
- **Happiness** because the directors 'got what they deserved'.
- **Mistrust** of the receivers.
- **Confusion** over who is in control. Who are these new people? Where should my loyalties lie?

Keeping the staff is essential to the continued operation of the hotel. Maintaining a motivated team is necessary to improve standards overall, and particularly of service. Both are difficult in a situation where the hotel will be sold: nobody knows when or who to. Assuming planning and other permissions are possible, the hotel could be sold for other uses. This is possible even though, by operating the hotel, the receivers are trying to maximise its value as a hotel and protect employees' jobs. The staff are usually aware that their jobs might not be safe once the hotel is sold and no one is more aware of this than the general manager, whose job is most at risk. If the hotel is sold and even if it continues to operate as a hotel after the sale, the new owners will often wish to put their own person in to manage. Despite this, the general manager's job during the receivership is to motivate the team. The receiver's challenge is to ensure that the general manager is motivated and in turn motivates the staff.

Maturity period of receivership

The needs and welfare of staff are usually neglected prior to receivership. Job and person specifications often do not exist, no training has been undertaken for months, an appraisal process normally does not exist and staff are demoralised. They often do not know what their responsibilities are, or what they are measured against.

case study continues ▶

case study continues

During the maturity period of receivership, it is important to address all these issues which help in raising staff morale and service standards:

- Job and person specifications must be prepared and used as the basis for recruitment. The job specifications clearly set out responsibilities and accountabilities for each employee. Systems can then be installed aimed at improving control, service and standards. Employees can then be held accountable for their responsibilities.
- Training needs must be identified and addressed.
- An appraisal process installed whereby staff are measured by clear and, if possible, measurable objectives.
- The appraisal process should be tied into the review system, where performance is measured against previously set objectives. The introduction of profit-related and loyalty bonuses at the Royal was critical in the motivation of staff and in the retention of personnel in key positions.

End of a receivership

As with customers, employees' concerns once the hotel has been placed on the market are similar to many of the issues faced during the initial period of receivership. Staff are concerned about the safety of their jobs and they wonder when and who are likely to be the new owners. Maintaining motivation once the hotel has been put on the market is difficult, particularly since this can be a long time. The 'end' of the receivership at the Royal lasted a year: the sale of the hotel was completed just over a year after the hotel had been put on the market. It is not unusual for staff to leave and recruiting quality new members of staff is difficult and can be costly if agency staff need to be used.

Suppliers

Initial period of receivership

Among the angriest of groups when a hotel falls into receivership are the suppliers. They are often owed substantial amounts of money. Their claims are known as 'unsecured creditors' which means that they will be paid a dividend only in the event that all secured creditors are repaid in full. A receiver need not honour any debts incurred by the company prior to its entering into receivership.

Nevertheless it is crucial to maintain the essential supplies to the hotel if it is to continue trading. It is not only provision suppliers and credit card companies who are critical, but also those who generate demand for the hotel, such as travel/conference/booking agents, and tour/coach operators. They are often owed substantial amounts of commission payments and will threaten to cancel bookings and not use the hotel if debts are not paid.

Maturity period and end of receivership

Many suppliers are unaware that payment is guaranteed for any supplies authorised by a receiver out of the proceeds of the receivership. However, the challenge is not only to

case study continues ▶

case study continues

secure supplies, but also to obtain the best possible prices. Some suppliers who are owed money might be tempted to claw back their debt by raising their prices once the hotel is in receivership. Those who are owed commission payments might raise their percentage charges.

Normal contracts with suppliers can sometimes be deemed to be too onerous by receivers. Long-term contracts are usually shunned simply because if the hotel is sold, the new owners may not wish to take over any or all the existing contracts. As such, the receiver might have to pay the penalties of early termination, which in turn reduces the pay-out to creditors. Thus, contracts are carefully scrutinised and short-term contracts usually preferred.

Without knowing exactly the length of time a receivership is likely to last, there are a number of difficult decisions to be made. This becomes increasingly the case when the hotel is close to being sold. For example, should additional cutlery be purchased or hired, given that if the hotel is not sold within the next three months or so, it would be much cheaper to buy the equipment? Should the hotel join a purchasing consortium? If there is a joining fee of say, £500, is the receivership likely to last long enough to recoup the £500 plus in savings from various purchases?

The debenture holder

By appointing a receiver a debenture holder places a great deal of trust on the receiver and the management team. The relationship with the debenture holder is one which requires confidence, management skills, diplomacy and a thorough understanding of the operational and strategic issues facing the hotel, leisure and tourism industries. The debenture holder will rely on the advice of the receiver regarding

- investment decisions
- when to sell the hotel.

Investment decisions

A hotel which is placed in receivership has often been starved of any investment for some time. If the decision is made to continue trading the hotel, a certain level of investment is sometimes essential to improve standards and thus enhance profitability. The receiver has to convince the debenture holder that such investment is needed and justified. A debenture holder appoints a receiver to stem its losses, yet when investment is needed in a property, it could be that the debenture holder/bank worsens its position at the outset.

In assessing any investment, the receiver needs to take into account the urgency in operational terms of the required maintenance/investment. For more substantial levels of investment, the receiver should consider whether the pay-back can be achieved during the time of the receivership. This is a difficult question to answer when the length of receivership is not known precisely. Finally, will the proposed investment increase the value of the hotel?

case study continues ▶

case study continues

When to sell the hotel

When advising the debenture holder on the timing of the sale of the hotel, the receiver needs to consider two factors:

- Whether the continued operation of the hotel will achieve further improvements in profitability levels. Since the value of a hotel is often calculated on the basis of a multiple of earnings, once a stabilised level of trading has been achieved, the value of a hotel is unlikely to increase further.
- The cyclical nature of the industry, whereby the value of hotel properties moves in tandem with the state of the general economy.

Planning and licensing authorities

The challenge of dealing with the authorities usually arises when investment is needed to meet their requirements. Such investment often does not enhance the value of the hotel or the operational efficiency and does not improve the overall standard of the hotel. It could even be detrimental to the operation.

The manager at the Royal, for example, was informed that due to complaints regarding noise from local residents, strobe lights and a cut-off system needed to be installed in the main function room at the hotel. A cut-off system would mean that as soon as the back doors in the function room were opened, any noise from the disco would automatically be stopped. The manager felt that this would quickly lead to complaints from customers.

The doors were opened when the room became hot, because the air conditioning system was not powerful enough. The obvious solution was to replace the air conditioning system in the hotel, but the investment could not be justified and would not pay back within the period of the receivership.

Thus diplomatic negotiations were needed to delay major investment. It was agreed that careful monitoring by the duty manager would take place to ensure that the back doors remained closed during evening events and strobe lights were installed – the cheapest option.

Local residents

The challenge of dealing with local residents is often similar to the relationship with local authorities.

At the Royal there was the noise issue mentioned above, and one of parking. Diplomacy and negotiation were used to deal with local residents' complaints.

The previous owners/directors of the hotel

The relationship between the receiver and the previous owners/directors of the hotel is most relevant in the initial phase of a receivership in terms of the management of the hotel.

case study continues ▶

case study continues

Previous owners/directors can interfere, confuse staff and try and woo customers away from the hotel, particularly when they have other hotels, restaurants or facilities which have not been placed in administrative receivership.

The directors at the Royal came into the hotel the day after the hotel had gone into receivership and ordered drinks from the bar, signed for them and were preparing to leave when an agent from the receiver requested payment. Such situations can be difficult for staff, where directors can become quite aggressive and demand service from a young, part-time, inexperienced waiter, as they had been used to prior to receivership.

All staff should be informed at the outset of a receivership what the new procedures are and who is entitled to sign for food and drink.

The security of cash, assets and negotiable assets is one of the first issues a receiver addresses. Staff must be made aware that no assets leave the premises without the knowledge of the receiver's agent. Depending on the site and building, it may be necessary to employ a security firm in the initial days to secure the building and the physical assets.

It is necessary to establish who has keys and access and that the requisite control systems are in place. It might be appropriate to change certain locks.

Possibly even more challenging is when previous owners/directors cause confusion among customers. This was the case at the Royal, where the directors withdrew customer correspondence relating to future functions, wrote to customers advising them that their contracts were with the previous company and that their functions could be serviced elsewhere. The job of the receiver in trying to win back such bookings was difficult. There was also the possibility that people attending a function could walk in without the knowledge of the management since all the correspondence had been removed. The receivers exercised their powers and the correspondence was eventually returned, but only once confusion, anger, uncertainty and mistrust had been instilled among customers.

The Royal

How far can a receiver build up a healthy business, invest in it and motivate the staff when there are budget constraints, conflicts of short- versus long-term decisions, an atmosphere of uncertainty and an incessant image problem during the period of receivership?

The receivership of the Royal lasted one year and nine months. Many of the issues explored above were faced by the receivers in the course of this period. There were a few key factors which helped the receivers:

- The hotel had been run down and starved of any investment.

- The staff were demoralised and fighting to survive from one day to the next. They were offering discounts to functions when they paid early and in cash – such that the money could be used to pay for supplies such as food for that night's function. The cash was critical – it meant they could spend it before the directors were able to take it out of the business. They worked in this way because of their loyalty to the guests and their colleagues, but were deeply unhappy.

- Customer complaints increased because of maintenance faults, the cleanliness of the hotel and service. It was the management of the hotel who dealt with such

case study continues ▶

case study continues

complaints, not the directors. But the complaints usually related to areas outside the control of the management of the hotel.

● Recently there had been only minimal marketing undertaken.

● As time went on, the level of trade diminished.

When the receivers arrived and within a week agreed with the debenture holder that all the curtains and carpets in the public areas should be cleaned, essential maintenance work should be carried out and all chandeliers in the banqueting rooms should be cleaned, the staff noticed an immediate change. The receivers dealt with suppliers and when supplies were ordered they arrived. Payment was dealt with by the receivers. Complaints reduced significantly. When there were complaints, they were generally to do with what was under the control of the general manager and his staff. Staff motivation increased and was enhanced by a new incentive scheme introduced by the receivers. This was a turnover and profit based incentive. The marketing activity was stepped up.

In what was a heavily banqueting dominated business, the receivers increased the number of ethnic functions from a total of twelve when they took the hotel over to twenty-seven the following year (1996). Fifty-two were booked for 1997 and thirty-eight booked for 1998 when the hotel was sold in November 1996. The number of other functions also increased significantly: when the hotel was sold in 1996, there were only two Saturdays available for weddings in 1997. Forward bookings for 1998 and 1999 were also coming in. Confidence in the marketplace had clearly been re-established despite nearly two years' of receivership. Room occupancy levels increased from around 30% when the hotel went into receivership to around 65%. Average room rates had also increased from £38 to over £45 when the hotel was sold.

There were staff changes during the period of the receivership. Key appointments included the head chef and the front of house manager. The general manager left some nine months after the hotel had been put on the market, but three months before the hotel was actually sold. He was replaced by a temporary, but highly experienced manager. This period was particularly difficult for the receiver – trying to maintain the momentum that had been created throughout the receivership, when the staff were fully aware that the sale of the hotel was due to complete imminently.

The hotel was sold at a reasonable price, although well below that paid by the directors. Within two months of the sale, all key managers had left the hotel.

Summary

This chapter has focused on the two important issues of financial management and marketing in the hotel industry. It identified the key financial elements of revenue and costs within the hotel industry and related these points to a case study containing industry data on the London five star hotel market. The discussion then considered the Uniform System of Accounts for the hotel industry. The central importance of both price and yield management was illustrated with a commentary on both the theory and practical applications of these twin topics. The second half of this chapter related the principles of marketing to the hospitality industry and special emphasis was placed on the planning process. There was a detailed discussion of the issues involved in managing a hotel in receivership.

Further reading

- Barclays de Zoete Wedd (1993a) *BZW Hotel Conference: Prospects for the UK Hotel Industry*, London: BZW.
- Barclays de Zoete Wedd (1993b) *The Hotel Sector: Focus on the UK*, London: BZW.
- Brassington F. and Pettit S. (1997) *Principles of Marketing*, London: Pitman.
- Brotherton B. and Mooney S. (1992) 'Yield management: progress and prospects', *International Journal of Contemporary Management* 11(1).
- Fenton L.S., Fowler N.A. and Parkinson G.S. (1989) *Hotel Accounts and their Audit*, 2nd edn, London: Institute of Chartered Accountants.
- Fill C. (1995) *Marketing Communications*, Hemel Hempstead: Prentice Hall.
- Hankinson G. and Cowking P. (1993) *Branding in Action*, Maidenhead: McGraw-Hill.
- Kotas R. (1986) *Market Orientation in the Hotel and Catering Industry*, London: Surrey University Press.
- Kotler P., Armstrong G., Saunders J. and Wong V. (1996) *Principles of Marketing: The European Edition*, Hemel Hempstead: Prentice Hall.
- Kotler P., Bowen J. and Makens J. (1996) *Marketing for Hospitality and Tourism*, New York: Prentice Hall.
- McDonald M. and Dunbar I. (1995) *Market Segmentation*, London: Macmillan.
- Mudie P. and Cottam A. (1993) *The Management and Marketing of Services*, Oxford: Butterworth Heinemann.
- NEDC (1992) *Costs and Manpower Productivity in UK Hotels*, London: National Economic Development Committee.
- Orkin E.B. (1988) 'Boosting your bottom line with yield management', *Cornell Hotel and Restaurant Association Quarterly* 28(4): 52–6.
- Palmer A. (1994) *Principles of Services Marketing*, Maidenhead: McGraw-Hill.
- Teare R., Mazanec J.A., Crawford-Welch S. and Calver S. (1994) *Marketing in Hospitality and Tourism*, London: Cassell.
- Zeithaml V.A. and Bitner M.J. (1996) *Services Marketing*, Singapore: McGraw-Hill International.

Chapter Six

Accommodation Operations

Objectives

After reading this chapter you should be able to

- Consider the elements of the hotel operation at a number of market levels.
- Identify the nature of accommodation operations within both front office and reservations.
- Understand the nature of the guest cycle.
- Recognise the importance of human resource management.
- Highlight the importance of computer technology within accommodation operations.

Hotel categories

Hotel properties can be classified in terms of three basic service level categories:

- economy
- mid range
- luxury.

Economy

Economy hotels are a growing segment of the hotel industry. These properties focus on meeting the most basic needs of guests by providing clean, comfortable and inexpensive rooms. Economy hotels appeal primarily to budget-travellers who want rooms with all the amenities required for a comfortable stay but without the extras they do not really need or want to pay for. Low design and construction costs and low operating expenses are part of the reason why economy hotels can be profitable. Many economy properties do not provide full food and beverage service which means guests may need to eat at nearby restaurants. Also, these properties do not usually offer room service or many of the facilities found at mid range and luxury properties.

Mid range

Hotels offering mid-range service probably appeal to the largest segment of the travelling public. Mid-range service is modest but sufficient and the staffing level is adequate without trying to provide overly elaborate service. Guests likely to stay at these hotels are business travellers on expense accounts, tourists or families taking advantage of special rates. These hotels generally offer a full food and beverage service. The property may have a speciality restaurant, coffee shop and lounge that caters to local residents as well as hotel guests. Typical hotel accommodation features one room and adjacent bathroom, a king-size bed or double bed and desk, dresser, modular units and one or two chairs.

Luxury

Luxury hotels provide restaurants, lounges, exquisite décor, concierge services, various meeting rooms and private dining facilities. Such hotels are typified by the Savoy Group of Hotels based in London. Primary markets for hotels offering these services are top business executives and other wealthy people.

Nature of the hotel product

The traditional view common to most marketing theory regards a product as a single entity. This is unrealistic if applied to a hotel. A hotel at any market level is really a combination of products combined within a system. In order to compete effectively the manager constantly needs to adapt and evolve the product under control in order to maintain customer interest.

Augmenting a product is the additional benefits and services which the product will provide. It will add to the core product of accommodation in order to enhance the product experience and enhance the customer's perception of receiving value for money. The provision of a leisure complex can be seen to fulfil these criteria (further discussion of leisure facilities is in Chapter 11). It may be that as consumer expectations change, the leisure club becomes an integral part of the expected product bundle.

The provision of these facilities can be considered to represent added value to the hotel product. With some companies it could be considered an essential product attribute. By emphasising both the tangible and intangible benefits of a hotel there is an extension to the traditional core product of accommodation. Such an approach can therefore lead to the achievement of an effective and competitive advantage.

Rooms division

The core product in any hotel is accommodation and the main operating department is in many hotels referred to as the rooms division. In large hotels the rooms division is often organised along functional lines with different employees handling separate operational areas. This sectional approach provides enhanced internal control of the operation and is to a great extent reflected in the design of the Uniform System of Accounts (see Chapter 5). Each area is responsible for only a segment of the guest's stay. This separation of duties may not be practical in a small hotel where it is common for one or two individuals to be responsible for all front desk operations.

Mission statement

All organisations, hotels included, must have a reason for existence. A mission statement defines the unique purpose that sets the hotel apart from other hotels and will differ from the hotel categories just discussed. It expresses the underlying philosophy that gives meaning and direction to the hotel's actions. Once the hotel has defined its mission and formulated it in a written statement, it should set objectives which are the ends in order to effectively carry out the hotel's mission. They should be specific and measurable. For example, specific objectives involving front office operations might include the following:

- Increase the hotel's average occupancy level above the previous years level by 2%.
- Increase the amount of repeat guest business by 10%.
- Reduce the average time it takes guests to check in and check out by two minutes.
- Reduce the number of guest complaints by 20%.

The rooms division is composed of departments and functions which play an essential role in providing the services guests expect during a hotel stay. In most hotels the rooms division generates more revenue than other divisions.

Front office

The front office is one of the departments within the rooms division. Front office is the most visible department in a hotel with the greatest amount of guest contact. Front desk, cashier, mail and information sections of the front office are located in the busiest area of the hotel's lobby. The front desk itself is the focal point of activity within the front office. Guests are registered, assigned rooms and checked out at the front desk.

Reservations

The reservations function is responsible for receiving and processing reservations for accommodation in the future. The reservation section must maintain accurate reservation records and closely track availability to ensure that no date is overbooked. Close co-ordination with the sales and marketing division is essential when large groups are booked into a hotel.

Telephone switchboard

The telephone switchboard function maintains a complex communications network similar to that of any large company. The hotel switchboard may have responsibilities beyond merely answering calls and connecting them to the appropriate extension. When long-distance calls are routed and priced through the switchboard, charges must be relayed to a front office cashier and posted to the proper guest account.

Housekeeping

Housekeeping is perhaps the most important front office support department (see pp. 153–5). The housekeeping department inspects rooms for sale, cleans the occupied and vacated rooms and co-ordinates rooms status with the front office. In some hotels the housekeeping function is considered an independent division from the rooms division.

The housekeeping department often has more personnel than other rooms division departments. Normally an executive housekeeper is in charge of the department and may be assisted by an assistant housekeeper, inspectors, room attendants and laundry managers. Room attendants are assigned to specific sections of the hotel and may be asked to clean from eight to eighteen rooms a day depending on the level of service expected, the room size and the task required. If the hotel has its own laundry, housekeeping departmental staff take care of the property's linen. To ensure speedy, efficient rooming of guests in vacant and ready rooms, the housekeeping and front office departments must inform each other promptly of any changes in a rooms status or availability. Close coordination and co-operation between the two departments help ensure guest satisfaction.

Uniformed service

Within the rooms division there is the uniformed service, i.e. parking attendants, door attendants, porters, limousine drivers and bell persons. Uniformed service personnel have a great degree of contact with guests. They greet and help guests to the front desk and to their rooms. At the end of the stay they take guests to the cashier, out of the front door and to their means of transportation. Such services are common in European hotels and resorts, but their introduction in American hotels is a relatively recent development. The basic task of a uniformed service is to serve as a guest liaison with both hotel and non-hotel services. In a sense, its function is an extension of the role of a front desk clerk. Some hotels find that front desk agents are too busy with other tasks to provide appropriate personal service.

Night audit

The night auditor checks the accuracy of front office accounting records and compiles a daily summary of hotel financial data. Traditionally this task is conducted at the close of the business on the hotel's night shift. The night auditor

- posts the room charges to guest accounts
- processes guest charge vouchers and credit cards
- posts any guest charge purchase transactions not posted during the day by the front office cashier
- verifies all accountings, postings and balances
- monitors the current status of coupon, discount and other promotional programmes
- summarises the results of the hotel operations in order to report to management.

The auditor tracks room revenues, occupancy percentages and other front office statistics and prepares a summary of cash, cheque and credit card activities. The data reflect the hotel's financial performance for the day. The hotel's accounting division use audit data prepared in the front office to determine the property's daily profile and report its findings to management. In many hotels, the night auditor is actually an employee from the accounting division.

The guest cycle

Guest transactions during a stay at a hotel determine the flow of business through the property. The flow of business can be divided into a four-stage guest cycle:

- pre-arrival
- arrival
- occupancy
- departure

Pre-arrival

During the pre arrival stage the guest chooses a hotel to patronise. This choice can be affected by a variety of factors including previous experiences with the hotel, advertisements, recommendations, location, etc. The guest's choice may also be influenced by the ease of making reservations and the reservation clerk's description of the hotel and its facilities, room rates and amenities. The attitude, efficiency and knowledge of the front office staff may influence a caller's decision to stay at a particular hotel. The proper handling of reservations information can be critical to the success of the property. If a reservation can be accepted as requested, the reservations clerk creates a reservations record. An effective reservations system helps maximise room sales by accurately monitoring room availability and forecasting rooms revenue. By analysing reservation information, front office management can develop an understanding of the hotel's reservation pattern.

Arrival

The arrival stage of the guest cycle includes registration and rooming functions. When the guest arrives at the hotel he or she establishes a business relationship with the hotel through the front office staff. It is the staff's task to clarify the nature of the guest–hotel relationship and the expectations of the hotel and the guest. A registration completed either as part of the pre-registration activity or at check-in is essential to an efficient front office operation. It can cover method of payment, planned length of stay and any special guest needs along with the assignment for room and a rate for each guest. The front office desk must learn of changes in the housekeeping status of a room as soon as possible to allow maximisation of room sales. Once it has been determined that a guest will be accommodated, the guest's method of payment becomes an important concern. The registration process plays an essential role in the guest accounting cycle by gathering information concerning payment for services rendered. Whether the guest will use cash, a cheque, a credit card or an alternative method of payment, front office should take measures to ensure eventual payment.

Occupancy

Throughout the occupancy stage front office represents the hotel to the guests. At the centre of front office activity, the front desk is responsible for co-ordinating guest services. Front office guest services may include providing the guests with information, equipment, supplies or services. A major front office objective is to satisfy guest needs in a way that will encourage a return visit. Another primary objective during occupancy is the issue of security. The occupancy stage of the guest cycle also produces a variety of transactions affecting guests and the hotels financial accounts. Most of these transactions will be processed according to front office account, posting and auditing procedures. The largest single guest account charge is usually the room itself. Additional expenses can be charged to the guest's account if the guest has established an acceptable credit at the front desk during the arrival stage. Many hotels limit the amount which guests can charge to their accounts. Guest accounts must be carefully and continually monitored to ensure that this limit is not exceeded. The night audit process is intended to review periodically and verify the accuracy and completeness of the front office accounting records. Computerised front office accounting systems may allow audits to be conducted at any time during the day, but many computerised properties still follow traditions and do it at night. Regardless of how or when it is performed, room charges are posted to guest accounts as part of the audit routine.

Departure

The fourth phase of the guest cycle is departure. Both the guest services and guest accounting aspects of the guest cycle are completed during this phase. The penultimate element of the guest service is checking the guest out of the hotel and creating a guest history record. The final element of guest accounting is settlement of the account. Once the guest has checked out, the rooms status is updated and the housekeeping department is advised. One primary concern of the front office during check-out is to determine whether the guest was satisfied with the stay and encouraging the guest to return to the hotel.

In terms of sales and marketing, the more information the hotel has about its guests, the better it can anticipate and serve their needs and develop marketing strategies to increase both revenue and profitability. Hotels often use expired registration cards as a basis for a guests history file. This information allows the hotel to better understand its clientele and provides a solid base for strategic marketing.

Front office and new technology

Integral to the development of the front office has been the introduction of technology. The technology used in this operating department for record keeping and equipment has evolved in three stages:

- non-automated or manual
- semi-automated or electro-mechanical
- fully automated and computer based.

Most hotels are fully automated with front office computerised record keeping. Computer systems designed for use in the hospitality industry were first introduced in the early 1970s. These initial systems tended to be expensive and were therefore attractive to only the largest hotel properties. During the following decade, computer equipment became less expensive, more compact and easier to operate. The development of versatile PCs provided the impetus for system vendors to approach smaller hotel properties. In the 1980s computer systems appeared cost-effective to hotels of all sizes.

At each stage of the guest cycle the influence of computer technology can be seen. The reservations module of an in-house computer system may directly interface with a central reservation network and automatically block rooms according to a predetermined pattern. The reservations module may also automatically generate letters of confirmation and pre-registration activities. The module may also generate lists of expected arrivals, occupancy and revenue forecasts, and a variety of informative reports. At the arrival stage, guest information is either copied from the computer reservation record or late arrival guests entered by the front desk agent. The guest may then be presented with a computer prepared registration card for verification and signature. The installation of on-line credit card authorisation terminals enables front desk personnel to receive and approve credit limits.

Throughout the occupancy stage, guests charge services consumed at revenue outlets, with the charge electronically transferred to the front desk and automatically posted to the proper account. Instantaneous postings, simultaneous guest accounts and departmental entries and continuous trial balances free the night auditor to spend the time auditing rather than just balancing guest accounts.

On departure the guest is presented with a neatly printed electronic folio. Depending on the method of settlement, the computer system automatically posts transactions to appropriate guest and hotel accounts. Once the guest account is settled and the postings are complete, guest information is used to create a guest history record.

Computer applications

Most chain hotels participate in computer-based central reservations systems. When the destination property uses a front office computer system, its reservations module can receive data sent directly from the central reservation system. An updated expected arrivals list can be produced just prior to the day's registration.

In any computerised system, front desk employees simply enter the room's number at a computer systems terminal and the current status of the room appears immediately on the terminal's display screen. Once the room has been cleaned and ready for occupancy, the housekeeping staff changes the room status by means of a terminal located in the housekeeping work area. Changes in room status are immediately communicated to the front desk. Management of reservations, room management and guest accounting systems will allow the generation of reports showing the day's expected arrivals, the number of rooms available for occupancy, and a combination of reservations and room management data. In addition to generating reports, this management of information serves as the central link between front and back office computer systems.

It is possible to implement front and back office software packages independently of each other. However, integrated front and back office systems offer the hotel the full range of control over all operational areas from room sales and payroll to guest and non-guest account analysis. An integrated system cannot produce complete financial statements unless all the required data are stored somewhere in the system's memory. The back office system's generation of reports depends on the front office systems collection of data. Several back office application modules are available including:

- An accounts receivable module which monitors guest accounts and account billing and collection when integrated with the front office guest accounting module.
- An accounts payable module which tracks the hotel's purchases and helps the hotel maintain sufficient cash flow to satisfy its debts.
- A payroll accounting module which processes such data as time and attendance records, pay distribution and tax.

- A financial reporting module which helps the hotel develop a chart of accounts in order to produce balance sheets, income statements and transactional analysis reports.

Other computer applications are available to a fully automated hotel property. Common interfaces include:

- a point-of-sales system which allows guest account transactions to be quickly transmitted from remote points of sale to the front desk for account folio posting
- a telephone call accounting system which directs prices and tracks guest room telephone use for resale and posting to guest accounts
- an electronic locking system which may interface with rooms management modules to provide enhanced guest security.

Sources of reservation

There are various reservation market sources within the hospitality industry. The four most common sources of reservation transaction are

- central reservation systems
- intersell agencies
- property direct reservations
- group reservations.

Central reservation systems

A large proportion of hotel properties belong to one or more central reservation systems. Industry wide, over one-quarter of all reservation transactions use central reservation systems. There are two basic types of systems – affiliate networks and non-affiliate networks. An affiliate reservation network is a hotel chain reservation system in which all participating properties are contractually related. Chain hotels link their operation to streamline and process reservations, and to reduce overall system costs. A non-affiliate reservations network is a subscription system designed to connect independent non-chain properties. Non-affiliate reservation networks enable independent hotel operators to enjoy many of the same benefits as chain affiliated operators. Like an affiliate reservation network, a non-affiliate network usually assumes responsibility for advertising its service. A central reservations office typically deals direct with the public by means of a free telephone number. Many of these systems use computers to connect the central systems office with member properties.

Intersell agencies

An intersell agency is a central reservations system that contracts to handle more than one product line. Intersell agencies typically handle reservation services for airline companies, car rentals and hotel properties. In this sense the system is taking 'a one call does it all approach'. Although intersell agencies typically channel their rooms reservation requests through a central reservation system, they may also be able to communicate directly with individual destination properties.

Property direct reservations

A large proportion of reservation transactions are handled directly by the hotel. These are described as property direct. Depending on the volume of direct customer contact at the property the hotel may staff its own reservation department. This department is responsible for handling all direct requests for accommodation, monitoring good communication links with central reservation systems and intersell agencies and maintaining updated room availability status reports.

Group reservations

Group reservations can involve a variety of contacts, i.e. meeting suppliers, convention bureaux, tour operators and travel agents. Group reservations typically involve intermediary agents and require special care. Usually when a group selects a hotel, its representative deals with the hotel's sales division. If space is available, an agreed number of rooms is blocked off and set aside for the group's members.

Housekeeping tasks

One section of the rooms division already mentioned is housekeeping. This essential department will now be considered in greater depth.

Efficiently managed housekeeping departments ensure the cleanliness, maintenance and aesthetic appeal of any hotel property. The tasks performed by housekeeping departments are critical to the smooth and daily operation of any hotel. Classifying hotels into types is not easy since hotels do not fit into any single well-defined category. The size and service level of the property determine the most important characteristics of the housekeeping section of the rooms division. The levels of housekeeping service offered by hotels vary tremendously across the whole of the industry.

Within the rooms division, housekeeping's primary communications are with the front office department, specifically with the front desk area. In most hotels the front desk clerk is not allowed to assign guest rooms until the rooms have been cleaned, inspected and released by the housekeeping department. Typically rooms are recycled for sale according to the following process.

Occupancy report

Each night a front desk clerk produces an occupancy report. The occupancy report lists rooms occupied that night and indicates those clients expected to check out the following morning. The executive housekeeper picks up this list early the next morning and schedules the occupied rooms for cleaning. These rooms are then available for arriving guests. At the end of the shift the housekeeping department prepares a housekeeping status report based on a physical check of each room in the property. This report indicates the current housekeeping status of each room. It is compared with the front desk occupancy report and any discrepancies are brought to the attention of the front office manager. Rooms status discrepancies can seriously affect a property's ability to satisfy guest requirements and maximise room revenue. To ensure efficient rooming of guests, housekeeping and the front office must inform each other of changes in room status.

Promptly notifying the front desk of the housekeeping status of rooms is a tremendous aid in getting early arriving guests registered, especially during high occupancy or sold out periods. Close co-ordination and co-operation are essential.

Computerised rooms status system

In a computerised rooms status system, housekeeping and the front desk often have instantaneous access to rooms status information.

When a guest checks out, a front desk clerk enters the departure into a computer terminal, housekeeping is alerted that the room needs cleaning through a remote terminal located in the housekeeping department. Next the housekeeping attendants clean the room and notify the housekeeping department when it is ready for inspection. Once the room is inspected, housekeeping enters this information into its departmental terminal. This informs the front office computer that the room is available for sale.

The problem in promptly reporting housekeeping status to the front office can be eliminated if the computer system is directly connected to the guest room telephone system. With such a network, a supervisor can inspect the room to determine its readiness for sale and then enter a designated code on the room telephone to change the room status in the hotel's computer system. No one needs to answer the phone since the computer automatically receives the relay and there is little chance for error. Within seconds, the room's updated status can be displayed on the screen of a front desk computer terminal. This procedure can significantly reduce not only the number of guests forced to wait for room assignment but also the length of their wait.

Team work between housekeeping and the front office is essential to daily hotel operations. The more familiar housekeeping and front office personnel are with each other's procedures, the smoother relationships will be between the two departments.

Maintenance

In some operations, housekeeping, engineering and maintenance personnel generally report to the same departmental manager. This makes a great deal of sense because these functional areas have similar goals and methods and must have a close working relationship. The housekeeping department often takes the first step in relation to maintenance functions for which engineering is ultimately responsible. There are three kinds of maintenance activities:

- routine maintenance
- preventive maintenance
- scheduled maintenance.

Routine maintenance

Routine maintenance activities are those which relate to the general upkeep of the property, occur on a regular, daily or weekly basis and require relatively minimal training or skills. These are maintenance activities which occur outside a formal work order system and for which no specific maintenance records are kept. Examples include sweeping carpets, washing floors, cleaning readily accessible windows, cleaning guest rooms and replacing lightbulbs. Many of these routine maintenance activities are carried out by the housekeeping department. Proper care of many surfaces and materials by housekeeping personnel is the first step in the overall maintenance programme for the property's furniture and fixtures.

Preventive maintenance

This maintenance consists of three parts:

- inspection
- minor corrections
- work order initiation.

For many areas within the hotel, inspections are performed by housekeeping personnel in the normal course of their duties. For example, room attendants and inspectors may regularly check guest rooms for leaking taps, cracked fixtures and other items which may call for action by engineering staff. Such maintenance protects the physical plant and contributes to guest satisfaction. Communication between housekeeping and engineering should be efficient so that the most minor repairs can be handled while the room attendant is cleaning the guest room. In some properties, a full-time maintenance person may be assigned to inspect guest rooms and to perform the necessary repairs, adjustments or replacements.

Scheduled maintenance

Preventive maintenance by its nature sometimes identifies problems beyond the scope of minor correction. These problems are brought to the attention of engineering through the work order system. The necessary work is then scheduled by the building engineer. This type of work is often referred to as scheduled maintenance activities, which are initiated at the property based on a formal work order or similar document. Work orders are a key element in the communication between housekeeping and engineering. In many properties work orders are numbered in three-part forms. Each part of the form is colour coded for its recipient. For example, when a member of the housekeeping department fills out a work order form, one copy is sent to the executive housekeeping and two copies to engineering. The chief engineer keeps one copy and gives the other to the tradesperson assigned to the repair. The individual completing the task indicates the number of hours required to complete the work, any parts or supplies required and other relevant information. When the job is completed a copy of the tradesperson's completed work order is sent to the housekeeper. If this copy is not returned within the appropriate amount of time, housekeeping issues another work order which signals engineering to provide a status report on the requested repair.

Equipment

Engineering generally keeps data cards and history records on all equipment operated by housekeeping personnel. Equipment data cards contain basic information about pieces of equipment. This information can include technical data, manufacturers' information, cost, special instructions, warranty information and references to other information as well. Equipment history records, detail the inspection and maintenance work performed on a given piece of equipment. Many properties have computerised these recording functions making it easier for the executive housekeeper to retrieve pertinent information when requesting replacement or new equipment items.

Planning and organising the housekeeping department

The range of duties and responsibilities of housekeepers of various sizes and types of properties vary enormously: many of the housekeeping management functions at small hotels may be carried out by the general manager. In the case of chain affiliated properties, many housekeeping management functions are performed by staff at corporate headquarters. This leaves the task of implementing standardised procedures to the general managers and head housekeepers at individual properties.

Inventory lists

Planning is probably the executive housekeeper's most important management function. It starts with creating an inventory list of all items within each area that will need the housekeeper's attention. These lists are the basis for developing cleaning procedures, training plans and inspection checklists. Inventory lists are bound to be long and difficult since most properties offer several different types of rooms. Separate inventory lists may be needed for each room type.

Frequency schedules

Frequency schedules indicate how often items on the inventory lists are to be cleaned or maintained. Items that must be cleaned on a daily or weekly basis become part of a routine cleaning cycle and are incorporated into standard work procedures. Other items are inspected on a daily or weekly basis but they become part of a general deep cleaning programme and thus scheduled as special cleaning projects. Items on an area's frequency schedule that are made part of housekeeping's general cleaning programme should be transferred to a calendar plan and scheduled as a special cleaning project. The calendar plan guides the executive housekeeper in scheduling the appropriate staff to perform the necessary work.

The housekeeper must take into account a number of factors when scheduling general cleaning of guest rooms or other special projects. For example, whenever possible, days marked for guest room general cleaning should coincide with low occupancy periods. Also, the general cleaning programme must be flexible in relation to the activities of other departments. For example, if the engineering department schedules extensive repair work for several guest rooms, the executive housekeeper should make every effort to co-ordinate a general cleaning of these rooms with engineering's timetable. Careful planning will produce good results for the hotel with the least possible inconvenience to guests or to other departments.

Performance standards

The housekeeper develops performance standards by deciding what must be done in order to clean or maintain the major items within an area. Standards are required levels of performance that establish the quality of the work that must be done. Performance standards state

- what must be done
- how the job must be done.

One of the primary objectives in planning the work of the housekeeping department is to ensure that all employees carry out their cleaning tasks in a consistent manner. The key to consistency is the performance standards that the housekeeper develops, communicates and manages. When performance standards are not properly developed, effectively communicated and consistently managed, the productivity of the housekeeping department suffers. This is because employees will not be performing their tasks in the most efficient and effective manner. The most important aspect of developing standards is gaining consensus on how cleaning and other tasks are to be carried out. Consensus can be achieved by having those individuals who actually perform the task, contribute to the standards that are eventually adopted by the department.

Performance standards are communicated through ongoing training programmes but however well written, standards are useless unless they are applied. The only way to get standards into the workplace is through effective training programmes. After communicating performance standards through ongoing training activities, the executive housekeeper must manage those standards.

Productivity standards

While performance standards establish the expected quality of the work to be done, productivity standards determine the acceptable quantity of work to be done by departmental employees. The key issue here is how long should it take for a housekeeping employee to perform an assigned task according to the department's performance standard.

Productivity standards must be determined in order to properly staff the department within the limitations established by the hotel's operating budget plan. Since performance standards vary in relation to the unique needs and requirements of each hotel, it is impossible to identify productivity standards that would apply across the board to every housekeeping department. As the duties of room attendants vary widely along economy service, mid-range service and luxury hotels the productivity standards for room attendants will also vary. Housekeepers must know how long it will take a housekeeping employee to perform the major tasks identified on the cleaning frequency schedules, such as guest room cleaning. Once this information is known, productivity standards can be developed.

The challenge is to balance performance standards effectively with productivity standards. A concern for productivity may not necessarily lower performance standards, it can sharpen and define current work methods and procedures. If, for instance, room attendants are constantly returning to the housekeeping area for cleaning and guest room supplies there is something wrong with the way they set up and stock their carts. Wasted motion is wasted time, and wasted time depletes the most important and most expensive resource of the housekeeping department – labour.

Equipment and supply inventory

After planning what must be done and how the tasks are to be performed, the executive housekeeper must ensure that employees have the necessary equipment and supplies to get their jobs done.

The housekeeper plans appropriate inventory levels for the amount of equipment and quantities of supplies needed for the housekeeping staff to meet the performance and productivity standards of the department. This ensures smooth daily housekeeping activities and forms the basis for planning an effective purchasing system, which must consistently maintain the required amounts of items stored within inventories controlled by the housekeeping department. Essentially the housekeeper is responsible for two types of inventories – recyclable and non-recyclable items.

Recyclable items are used many times during the course of hotel operations. Non-recyclable items are consumed or used up during routine activities of the housekeeping department. Due to limited storage facilities and the management's desire not to tie up cash in overstocked inventories, the executive housekeeper must establish reasonable inventory levels of both recyclable and non-recyclable items. Recycled inventories include linen, most equipment items and some guest supplies. Recycled equipment items include room attendant carts, vacuum cleaners and carpet shampooers. Recycled guest supplies include such items as irons, ironing boards and cots that guests may need during the course of their stay. Non-recycled inventories include cleaning supplies, guest room supplies such as bath soap and guest amenities which may range from toothbrushes, shampoos and conditioners to scented bath powders and colognes.

Since these items are used up in the course of operations, inventory levels are closely tied to the purchase ordering system used at the hotel. A purchase ordering system for non-recyclable inventory items establishes a number that is based on two figures; a minimum quantity and a maximum quantity.

Job lists and job descriptions

If the housekeeper has planned the work of the housekeeping department properly, organising the department's staff becomes a relatively straightforward matter.

Housekeepers use information gathered from earlier planning activities to identify the number and types of positions that are needed, and to develop job lists and job descriptions for these positions.

Job list

A job list identifies a task that must be performed by an individual occupying a specific position within the department. The tasks on the job list should reflect the total job responsibilities of the employee. However, the list should not be a detailed breakdown of the procedures that the employee will follow in carrying out each task. The job list must simply state what the employee must be able to do in order to perform the job.

Job description

Some types of job descriptions simply add information from the appropriate job lists. This information may include reporting relationships, additional responsibilities and working conditions as well as equipment and materials to be used in the course of the job. To be effective, job descriptions must be tailored to the specific operational needs of individual hotels. Therefore the form and content of job descriptions will vary among housekeeping departments.

Since job descriptions may become inappropriate as work assignments change, they should be reviewed at least once a year for possible revision. Properly written job descriptions can ease employee anxiety by specifying responsibilities, requirements and peculiarities of the job. Employees should be involved in writing and revising job descriptions for their positions. All employees of the housekeeping department should be given a copy of the job description for their own position.

Job breakdown

Job lists and job descriptions form the basis for developing job breakdowns, i.e. specific step-by-step procedures for accomplishing a task. They also provide the elements for training plans and effective performance evaluation.

> ### Case Study: Energy management in the international hotel industry

In many areas of the rooms division an important consideration for management is the control of energy. This matter will now be considered with a case study focusing on energy management in the international hotel industry.

This case study presents a commentary on three energy efficiency issues in the international hotel sector:

- heating, ventilation and air conditioning
- lighting
- renewable energy sources.

It does not deal with wider environmental issues which are covered in Chapter 12. However, many writers about environmental or green issues, particularly environmental management, include within that topic the coverage of energy.

Heating, ventilation and air conditioning

Heating, ventilating and air conditioning (HVAC) is a very wide subject; the literature on HVAC is vast. Only some of it deals with energy efficiency issues, and only some of it applies to the hotel industry. Literature dealing specifically with energy efficiency of HVAC systems in hotels is quite manageable, but narrowing it down in this way has the disadvantage that some important aspects of HVAC systems are not dealt with in the specific context of hotels. For example, few writers consider the maintenance of hotel HVAC systems, even though maintenance is an important aspect of minimising fuel waste in buildings.

Heating boilers

Most UK hotels are heated using a low pressure hot water (LPHW) system. Water is heated in one or more boilers that are often gas-fired but may alternatively use oil, and then pumped around the building at low pressure to radiators and other heat emitters. Generally, the same boiler provides hot water to one or more calorifiers which store hot water and supply it to taps and showers. The potential for wasting part of the fuel which is burnt exists in most of the elements of these systems. If the boiler is not maintained adequately, its combustion efficiency may drop over time and should be regularly checked in accordance with good maintenance practice. Most systems of this type are sized to provide adequate heat during cold mid-winter weather when they operate at near-maximum output and at their highest efficiency. But at other times they need to be controlled to ensure that their heat output matches the heat requirements of the building.

case study continues ▶

case study continues

In spring and autumn for example, many hotels are overheated and guests are likely to open windows to reduce the temperature, resulting in heat being wasted.

The products of combustion from a boiler have to be exhausted to the outside, taking with them some of the heat output from the boiler. Condensing boilers extract heat from exhaust gases and are therefore more energy efficient than conventional boilers.

Air conditioning systems

Air conditioning should not be confused with mechanical ventilation. Ventilation provides fresh air using fans, vents and ducts. The fresh air may be pre-heated before being delivered to the rooms it serves. Air conditioning, by contrast, implies cooling. Relatively few UK hotels use air conditioning in guest rooms, but it is often used for some of the public areas, such as lounges and restaurants. Air conditioning may be provided by a centralised system or by individual air conditioning units.

Thermal storage for air conditioning systems involves generating cooling capacity at off-peak times and storing it for future use. It is claimed that ice storage has an advantage over chilled water. One example is the use of thermal storage at a complex in San Diego including a twenty-seven-storey hotel. Another example is the use of ice thermal storage in a retrofit to an air conditioning system at the Worthington Hotel in Fort Worth, USA. Here a system incorporating three heat pump chiller packages and seven ice-on-pipe thermal storage tanks were modified by deleting the heat pump mode and enhancing the ice storage system; substantial energy savings were reported. These units are commonly found in US hotel rooms placed under the windows. They are through-the-wall combination heating/cooling units. Although they have been around for decades, they are experiencing a new phase of growth in popularity for applications in hotels, motels and other commercial buildings where zone control is important. They offer improved energy efficiency, greater dependability and quieter operation. Properly applied equipment, electronically controlled by a building energy management system, could help air-conditioning units rid themselves of their cheap hit-and-miss image.

At the Swindon Holiday Inn hotel, individual packaged thermal units were costed and found to be justifiable on capital cost grounds without a significant running cost penalty when compared with four-pipe fan coil units. There is, in addition, a tempered warm air supply into each guest room. All 160 guest rooms are heated and cooled on an individual basis using these units.

Heat pumps

Heat pumps operate on the same principle as the domestic refrigerator. They transfer heat (or cool) from one place to another. They can extract the latent heat (even from something which appears to be already cool like a lake) and use that heat to warm something else, like a hotel interior. Heat pumps can be run in reverse too, to cool a hotel interior and transfer the heat to a lake. For instance the use of heat pumps in three Norwegian hotels deliver heat for room heating and water heating and are used for cooling in the summer. The heat sources are brackish water, sea water and extract air. A UK demon-

case study continues ▶

stration project employed air-to-water heat pumps in six public houses. They were used to keep the cellars cool and the heat extracted used to heat the domestic hot water supply.

In Hawaii conventional central service water-heating systems were replaced by central heat pump water-heating systems in a number of buildings including fifteen hotels. Monitoring of about twenty installations was undertaken by the electricity utility and used to assess the savings. Payback periods for the capital costs of the heat pumps were reported as reasonable.

Heat recovery

Heat recovery systems extract heat from hot water or warm air and use the heat extracted to warm some other air or water. Compared with the active mechanical systems used in a heat pump, they are passive systems so they are not reversible, but they do not have the running costs associated with the compressor used in a heat pump. Examples of heat recovery are mostly from Germany, but there are older examples from Switzerland.

Hollow floor blocks

Hollow floor blocks can be used as a means of cooling a building. The blocks absorb heat during the day when the building gets hot and thereby limit peak temperatures. By mechanically ventilating the hollow cores the blocks can be cooled. Their use is predominantly in offices but they have been used in hotels.

Laundries

Even though laundries use energy and water intensively, there appear to be very few publications about energy efficient appliances or practices. Unless the laundry operation is controlled, costs rise as gallons of water go down the drain. Laundry equipment manufacturers are introducing continuous batch washing machines whose designs feature a split valves system which allows water re-usage. Water consumption can be reduced from 2.5 gallons per pound of laundry to a claimed value of 1 gallon. There is also the availability of energy saving equipment which measures when laundry is dry so over-run time can be reduced.

Lighting

The efficiency with which electricity is used in hotels depends, broadly, upon three main factors:

- availability and exploitation in practice of natural daylight
- lighting controls, including whether they ensure that lighting is used only when and to the extent it is required

case study continues ▶

case study continues

- efficiency of the electrical components of the lighting systems – lamps, ballasts and luminaries (lamp holders), including the maintenance regime.

Maximising daylight

These matters of lighting are primarily a management and operating issue. In order to maximise the use of daylight, windows should be kept unobstructed by nets, curtains and furniture; light colours should be used to maximise reflections from wall and ceilings. Hotel management should establish a routine for checking the use of artificial lighting periodically and if sufficient natural daylight is available, switch lights off completely or reduce the quantity of artificial lighting. Alternatively, photocells or other sensors can be used. In new build, there are a number of opportunities to ensure daylight can be used as far as possible. Windows, roof lights and other glazed apertures should be

- positioned in relation to the rooms they serve
- have their proportions set
- be sized such that they give a high level, and an even distribution, of illumination.

Illumination should be checked using appropriate design tools, of which there are many available. The risks of glare and solar overheating should also be assessed.

Lighting controls

There are four basic methods of controlling lighting:

- daylight linked control
- time based control
- occupancy linked control
- localised switching.

Lighting control systems usually combine a number of these four strategies. It is important that staff are informed and trained about the use and operation of these systems if they are to be effective in use.

Photoelectric cells may be used for switching or for dimming. The cells may sense daylight outside or the light available inside the space. Photoelectric switching causes lights to be turned on and off depending on conditions; time delays prevent repeated rapid switching. Photoelectric dimming is less obtrusive and adjusts the artificial lighting to top up daylighting as required. Signals are transmitted to the luminaries from, for example, a building management system or a more simple timing device. Lights are switched on and off at pre-set times. Local override ensures lights can be restored when needed.

Occupancy linking is achieved using sensors which can detect movement or noise in a space. The sensors bring on lighting when occupancy is detected and switch off when they have failed to detect an occupant for a set time.

Localised switching is important where only part of a large space needs to be lit artifi-

case study continues ▶

cially, either because other parts are unoccupied or because daylight there is adequate. It is also important to ensure that local switches are clearly labelled so that any unnecessary lighting can be switched off unobtrusively leaving other lights unaffected.

Lighting systems

There have been major innovations since the mid-1980s in the types of lamps available. In particular the advent of compact fluorescent lamps with their far greater ratio of light output to kilowatt hours of electricity consumed offers the potential for considerable reductions in electricity consumption due to lighting. Compact fluorescent lamps are available in a wide range with some having integral control gear and are intended as replacements for tungsten lamps. Where new luminaries are being installed it is more cost-effective to use a lamp with separate control gear, since the life of the control gear is longer than that of the lamp itself. Compact fluorescent lamps are particularly suitable in bulkheads and other similar fittings used in corridors. However, there are decorative fittings which allow them to be used in guest rooms and other front of house locations.

The colour rendering of compact fluorescent, once believed to be inferior to tungsten, is continually being improved. Although their initial costs are higher, the rated life is around eight times longer, reducing the frequency with which they have to be replaced, with a consequential saving in staff time and in the storage of replacement lamps. Furthermore, their light output per watt is higher than tungsten, so less electricity is needed to achieve the same level of illumination.

In addition to these changes, there are more energy efficient lamps available suitable for standard linear fluorescent luminaries. Increasingly energy efficient tungsten halogen lamps with good colour rendering are available for decorative interior lighting, and for external lighting, metal halide and high pressure sodium lights are available. Finally, the efficiency of luminaries (lamp holders) is also improving, for example, increased reflection to direct the light to where it is required.

Compact fluorescent lamps were installed in the Grand Hyatt Hotel in San Francisco where $48,000 was invested with a pay-back of one year; a rebate from the electricity utility was also obtained. Marriott Hotels have also retrofitted low energy lighting wherever it is cost-effective and aesthetically acceptable to do so.

Renewable energy sources

Renewable energy sources, as applied to hotels, may comprise

- use of solar power (and/or wind)
- geothermal energy (hot rocks beneath the earth's surface)
- waste incineration.

The potential use of solar power in hotels received some coverage in the early to mid-1980s. Examples include the solar restoration of a hotel in Athens, hot water from the sun in Milan, and harnessing of solar power in a hotel in Cambridge. These three examples describe the use of solar energy for two possible purposes:

case study continues

- space heating (using so-called passive systems, in which the orientation of the building and the size and form of windows allows benefits to be had from solar gains).
- hot water heating (so-called active systems with water circulating through panels, typically roof-mounted, exposed to solar radiation).

One hotel in the US Virgin Islands was built with recycled and reusable materials and is powered by solar and wind power. An alternative way of exploiting solar energy is its conversion into electricity using photovoltaic cells. Two Accor-owned UK hotels in Southampton, the Novotel and Ibis, have been included in an expansion of Britain's first geothermal district heating system. Hot water at more than 70°C is pumped from 5,500 feet below the earth's surface to supply the district heating system.

Human resource management

One aspect that impinges on all areas of a hotel operation including the rooms division is the topic of human resource management (HRM). The management of the human resource or personnel within a hotel operation can be both a generalist function and a specialist department. All managers in both operational and supporting departments have to manage people within their particular section. Equally, specialist advice on such matters as employment law, interviewing or training are usually the responsibility of the human resource department. Four features of the industry can be identified as having implications for human resource management:

- **Fluctuation in customer demand**. Business fluctuates by the week, the day, the hour. This means an irregular work flow and from an operational point of view the problem of adjusting labour supply to demand. In this respect many hotels make use of casual or part-time labour.
- **Direct demand for labour**. Labour is demanded in the industry for what it can produce which means that productivity is based on personal ability and effort, and so there are differences between worker's output and a judgement on human capacity.
- **Subjective nature of standards**. Concepts like hospitality, service and cleanliness are all matters of subjective judgement, which means that every worker's output is judged subjectively. This affects the management–worker relationship. Within this relationship there is a requirement for standards and the implicit subjectivity means that standards are open to interpretation. However in the absence of standards, there is a potential for conflict.
- **Transferability of skills**. Skills required for the industry are generally confined to the industry. The relatively unskilled nature of some of the work encourages high labour mobility within the industry.

The role of HRM

HRM can play a key role in ensuring that the total strategy of the hotel is successful. It is the guardian of management style thus protecting image and culture with regard to people and is therefore the co-ordinator of a powerful asset. It has influence over the company's ethos, principles and management style. HRM has strategic control over recruitment procedures and determines content and style of induction training along with management development. As a co-ordinating activity HRM is of prime importance in management development and succession planning.

Hotels often have a very similar product, so it is in many cases the human element that captures success for one hotel over another and gives that crucial competitive edge. Human resource management is therefore an investment, not a cost.

HRM should be seen as a development in philosophy from the traditional ideas of staff management and it demands that people are considered as a key resource or asset to a business. Human resource specialists need to be proactive in assessing the needs of the business and workforce and presenting operators with the up-to-date issues, trends, information and proposals upon which they can make better decisions.

Planning

This general philosophy of HRM requires human resource planning as part of the overall business planning process that normally occurs on an annual basis and must take into account local and national trends and factors. Proactive management planning minimises the chaos and begins to ensure that the competitive edge is maintained through optimum staffing levels and optimum wage costs to sales revenue while assuring an agreed quality in product and service.

These highly competitive objectives of getting and keeping the best staff available demand that the hotel addresses the issue of workforce public relations. Every interaction with a potential employee is an opportunity to establish and reinforce the hotel's standing as an employer. The HRM's market is therefore the potential and existing workforce. Wherever the labour force comes from, the hotel must have the right package of terms and conditions. The hotel must attract them using the most effective media and then satisfy and retain them.

Employment process

Training is often referred to as the structured development of knowledge, skills and attitudes; knowledge may be gained by reading, listening and experiencing. When considering the training of new skills and different but appropriate attitudes, the human resource function is in a situation of actually changing the ways in which an individual behaves. Employees come to an organisation with a range of experiences, a set of attitudes built from their varying levels of knowledge. Training is adapting that mixed bag of attributes into a very systematic job-oriented set of qualities demanded by the standards and methods of the hotel. However, knowledge in isolation is of only partial use to the hospitality industry. The business demands technical skills and social skills, and staff are in constant behavioural involvement with the customer, so training that happens must reflect this consistently and significantly should have an emphasis towards interaction and behaviour. Alternating sessions on job or off job must link the technical skill of the task to the social skill involved. This will involve the use of role plays and realistic simulations wherever possible in the training process. Role plays can be very effective if linked to earlier knowledge demonstration sessions; if the role play is well prepared and constructive and feedback given, the training process will be considered a success. Such sessions lend themselves well to the use of a video camera and recorder as it can be powerful in encouraging people to consider their own behaviour. Training within groups assists interaction and discussion along with consideration of behavioural issues.

Customer care

All staff within a hotel work either in direct contact with the guests, or provide an important service which will influence the final product or service. All these people need to have a full awareness of customer care with constant reinforcement. Customer care is a major training and cultural effort in most companies in the hotel sector. It has a major part in attaining a competitive edge over companies offering a similar product to the market, with the difference to a hotel in many cases being the human element. In a recession where a buyers' market prevails, guests will choose to return to the hotel or restaurant that give them better service. Better customer care gives the customer added value. The entire training programme of any hospitality enterprise must feature prominently customer care as an issue of the utmost significance to every member of staff. Customer care should be part of induction and all on and off the job training. It should be reinforced in staff notices, staff meetings, management meetings and at every conceivable opportunity. Supervisors should be generally more vigilant in the observation and correction of social skills; frequently they supervise only incorrect technical factors. Back of house staff must realise that they are a vital link in the customer care chain, aware of the motto that 'if you are not serving a customer you had better be serving someone who is'. Customer care is also a frequent topic for refresher training as the pressure and bustle of constant customer contact can often lead to understandable complacency. The role of management in this area must be set to a high quality. Their actions and decisions should seek out and recognise people who provide an exceptional example of customer care. Too often management are seen as concerned only about profit, reducing costs and reviewing guest services in the light of purely financial considerations. The management team must share customer complaints so that positive lasting corrective action can be taken. They should also share the compliments and thank you letters at staff briefings and meetings; copies should be posted on the notice boards as well.

Career development

All members of staff should have the opportunity to develop their abilities and to improve their career and job prospects. Most people are motivated by this possibility and many staff will seek extra responsibility. Giving recognition of success through promotion engenders a very real increase in status and reward that comes with such progression. For the employer this should also be positive and helpful as people who truly believe that hard work and achievement will be recognised in tangible ways like promotion and job prospects are motivated to stay with their employer for much longer. However, there will be a range of employees from vigorously ambitious people, determined to reach the top, to the highly competent people who value stability and security much more than managerial status and responsibility.

Opportunities for in-company advancement clearly vary with the size and nature of the organisation. Multi-unit companies may have sophisticated internal transfer and training schemes; these should be fully promoted to employees as a real and valuable benefit, so that their career prospects can develop within one firm, assuring continuity of service and associated employment rights. For single unit operations, the crucial element is the realisation that for employees to develop, it may be necessary for the individuals to leave the organisation for a job more in keeping with their abilities and ambitions. If internal promotion and development are not possible, it is no use ignoring the situation hoping that people will stay and revise their career plans. This is unwise as the person will eventually become frustrated, demotivated and a less than productive worker, and may leave in an unplanned and often acrimonious fashion.

Summary

This chapter has discussed elements of the hotel operation, with respect to front office, reservations, housekeeping and human resource management. The hotel's relationship with the outside environment and its potential clients was also considered. It was also shown that developments in computer technology impinge on a number of operating departments. A case study focused on energy management within the hotel industry with a special emphasis on rooms division.

Further reading

- Brander-Brown J. and McDonnell B. (1995) 'The balanced score card: short term guest or long term resident?', *International Journal of Contemporary Hospitality Management* 7(2/3): 7–11.
- Gamble P.R. (1984) *Small Computers and Hospitality Management*, London: Hutchinson.
- Gamble P.R. (1991) 'An information strategy for the hospitality industry in the 1990s', *International Journal of Contemporary Hospitality Management* 3(1): 10–15.
- Geller A.N. (1985) 'Tracking the critical success factors for hotel companies', *Cornell Hotel and Restaurant Association Quarterly* 24: 76–81.
- Gilbert D. and Arnold L. (1989a) 'Budget hotels part 1', *Leisure Management* 9(2).
- Gilbert D. and Arnold L. (1989b) 'Budget hotels part 2', *Leisure Management* 9(4).
- Gilbert D. and Lockwood A. (1990) *Budget Hotels: The USA, UK and France Compared, Travel and Tourism Analyst no 3*, London: Economist Intelligence Unit.
- Gilbert D. and Zok S. (1992) 'Marketing implications of consolidation in the hotel industry', *Journal of Hospitality and Leisure Marketing* 1.
- Hirst M. (1992) 'Creating a service driven culture globally', *International Journal of Contemporary Hospitality Management* 4(1).
- Hubrecht J. and Teare R. (1993) 'A strategy for partnership in total quality service', *International Journal of Contemporary Hospitality Management* 5(3).
- Johns N. and Edwards J.S. (1994) 'Operations management for the hospitality industry', London: Cassell.
- Jones P. (ed.) (1989) *Management in Service Industries*, London: Pitman.
- Jones P. and Lockwood A. (1991) *The Management of Hotel Operations*, London: Cassell.
- Johns P. and Pizam, A. (eds) (1993) *The International Hospitality Industry: Organisational and Operational Issues*, London: Pitman.
- Lockwood A. and Jones P. (1994) *People and the Hotel and Catering Industry*, London: Cassell.
- McGuffie J. (1990a) *CRS Development and the Hotel Sector – Part 1, Travel and Tourism Analyst, no. 1*, London: Economist Intelligence Unit.
- McGuffie J. (1990b) *CRS Development and the Hotel Sector – Part 2, Travel and Tourism Analyst no. 2*, London: Economist Intelligence Unit.

● Mullins L. (1992) *Hospitality Management: A Human Resources Approach*, London: Pitman.
● Riley M. (1991) *Human Resource Management*, London: Butterworth Heinemann.
● Sternberg L.E. (1992) 'Empowerment: trust vs control', *Cornell Hotel and Restaurant Association Quarterly* 33(1): 69.

Chapter Seven

Legislation

Objectives

After reading this chapter you should be able to

■ Recognise the background to the legal system in the UK and EU, and to concentrate on a number of legal issues which are of direct relevance to the hospitality industry.

■ Identify the issues with respect to food hygiene in the hospitality industry.

■ Consider at an introductory level issues to do with health and safety, liquor and planning legislation.

Legislation relevant to the hospitality industry is continually evolving. Students of the industry are strongly recommended to consult the further reading at the end of this chapter, along with recognised texts in law, available in most reference libraries.

Definitions

Law can be defined as a body of rules, enforced among the citizens of a given state by the sovereign body. State in the UK means England and Wales, as Scotland has a different legal system. Sovereign body means the Queen in Parliament.

Historical development in the UK

The development of legislation in the UK can be set within a historical context. The topic of common law was established by a process of upholding good local customs; in time, some ancient customs became common law. When a decision had been made on a new problem it had to be followed in all subsequent cases. This approach added consistency to the application of the law and established the principle of judicial precedent.

Judicial precedent means in practice that one judge does not lightly set aside the decisions of another judge. The basic rule to stand by past decisions was established as the general doctrine of 'let the decision stand': a precedent set by a higher court must be observed in lower courts.

The defect in common law is that the award of money was, and still is, the only remedy. A development in this situation is 'equity' which is a refinement on common law. There are a number of equity remedies such as specific performance or an injunction to resolve a breach of common law.

Statute law

The power of Parliament arose out of the need to erect a system of controls and balances within the nation-state, in order to ensure that no one individual body could hold all the power. A statute is a body of written law drawn up by the legislative body Parliament, which was the supreme law-making body in the UK; now there is the increasing influence of the EU.

Once an Act of Parliament has become law, an English court must interpret and apply the law as it stands. Every Act of Parliament starts life as a Bill, which must be approved by the House of Commons, the House of Lords and then receive royal assent.

The court system

The Supreme Court Act 1981 sets out the court system as it works in England and Wales. The system includes, going from higher to lower courts

- House of Lords
- Court of Appeal
- High Court
- Crown Court
- County Court (including the small claims court)
- Magistrates Court

The House of Lords is the highest court in the UK and is the final court of appeal in civil and criminal matters, with the exception of Scottish criminal law. There is no higher authority except the European Court of Justice, which has jurisdiction over EU matters.

Many matters concerning the hospitality industry, such as licensing law and food hygiene offences, are considered in the magistrates court, which deals with more cases than any other court. There are two kinds of magistrates – lay and stipendiary. A lay magistrate is a local non-professional magistrate, a person well respected in the community, but not from the legal profession. A stipendiary magistrate is a full-time professional magistrate. They are professionally trained barristers or solicitors of at least seven years' standing. Each magistrates court has a clerk to the justice, who is a barrister or solicitor of at least five years' standing. The clerk's functions are numerous and include all general administrative work of the court, issuing summons, warrants granted by magistrates and collecting and accounting for the fines imposed.

The magistrates court may sit as a trial court to make decisions on cases in its own right or as a court of preliminary investigation with the case proceeding to the crown court if it is found there is a case to answer. The magistrates court also has certain other duties, particularly with respect to licensing matters.

European Union legislation

EU law is becoming increasingly relevant to the hospitality industry, for example food hygiene legislation, employment legislation, e.g. Working Time Directive (restrictions on how many hours in a week you work), health and safety legislation. The original basis for much of this legislation is the Treaty of Rome, the Single European Act and the Maastricht Treaty.

Treaty of Rome and Single European Act

The European Economic Community (EEC) was established in 1957 by the signing of the Treaty of Rome. Since then modifications have been made to the Treaty, for instance by

The Community shall adopt measures with the aim of progressively establishing an internal market over a period expiring on 31 December 1992. The internal market shall comprise an area in which free movement of goods, persons, services and capital is ensured in accordance with the provisions of this treaty.

Figure 7.1 Single European Act 1987 Article 8A

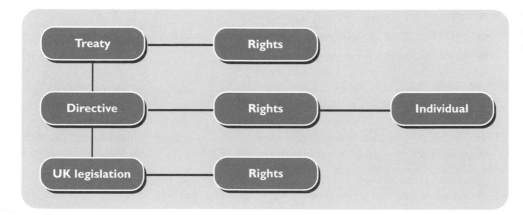

Figure 7.2 Legislative framework

the signing of the Single European Act in July 1987. This Act inserted a new Article 8A to the Treaty of Rome, establishing the single European market as illustrated in Figure 7.1.

Legislation within the EU takes one of two forms, the Regulation or the Directive. A Directive requires member states to incorporate its provisions into its own national legislation before it takes effect. The majority of measures affecting the internal market take the form of a Directive. The Directive is transformed into a Bill in the British Parliament and implemented into UK law. This relationship is illustrated in Figure 7.2.

Within the EU there are basically three organisations involved in the legislative process:

- European Commission (EC)
- European Parliament
- Council of Ministers

It is the Commission that proposes legislation. In general terms the European Parliament debates and the final decision rests with the Council of Ministers.

Single Market measures are subject to qualified majority voting and under the Single European Act, Single Act measures have two readings in the European Parliament; this point changed with the Maastricht Treaty.

Social Charter

The EU Social Charter is an attempt to balance the free market ideals of 1992 with an improvement in the well-being of chiefly employed people. The Social Charter was adopted in December 1989 by eleven out of twelve member states, which means that the charter is not legally binding. However, the Commission has been pressing ahead with its action plan. It should be noted that the action plan has preceded the Social Charter in terms of the Commission's short-term social policy, but the Social Charter contains the long-term intentions of both the Commission and eleven out twelve member states. The Social Charter action programme covers basically seven areas:

- employment and remuneration
- improvement of living and working conditions
- freedom of movement
- social protection
- information, consultation and participation
- equal treatment for women and men
- health and safety protection for workers

Employment legislation in the EU

EU employment legislation is a complex subject in its own right. In the space available it is not possible to do more than indicate the scope of EU employment legislation and look at four EC Directives which have been passed:

- Principle of equal pay for equal work
- Principle of equal treatment of women and men
- Preservation of employees' rights in the context of transfer of undertaking
- Rights in relation to health and safety at work

Principle of equal pay for equal work
This principle is established by Article 119 of the Treaty of Rome (see Figure 7.3).

Supplementary legislation has given effect to these treaty obligations. This includes the Equal Pay Act 1970, Equal Value Regulations and the Sex Discrimination Act. The purpose of the equal pay Directive is to facilitate the practical application of the principle of equal pay for same or like work to include work of equal value. This principle has been further extended by the cases in connection with pensions and part-time work.

Principle of equal treatment of women and men
This Directive not only provides for equal access to employment, vocational training, working conditions, promotion, but also prohibits discrimination by reference to family or marital status. This Directive has been the springboard for other European Court of Justice decisions, in respect of which it was held that to treat a woman less favourably than a man because she is pregnant was in breach of EU legislation. It has been held un-

Figure 7.3 Article 119 Treaty of Rome

Each member state shall maintain the application of the principle that men and women shall receive equal pay for equal work.
... pay means the ordinary basic or minimum wage or salary and any other consideration whether in cash or kind, which the worker receives, directly or indirectly, in respect of his employment from his employer.

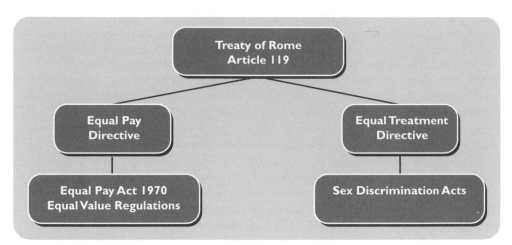

Figure 7.4 Giving effect of treaty obligations Article 119

lawful to have different compulsory time off for men and women. This link between Treaty, Directive and UK legislation is shown in Figure 7.4.

Preservation of employees' rights in the context of transfers of undertaking

This introduces the central principle that the rights and obligations under a contract of employment of those employed in the business would bind the person purchasing the business, i.e. the transferee. This Directive goes on to suggest that any dismissals arising out of the transfer must be for economic, technical or organisational reasons. Where the business transferred retains its autonomy the position of employee representatives must be preserved. The Directive also requires advanced information on the transfer to be given to employee representatives. This relationship between Treaty, Directive and UK legislation is shown in Figure 7.5.

Rights in relation to health and safety at work

EU legislation on issues of health and safety is also a complex subject in its own right. It originates from Article 118 of the Treaty of Rome. Much of this Article is aimed at particular industries and work situations. This area received much attention after the inser-

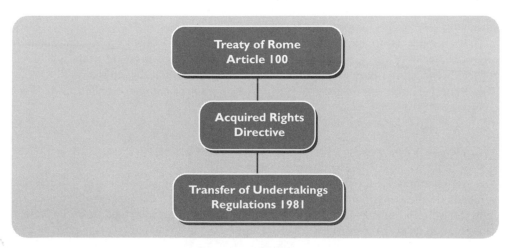

Figure 7.5 Giving effect of treaty obligations Article 100

tion of Article 118A into the Treaty of Rome by the Single European Act and is rapidly developing. Because of the broad consensus among most member states on health and safety issues, qualified majority voting in Article 118A has made it easier for legislation to be passed. In June 1989, the Council of Ministers adopted a directive to require EU countries to introduce new health and safety laws by 31 December 1992. A wide range of regulations and supporting codes of practice under the Health and Safety Act 1974 were introduced on 1 January 1993 in order to implement the EC Directive. Some will apply to temporary workers, fixed duration workers and agency workers. New regulations require positive steps to be taken by employers to carry out health and safety risk assessments. Managers within the hotel and catering industry are now faced with a number of major new health and safely regulations plus subsidiary approved codes of practice or guidance which effectively rewrite most of the UK health and safety legislation developed in the 1970s and 1980s. These new requirements should be considered an amplification of how to achieve the requirements of the Health and Safety at Work, etc. Act 1974.

The common theme throughout all these health and safety issues is the need to carry out an assessment as a way of ensuring that the safeguard is closely tailored to the real need or risk. The general provisions regulation contains a requirement for the employer to adequately assess the risk arising from all work activities in addition to those for which there is already a specific requirement. This requires an assessment of risks and a review of the control arrangements over any hazard. Another common theme is the requirement to inform and train operators and those who manage and supervise them. There is an overriding requirement for employers to ensure they have provided appropriate health and safety training of employees when giving them work activities and to take into account their health and safety capabilities in their work placement. Vocational training qualifications and competencies form part of meeting that duty. The regulations also envisage a more specific and increased role in health and safety for employees, who must use machines and tools as instructed and trained, reporting defects and unsafe situations. For them to assist management in this way, clearly more information and training will have to be given to them on the hazards with which they are working and the control regime instituted in the first place.

Food safety legislation

The 1980s saw an exceptional rise in the number of reported food poisoning cases which indicated a rising trend of food poisoning outbreaks between 1980 and 1990. Throughout the 1990s that trend continued, although it was not clear if this was due to increased food poisoning cases or the reporting of them.

There is evidence to suggest that food poisoning caused by caterers is greater than in any other sector of the food industry. Consultation by the government in the mid-1980s revealed several important aspects that needed attention within the legislation of the day. The White Paper on Food Safety in 1989, *Protecting the Consumer,* resulted in the Food Safety Act 1990.

Food Safety Act 1990

This Act sets the legal framework for food safety and consumer protection. The Act concentrates on the fundamentals leaving the details to be filled in through regulations and codes of practice, and in doing so is also more flexible and adaptable to future needs. The broad aims of the legislation cover five areas:

- to provide safety controls through the food chain from source to ultimate consumption
- to continue to ensure that food produced for sale is safe and not misleadingly labelled or advertised
- to reinforce present powers, penalties and ensure consistency of enforcement
- to ensure that new European Union directives on food can be implemented
- to simplify and streamline the legislation by combining the Acts which apply in England, Wales, Scotland and Northern Ireland.

Part Two of the Act contains the main provisions. It includes the food safety offences, enforcement powers, consumer protection, regulation making powers and defences.

Food safety offences

The first two offences contained within Section 7 and 8 of the Act deal with food safety. The principal offence is in Section 8 and created the new umbrella offence of selling food that does not comply with food safety requirements. Food fails to comply if it has been rendered injurious to health, if it is unfit for human consumption or if it is so contaminated that it would not be reasonable to expect it to be eaten in that state.

If any one of these conditions is breached an offence may have been committed. This definition of food safety requirements was made as wide as possible because it also acts as a trigger for further action. If food safety requirements have been breached, enforcement officers may use their detention and seizure powers under Section 9.

The first two elements of Section 8, injurious and unfit, are familiar; they had been retained on purpose so that the existing body of case law would remain relevant. The third element, contamination, was new. It had been added so that contaminated food can be dealt with as soon as it appears to be unsafe. Under previous legislation, having contaminated food on the premises was not an offence unless it was actually sold. The other new feature of Section 8 is a presumption that where any part of a batch of food fails to comply with food safety requirements, the whole batch will be presumed not to comply, until the contrary is proven.

Consumer protection

In terms of consumer protection, Section 14 of the Act re-enacted the well-known offence of selling any food for human consumption which is not of the nature, substance or quality demanded by the purchaser.

The wide application of this section is apparent. Offences of substance or quality may be an alternative to proceedings under Section 8. In the past the offence of substance has often been used to deal with mould or foreign bodies in food.

Section 15 of the Act contains the offence of selling or displaying food with a label that is false or is likely to mislead as to the nature, substance or quality of the food in question. Section 1 of the Trade Descriptions Act 1968 is frequently used as an alternative to proceedings under this section. These offences are mainly consumer protection offences which are enforced by Trading Standards officers. However under Section 14 an environmental health officer may become involved.

Enforcement in England and Wales

Section 9 entitled 'Inspection and Seizure of Suspected Food' makes provision for the issue of notices by authorised officers. The authorised officer may inspect food at all reasonable times, at any stage between production and distribution, to check whether it complies with food safety requirements. Where a detention notice has been served the officer must decide as soon as is reasonably practicable and in any case within twenty-one days whether the food complies with food safety requirements.

Section 10 confers upon enforcement authorities the power to issue notices to prevent and control the risks to health arising from contravention of hygiene or processing regulations. It empowers an authorised officer of an enforcement authority to issue an improvement notice where the officer has reasonable grounds for believing that the proprietor of the food business is failing to comply with certain regulations. The notice would include details of the offence, the reasons for the notice, measures to be taken and the time limit. Also a notice under this section would be issued where there is *no* imminent risk of injury to health.

Section 11 gives powers to the courts to make prohibition orders. These powers allow a court (before whom the proprietor of the food business has been convicted) on being satisfied that the health risk condition is fulfilled can issue a prohibition order against processes, equipment or premises. Additionally, the court may prohibit the food business proprietor or manager who has been convicted from participation in the management of any food business as specified in the order.

Section 12 provides for emergency prohibition notices and orders to deal with circumstances which pose an *imminent risk of injury to health*. An emergency prohibition notice may be issued by an authorised officer who is satisfied that there is a serious health risk.

The emergency prohibition notice must be confirmed as an order in an application to a court within a three-day period. The authorised officer must also give at least one day's notice of the intention to apply for the order to the proprietor of the food business. The issue of an emergency prohibition notice ensures the immediate closure of the premises or the immediate cessation of use of a particular piece of equipment or process.

An integral part of food safety legislation is the enforcement process, which will now be explored with a case study on the role of enforcement officers in respect of food safety.

Case Study: The role of enforcement officers in respect of food safety

The framework for EU foodstuffs legislation is well established as part of the single European market with its central reason being the protection of the consumer through the provision of safe food. With the issue of EC Directives it is for the individual member states of the EU to implement such Directives into legislation at a national level. The focus of this case study is on food legislation with particular emphasis on enforcement within the UK. A background to the role of such officers will be given, based on interviews; comments will be given on trends in enforcement practices. It is self-evident from considering practices in other European countries that a number of them approach the subjects

case study continues ▶

of food safety, consumer protection and enforcement in different ways, while seeking to achieve the central objective of ensuring the provision of safe food.

Enforcement

The importance of enforcement comes from the reported level of food poisoning cases, some, like the E-Coli outbreak in Scotland in 1996, have been very serious and resulted in deaths. The rise in food poisoning since the Food Safety Act 1990 must be regarded as a cause for consumer concern. There has been an increase in food poisoning, but this could be reflected in a greater level of reporting by family doctors and so a clear reason for this rise has not been determined.

The enforcement of food health and hygiene issues is generally undertaken by environmental health officers (EHOs) and fraudulent trading practices are the concern of trading standards officers (TSOs). The inspection of food enforcement functions is carried out by either TSOs or EHOs, but the analysis of food is done by public analysts or the Public Health Laboratory Service. Public analysts are required to analyse samples of food to identify their nature, substance and quality, for compositional irregularities, additives, contaminants and nutritional claims. They also comment on matters concerning labelling and advertising.

This division between EHOs and TSOs is discussed in greater detail within the Code of Practice no. 1 issued under Section 40 of the Food Safety Act 1990. The appointment of such authorised officers is a statutory requirement under the Food Safety Act 1990 Section 5. Under Section 40 of the Food Safety Act 1990, statutory codes of practice have been issued and generally enforcement officers follow a staged approach in their inspection. For instance, with the matter of temperature EHOs first consider the temperature monitoring systems. They will take air temperatures and between-pack temperatures of food within refrigeration equipment. If not satisfied with the results, they will then measure actual food temperatures. If an EHO believes an offence has been committed the issue of improvement notices, prohibition notices or emergency prohibition notices may follow under the relevant sections of the Food Safety Act 1990. The proprietor may also be prosecuted and in extreme circumstances banned from running a catering business.

Much of the legislation generated by either the EU or the UK government and directed at the hotel, catering or food service industries, overlaps with the wider food industry; this is reflected in the duties of both EHOs and TSOs whose enforcement interests are not solely directed at the hotel and catering industry. The link with EU legislation is contained within Section 17 of the Food Safety Act 1990.

Enforcement in Scotland

The relevant professional body for Scotland is the Royal Environmental Health Institute of Scotland (REHIS). Formed in 1983 following the amalgamation of two older professional bodies and based in Edinburgh, the central aim of REHIS is to promote the advancement of all aspects of health and hygiene. Like its counterpart in England and Wales, the Institute of Environmental Health Officers, the REHIS runs a series of food hygiene training courses at three main levels: training is a requirement under food safety

case study continues

legislation. In Scotland EHOs employed by district or island councils enforce all parts of food safety legislation.

The principal food safety legislation in Scotland is the same as in the rest of the UK; it is similar in content to the English and Welsh equivalent but there are marked differences in a number of aspects, for example the reheating of foods to a relevant temperature.

Uniformity in enforcement

The Local Authorities Co-ordinating Body on Food and Trading Standards (LACOTS) is a local government central body whose purpose is to co-ordinate trading standards, food safety and hygiene activities throughout the UK. One aspect of its work is the catering industry where its central aim is to provide a uniform interpretation of local authority law enforcement and a liaison point between trading standards officers, environmental health officers and public analysts. Issues referred to LACOTS are considered by panels; two panels of particular interest to the catering industry concern food safety and general hygiene. LACOTS is well placed to liaise, collaborate and share information with its sister organisations throughout Europe on food safety and food hygiene matters.

A frequently voiced criticism of food safety legislation is that there is not uniform enforcement. One area in which LACOTS takes particular interest is the principle of the **home authority**, which is designed to encourage efficiency, promote uniformity, reduce duplication and assist businesses to comply with the law. The principle applies to food safety and trading standards issues and commands the support of local and central government, industry, trade and enforcement professional bodies.

Trends in enforcement

A number of trends in enforcement practices can be detected. A clear distinction can be drawn between two principal types of legislated controls on the hygienic production of food. Traditionally, but only for the production of foodstuffs of animal origin, prescriptive requirements have been laid down in considerable detail to ensure that all stages are closely regulated. This resulted in a wealth of provisions which were not always appropriate or necessary in particular establishments and to this extent can be considered as being disproportionate or over regulatory. Steps over the years have been taken to eliminate such excesses where this is practicable. More recently, it has become more acceptable to rely on the operators of businesses, approved and monitored appropriately by the EHO, to provide adequate hygiene controls within a framework of varying complexity, often based on critical control points (the principles of Hazard Analysis Critical Control Points). Almost inevitably at this early stage in the development of this type of control system, it has been necessary to supplement these sophisticated legislative elements with a number of basic obligations. Thus limited detailed rules are to be found allied to provisions based on generalities, routine monitoring is associated with irregular auditing, and flexibility is surrounded by historic rigidity. Over the next few years, it is suggested that there will be a reliance on a greater degree of audited self-regulation and less on specific fundamental discipline provided by EHOs. As developments continue, the opportunity must be taken at each phase to challenge every rule, and to eliminate legislative pro-

case study continues ▶

visions that can be safely left to be applied flexibly by responsible businesses, while ensuring that the process can be monitored and controlled by the environmental health officer.

Within this context, it is argued that while there is a useful trend towards adopting risk assessment and monitoring controls based on critical control point techniques, uniformity could be improved, perhaps through the continued support of LACOTS. Also, ensuring safety in production at the early stages of the food chain leads on naturally to the next stage – controls on finished products within the catering business.

Enabling powers

The Food Safety Act contains enabling powers throughout the text linked with the main provisions to which they relate. The main enabling powers are contained in Sections 16 to 19 of the Act. There are powers to issue regulations under Section 16 on Food Hygiene Training (discussed later in this chapter). Training is an important element of the defence of due diligence which is identified under Section 21 of the Food Safety Act.

Due diligence

The concept of due diligence and all reasonable precautions lies at the heart of the Act and examples can be seen of this defence in other statutes such as Section 24 of the Trades Description Act 1968. It was because absolute or strict liability offences are anathema to most lawyers, as they are regarded as oppressive, that the concept of due diligence was introduced into food safety law.

It is the hotelier's responsibility to ensure that a safe and efficient system of food handling exists and that all reasonable precautions are taken to avoid food contamination during handling. Hoteliers have little to fear from food safety law if they can show that the due diligence system is effective in operation, and that it can withstand the critical scrutiny of enforcement authorities. The type of due diligence system in an establishment must be geared to the size and type of the particular operation.

The objective contained within Section 21 of the Food Safety Act was to modernise the system of defences and bring it into line with other consumer protection legislation. In legal terms, offences of absolute liability are employed in trading legislation because it would be nearly impossible to secure a conviction if the prosecutor was obliged to prove guilty intent in every case. However, conscious that absolute liability could bear down harshly on traders, a series of statutory defences have been introduced over the years which would, subject to proof that the criteria in each case had been fulfilled, enable a court to acquit a trader even though an offence had been committed. Statutory defences have evolved over time and the Food Safety Act 1990 brought those relating to food offences up to date.

Such a defence can be extended to persons who neither prepared nor imported the food and who are accused under Sections 8, 14 or 15. Within this offence the objective is to put responsibility for food upon the persons who have the greatest influence over the final product.

Nobody can escape conviction simply by producing a warranty from their supplier. There is however a difference between warranties and written assurances from suppliers.

It is the duty of a food business to seek written assurances from suppliers that the products being supplied comply with all legal requirements. Such assurances are an essential first step in the establishment of a due diligence system, but are not warranties as defined within the Food Act 1984. Such assurances should not go beyond the competence of the supplier.

The burden of proof rests with the defendant. While there is no requirement for a due diligence system, it is however recommended good practice that every food business should establish and maintain an adequate due diligence system. A control system which is not written down and not recorded creates great difficulties of proof in a court no matter how comprehensive it may be.

While the decision of the courts cannot be predicted, case law on due diligence under other consumer protection legislation gives some clues. The courts have expected defendants to prove that they have *actively* taken some steps. The amount of checking necessary has depended on the size and nature of the business. It was not until 1994, some three years after the Food Safety Act came into force, that a law report was published on the due diligence defence, namely *Carrick District Council* v. *Taunton Vale Meat Traders Ltd 1994*. The case reached the High Court in London. The key point in this decision is that the company relied on a meat inspector's inspection without having a separate system of checking. The court found that the company claim of due diligence was proven. While going against the tone of previous case law on due diligence, this decision may also affect an officer's willingness to give specific advice to caterers, because such willingness to give advice may eventually be used in a due diligence case.

Quality control

The development of quality control systems to satisfy the test of due diligence will probably be one main consequence of the Act. Businesses are likely to pay greater attention to the quality of their supplies and to the quality control systems of their suppliers. If so, enforcement officers will need to do the same and this could have significant effects. Interestingly, there is a case in which the food manufacturers and distributors in question had obtained British Standard 5750 – Quality Management Systems (now referred to as ISO9000 series, the European equivalent being EN29000) yet were still not successful in claiming a due diligence defence in a prosecution on a food safety matter. In general terms, quality assurance in this context can be considered under three headings.

Risk assessment
The system must be based on an identification of risk areas throughout the catering processes and procedures. Typical areas include cleaning and pest control; ordering and specification of food; storage and stock rotation; food preparation and cooking; temperature control; refuse disposal; personal hygiene and training. This assessment should be kept constantly under review. If the system is written down, it will assist in any due diligence defence.

Management control
It is necessary to set up a programme of monitoring and control to ensure the due diligence systems which have been instituted actually operate in practice.

Staff and due diligence
It is important to remember that staff fault can never be the basis of a third party due dili-

gence. The systems (precautions) and monitoring (due diligence) which are established by the employer must be such as to avoid commission of the offence not only by the employer, but also by the employee. This means that the controls must take some account of the possibility of staff aberrations. The fact that staff were not properly trained or supervised, or did not know what to do or were just plain incompetent for the job, may tend to show that the employer has not taken all proper steps in being able to prove the due diligence defence.

Food hygiene regulations

The Food Safety Act 1990 is a relatively recent issue within the topic of food legislation; other related regulations have a much longer history.

A central plank of food safety law, up to September 1995, was contained within the Food Hygiene (General) Regulations 1970, as amended, which applied to all food premises. These were reviewed and consolidated in 1995 with the implementation of the EC Directive on the Hygiene of Foodstuffs, under the Department of Health's copy out principle.

An examination of the 1970 regulations shows them to be non-specific in using words such as sufficient, suitable and adequate (not dissimilar from the Directive on the Hygiene of Foodstuffs). Both the 1970 and 1995 regulations relate to premises and equipment, food handling practices, personal hygiene, construction, repair and maintenance of premises, water supply and washing facilities, waste disposal, and temperature control of certain foods. There is a clear link between the 1990 Act and the 1995 regulations; a breach of these regulations could result in the enforcement authorities taking action.

Food Safety (General Food Hygiene) Regulations 1995

As part of its implementation of the EU Food Hygiene Directive, the government issued the Food Safety (General Food Hygiene) Regulations 1995. These regulations apply equally to England, Wales and Scotland and repealed the bulk of the existing sets of regulations. The only exception were those regulations relating to temperature control (discussed later in this section).

The layout of the regulations follows that of the EU food hygiene directive very closely. The main requirements of these regulations are as follows:

- Regulation 2 defines some of the expressions used in the regulations. 'Food Business' means any undertaking (private or public) that carries out any activity relating to the preparation, processing, manufacture, packaging, storage, transportation, etc., of food. 'Hygiene' means all measures necessary to ensure the safety and wholesomeness of food during any of the activities listed above. 'Wholesome food' means food that is fit for human consumption as far as hygiene is concerned and 'wholesomeness' shall be construed accordingly. These regulations do not apply to those food businesses that are covered by regulations made under 'vertical' directives. Such vertical or product specific regulations include red meats, poultry meat, meat products and dairy product manufacturing plants. However, the training requirement of these regulations will apply if the 'vertical' regulation contains no such requirement.

- Regulation 4 is a general requirement that proprietors of food businesses are required to ensure that all food handling operations are carried out in a hygienic manner.

- Regulation 5 provides the link with the requirements in Schedule 1. Hoteliers must ensure that the requirements in Schedule 1 relating to equipment, food waste, water supply, personal hygiene and training are complied with. Compliance with these requirements is a provision of Regulation 5. The requirements are set out in ten chapters.

- Subsequent regulations require the identification and control of potential food hazards based on the principles set out in Schedule 2. This schedule lays down the principles whereby the potential food hazards in any food business can be identified and controlled.

- Provided within the legislation is the need for the notification of food handlers suffering from certain infections to the appropriate local authority and is unchanged from the similar requirement in the existing legislation.

- Contravention of the regulations can incur in some cases a fine (unlimited) or imprisonment for not more than two years, or both.

- The enforcement authorities must have due regard to any relevant Industry Guide to Good Hygiene Practice when enforcing these regulations.

Temperature control

Temperature control was not included in the 1995 regulations but has a long history of development in the UK.

The Food Hygiene (Amendment) Regulations 1990 came into force on 1 April 1991 and specified temperature controls for certain foods. Further amending regulations, the Food Hygiene (Amendment) Regulations 1991 came into force on 5 July 1991. Similar temperature controls apply to foods in transit and to catering operations using temporary or mobile facilities as covered in the Food Hygiene Market Stalls and Delivery Vehicles Regulations 1966. The amendments produced a complex set of controls for storage temperatures of prepared foods. Foods defined within the regulations were divided into categories, some of which must be kept at 8°C or colder and some that should be kept at 5°C or colder.

Further to these amendments, the UK government announced on 23 February 1993 their intention to review statutory temperature controls in order to identify how they might be simplified and rationalised without compromising public health. It considered options, looking both at domestic legislation and legislation that results from EU Directives or international agreements. The government issued proposals on this subject for public consultation in October 1993 and the results of the consultation were made available in the spring of 1994. In essence the results of the consultation was that the two tier temperature control system was abandoned and a single temperature requirement of 8°C introduced in September 1995. Such a temperature contrasts with France's 3°C and Netherlands's 7°C. It is this inconsistency in the temperature control within member states that will eventually have to be resolved on a European-wide basis. This means that the UK's 8°C within the 1995 regulations may be subject to change in the medium term.

The Food Safety (General Food Hygiene) Regulations 1995 initially omitted references to temperature control provisions as these were still under consideration by the European Commission. The temperature regulations came into force on 15 September 1995, the same day as the Food Safety (General Food Hygiene) Regulations 1995. These regulations implement Paragraphs 4 and 5 of Chapter 9 of the Annexe to the Food Hygiene Directive issued in June 1993 as well as containing certain national provisions relating to food temperature control. The regulations are separated into four parts with some requirements applying to England and Wales and separate requirements applying to Scotland.

Regulation 2 is an interpretation provision and details the meanings of a number of terms used in the regulation. Many of the terms relate back to the Food Safety Act 1990, the EU Food Hygiene Directive of June 1993, the Food Labelling Regulations 1984 and the Food Labelling Scotland Regulations 1984.

The regulations apply to all stages of food production except primary production and fishery products.

Chill holding requirements
Food which needs to be kept chilled because it is likely to support the growth of pathogenic micro-organisms or the formation of toxins is required to be kept either at or below 8°C. This does not apply to mail order food which is subject to a separate offence. There are certain exemptions to this general requirement.

Regulation 5 contains general exemptions from the chill holding requirements just identified. The 8°C requirement does not apply to food which has been cooked or reheated or is for service or on display for sale, or to food which is being or has been subject to a process such as dehydration or canning intended to prevent the growth of pathogenic micro-organisms at ambient temperature. A provision can be introduced which allows for the upward variation of the standard temperature of 8°C in appropriate circumstances. Any such variation must be based on a well-founded scientific assessment of the safety of the food at the new temperature.

Other parts of the legislation allow for chill holding tolerance periods and identify that there are defences which relate to the tolerance periods for which food may be held outside temperature control. For instance it is not an offence to keep food for service or on display for sale for a period of less than four hours and above the 8°C temperature requirement. It is however not allowable for such food to be displayed on more than one occasion. Equally if food has been transferred to a vehicle or there has been a temporary breakdown of equipment it is again a defence to keep food above the 8°C temperature requirement.

Hot holding requirements
Hot holding requirements are also referred to and the legislation notes that food that has been cooked or reheated should not be kept below 63°C. This is in order to control the growth of pathogenic micro-organisms or the formation of toxins. There are defences which allow for downward variation of this minimum 63°C temperature in appropriate circumstances and for a tolerance period of two hours.

General requirements
Regulation 10 adds a new general temperature control requirement which prohibits keeping perishable food stuffs at temperatures which would result in a risk to health. For instance, even if food is kept at or below 8°C there still could be a breach of food safety legislation under this general requirement contained within Regulation 10.

Regulation 13–16 refers to temperature control requirements in Scotland and Regulation 13–15 re-enact with minor and drafting modifications to food temperature control requirements previously contained in the Food Hygiene (Scotland) Regulations 1959. Regulation 16 adds a new general temperature control requirement which prohibits keeping food stuffs which are likely to support the growth of pathogenic micro-organisms or the formation of toxins at temperatures which would result in a risk to health.

The Department of Health has issued guidance which is intended to help explain for both food businesses and enforcement authorities the food temperature control requirements which will operate in England and Wales. It contains advice on the types of food which are required to be held under temperature control. It also gives guidance on the circumstances when the regulations allow some flexibility from the temperature requirements. While the guide is intended to be helpful, it does not provide any authoritative interpretation of the law and there is no substitute for an understanding of the legal requirements. Advice on the approach to enforcement of the temperature control requirements of the food hygiene regulations is found in the Food Safety Act 1990, Code of Practice no. 10.

Hazard analysis

Unlike previous food temperature control regulations, these regulations do not list specific foods which need to be held under temperature control conditions. The businesses themselves need to consider which food needs to be held under temperature control. There is a clear link between these regulations and the Food Safety (General Food Hygiene) Regulations 1995 and the topic of hazard analysis. The temperature control requirements should be understood in the general context of hazard analysis requirement contained in Regulation 4 of the Food Safety (General Food Hygiene) Regulations 1995. This requires food businesses to identify food hazards and to ensure that controls are in place to eliminate or minimise risks to consumers. Hazard analysis systems have an important part to play in helping to ensure that food is produced safely and chill control, in particular, is very often critical to food safety.

Guidance notes

There is more detailed sector-specific guidance in the UK industry guides to good hygiene practice and in an EU industry guide to good hygiene practice which are recognised by the UK government and the European Commission respectively as providing aids to compliance with the regulations. The guidance notes make the link with product-specific food hygiene regulations. A number of these regulations require food to be kept at prescribed temperatures or for the manufacturer to prescribe a temperature. Where a product-specific regulation applies, the provisions of the Food (Temperature Control) Regulations 1995 generally do not apply. The guidance gives examples of foods which need to be kept at or below 8°C. It is important to note that the requirement is for the temperature of 8°C to be applied to the food, not the air in the storage facility. The regulations allow a variation upwards from the 8°C maximum chill temperature but require a necessary scientific assessment. Detailed comments are included in the guidance notes on what processes should be contained in that scientific assessment. Discussion in the guidance notes then progresses to the issue of exemptions from the 8°C requirement and chill holding tolerance periods as well. Hot holding controls and hot holding tolerance period is also referred to in the guidance notes. An interesting requirement within the regulations is Regulation 10, which effectively means despite complying with the 8°C requirements, in some cases the food can result in a risk to health. There will be some foods where the general requirement of 8°C might require the food to be stored at a chilled temperature lower than 8°C for safety reasons, taking account of the allocated shelf life. Vacuum packed extended shelf life food, such as sous vide products, may be an example.

Food hygiene training

Contained within the Food Safety (General Food Hygiene) Regulations 1995 is a requirement for food hygiene training which mirrors the training requirements under the EU

Directive on the Hygiene of Foodstuffs of June 1993. This requires staff to be trained appropriate to their level and experience. On the subject of training there are six areas in which the majority of food handlers should have an understanding:

- how bacteria multiply
- conditions for bacterial growth
- prevention of food poisoning
- personal health and hygiene
- cleaning of premises and equipment
- pest control.

The basic training requirement is equivalent to the six-hour examined and certificated course run by the three main examining bodies:

- Institution of Environmental Health Officers (IEHO) Basic Food Hygiene Certificate
- Royal Society of Health (RSH) Essential Food Hygiene Certificate
- Royal Institute of Public Health and Hygiene (RIPHH) Primary Certificate in Essential Food Hygiene.

Registered trainers are required to run these courses; to apply for registration an individual has to have food hygiene qualifications equivalent to the IEHO Advanced Level. There are three main ways in which the training of staff can be recorded:

- incorporation into basic staff training programmes
- incorporation into existing catering qualification
- certification by the three main examining bodies

Another important point to consider is the attitude of EHOs to training as part of a routine inspection.

Although not a legal requirement **operating instructions and training** are considered part of a checklist of points to be used by an EHO. This is in order to comply with the statutory code of practice on **food standard inspections** issued under Section 40 of the Food Safety Act 1990.

A similar requirement is included in the statutory code of practice on **food hygiene inspections** also issued under Section 40. EHOs will want to know if staff receive training in food hygiene and to what level. Such answers may determine the frequency of inspection.

Food premises registration

The introduction of regulations on 1 May 1992 required nearly all existing food premises to be registered with the local authority and new food premises may not be opened or used without an application for registration having been made at least twenty-eight days in advance.

The process of registering food premises is relatively simple, requiring a one-page registration form, available from the local authority; there is no registration fee.

The Food Premises (Registration) Regulations 1991 creates a range of criminal offences from failure to register or to notify notifiable changes, through to giving false information. A food business is not just one run for profit and so can include a school, hospital, charity subsidised canteen and public services.

There are two types of premises: permanent premises, which include land and buildings, and moveable (not fixed) premises, which include ice-cream vans, office drinks trolleys, market stalls, hospitality trailers and even food delivery vehicles. The registration requirements for these two types of premises are different.

At the simplest level, any food premises used by one food business must be registered by the proprietor of that business. Food does not necessarily have to be the principal aspect of the business in order for registration to be necessary and so nursing and rest homes, hospitals, schools and such like also have to register.

Where permanent food premises are within larger premises, for instance a works canteen in a factory, then the smaller premises must be registered by the proprietor of the food business.

Where permanent premises are used by more than one food business, for example the community hall which is let out for wedding receptions, the person, authority or company who hires out or allows the premises to be used by different food businesses must register those premises.

The registration regulations apply only to what are termed 'relevant moveable premises'. This term excludes the following: passenger vehicles for no more than eight people (including the driver). marquees, awnings, etc.

Almost any other temporary or mobile structure will be within the category of relevant moveable premises. Unlike permanent premises (and apart from market stalls) it is not the moveable premises themselves which are registerable but the place where they are normally kept stored or garaged. It is the responsibility of the proprietor of the food business to register the premises where the moveable premises are kept even though he or she may not own those premises.

Market stalls and stands are different. If the market controller supplies the stalls, then as a generalisation the market controller is responsible for registering the market. If a market trader, for example, a hamburger stand or a mobile tea bar, uses the market then that market trader must register the moveable premises. This applies even if the market controller has also registered the whole market.

The regulations list over twenty exemptions in five different categories, the main one being premises used (whether by the same or different food businesses) fewer than five days in any five consecutive weeks.

Case Study: EC Directive on the Hygiene of Foodstuffs: implications

The subject of food safety law is ever changing, no more so than with the effect of EU legislation. The EC Directive on the Hygiene of Foodstuffs was adopted June 1993. It makes reference to Food Hygiene Training, Hazard Analysis Critical Control Point and Industry Codes of Practice. All these issues were introduced into legislation within the UK in 1995.

One significant directive that is having implications for the European hotel and catering industry is the EC Directive on the Hygiene of Foodstuffs. Adopted in June 1993 by the EU, member states have had thirty months in which to implement its requirements into national legislation. This Directive in particular illustrates a change in EU food law, the attitudes of individual member states to this issue and prompts questions on the diversity of food law enforcement.

case study continues ▶

case study continues

Development of EU food law

The initial approach of the European Commission to food law was based on the concept that a national law needed a community law in order to ensure the free circulation of goods. For many years EU food legislation pursued the path dictated by this approach using Article 100 of the EEC Treaty which called for unanimity; however the unanimity rule was not the main obstacle to progress. Although food law in member states had common objectives the approach and structure was rooted historically in the culinary and cultural traditions of member states. The diversity of climate and agriculture in the EU meant that the nutritional needs of the population were met in a variety of ways and even in areas having access to the same raw materials, methods of preparation of food varied widely. As labelling was only in its infancy, the interests of consumers and also producers was served by using a food name or denomination based on these traditions as the vehicle to inform the consumer, and legally reserving this name for a particular specification or recipe. It was inevitable that the concepts of 'good beer, good sausages and good bread' should conflict in a society as diverse as the EU. Early attempts to legislate were focused on the harmonisation of product specifications and met with little success since they were perceived as a direct assault by bureaucrats on long hallowed traditions. It took some time to understand that the root of the problem lay in the fact that if recipes were embodied in law then the point of attack should be on the law not on the food.

It was for this reason that there has been a shift away from product specific directives to general horizontal Directives, an example being the EC Directive on the Hygiene of Foodstuffs 1993.

Diversity of food law enforcement

The problems of consistent enforcement of this Directive are ongoing throughout the EU and can be related to the structure of the enforcing authorities. In Denmark, Netherlands and the UK, control rests with one government organisation, while responsibility for inspection is devolved by region, legislation can not be determined by region. In the UK, food hygiene matters are dealt with by a separate government organisation. In Italy the Ministry of Health takes responsibility for food law enforcement. Italian food legislation is highly complex and difficult to interpret and much has become outdated as the country's cumbersome legislative process has failed to keep up with the need for change. This is partly a result of a post-war constitution concerned to establish safeguards against arbitrary abuse of power, but it has made it more difficult for Italy to implement EU legislation. In Spain, food law is based on the *Codigo Alimentario* which was enacted in 1967 and came into force in 1974. The *Codigo Alimentario* contains a description of the regulatory aims and scope of the legislation, definitions of the most fundamental concepts of food law and a list of the persons and organisations affected by the regulations. It is supplemented by a host of decrees, ministerial orders, product standards and sanitary regulations. The responsibility for food control is divided up between central government, the *communidades autonomas* and the local authorities. Food issues are regulated by a number of ministries and unless competence can be clearly imputed to one of them, the committee for the regulation of food matters will intervene. This organisation co-ordinates any action taken in this field by the different ministries.

case study continues ▶

case study continues

It is these differences in enforcement that make it difficult to implement EC Directives into national legislation.

The Netherlands

Issues concerning the implementation of the EC Directive can be illustrated with reference to the Netherlands. On 12 December 1994 the Commodities Act Order on the Hygiene of Foodstuffs was issued to implement the Directive on the Hygiene of Foodstuffs 1993; it came into force in December 1995. Article 1 of the Dutch Order implements the definitions of hygiene and of food businesses (Article 2 Directive) by copying them out literally. As with Dutch law there is no European definition of food.

The identification of methods (control on food safety hazards) is a central part of the legislation and is covered with the use of Hazard Analysis Critical Control Points (HACCP). An important difference between the HACCP principles contained within the Directive and the codex guidelines for the application of the HACCP system is that the EU principles do not contain the obligation to establish documentation concerning all procedures and records related to HACCP principles and their application. Although this record keeping requirement had been proposed by the European Parliament in 1992, it has not been included in the Directive itself. An important additional obligation for the Dutch is that Article 30 Section 2 obliges businesses to keep records of their HACCP system and that this should be available to supervising officials. HACCP will bring about changes for both food operators and a need for a flexible attitude by inspectors – they will need a capacity to monitor.

Article 5 of the Directive contains provisions concerning both so-called national and European guides to good hygiene practice. Article 31 of the Dutch Order implements the community provisions on national guides. Since 1987 the Dutch government has stimulated the drafting of guides to good hygiene practice. In the late 1990s there are some fifteen Dutch guides to good hygiene practice, many (but not all) of which contain several elements of the HACCP principles. The use of the guides raises several questions in Dutch law. A first question concerns the way in which the guides will be viewed by the monitoring authorities. Article 32 requires the authorities to take proper account of the guides. A second question deals with the fulfilment of the HACCP requirements by the application of a hygiene guide. A third question concerns the nature of the relationship between national and European guides. Must the contents of the national guides be in accordance with the contents of the European ones?

The Directive also gives member states a lot of freedom to decide on the organisation of the national monitoring and enforcement system. In the Netherlands the Inspectorate for Health Protection is the main authority for food monitoring.

The hygiene Directive allows the member states to designate their own system of penalties, whether it is of a criminal, civil or administrative law nature. In the Netherlands, violations against food legislation come under criminal law and the relevant authorities have criminal investigation powers.

From the description of food law in the Netherlands and the agencies monitoring the law it is obvious that the system is highly complicated. Moreover the ministries involved disagree on the division of powers. This has resulted in discussions on what form legis-

case study continues ▶

case study continues

lation should take and on the division of powers concerning the monitoring of such legis-lation. It is perhaps inevitable that all government institutions will be brought together into one Dutch Control Agency of Foodstuffs.

Trends in food law

It could be argued that there is a need for a transparent and simpler EU food policy with a preference for horizontal legislation and only limited vertical legislation. According to some experts, deregulation and subsidiarity should be the leading principles in such a way that the EC regulates the main issues clearly and with one voice and that member states are responsible for the application and more detailed provisions. Another aspect is the use of instruments, regulations and directives. One view is that the regulation should be considered more often in addition to the directive. First, because a regulation does not need to be transposed into national law, and second, a regulation promotes a more uni-fied application of community rules in the EU especially where community legislation does not leave any discretionary power to the member states.

Liquor licensing legislation

The sale of alcoholic drinks in the UK is controlled by a system of licences under the Licensing Act 1964, as amended by the Licensing Act 1988.

The 1964 Act licenses the person at premises authorised by the licence. It is the local licensing justices who grant licences at either the annual licensing sessions held in February each year or at any of the transfer sessions which are held throughout the year. The licensing system described in this section operates in England and Wales. The law in Scotland is different and is governed by the Licensing (Scotland) Act 1976. The law per-mits the sale or supply of alcoholic drinks at certain times.

Types of licences

Licences are broadly divided into on-licences and off-licences. The typical on-licence will permit off-sales as well, so a public house will usually be able to sell drinks for drinking on the premises as well as selling drinks to be taken away. A full on-licence permits the licensee to sell alcoholic drinks for consumption on or off the premises and with or with-out meals. On-licences are divided into five categories according to the type of alcoholic drinks which are licensed to be sold.

Restaurant licence

A variety of on-licence is a restaurant licence. The condition imposed on such a licence is that drinks may be served only to diners taking table meals. A licensee under a restau-rant licence can generally obtain a supper hour certificate which will extend the permit-ted hours by one hour per day. The permitted hours include the afternoons on Sundays, Christmas Day and Good Friday, so there is no need to close the restaurant or cease the service of alcoholic drinks with meals during the period 3p.m. to 7p.m. on such days. Off-sales are not permitted under a restaurant licence.

Residential licence

A residential licence is another variety of on-licence and is suitable for hotels and guest houses which provide bed, breakfast and at least one other main meal. It allows drinks to be served to residents and their friends. The normal permitted hours do not apply so that residents may buy and consume alcoholic drinks at any time of the day or night.

Combined licence

A further variety of on-licence is the residential and restaurant licence often known as a combined licence, suitable for a hotel operating a restaurant open to non-residents.

Occasional licence

An occasional licence is granted to a person who has an existing on-licence other than a residential or club licence; it allows the licensee to sell drinks somewhere other than the licensed premises. It can be granted for a maximum period of three weeks. These licences are not available on Christmas Day, Good Friday or any other day appointed for public fast or thanksgiving.

Occasional permission

Occasional permissions enable non-profit organisations to run a bar at a fund-raising event without having to get a licensee to run the bar. The bar must not be carried out for private gain and such drinks can not be served for more than twenty-four hours. An organisation can apply only for up to four permissions in any twelve-month period.

Permitted hours

The generally permitted hours for on-licensed premises are

- Sundays, Christmas Day and Good Friday: 12 noon to 3p.m. and 7p.m. to 10.30p.m.
- Other days: 11a.m. to 11p.m.

It is an offence to sell or supply alcoholic drinks on licensed premises outside the permitted hours.

A licensee is not obliged to keep the premises open throughout the permitted hours. There are various exceptions to and methods of extending the general licensing hours in particular circumstances but it should also be noted that the permitted hours in registered clubs may be different.

Orders of exemption

The 1964 Act allows local magistrates to grant a general order of exemption to the licensee of on-licensed premises. Such an order can specify additional hours every day or for certain days of the week or month. They usually happen within the neighbourhood of, for instance, a public market. Special orders of exemption are similar to general orders of exemption in that they extend the permitted hours but as their name implies they are only for special occasions rather than continuous or recurring events. The order is therefore for a specific event or occasion and such an occasion has to be special. The magistrates have complete discretion on whether to grant a special order of exemption.

Supper hour certificate

The licensee of on-licensed premises can apply for a supper hour certificate to serve drinks with a meal for an extra period after the permitted hours on a continuing basis that is not just for a particular day. In practice this certificate is granted only to a restaurant or dining area.

Extended hours order
If the premises have a supper hour certificate then it is possible to extend the permitted hours for the premises even longer by having live music or other entertainment. In such a case an extended hours order may be granted which will extend the permitted hours for the premises until 1a.m. the following day. The order operates on a continuing basis but only when entertainment is provided. An important requirement of this is that the music must be *live*.

Special hours certificate
The effect of a special hours certificate is to extend the permitted hours to 2a.m. the following morning and 3a.m. in certain parts of Central London. The one exception is Sundays into Monday mornings. This type of certificate is appropriate to a nightclub. It is not necessary that there are table meals but there must be an entertainment licence and the regular provision of music for at least fifty weeks of the year.

Drinking up time
At the end of the permitted hours there is a further drinking up time of twenty minutes in public houses and bars, and thirty minutes if alcoholic drinks are being consumed ancillary to a meal. The drinking time applies at the end of the period when drinks may be lawfully sold.

Licensing procedure

The licensing procedure is administered by the licensing justices who are appointed from the local magistrates and conduct their proceedings in the local magistrates courtroom. Many of the applications under the 1964 Act require notice not only to the licensing justices but also to the police and sometimes to the local fire service.

The application for any type of justice licence involves a procedure of giving notice and advertising the application prior to consideration of the application by the justices. In every case a licence can be granted only if the applicant is a fit and proper person to hold a licence, an issue which is for the justices to decide. A provisional licence, which is not a licence to sell drink, may be granted on the basis of deposited plans of a proposed development. The issue of the licence being made final would then focus on whether the applicant was a fit and proper person. Licences are renewed every three years at which time justices have powers to revoke the licence. The transfer of a licence may be made at the annual sessions or at the quarterly transfer sessions. Transfers may happen due to ill health, retirement, death or perhaps the sale of the business. In these circumstances the issue is whether the incoming licensee is a fit and proper person. As there can sometimes be a gap between licensing sessions, protection orders may be granted by the local magistrates court in order to cover the period up to the next licensing session.

Criminal offences

The 1964 Act also concerns itself with the conduct of the licensed premises and in certain circumstances imposes a range of criminal offences. Children under 14 are prohibited from being in a bar during the permitted hours (unless they are the landlords children). It is a criminal offence for a licensee or employee to sell alcoholic drinks to anyone under the age of 18 and it is an offence for an underage person to buy or attempt to buy such drinks. Anyone over 18 buying a drink for someone under 18 on licensed premises is committing an offence. One general exception is that a person over 16 can purchase beer, porter, cider or perry for drinking with a meal. Finally it is an offence if a licensee employs a person under 18 in a bar when it is open. The word *bar* is defined as a place which is only or mainly used for selling and drinking alcoholic drinks, except a bar serving only diners who are taking table meals.

Health and safety at work

The section of this chapter devoted to EC legislation has already mentioned health and safety. This subject will now be discussed further within a UK context.

Statutory obligations under health and safety arise out of the Health and Safety at Work etc. Act 1974, which created criminal responsibility with certain general duties on employers and employees.

Section 2 states that it shall be the general duty of every employer to ensure so far as is reasonably practicable the health, safety and welfare at work of all employees. Section 7 of the Act places a similar duty of care on employees. Reinforcing these duties are further obligations:

- preparing and keeping up to date a written health and safety policy and bringing it to the attention of employees
- displaying a poster or distributing a leaflet about the general duties required under the Act
- making available facilities, including time off for training safety representatives.

Enforcement of the Act is made by local authorities and the Health and Safety Executive, the latter having the power to issue improvement notices and prohibition notices. Contained within the Act is the power to issue regulations and approved codes of practice.

Following on this theme of safety is the Control of Substances Hazardous to Health Regulations 1988 (COSHH) which created duties owed by employers to employees concerning substances hazardous to health. These regulations require the employer to carry out a risk assessment of any work practices where employees might be exposed to any substances that might be hazardous to their health and to decide what steps should be taken to eliminate or reduce the risk.

Employers are obliged to report certain injuries and dangerous occurrences as covered by the Reporting of Injuries, Diseases and Dangerous Occurrences Regulations 1988. Normally these are reported to the local authority. Also every employer is required by the Health and Safety (First Aid) Regulations 1981 to provide adequate equipment and facilities for first aid for employees who are injured or become ill at work.

Planning legislation

Town and country planning legislation has been around in substantially its present form since 1947 and is administered by local authorities. Legislation concerning planning is mainly controlled in the UK by the Town and Country Planning Act 1990 as amended by the Planning and Compensation Act 1991.

There are two elements to this control on development: building on land, and a change in use of buildings or land. Planning permission is required for any development and so an application has to be made to the local authority. Failure to obtain planning permission when it is required may lead to the issue of enforcement action which may result in the building being removed or the original use restored. It is only a material change of use that triggers the need for planning permission in the case of a change of use. It will generally be the case that a change from one class to another will require planning permission. The relevant order is the Town and Country Planning (Use Classes) Order 1987, which lists the various uses under various orders.

There are special controls which affect buildings designated as being of special architectural or historic interest along with controls on areas of special interest. Finally there are controls concerning the display of outdoor advertisements.

Summary

This chapter has sketched a background to the UK legal system and the effects of the European Union and described certain areas of legislation that have a direct effect on the hospitality industry. The emphasis has been on food safety at both UK and European level. Comments have been made on liquor licensing, health and safety and planning legislation.

Further reading

- Acton C. (1993) *EC Food Hygiene Directive on the Safety of Foodstuffs*, 13 August, Circular Letter, London: Department of Health.
- Coopers and Lybrand (1992) *Employment Law in Europe*, London: Gower Press.
- *Croner's Catering Manual* (1992a) New Malden: Croner Publications.
- *Croner's Practical Food Hygiene Manual* (1992b) New Malden: Croner Publications.
- Department of Health (1994) *A Template: Industry Guide to Good Hygiene Practice*, London.
- Department of Health (1994a) *Management of Outbreaks of Food-borne Illness*, London: HMSO.
- Department of Health (1994b) *Assured Safe Catering*, London: HMSO.
- Knowles T. (1994) 'Some aspects of UK and European food legislation', *Hygiene and Nutrition in Food Service and Catering*, 1(1): 49–62.
- Knowles T. (1992) Effect of the EEC Law on the Hospitality Industry, Discussion Paper, Leeds Polytechnic, October.
- Local Authorities Co-ordinating Body on Food and Trading Standards (1995) *Food Hygiene Risk Assessment: Guidance to Local Authorities on the Application of Risk Assessment Principles to Food Hygiene Inspections*, Croydon: LACOTS.
- Ministry of Agriculture, Fisheries, and Food (1989) *Food Safety: Protecting the Consumer*, Cmnd 732, London: HMSO.
- NEDC (1991) *The Planning System and Large Scale Tourism and Leisure Developments*, London: National Economic Development Office.
- *Pattersons Licensing Acts* (1992) London: Butterworths.
- Peters R. (1992) *Essential Law for Catering Students*, London: Hodder and Stoughton.
- Selwyn N.M. (1991) *Selwyns Employment Law*, 7th edn, London: Butterworth.
- Sheard M.A. (1986) 'HACCP and microbiological quality assurance in catering', in *The HACCP Concept and Quality Assurance in Food Manufacture and Catering*, SOFHT Proceedings, pp. 20–43.
- Thomas R. and Thomas H. (1990) *Not an Appropriate Area: The Consideration of Planning Applications for Hot Takeaway Areas*, Leeds Metropolitan University.

Chapter Eight

Restaurant and Fast Food Industry

Objectives

After reading this chapter you should be able to

▪ Identify and quantify the main sectors of the consumer catering market.

▪ Examine major developments and the major participants within the market.

▪ Consider the management of food and beverage operations from the purchase of supplies, through storage and preparation, to the final service of the finished product to the ultimate consumer.

Catering market

The structure of the catering industry of which restaurants and fast food outlets represent an important sector expanded substantially in the late 1980s. In the late 1990s it is no longer possible to define a single type of catering establishment which falls into either the restaurant or fast food market. Indeed, the catering market consists of various restaurants: fast food outlets which offer full table service such as Pizza Hut, up-market gourmet premises, pub restaurants, in-store outlets, cafés and bars, all of which come within the definition of the consumer catering market.

Whereas major operators such as McDonald's or Burger King are easily identifiable as fast food chains, there are thousands of restaurants, public houses and other establishments which have catering facilities offering fast food. Therefore the distinction between full service, eat on the premises outlets, self-service outlets and take-aways is becoming increasingly blurred. For the sake of simplicity, this chapter will concentrate in the main on the commercial profit sector.

Sources of data

Although in the UK there are official government figures available covering the catering market they come from a number of sources and the end results are impossible to reconcile in some cases. In addition, there are problems concerning the coverage of the data so far as consumer catering is concerned and some data are not up to date.

The main source of official data are the *Consumer Expenditure Figures,* the report series *Catering and Allied Trades in the Business Monitor* (based on an industry survey covering the VAT registered businesses) and the *Family Expenditure Survey* (a consumer survey based on records of expenditure). Also of some use in attempting to gauge market growth are the *Retail Prices Indices* covering the catering industry and the *National Food Survey* which provides data on the number of meals eaten out per person per week.

The most useful in providing market size figures for consumer catering are those published in the Business Monitor series. The figures are fairly comprehensive excluding only those businesses not registered for VAT and businesses whose main activity is not catering. The figures are based on the turnover of catering businesses which is easily measurable. Not only are the figures broken down by broad catering sector but also in some years by a source of turnover. One problem with the Business Monitor series is that they are not kept up to date in terms of the food figures published. Also significant industries such as contract catering fall outside the scope of the report.

Analysing the general environment

The consumer catering market has a wide customer base, and so, is strongly influenced by general environmental trends within the country. The consumer catering market during the first half of the 1990s was severely affected by the economic recession, particularly by its impact on disposable income. Consumers appeared to be less willing to eat out, with the frequency and amount spent per visit declining. Problems caused by the economic downturn had been compounded by other factors. The impact of the introduction of the uniform business rate, the falling value of restaurant property prices and rent reviews combined to result in a dramatic reduction in profits during this period. Additional investment, because of political and legislative factors, has also been required to comply with the Food Safety Act 1990 which came into force in 1991, along with food hygiene and temperature regulations which came into force during 1995. The influence of the EU will continue to affect the consumer catering market.

During the second half of the 1990s many of these factors, particularly economic, were reversed and profitability returned to the consumer catering market.

Three main demographic factors will influence the market during the period up to the millennium and beyond. The increase in child population should benefit those sectors with a strong appeal to children or families, such as fast food, travel related catering, pub catering and family restaurants. The drop in the number of 16–24 year olds, as well as possibly creating staffing problems throughout the sector, will impact on theme restaurants where this group forms an important potentially high spending market. Theme restaurants are likely to pitch for slightly older customers aiming particularly at those with a higher level of disposable income. Older age groups, especially 'empty nesters', represent a more difficult market as they tend to eat out infrequently and in expensive restaurants. Fast food operators in particular are likely to find it difficult to appeal to this group.

Catering sectors

The consumer catering market in the UK is worth an estimated £15 billion. The various sectors of the market have experienced varying fortunes with particularly pub catering buoyed by the general movement downmarket.

There are some 207,000 consumer catering outlets in the UK. The total has been in decline in recent years as some of the large, long established sectors have been gradually rationalised. The number of catering businesses totals some 124,500.

Fast food and take-away is the largest sector of the market by value with a 34% share. This growth is attributable to the expansion of the fast food market. The pub and club sector, the second largest, has also seen a gain in share. The fastest growth in potential terms has been in the small retail catering sector, thanks to the rapid development of outlets in the late 1980s. The levels of growth moderated in all sectors during the early 1990s as a result of the economic downturn with the restaurant/café and accommodation sectors being most severely affected.

The largest sectors of the consumer catering market in terms of outlets are pubs and accommodation establishments although of course these are not dedicated to catering establishments. Fast food has been the only consistently expanding sector thanks to the high penetration of major brands with funds for ongoing expansion. Sectors where there is a large proportion of independently run businesses such as restaurants, cafés and take-aways have seen a steady rationalisation of outlets over the past few years. The pub sector is likely to see a sharp drop in total number of outlets, as the major brewers have been forced to sell off premises to meet the recommendations of the Monopolies and Mergers Commission Report, although in turn, this has seen a growth in the medium sized regional pub retailers. The major brewers are concentrating on fewer but larger and profitable outlets.

The overall fast food and take-away sector has seen considerable growth. **Burger bars** are the major sector in the fast food market with a 50% share of total turnover of the sector. The most dynamic growth sector in fast food has been chicken.

Pub catering has been a strong growth area as brewers have emphasised this side of business to capitalise on all-day opening hours and guard against any fall in the core alcoholic drinks markets. Catering currently accounts for around 25% of sales through pubs. Within the pub food market, bar food and food counter sales have registered the highest growth rate reflecting the fact that they are generally less expensive than other consumer catering sectors and are regarded by many as value for money.

The **restaurant and café sector** encompasses a wide range of outlets ranging from the upper end restaurants to down market cafés. Overall the sector saw an increase in sales, although fortunes have varied widely between the individual sectors. **Steak-house and family chains** continued to expand, but the strongest relative growth was in the theme restaurant sector. The latter are generally American and are targeted at younger, more affluent consumers. The family chain sector has experienced some rationalisation with the withdrawal of Berni Inn from the sector by Whitbread, and its incorporation within the Beefeater Brand. Cafés such as Whitbread's *Café Rouge* have seen a relatively strong growth through trading down from other higher priced sectors and through an increasing number of upgraded premises.

The **accommodation catering** sector as a whole is directly affected by the travel and tourism market and indirectly affected by the consumer catering market. The rise and fall in visitors to the UK during the 1990s has affected a number of potential customers for these catering outlets.

The **travel catering** sector incorporates rail and roadside outlets. Growth is directly related to the market for passenger travel particularly in the onboard sector. Station outlets cover a range of concepts such as snack bars, bars and hamburger outlets while large city stations tend to contain a number of different styles of catering outlets, many of which are controlled in the UK by Travellers Fare, a division of Compass plc.

Most **leisure catering** is accounted for by the catering facilities offered by leisure centres. There has been a steady growth thanks to newly built or upgraded centres and the growing interest in sport and fitness.

The **retail catering** market has experienced rapid growth through facility developments which have expanded the market considerably beyond the **in-store restaurants** traditionally found in department stores. However, in line with other sectors, growth is constrained by the economy and the performance of high street retailers. **Food courts** which currently number around fifty have been the fastest growing sector. They have been included in many out-of-town shopping centres and are thought to appeal to customers who would be unlikely to use other catering outlets. This sector has shown its potential for growth as the economy began to recover in the mid-1990s. **In-store cafés** have some potential for growth largely because of their incorporation into out-of-town developments by the major grocery multiples.

Consumers

Having identified the sectors of the consumer catering market and some of the factors which affect their growth, we will now consider the sort of people who eat out in the UK, the type of food and meals they purchase and consume and how much they spend, including places where people eat, frequency of visitation, reasons for eating out and factors which influence the choice of new restaurants.

Some 30% of consumers eat a meal in a fast food restaurant every month, demonstrating the extent to which this form of eating out has become accepted by the British consumer. However, the restaurant remains the most popular place to eat out either in the evening or at lunchtime. Almost the same number using fast food outlets had eaten in a restaurant in the evening while a significant proportion of consumers also eat in a restaurant at lunchtime. Pubs remain an important place to eat out especially at lunchtimes, with some 25% eating in these outlets every month.

Another sector of significance is cafés, including sandwich bars which, particularly in the major cities, are a popular place to eat at lunchtimes. In addition, there are a number of cafés positioned on or near main roads, which draw their custom from the commercial sector such as lorry drivers. This sector has tended to dwindle with the development of motorways and major trunk roads which are served by motorway service stations or the leading roadside restaurant chains such as Little Chef.

Gender

One can extend these comments further by considering the demographic trends. The main points to emerge by gender is that eating out in fast food outlets is slightly more popular among men than women. Restaurants have a broad appeal with similar proportions of men and women eating in them. In contrast, eating out in pubs has a strong bias towards men both at lunchtime and in the evening.

Age groups

The figures can also be analysed by age groups. The results show some significant variations in the pattern of eating out between the different age groups. Fast food outlets have a very strong bias towards those from the younger age groups, particularly those in the 15–24 age bracket and fall off slightly among older consumers. Those from the 20–24 age group are the most likely to have eaten a meal in a restaurant in the evening, although there is a strong core of restaurant visitors aged between 20 and 54. There is no significant difference in the level of eating in restaurants at lunchtime between the various age groups. Those from the 20–24 age group are also most likely to have eaten in a pub both at lunchtime and in the evening. Like fast food outlets, eating out in cafés has a strong bias towards those from the younger age groups particularly those aged 34 and under. Eating out in restaurants and cafés in a shop is most prevalent in respondents aged 20–34. This group is most likely to be young adults and especially young mothers who are not working. Those having not eaten away from home come from the older age groups with almost half of those aged 65 and over saying that they had not done so.

Socio-economic groups

Fast food outlets have a broad appeal across all socio-economic groups peaking among those respondents from the C1 group and only really falling off among those from E group, many of whom are elderly or unemployed. Eating out in a restaurant both in the evening and at lunchtime is strongly biased to those in the higher earning A and B groups and to a lesser extent C1 groups. It falls off noticeably in those from the D and E groups who are least likely to have eaten out. Those eating out in pubs at lunchtime are most likely to be from the A, B and C1 groups. This trend is less pronounced with eating in the pub in the evening, which has a broader appeal across most groups. The level of eating out in a café is fairly even across all socio-economic groups, peaking among those from the E group who are those living at the lowest level of subsistence e.g. elderly and unemployed people. Eating out in a restaurant or café within a shop is most prevalent among those from the AB and C1 groups.

Regions

The level of eating out in fast food restaurants peaks in the London region where the concentration of such outlets is at its highest in the UK. It is lowest in areas where the concentration of restaurants is at its least dense. The level of eating out in each type of establishment considered is higher than average in almost all cases for people living in the London region. The highest level of consumers visiting a restaurant in the evening was among individuals from the London area. Eating out at lunchtime and in the evenings in pubs is most prevalent with consumers in the Yorkshire and Tyne Tees regions although an above average level can also be noted among those from the London region for lunchtime eating. Eating out in pubs in the evening in Scotland is not a popular activity: the level for this region is considerably below average. The level of eating out in cafés is highest in the far northern and western regions of the UK and slightly below average in the London region.

Working status

When one considers places eaten in by consumers' working status, not surprisingly people who are working have a higher level of visiting eating out establishments than those who are not, with the exception of cafés. Those who are retired have a low overall level of eating away from home.

Children

Fast food restaurants are significantly more likely to be visited by respondents with children than those without, while cafés are slightly more likely to be visited by those with children. Restaurants and pubs are slightly more likely to be visited by those without children. The presence of children is clearly an important overall influence on the propensity to eat out. Marital status is less of a significant influence. This is because those who have not married are mainly from the younger age groups and who tend to have the highest levels of visiting these types of outlets.

Suppliers

An important element of the consumer catering market are the firms that supply it. Since the mid-1980s as the concentration of the consumer catering market has fallen increasingly into the hands of a limited number of larger chains, so the power of food manufacturers, sales and transport resources have been affected accordingly. The change in power that this concentration has afforded the leading catering retailers has rendered this market an increasingly unprofitable proposition for food suppliers who are now turning more and more towards the independent catering sectors, in order to achieve viable margins among other things. Currently direct food manufacturing business accounts for only 7% of caterers' purchases of food, soft drinks and other consumables while the delivered wholesalers supply an estimated 75% of the market. Delivered wholesalers who have seen their business with multiple catering retailers shrink in recent years have been going through a period of redevelopment and restructuring resulting in companies which are both larger in size and more professional in outlook and operations. At the same time the cash and carry trades have been developing their influence among independent and small caterers. In common with this trend, the delivered wholesale trade and cash and carry businesses are increasingly dominated by a few key players. Thus, as manufacturers are tending to rely significantly on wholesalers to distribute to a more fragmented market, those wholesalers are becoming fewer in number. It is crucial therefore for the food suppliers to understand more about the way in which the distribution market works, the leading players within it and the ways in which the distribution sector is likely to develop and in addition its relationship with the consumer catering market.

The trend during the 1990s has been for fewer catering businesses to rely on wholesale deliveries, with specialist retailers and to a lesser extent cash and carry and general retailers being the main beneficiaries. Indeed the attraction of supermarkets such as Sainsbury's for smaller businesses is increasingly obvious: the range of produce including the exotic is increasingly varied. Restaurateurs can buy a small quantity, the prices are competitive and it seems it is the small operators that are buying from such retailers. With fresh meat and fish, however, it is the specialist retailer, the butcher and the fishmonger who are taking a major slice of business and the indications are that it is more broadly across the consumer catering market. Only in the big catering outlets do the wholesalers and indeed the food manufacturers gain significant levels of business.

Major operators

The UK catering industry is dominated by a large number of small mainly independent operators; however, the number of chains has increased in recent years and many large catering companies now have key positions within the market. The chains are operated by three types of companies:

- Brewers and public house owners who are specially strong in the steak-house sector.
- Leisure specialists who concentrate on the fast food theme sectors.
- Hotel groups which specialise in the fast food roadside market.

Having considered the major sectors within the consumer catering market and their consumers the history and development of a number of major operators will now be discussed.

McDonald's

McDonald's was founded in 1955 in the USA by Ray Kroc. Since then it has expanded to become the world's largest and fastest growing restaurant chain with over 12,750 outlets in 62 countries, including an outlet in Moscow. In the UK, McDonald's opened its first outlet in Woolwich, South London, in 1974. By the mid-1990s the number of McDonald's in the UK had reached some 500 and is certain to be even higher in the years to come. Not only is the company clear leader in the burger market with a share of almost 40%, it is also the largest catering chain in the UK. While the McDonald's red and yellow fascia is a familiar sight throughout cities and towns in the UK, the company has shown some sensitivity to its surroundings with a few of the outlets in architecturally sensitive areas not being fronted with the McDonald's usual colourings and logo. Another major change of policy has been McDonald's decision to stop using its famous foam plastic burger boxes; the company has finally given in to pressure from environmentalists. While the majority of the restaurants are company owned, up to forty in the UK are franchised. The company has made considerable efforts to diversify its product offering away from the central product of beef burgers. This has involved appealing to a wider clientele with the introduction of such products as Filet o Fish, Chicken McNuggets, McChicken Sandwich and Fruit pie. Salads were introduced and pizza has been tested.

Grand Metropolitan

Grand Metropolitan used to be considered the UK's leading challenge to McDonald's in the domestic fast food market; a more accurate description would be to describe it as McDonald's leading challenger in the hamburger chain sector of the fast food market. In this sector Grand Metropolitan owns Burger King which it acquired in its purchase of the Pilsbury Corporation in late 1988. At the time, Burger King had thirty outlets in the UK, a number that grew considerably during the 1990s. Burger King is the world's second largest hamburger restaurant chain after McDonalds. In the UK some are company owned and others are franchises. In addition to its rapid expansion in number of outlets, the company has been expanding its menu base to broaden its appeal. In addition to vegetarian burgers being introduced, a breakfast menu is now available. Just like McDonald's, Burger King has attempted to appeal to a younger age group along with a similar environmental policy. World-wide Burger King has over 6,000 franchised and managed outlets in over forty-one countries, although most are in the USA.

In April 1990 Grand Metropolitan sold 216 table service Wimpy outlets to a management buyout for £20 million, while retaining 100 counter service Wimpy outlets. In 1991, Grand Metropolitan divested itself of its interest in the pizza sector of the fast food market. It sold its pizza delivery chain Perfect Pizza to Canadian group Scotts Hospitality (there were 161 Perfect Pizza outlets at the time of this acquisition). Also in 1991, Grand Metropolitan sold its ailing 101 Pizzaland restaurant chains and its 18 Pastafichio pasta specialist restaurants to Bright Reasons, a company set up by the former Mecca Chairman Michael Guthrie.

Granada

Granada plc's division Forte operates among its portfolio the Little Chef and Happy Eater chains of roadside diners. The Little Chef chain started in 1958 and is the largest chain in the sector. The concept is targeted at the travelling family as well as individuals and couples. The Happy Eater chain of roadside diners acquired in 1986 is geared even more to the needs of travelling families. They have greater restaurant space, wide menus and children's play facilities.

Whitbread

Whitbread is a major force in the consumer catering market with a substantial presence in the pub catering, steak-house and other niche restaurant sectors, as well as a 50% share in the UK's largest pizza chain Pizza Hut. Whitbread's major brands are Pizza Hut, TGI Friday's, Beefeater (now incorporating Berni Inns), Brewers Fayre, Mulligan Fish Bar and Henry's Café. Pizza Hut was established in 1958 with the first UK outlet opening in 1973. In 1982 Pizza Hut (UK) Ltd was established as a joint venture operation between the UK brewers Whitbread and the US soft drinks giant, Pepsi Cola. Pizza Hut is the clear leader in the pizza restaurant sector. The first UK Pizza Hut opened in Islington, London, in 1973; the company has over 200 full service restaurants in the UK and a number of fast growing specialised delivery outlets. Pizza Hut has undergone a complete refurbishment which aims to give outlets a softer plainer look in order to appeal to the family and the older market. In addition to dine-in restaurants the company has developed other sectors of the market, including take-away, home delivery and Pizza Hut Express. Launched in 1987, home delivery has been one of the areas identified as offering high growth potential. In addition to Pizza Hut, the Whitbread Group is responsible for the catering activities of Beefeater, the largest chain of branded steak-houses in the UK, a strength boosted in 1990 with the acquisition of 53 Berni restaurants. The product offering at Beefeater can be segmented in terms of clientele with family customers coming in for Sunday lunch and for early evening meals, older customers, typically the more affluent and retired people, who visit Beefeaters on weekday lunchtimes and the celebratory group, often C2 and D groups, visiting the restaurant on Friday, Saturday or Sunday evenings.

Allied Domecq

The Allied Domecq group has catering interests in a number of restaurants, public houses and operates both company owned and franchised outlets. The Beer and Retailing Division includes not only pub catering operations of the group's estate of public houses, but also a number of branded catering chains. The company has been developing its Big Steak concept of public house steak-houses. The group operates the Porterhouse restaurants, and its other catering brands include Calenders, Brasseries and Exchanges.

Bass

The restaurant division of Bass Brewery group, Toby Restaurants, was established as a brand in 1985. The division comprises of Toby Grills, Toby Carving Rooms, Toby Hotels and American themed restaurants, as well as a number of unbranded outlets. Toby Grills offer a range of steak, chicken, fish and vegetarian dishes. The company's Toby Carving rooms offer self-service traditional roast and vegetable meals. Toby Restaurants also operates two American themed mini-chains. The first is TJ's Rib Place. TJ's is conceptualised as a casual medium-priced fun bar with rock and roll music and a heavy emphasis on classic American nostalgia. The second is Jeffersons Bar and Restaurant. The theme of the restaurant is fun, relaxed and contemporary southern style USA. Themed dining areas include the Veranda Library, Kentucky Gardens and Cotton Club, with Italian, Oriental, Mexican, Cajun and Barbecue food.

Key trends and developments in the UK catering market

Five key trends will be discussed:

- internationalisation
- pub catering
- ethnic trends
- hotel catering
- healthy eating

Internationalisation

International catering concepts which have achieved mass market status in the UK have tended to come from the USA. The most pervasive have been the spread of US-style fast food outlets pioneered by the arrival of Kentucky Fried Chicken in the late 1960s and McDonald's in the mid-1970s. Hamburger restaurants existed before this, e.g. the Wimpy chain, but McDonald's in particular set new standards of presentation and fast service. The UK market for fast food hamburger outlets has still not reached saturation with the major players continuing to expand their network of outlets.

Another example of this internationalisation effect are pizza chains which have risen in popularity since the mid-1980s, with home delivery being the most dynamic sector as it requires small overheads initially and comprises businesses that are relatively easy to establish. However, when pizza markets become saturated there is no sign of any other international fast food concept that will equal their success. Outlets such as salad bars and those serving Mexican food, which have proved to be extremely popular in the USA, are not likely to catch on in the UK in the short term.

The key international brands in the UK catering market are all in the fast food sector, in hamburgers, chicken and pizza. Grand Metropolitan owns the Burger King brand which it acquired with the US food company Pilsbury. The bulk of the UK chain was created by converting counter service Wimpy outlets to the Burger King format. PepsiCo's two brands in the UK are Kentucky Fried Chicken and Pizza Hut. Outside the brand oriented fast food sectors, international catering concepts tend to be localised and mainly limited to large cities. These include European-style bistros, which offer an all-day menu and also cater for customers who want only a drink, and wine bars which offer a large wine selection. The growing theme restaurant and bar sector borrows heavily from US-style decoration. There are a number of foreign brands which have a limited presence in the UK market, for example Whitbread has the UK franchise for TGI Friday's, a bistro theme bar owned by the US-based Carlson group.

Pub catering

Pubs and fish and chip shops are both large in terms of number of outlets, but vary significantly in terms of market value.

Pub catering is currently the focus of several important developments; around 96% of the UK's pubs serve food of one sort or another, from cold bar food to a full sit-down restaurant. Running costs are lower than for stand alone restaurants and an increased emphasis on food is helping to safeguard against any decline in the alcohol market, to draw family custom and to capitalise on all-day opening. Throughout the first half of the 1990s, pubs benefited from trading down in the consumer catering market, taking business away from the higher priced outlets. The report by the Monopolies and Mergers Commission (MMC) into the supply of beer during that period forced the major brewing groups to reorganise their pub estates and has prompted several large brewers to withdraw from beer production in order to concentrate on pub retailing and catering. Many of the major brewing groups responded to the MMC by branding a part of their managed pub estates, pitching them at a more closely defined target market, particularly families, and emphasising their food offer.

Whitbread has made the most progress in this respect, in identifying three business streams, locals or community inns, pub restaurants such as Brewers Fayre and Wayside Inns and specialised destination venues like Hanrahan's and Mulligan's fish restaurants. A further example is Allied Domecq Retailing, which runs Tetley, Ansells, Ind Coope and Taylor Walker pubs under four separate pub retailing companies. All four operate the pub chains of Firkin, Big Steaks, Exchange Bar Diners and Mr Q's. Cooks Platter, Farmhouse Platter and Landlords Choice are to be found throughout the various Allied Domecq Retailing estates. Other food brands are found on a regional basis such as Clutterbuck's and Arkwright's Wheel. The other effect of the MMC report has been to create a surplus of pub premises that are well suited for development into more specific catering outlets such as branded restaurants.

Ethnic trends

There has been an increasing willingness by consumers to experiment with different types of food with consequent rapid development of a wide variety of national and ethnic cuisine. Consumers have become generally more adventurous as a result of greater numbers travelling abroad and also the growing number of television cookery programmes which increase knowledge about more exotic foods. Chinese and Indian restaurants have had the most impact followed by Italian. The trend is particularly pronounced in London which tends to be more cosmopolitan than the rest of the UK, but English restaurants still prove the most popular in all regions, with the exception of Greater London and Scotland where Chinese is slightly ahead. Other types of restaurants which are growing in popularity are Thai, Vietnamese, Japanese, Spanish, Middle Eastern, Afro-Caribbean, Jewish, Middle European and American.

Hotel catering

The overall accommodation market and its catering businesses were severely affected by the Gulf War in 1991 which exacerbated the adverse effects of the economic downturn in the period 1990–4. This resulted in a dramatic fall in business travel and a cancellation of a large number of holiday bookings. In general hotel catering has suffered from its image of being overpriced and many companies have attempted to reposition and rationalise their property portfolios in order to capitalise on the move down market. Budget travel lodges have proved to be one of the most resilient sectors and therefore became a major focus for development by several major operators. The major budget hotel operators also operate stand-alone catering brands; such hotels are generally sited near to one of these which offers convenient catering facilities. All Forte's Travelodges are located near to a Little Chef or Happy Eater.

Healthy eating

There has been a growing consumer interest in healthy eating which has encouraged a move away from red meat towards lighter foods. For example in the mid-market steak-house family restaurant sector, steak generally accounts for some 30–40% of sales in the late 1990s, compared with 75% in 1980. A greater variety of poultry, fish, ethnic and spicy dishes and vegetarian meals are included in the menu. Fast food operators have also moved in this direction by providing salads, skinless chicken and leaner burgers. Vegetarians currently account for around 9% of the UK population, a proportion which is continuing to grow. Vegetarian restaurants have risen in popularity although a number of specialist small chains have found the trading climate difficult.

Food and beverage management

The experience of eating out is sometimes described by the term meal experience. This is defined as a series of events both tangible and intangible that a customer experiences when eating out, with the main experience beginning when customers enter the restaurant and ends when they leave. By tangible elements what is referred to is the product itself i.e. food and drink, and intangible aspects are covered by such elements as service, atmosphere, mood etc. The aim for the caterer is to create a meal experience which includes both tangible and intangible aspects integrated together to create a whole product service mix. This section of the chapter identifies some key issues, discussed in greater detail by Davis, Stone and Lockwood in their book *Food and Beverage Management* (listed in further reading at the end of this chapter).

Customer choice

Prior to customers entering a catering unit they will already have decided on the type of meal they want and what would be appropriate for that particular occasion. The general factors affecting a customer's choice of a meal experience include a range of issues such as social, business, convenience and time, atmosphere and service, price and the menu. There is to some customers a trade-off point between the task and cost of preparing a meal at home or paying for a meal out. Generally speaking, the higher the disposable income, the higher the trade-off level. Finally, the menu at the restaurant depending on its content will appeal to different types and groups of customers. All these factors will affect the buying decision.

Elements within the meal experience

The choice of food and drink revolves around the **menu**, be it limited or extensive, and whether it concerns a particular product, if there is a varied choice, and the quality of the product offered, be it fresh or convenience. Other factors include portion sizes and the availability of children's menus along with consistency, range of tastes, textures, aromas and colours and presentation of the food and drink.

The **price** of the meal should be related according to perceived value for money and be in line with customers' expectations. The variety of menu choice offered is related to the market level of the restaurant in question. The factors of price, choice and time spent consuming the meal are all interrelated, along with service and production facilities and the skills of the staff. Broadly speaking, the higher the cost of the meal, the more service the customer expects to receive. Most customers will frequent a restaurant not only because of its food and service, but also because they feel the price they are paying represents value for money.

The **interior design** of a restaurant is one of the first physical aspects of a catering operation the customer will come into contact with. Interior design includes the size and shape of the room, the furniture and fittings, the colour scheme, lighting, air conditioning, etc. The colour scheme of the restaurant should blend and balance, and be enhanced by lighting arrangements, tables and chairs, designed so that they not only satisfy their functional purpose, but also look attractive. The interior design of a restaurant contributes greatly to the creation of its image.

The **atmosphere** or mood of a restaurant is often described as an intangible *feel* inside a restaurant. The atmosphere of a restaurant is affected by many different aspects, including décor, interior design, table and seating arrangements, the service accompaniments, the dress and attitude of the staff, etc. The harmony between the product itself, service and the overall environment is important. A single customer or group of customers, arriving at a restaurant for a meal, bring with them a series of expectations, which can include the type of service they will receive, the price they will pay, the expected atmosphere and the mood of the restaurant.

The **location** of the food service facility may be said to be the most important feature. Services which are not appropriately located may not successfully perform. The siting of a catering outlet must be made after careful identification of the location of the market segment which it is catering to, and can be related back to the socio-economic groups it wishes to attract. The restaurant's location in relation to its present market should be considered and also its location to possible future markets. A road-side restaurant trade for instance would be affected by the expansion or relocation of the major road nearby, with a consequent increase or decrease in the volume of traffic and hence customers. The **accessibility** to a catering operation is also another important factor: customers arriving by car will expect adequate car parking facilities. If a high street take-away facility expects a large percentage of its business from passing trade, there should be a heavy pedestrian flow past its stores. **Staff** employed by a restaurant operation should complement the meal experience of the customers. The number of staff serving in the restaurant is closely related to the prices charged by the establishment and the level of service that it offers.

The type of meal experience offered by a food service facility is therefore tailored around the requirement and expectations of the customer. This begins with the basic marketing questions of who are the customers and what do they want? By seeking to answer these questions, caterers are able to determine their position in the market and to offer the right product at the right price to the identified market segments.

Food and beverage control

Food and beverage control may be defined as the regulation of costs and revenue in operating a catering activity. Food and beverage sales count for up to half the total revenue in hotels, while in restaurants it is the main or only source of revenue. The cost of food and beverages in the commercial sector is usually in the region of 25–40% of the total sales.

The amount of control required in such units is related to the size of the operation. A large group operation obviously requires much more precise, detailed up-to-date information than a small operation such as an owner-operated restaurant that often cannot afford nor does not need the same level of sophistication of control. In both instances the type and volume of data required need to be selectively determined if control is to be meaningful and effective.

An effective food and beverage control system is dependent upon correct up-to-date policies and operational procedures. The system should be able to identify problems and trends in the business. A control system will also require constant management supervision to ensure that it is functioning efficiently, and finally management will need to evaluate the information produced and to act upon it.

The objectives of food and beverage control can be summarised as follows:

- analysis of income and expenditure related to food and beverage operations
- analysis of revenue by each selling outlet according to volume of food and beverage sales, sales mix, average spending power of customers at various times of the day and number of customers served
- analysis of costs including departmental food and beverage costs, portion control and labour costs
- performance of each outlet expressed in terms of profit.

The basis for the operation of any food and beverage outlet is the establishment of a set of standards which would be particular to an operation. Unless standards are set, no employee would know in detail the standards to be achieved, nor could the employees' performance be effectively measured by management. Another important objective of food and beverage control is to provide a sound basis for menu pricing: food menu and beverage list prices must be calculated in the light of accurate food and beverage costs, other main establishment costs, and general market considerations. In order to achieve performance standards for an establishment, targets are set for revenue cost levels and profit margins. To achieve these levels of performance it is necessary to prevent wastage of materials caused by such things as poor preparation, overproduction and failure to use standard recipes. Equally, it is necessary for a control system to prevent or at least restrict the possible areas of fraud by both customers and staff. Finally, a system of control is an important task to fulfil in providing accurate up-to-date information for the preparation of periodic reports for management.

Customer demand

Food, whether raw or cooked, is a perishable commodity and has a limited life and so caterers have to ensure that they buy produce in the correct quality and quantity in relation to customer demand and that it is correctly stored and processed. Sales instability is typical of most catering establishments; very often a change in volume of business from day to day and in many establishments from hour to hour will affect purchasing, preparation and levels of staffing required. This implies a requirement for some form of volume forecasting.

Policies

It is difficult to run an effective catering operation without defining the basic policies. A catering operation should have its policies clearly defined before it commences business and redefined whenever a major change takes place. In a large organisation, the policies should be written down and periodically reviewed in relation to the current business and future trends. There are three basic policies which need to be considered:

- The **financial policy** will determine the levels of profitability, subsidy or cost limits to be expected from the business as a whole, and the contribution to the total profit.
- The **marketing policy** will identify the broad market that the operation is intended to serve, and the particular segment of market on which it intends to concentrate.
- The **catering policy** normally evolves from the financial and marketing policies. It will define the main objectives of operating the food and beverage facilities and describe methods by which such objectives are to be achieved.

Having defined the policies, it is then necessary to outline how they are to be interpreted into day-to-day control activities of the catering operation. The next stage of the cycle occurs after the event when there is a need for food and beverage cost reporting. Finally, there will be an assessment by management of the reports generated and a comparison with the budget for the period.

Operational phase

The operational phase can be considered as six stages:

- purchasing
- receiving
- storing
- issuing
- stocktaking
- preparing

Purchasing

Purchasing can be defined as the function concerned with the search, selection, purchase, receipt, storage and final use of a commodity in accordance with the catering policy of the establishment. The purchasing procedure can be broken down into a number of steps, with the start being a requisition form from an authorised member of staff which will inform the purchasing manager of the level of stock items. The purchasing manager will then identify a source of supply, enter into a contract with the supplier by phone or in writing and negotiate the price to be paid, along with a satisfactory delivery performance. Particular reference will be made to the time, date and place of delivery. The goods will be delivered and any discrepancies will be noted in terms of quality or quantity of the goods delivered. Finally the commodities will be transferred direct to the kitchen, the stores or the cellar. A supplier can be easily selected from among those that the buyer has previously purchased from in that the quality of goods received, price and service offered would be known. When seeking a new supplier, caution must be exercised and detailed enquiries made. When purchasing food, it is necessary to consider what the true cost of the item will be in relation to the printed price list from the supplier. **True cost calculation** must take into account the invoice price less any discounts claimable, storage cost of the item and the production costs. The calculation of a true cost may well indicate that it is cheaper to buy in five-case lots as against a fifty-case lot at a lower price.

Purchasing specifications should be used whenever possible in purchasing. A **purchase specification** is a concise description of the quantity, quality, size and weight required for a particular item. Each specification should be particular to an establishment and would have been determined by members of the management team who will have referred to the catering policy, the menu requirements and its price range. The reasons for preparing specifications are that it establishes a buying standard of a commodity for an establishment. It also informs the supplier in writing precisely what is required and aids the storekeeper deciding the standard of goods to be accepted.

Receiving

It is important to realise that all goods being received to an establishment have a monetary value, and that it is essential to ensure that exactly this value in goods is properly accounted for and received. What is also important to remember is that often these goods will have a selling value several times their original purchase price. The storekeeper should ensure that the quantity of goods delivered matches the quantity which has been ordered. Equally the quality of goods delivered should be in accordance with the specification stated on the purchase form. The delivery note should be checked to ensure that the prices stated are in accordance with the prices on the purchase order form. If there is a discrepancy, there should be a request for a credit note. Finally, an accurate record should be made for goods received.

Storing

The main objective of a food store is to ensure that an adequate supply of food for the immediate needs of the establishment is available at all times. Perishable items tend to go straight to the kitchens where they would be stored in either refrigerated or cold rooms depending on the item. Non-perishable items such as canned foods go to a food store.

Issuing

The issuing of food should take place at specific times during the day and only against a requisition note signed by an authorised person within the establishment. The pricing of issues is usually at the as-purchased price. The pricing of perishable items is often done by the control office after they have been issued, as they have access to the suppliers' invoices.

Stocktaking

The purpose of stocktaking is to determine the value of goods held in stock. This will indicate if too much or too little food is held in stock and if the total value of stock held is in accordance with the financial policy of the establishment. These figures are also required for the profit and loss account and the balance sheet of the organisation. Stocktaking compares the value of goods actually in store at a particular time with the book value of the stock which will have been calculated. This will highlight any differences and indicate the efficiency of the storekeeper and of the system used to obtain goods when the storekeeper is off duty. Stocktaking also brings to the attention of management a list of slow moving items along with determining the rate of stock turnover.

The process can also compare the usage of food with food sales to calculate food cost percentage and gross profit and can be seen as a deterrent against loss and pilferage. Stocktaking will be done every trading period by management and will usually take place in the evening or early in the morning. Professional stocktakers are often used.

Preparing

Food production is mainly concerned with the processing of raw, semi-prepared or pre-pared food stuffs. The resulting product may be in a ready-to-serve state, for example in the conventional method, or it may undergo some form of preservation, for example cook-chill, or cook freeze before being served to the customer. There is a fine dividing line between production and service which is not always distinguishable. The decision as to which food production method to use in a particular catering operation is taken at the initial planning stage; this comes from the market to be catered for. The initial planning of a food service facility is critical for the long-term success of the operation and one which should be afforded considerable time, effort and finance.

Planning a catering facility

Objectives

The first step in the planning of a catering facility is a written statement of the operation's objectives. The primary objective must be to serve a particular market segment of the population allied to other objectives such as a return on capital in the shortest possible period. This latter objective may not be required in the case of an industrial cafeteria, for example.

Costs

Whatever the type of catering facility, costs must be controlled. In a catering operation, these include the initial planning and building costs and the daily running costs such as food, labour and fuel. Such costs should be kept to a minimum so that any profit made may be put back into the operation and hence reduce the overall cost of the product to the consumer.

Layout

The catering operation should be designed to facilitate production and service. This involves designing the layout of production and service areas and equipment both in the kitchen and the restaurant.

Materials handling

The movement of materials in the catering operation should be planned so that minimal handling is involved. If possible the materials flow should be as direct as possible.

Labour utilisation

The planning of efficient labour utilisation involves identifying the tasks that are to be performed in the production and service areas of the catering operation, along with the most efficient method of doing these tasks. At the planning stage, consideration should also be given to the task of supervising and managing the catering operation particularly the production and service employees.

Hygiene and safety

Hygiene and safety standards must be built into a catering operation at the planning stage. Food safety, hygiene regulations and health and safety regulations must be taken into account and be observed by all catering establishments. Closely related to safety is consideration at the planning stage for easy cleaning and maintenance of the premises.

Food production methods

Food production methods in the catering industry have evolved over a period of time. In the past there was an abundance of labour and the design of the traditional kitchen, first introduced into the UK in the latter half of the nineteenth century, grew up around the division of tasks into parties, i.e. similar tasks with numerous foods were carried out by a particular group of people. This was the development of the **partie system**.

It is only since the mid-1960s that changes in the old traditional methods have evolved. These changes were slow to appear and started in the manufacturing industry rather than in the kitchens of hotels and restaurants. In 1966 the first cook-freeze operation in the UK began and from this, derivatives have evolved from both cook-freeze and cook-chill methods.

Convenience foods

One development has been the introduction of convenience foods into a traditional production kitchen. Conventional production using convenience foods may range from a partial to virtually complete reliance on the use of a wider variety of convenience foods now available. A major problem with the traditional food production system is that there is no separation between those activities of production and service, causing major problems. Once the link between production and service has been severed the catering operation can be completely reorganised, in particular the production activity can be separated from the service by place and by time. Instead of a number of small self-contained operations producing food, these can be streamlined to some extent, with the kitchens being reduced in size of activity. They can be converted into end kitchens or satellite kitchens each equipped to provide most of the food for each unit by the regeneration of frozen or chilled foods supplied from a central production kitchen. The central production unit will require skilled production staff while the satellite kitchen will not require such skilled staff. The introduction of a storage stage between production and service allows the production unit to work to maximum efficiency in order to achieve a better utilisation of staff and equipment.

Cook-freeze and cook-chill

The term cook-freeze refers to a catering system based on the full cooking of food followed by fast freezing, with storage at a controlled low temperature of $-18°C$ or below, followed by subsequent complete reheating close to the consumer prior to prompt consumption. The term cook-chill refers to a catering system based on the full cooking of food followed by fast chilling with storage in controlled low temperature conditions just above freezing point and between $0°C$ and $+3°C$ followed by subsequent complete reheating close to the consumer prior to prompt consumption. It has a short shelf-life compared to cook-freeze of only five days including the day of production, distribution time and regeneration.

Sous vide

Sous vide is a more recent processing technique developed in the late 1970s which lends itself readily to adaption of a cook-chill variant. The system involves the preparation of quality raw foods, precooking when necessary, putting the raw foods into special plastic bags, vacuuming and sealing the bags and then steam cooking to pasteurisation temperatures. The food product can be served direct to the customer at this stage or rapidly chilled to between 1°C and 3°C and stored at between 0°C and 3°C for a maximum of twenty-one days. The shelf-life of the food is extended not only because of the vacuumising of the product but also because the food is cooked to pasteurisation temperatures, which aids the destruction of most micro-organisms. However, exceptionally high standards of hygiene are fundamental to the system as it is potentially more dangerous than conventional or cook-chill methods.

Food service methods

The food service stage is concerned with the presentation of food to the customer after completion of food production and may include transportation. As with food and beverage production, there are a number of food and beverage service methods but unlike production, service is the part of the catering operation that the customer actually sees and it can therefore make or break an establishment's reputation. The system chosen must be in keeping with the total concept of the catering facility and represent value for money to the customer. It must be able to provide a fast and efficient service appropriate to the market level of the catering outlet. Good standards of hygiene and safety must be maintained; if necessary, food should be displayed in appropriate equipment which will maintain the temperature, appearance and nutritional quality of the product. Finally the unit should operate within the cost and profit targets of the establishment as detailed in the catering and financial policies.

Traditionally, full waiter service was the predominant method of food service. However a greater degree of informality when eating away from home and the need for increased productivity due to rising costs have led to other food service methods and styles being developed. These can range from the traditional cafeteria, counter service take-away foods, vending and numerous trade service systems used, particularly in the welfare sector. The mode of food service employed by an establishment will depend on a number of interrelated factors. Sometimes more than one type of food service is offered in the same establishment. In contract catering there may be a cafeteria for the majority of staff and a waiter service restaurant for top-level management, both supplied by only one kitchen.

Summary

This chapter has taken a two part approach to the restaurant and fast food industry. The first half concentrated on the main sectors of the industry and the major operators within it. It gave an indication of structure and market size along with trends for the future of the industry. The section investigated the UK consumer catering market, an industry which covers a wide range of sectors and companies. It showed that consumers are increasingly willing to experiment with different types of food and that consumers attach a high priority to what they *perceive* as healthy eating practices. International catering concepts which have achieved mass market status in the UK have tended to come from the

USA, the most pervasive being the spread of US-style fast food outlets. The second half of the chapter focused on the management of food and beverage operations. It analysed the meal experience enjoyed by consumers and went on to consider the elements of control within a food operation. It described the food cycle from purchasing through receipt, storage and issue to production and service.

Further reading

- British Hospitality Trends and Statistics 1998, Editor, Miles Quest, published by the British Hospitality Association, London.
- Campbell-Smith G. (1967) *Marketing the Meal Experience*, Guildford: University of Surrey.
- Carmin J. and Norkus G.X. (1990) 'Pricing strategies for menus: magic or myth?' *Cornell Hotel and Restaurant Association Quarterly*, November: 45–50.
- Davis B. (1989) *Food Commodities*, 2nd edn, London: Heinemann.
- Davis B. and Lockwood A. (1994) *Food and Beverage Management: a Selection of Readings*, Oxford: Butterworth Heinemann.
- Davis B., Stone S. and Lockwood A. (1998) *Food and Beverage Management*, 3rd edn, London: Butterworth Heinemann.
- Dixon S. (1994) 'Bar billions', *Hospitality* December: 23–5.
- Euromonitor (1992) *Consumer Catering: the International Market 1992*, London: Euromonitor.
- Green E.F. *et al.* (1987), *Profitable Food and Beverage Management Planning*, Jinks, OK: Williams Books.
- Jones P. and Atkinson H. (1994) 'Menu engineering: managing the foodservice micro-marketing mix', *Journal of Restaurant and Foodservice Marketing*, 1(1): 37–56.
- Key Note (1996a) *The UK Catering Market*, London: Key Note.
- Key Note (1996b) *Fast Food Outlets*, London: Key Note.
- Knowles T. and Ware-Lane, B. (1994), New Product Development in Food and Beverage Operations in Readings in Food and Beverage Operations, Editors, Davis B. and Lockwood A. Butterworth Heinemann, London
- Mintel (1992) *Roadside Catering, Leisure Intelligence Report*, vol. 2, London: Mintel.
- O'Connor J. (1993) 'A review of dining out patterns in Britain', *International Journal of Contemporary Hospitality Management*, 5(5): 3–9.
- Powers T.F. (1985) 'Concept selection for independent restaurants', *Cornell Hotel and Restaurant Association Quarterly* December: 59–72.
- Price S. (1993) *The UK Fast Food Industry*, London: Cassell.
- Silverstone R. (1993) 'Wither fast food?', *International Journal of Contemporary Hospitality Management*, 5(1): 1–3.
- Teare R. with Adams D. and Messenger S. (1992) *Managing Projects in Hospitality Organisations*, London: Cassell.

Chapter Nine

Contract Catering Industry

Objectives

After reading this chapter you should be able to

▬ Comment on the history of the sector.

▬ Provide an overview of the contract catering industry in the UK.

▬ Give an analysis of the industry's subsectors, products and markets.

▬ Understand the concept of outsourcing.

Historical development

At the beginnings of the early industrial revolution in the late eighteenth century, the tradition of rural communities, from where the first industrial workers migrated, was one of self-reliance. Workers were happy to bring a packed meal to be eaten during a short midday break, or during their labours at the loom, just as they had been accustomed to do when working as agricultural labourers in the seventeenth century.

In the Victorian age from the mid-nineteenth century on, it was the era of the paternalistic industrial employer along with those who were purely exploitative. The former saw that the provision of food in the workplace, along with other benefits, was good for business. Well-fed workers were perceived to be more productive than those who were unfed. Loyal workers who worked for basic sustenance were more likely to be prepared to commit themselves to the purposes of their employer. The enlightenment of the Victorian paternalists was self-interested in the best sense of the term. Cadbury's, Lever Brothers, Frys, Rowntrees, Colman's and others were happy with the concept of meal breaks and later the idea of low-cost lunches provided by the company. It was not long before they set up some of the earliest canteens.

Legislation led to the spread of canteens from the few enlightened employers to the rest. From the mid-nineteenth century onwards, the government reacted to growing public concern about the living and working conditions of industrial workers. Employers were encouraged to look after the welfare of employees and in due course, workers ate better food at work than they did at home.

The significance of government legislation as a factor in improving the diet of workers was much clearer in wartime. Most government factories established at the end of the 1930s were built with canteen facilities, although in the 1930s the majority of industrial workers still ate sandwiches made at home for their midday meal as employers offered no catering facilities. The traditions of the early rural stages of the industrial revolution when workers were expected to be self-sufficient, living in their own communities, took a long time to fade away. In 1940, the government's Factory Canteens Order made it compulsory for factories employing more than 250 people to provide dining rooms where wholesome meals at reasonable prices were available.

The origins of the contract catering industry can be traced back to the early 1940s. In wartime, the home was no longer able to provide food as effectively as government-supported central kitchens. The Factory Canteens Order 1940 provided the spark for businesses to offer catering service under contract. Such statutory requirements have long since disappeared. The Second World War acted as a major catalyst, introducing the canteen as the focal eating point for the whole nation. Wartime meant food rationing and the scarcity of energy and food supplies made the provision of meals from a central kitchen at the workplace economic sense. The contract catering industry was called in by employers to help them meet the requirements of government legislation. An interesting by-product of these changes from domestic to public eating facilities was a significant increase in the overall health of the population. Present-day problems of unbalanced diet, obesity and other food-related disorders were minimal, if they existed at all.

If the demands of war forced the expansion of contract catering, the coming of peace led to a period of relative stagnation. After the war, contract catering grew slowly. However, employers at a time of full employment saw the provision of services like food as a way of attracting and keeping employees. The provision of subsidised food at the workplace became a recognised employee benefit.

The period between the late 1940s and the 1960s was one of little growth for the British contract catering industry. Trends in industrial development in the 1960s and 1970s were not conducive to the expansion of contract catering as there was a decline of heavy industry in favour of light industry and the service sector accelerated during these years. Service sector companies employed fewer people on one site and had a more mobile and independent workforce usually with access to off-site facilities. These smaller firms were less prepared to invest in on-site facilities or to invest in what they regarded as non-earning overheads.

In this context, it is not surprising that in the 1990s, the contract catering industry in the UK still has a relatively low percentage of the potential commercial market. There are signs, however, of a significant shift in management practice which augurs well for the expansion of contract catering in the future. There is a growing trend in management thinking to subcontract all activities other than the core business activity to specialists, sometimes referred to as **outsourcing**. Supplying food to the workforce, the argument goes, should no longer be the direct concern of management of non-catering companies.

The political aid of privatisation from the late 1980s to mid-1990s created the prospect of major new market opportunities for the contract catering industry. Once again government, but this time in peacetime, acted as the catalyst in encouraging the public sector to use contract caterers on a large scale and in new ways. The management of the new privatised companies was more accountable to deliver profits to satisfy the City and their new shareholders. The introduction of catering contractors allowed them to introduce lower staffing levels without reducing the quality of service, allowing significant cost savings in the first few years of operation as a private entity.

The same drive to reduce the cost of ancillary services, like catering, encouraged the government to introduce contractors into services directly financed by the government, e.g. like health, defence and local government. The government term for this approach is one of **market testing**. These services are unlikely to be sold off but are either contracted out completely or put out to competitive tender with the consequence that the scale of this new business opportunity for the contract catering industry is huge. The local government market alone, which came on stream in August 1989, added a further 30,000 potential catering opportunities. The catering market worked by contract caterers could triple around the millennium. A close look at the different market segments show how social and economic change is working in favour of the spread of contract catering.

Since those wartime beginnings, the 1990s have seen the industry change with the terms 'staff restaurant' and 'dining room' replacing 'canteen'. Indeed many use the term 'food service management' as opposed to 'contract catering'. There is a growing demand for style and quality of service in the workplace on a par with that of a restaurant outside. The trend towards healthy eating is also noticeable and such dietary matters are considered important. Employers see the provision of a lunchtime experience as an effective form of internal public relations, establishing their credentials as caring and well organised.

This expansion of contract catering will now be illustrated with a case study on outsourcing that will show how the industry is increasingly looking for opportunities within the hotel sector.

Case Study: **Expansion of contract catering: the case for outsourcing**

Outsourcing can be seen as an opportunity to leverage higher returns by concentrating on core activities. There are considerable opportunities in industry as a whole and indeed in some sectors of the hospitality industry to consider employing contract catering firms.

From a financial perspective this management approach involves the transfer of part, or in some cases all, of the business to niche market operators, i.e. contract caterers, with the objective of achieving higher financial returns, particularly in the firm's core activities. The firm needs to distinguish its core activities from those that it regards as peripheral. Such a decision is strategic in nature and should not be taken in a haphazard or opportunistic way. The relationship between the core firm and the catering contractor should be regarded as a partnership by which the contractor must retain the capacity to manage, while the core firm needs to be able to protect its reputation, brand image, core skills and property rights.

Niche catering operators are in many cases better geared and competent to react to rapidly developing consumer needs at a quicker pace than the traditional operator. Even within the hotel industry new outsourcing developments have been seen with restaurants in hotels and in catering for staff. Although the focus here is on catering, outsourcing has been extended to security and grounds maintenance (facilities management), and many contract catering firms offer these services. Outsourcing in the hotel industry developed with the provision of leisure facilities by specialist contractors.

Critical to the success of outsourcing is the need for a strong level of trust and co-operation between the two parties. The agreement must become a partnership between the core operator and catering contractor working together as a team. The type of agreement between the two parties can take four main forms:

- lease or rental agreements
- restaurant brand franchises
- full food and beverage outsourcing to a contractor
- joint ventures with a contractor

In all these forms management of the food and beverage operation is devolved; in many cases the operator pays the core firm a guaranteed rental income, or share of profit, or a reduction in the cost burden, or a combination of these benefits. Whatever the approach

case study continues ▶

case study continues

adopted, the customer using the food and beverage service should be generally unaware of the contracting out position.

A final and perhaps pivotal argument for outsourcing is profitability, which can be analysed with the key financial ratios of

- gross profit (GP)
- departmental operating profit (DOP)
- departmental net operating profit (DNOP)
- departmental return on investment (DROI)

According to the UK based consultancy Pannell Kerr Forster an average UK provincial three or four star hotel with 153 rooms turning over £1.7 million in food and beverages makes:

- GP   71.3%
- DOP   31.9%
- DNOP 8.7%
- DROI 7.1%

These ratios are drawn from Table 9.1 and give a clear indication of departmental profitability within hotel food and beverage.

Table 9.1 Estimate of departmental profitability: hotel food and beverage

Revenue/expense category	PAR	Assuming 150 rooms	Ratio to dept revenue	Ratio to hotel revenue
Revenue	(£)	(£000)	(%)	(%)
Total hotel revenue	30,461	4,569	–	100.0
– Food and beverage revenue	11,489	1,723	100.0	37.7
Operating expenses				
Cost of sales	3,297	495	28.7	–
Gross profit	8,192	1,229	71.3	–
– Payroll and related expenses	3,591	539	31.3	–
Dept operating expenses	938	141	8.2	–
Departmental operating profit	3,663	549	31.9	–
Undistributed operating expenses				
Admin and general	1,008	151	8.8	–
Sales and marketing	453	68	3.9	–
Repairs and maintenance	221	33	1.9	–
Energy costs	179	27	1.6	–
Nominal fixed charges				
Nominal rent	345	52	3.0	–
Nominal finance charges	115	17	1.0	–
Replacement of FF & E	345	52	3.0	–
Departmental NOP	997	149	8.7	–

Source: Pannell Kerr Forster Associates (1996) Hotel Food and Beverage: For Prestige or Profit?

case study continues ▶

case study continues

	Food and beverage	Rooms department	Other departments	Total hotel
Investment/construction				
Cost (£PAR)	14,000	52,500	3,500	70,000
Departmental revenue (£PAR)	11,489	16,327	2,645	30,461
Ratio to total hotel revenue (%)	37.7	53.6	8.7	100.0
Departmental operating profit (£PAR)	3,663	12,041	1,484	17,188
Departmental operating profit (%)	31.9	73.7	56.1	56.4
Departmental NOP (£PAR)	997	6,884	N/A	9,180
Department NOP (%)	8.7	42.2	N/A	30.1
Departmental ROI (%)	7.1	13.1	N/A	13.1

Table 9.2 Estimate of return on investment: hotel food and beverage

Source: Pannell Kerr Forster Associates (1996) Hotel Food and Beverage: For Prestige or Profit?

Table 9.2 compares the return on investment between the three main departments of the hotel – food and beverage, rooms, and other. The figures illustrate that there is a clear gap in both revenue and profitability between food and beverage, and rooms.

The conclusion from Tables 9.1 and 9.2 is that food and beverage is considerably less profitable than the hotel rooms operation; in many cases within the industry food and beverage may actually lose money. The food and beverage department distracts from the operation of the more profitable rooms division and therefore the influence of the contract catering firms in taking over this element of the operation may continue its development over the next few years.

Food service management

A number of publications, including the British Hospitality Association's *Contract Catering Survey,* use the term 'food service management' in preference to contract catering yet both terms can be regarded as having similar meaning. However, food service management reflects the wider interests and appeal of this particular industry sector as it has expanded its interests away from the traditions of institutionalised catering. The British Hospitality Association's survey should be regarded as the most accurate and comprehensive source of comment and statistical information on the industry.

Food service management, where the provision of meals is not the main activity of the outlet, covers such areas as feeding people at work in business and industry, catering in schools, colleges and universities, hospitals and health care, welfare and local authority catering and other non-profit-making outlets. The sector also includes catering provided for the public in such outlets as leisure centres, department stores, exhibitions, places of entertainment and a large number of one-off or other temporary events. This market sector is valued at an estimated £60 million turnover.

The traditional sectors of the industry are called cost, non-profit-making, non-commercial catering or social catering. Because contract caterers are also developing their interests in commercial catering (catering for the public represents 4.3% of outlets and some 8% of meals served), the term food service management is used to define the total business sector.

Primary markets in the UK

Private sector

The main market for contract catering in the UK is in industrial and commercial locations with 200 or more employees. This category of contract includes some interesting developments where smaller companies share facilities on an industrial estate or within an office building. There are estimated to be 20,000 sites employing more than 200 people, of which less than 50% currently use contract caterers to provide facilities.

The next most significant market are the 40,000 locations with between 50 and 200 people on site. Normally they rely on a delivered food service or vending rather than canteens, but a growing exception to the rule that the lower the number of employees, the lower the investment in catering facilities, is the emergence of the dining-room concept. This in-house restaurant facility supplied by a contract caterer is being used by the more sophisticated small companies employing high calibre staff. The benefit is that it can be used for both internal and external marketing purposes. In these and other examples quality contract catering, matching the highest restaurant standards in both gastronomic terms and service, is replacing the canteen as the growth market. An area that has attracted the industry is the financial service sectors in the City of London, corporate headquarters and sales and marketing centres, which entertain a constant flow of visitors, with such clients representing a growing low-turnover high-profit market.

Contract caterers know that these smaller secondary-niche markets are growing faster than the primary single-site markets. The economy is tending to favour the emergence of new industries and small businesses. An alert contract caterer can exploit these new markets as effectively as those of large single sites.

In France, a development shows how economies of scale can be applied to the small company sector. Developers of a major trading estate, science park or office complex include a large catering facility in the central plans. This facility is let on a long-term contract to one central supplier who offers catering services to all employees on the site.

The largest company in the contract catering industry, Gardner Merchant/Sodexho is now operating many of these units in both Paris and Lyons. The essential idea behind this French development is applicable to the UK. Employee care is a top priority for the new high-technology companies in search of scarce technologists and technicians. The supply of a top quality lunchtime experience is an important part of the employee package. The French type of central catering facility on a trading estate makes it possible to provide good food at a reasonable cost.

Catering contractors have little control over the factors changing their market. The demand for a different type of catering service reflects deep-seated developments in society and the economy. The decline in employment in heavy industry leading to the overnight closure of large industrial centres immediately affects all suppliers including contract caterers. The contract catering industry has to be market-led and be able to respond with imagination to thrive profitably amid all this change.

Public sector

Throughout the 1980s and into the late 1990s the public sector was a major market in the UK for the contract catering industry. The Conservative government which lost office in May 1997 was committed to the involvement of the private sector in order to reduce public expenditure across all government financed institutions. Hospitals, universities, local government, prisons, colleges of further education, schools, Ministry of Defence establishments as well as the police and fire service made up an impressive list of potential business. There are in excess of 2,500 National Health Service (NHS) hospitals alone.

Progress during this period of involvement within this public sector market has been slow for caterers. The difficulty has arisen from the dislike by government of cost-plus contracts (a topic discussed later in this chapter). The contract catering industry has most of its contracts in the commercial world as **management fee contracts**, the term they use for cost-plus contracts. Experience has shown that both parties gain from contracts which recharge all costs incurred, allow for a small fixed profit or management fee, and are controlled by an open-book accountancy system. Despite extensive lobbying, the government has continued to favour fixed price contracts for all ancillary services including catering. The contact catering industry in response agreed to respond to fixed price tender contracts, but only if there was no in-house tender. All fixed price invitations with an in-house bid have been rejected by the vast majority of catering contractors.

One market for the industry which is particularly attractive is the Ministry of Defence, despite the contracts being let on a fixed price because the service is contracted out with no in-house bid. A central contract unit makes sure that the flow of contracts are put out in line with the resources of contractors who are invited to respond. The NHS market, very much bigger than the Ministry of Defence, has been disappointing. The choice of competitive tendering linked with fixed price contracts has led to few catering contractors competing. Gardner Merchant/Sodexho has restricted its tendering activity to large district-wide management-fee contracts as and when they become available.

The local government market has been slow to develop. The Department of the Environment followed the example of the Department of Health and opted for competitive tendering. Fixed price contracts are favoured. Many catering companies are unwilling to tender for fixed price contracts and it will take time for the political orientation of the market to be replaced by a true commercial partnership.

The public service catering market is evolving into new niche markets in the same way as the commercial and industrial markets. The latest development is to merge catering with other ancillary services to create a hotel services contract. The advantage to the client is a higher rate of saving in terms of management time and overall cost. The contractor gains because of the higher value of the contract being managed essentially by the same management team. The central problem facing contractors in such an approach is how can they offer a hotel service without the operational experience of other ancillary services like cleaning. Contractors can make alliances with other specialist companies or alternatively they can set up their own operation to offer all the staff needed. The advantages to the client of the hotel-type contract are clear and it is likely to spread from the Ministry of Defence and a few NHS health authorities to the whole public sector market. Another term for this approach is **facilities management**.

The problems of these government markets are their size with catering contracts worth £1 billion on offer. Even if only a very small proportion of these are won by contractors, the strain on the skilled management and specialist back-up service of the industry will be intense. The opportunities for new business in commercial, industrial and public sector markets in the UK is matched by the opportunities abroad, especially in Europe.

European and other markets

The contract catering industry, like many other industries, in Europe has changed since 1992. The creation of a single European market removes any legislative barriers to British contract caterers expanding into other European markets. Previous to 1992 for example, in Germany, the government restricted the expansion of contract caterers of the British type through legislation as the allowance for feeding workers was fixed by law and any expenditure over this figure was taxed very heavily. This approach is slowly changing in the 1990s. In other countries, however, the barriers will be more cultural than legislative. A caterer will need to be very sensitive to special attitudes towards food and its consumption. Is the main meal at lunchtime or in the evening? Do people prefer to eat hot or cold foods? How long do they take for a lunch break? Is it normal for lunchtime to be used by management to influence the attitudes of employees? What hours of working are normal?

The answers to these questions vary from one European market to another, and also from region to region within some countries. For the French, eating is a way of life. Italians eating at work regard it as topping up the fuel levels. In Northern Europe, heavy meals with a large meat content tend to be the norm. In Southern Europe, it is not unusual for the working day to be organised with either a finish in mid-afternoon, when employees prefer to go home to eat, or a long two or three-hour break at midday when employees tend to go off-site.

Working in Europe means the problem of managing a European group with a wide range of nationalities each with different attitudes and management skills. A responsive management strategy is needed to handle cultural differences. A caterer has to be flexible and fit in with local realities rather than to try to change them. Experience of regional variation in the British market reinforces this point of view.

The effect of the single European market will be to increase markets. The major contract caterers will have to increase the sophistication of their management to cope with the complexities of working on a European scale. This section focuses on contract catering in various countries:

- France
- Germany
- The Netherlands
- USA
- Japan

France

There are some 249,000 food service outlets in France with almost 178,000 in the profit sector and 71,000 in the cost or non-commercial sector. In 1996, the French public ate 6.5 billion meals away from home. Growth is averaging just under 1% in the total eating out market but the contract sector is growing faster than this. The contracted sector served over 640 million meals in 1996 from 20,600 outlets, with business and industry accounting for 44% of outlets but 42% of meals. Education and health care combined have 52% of outlets and 56% of contracted meals. Sodexho is the largest contractor in France in terms of turnover. Generale de Restauration is second and Eurest is third.

Germany

Germans consume 9.7 billion meals away from home each year; almost 57% of these representing 5.5 billion meals in 1996 were eaten in the profit sector and 4.2 billion in the non-commercial sector. Overall developments in the food service sector have been strongly influenced by the general situation in the German economy as a result of reunification in the early 1990s and more recently in the run up to European Monetary Union. One of the major effects has been cut-backs in employee feeding, resulting from increasing unemployment and also from efforts to cut costs. This has not been so noticeable in other countries, especially France and UK, where contract catering is seen as an opportunity to enhance employee prospects while increasing control over costs. This difference in reaction underlines the lack of progress that contract catering has made in Germany to date. The contracted sector served fewer than 60 million meals in 1996 compared with ten times that number in the UK and France, whose economies are less than two-thirds than that of Germany. The largest contractor in Germany is Eurest, which operates almost 19% of contracted outlets, followed by Aramark and Pedus (both at 12%).

The Netherlands

Although significantly smaller than other European countries, the Netherlands is nevertheless a rich and dynamic country with one of the healthiest economies in Europe. There are almost 40,000 places to eat out. Of these just under 32,000 (82%) are in the commercial sector and they served 1.8 billion meals in 1996, while the non-commercial sector served a further 0.6 billion meals. In the same year, contractors served just over 130 million meals representing a reported growth rate of over 5% on the year before. Van Hecke, with over 1,100 outlets, is the largest contractor. Eurest is second and operates 725 outlets. BRN Groep has 375 outlets (12%) and Service One Group operates 350 outlets (11%).

USA

The US food service sector was worth some $321 billion in 1996 and represents 52% of the total (retail plus food service) consumer food dollar. The market has grown at a steady rate of between 1.5 and 2.5% every year since 1986. The commercial segment which approximates to the profit sector in the UK accounts for 69% of all food service sector food purchases; the balance is made up from the non-commercial sector which includes business and industry, education, health care, prisons, and the army. Marriott is the largest contractor with some 3,600 outlets (19%) followed by Aramark (12%), Sodexho (8%) and Compass (7%)

Japan

There are in excess of 360,000 food service outlets in the commercial sector in Japan, the majority of these are sit-down restaurants and bars, although US-style take-aways are very much a feature of the market. One noteworthy aspect of the Japanese market is the comparative lack of hotels and lodging places in comparison to Europe and the USA. The non-commercial sector is also significant: there are about 35,000 health-care sites although this is only slightly more than in the UK, which has only 45% of the population.

Contracting is very much a feature of the business and industry sector where some 13,000 outlets are contracted, representing 72% of workplaces which supply meals. In contrast, contracting in the education and health-care sectors achieves only 8% in both cases. The Uwokuni Group is the largest contract caterer with over 1,820 outlets in Japan.

Catering contracts

The contract between catering contractors and their clients tends to be precise in terms of the legal obligations of both parties, while mentioning in only broad terms the operational obligations of contractors. This may be due in part to the difficulty of defining standards of food and service and of the environment in which the products are to be served and consumed. The length of retained contracts with clients is dependent on the degree of success of the relationship between contractor and client. The average length of contract before it is lost is usually between three and five years. Renegotiation of fees and budgets is normally on an annual basis.

There are two main methods by which contractors are remunerated – fixed fee system and a cost-plus system.

In the **fixed fee system**, the contractor quotes an overall fixed cost to the client usually calculated and tendered as a cost per potential customer. This fee is the total sum payable by the client to the contractor and therefore covers reimbursement for all operating costs plus an element for profit. The benefit of this approach is that it helps protect the client against mistakes or inefficiency especially if the agreement is tied to guarantees of performance. However the contractor may end up cutting corners to rectify tendering errors.

Those contracts who are on **cost-plus terms** or **management fee** are reimbursed for costs and in addition are paid a management fee plus a percentage of unit revenue or unit operating cost or a percentage of gross revenue. The essence of this approach is a partnership between contractor and client. With this approach the client frequently has the power to require a contractor to produce supplier documentation and so price changes can be monitored. It is therefore in this sense that the management fee approach focuses on value for money as opposed to lowest cost. Table 9.3 illustrates the types of contracts in operation within the UK and shows that there has been a significant shift in the types of contract which contractors are winning. The two main types of contracts, cost-plus and fixed fee, have already been discussed. Others such as partnership contracts (where the client and caterer are partners in the operation, sharing costs and revenues) and contracts based on concessionary rent (in which the caterer pays a rent to the client perhaps based on a percentage of turnover and/or profit) are also becoming prevalent. The number of outlets operated under the more traditional cost-plus contract has declined between 1994 and 1997 from 59% to 41%, while the number of outlets on some form of fixed fee contract has risen by the same amount. There is doubt that this trend will continue.

Apart from the fee, an additional method of remuneration is the retention of discount allowed by suppliers for bulk purchases dependent on size. Clients are surprisingly ignorant of this facet of the contract catering industry and whether they derive any benefit from the contractors receiving such a discount. There has in recent years been more open discussion of these discounts with contractors willing to discuss their size and value.

The primary obligation of the contractor is to operate the designated unit or units in compliance with the contract. The recruitment selection and training of staff adequate to the operation of the unit is an essential obligation of most contracts. The staff are employed by the contractor as principals, not agents of the client. Responsibility is therefore on the contractor to ensure compliance with employment law.

Table 9.3 Types of contracts

	1994	1995	1996	1997
Cost plus	7,958	7,925	7,637	6,762
Performance guarantee	529	654	950	1,342
Fixed fee	4,018	5,493	6,224	8,070
Partnership	72	101	86	131
Concession rent	777	741	735	671
Total	13,354	14,914	15,632	16,722

Source: British Hospitality Association (1997) Contract Catering Survey 1997

Normally the provision and maintenance of premises and equipment is primarily the responsibility of the client. Control of stock and cash receipts along with budgetary control is the responsibility of the contractor. Contractors customarily carry out initial feasibility studies on the unit for which they are tendering for. This approach is more in the context of a right (to protect themselves by for example assessing potential sales and estimating fees chargeable) than as an obligation to the client. Where further catering assistance or advice is required there is a tendency for contractors no longer to regard the provision of such services as an automatic obligation within the contract but as an extra benefit for which the prospective client should pay.

In comparison with the extensive formal or implied obligations of contractors, their rights are considerably fewer. Right of access to a properly equipped constructed and designed property with properly supplied services is one aspect. Similarly the right to prompt payment of invoices rendered is another right of contractors. Finally, the contractors normally retain a right to terminate the contractual agreement if the client company is liquidated, if a receiver is appointed or if there is a material breach of the agreement.

Industry supply

Number of outlets and meals served

It has been estimated that the total number of outlets in the food service management sector is 83,340; on this basis, catering contractors are responsible for 16,722 of the market (18.6% of the total). In terms of meals served the total figure is 2,685 million, and for contractors 1,111 million. Catering contractors in the UK have some way to go before they match the average 80% share of the US business and industry market; the European average, however, is nearer 30%.

While the economic recession of the early 1990s resulted in contractors suffering a slight decline in market share in the number of outlets in business and industry, contractors did increase their share of the number of meals served in the sector. Catering contractors tend to operate in the larger outlets in this sector. This point is illustrated in Table 9.4 with reference to outlets and Table 9.5 with reference to meals. By outlets, it is meant any catering unit (or part of a catering unit) which is separately operated and managed; a catering unit could have a number of different outlets.

The biggest sector in food service management is education, followed by health and welfare, and business and industry. This structure is not reflected in the share of the contract catering market where contract caterers have a greater share of business and indus-

Table 9.4 Number of outlets 1990–7

	1990	1991	1992	1993	1994	1995	1996	1997
Business and industry	7,089	7,058	7,775	7,671	7,132	7,473	7,574	7,586
Health care	250	365	337	379	405	459	397	483
State education	242	465	450	490	2,383	4,603	4,957	6,140
Independent schools	492	610	620	733	587	579	578	545
Local authorities	262	362	463	362	261	295	451	357
Ministry of Defence	68	132	190	210	265	267	393	395
Public catering	116	233	324	475	619	1,002	971	1,034
Oil rigs, training centres, construction sites	62	163	246	242	302	263	311	182
Total	8,581	9,388	10,405	10,562	11,954	14,941	15,632	16,722

Source: British Hospitality Association (1997) Contract Catering Survey 1997

Table 9.5 Number of meals (million) 1990–7

	1990	1991	1992	1993	1994	1995	1996	1997
Business and industry	304	320	322	401	408	456	465	455
Health care	29	42	38	68	65	77	81	121
State education	15	26	30	31	94	163	172	206
Independent schools	59	66	81	111	100	99	99	84
Local authorities	22	30	31	28	20	15	18	17
Ministry of Defence	22	47	55	67	92	86	92	86
Public catering	24	50	62	69	120	130	134	128
Oil rigs, training centres, construction sites	10	27	25	29	41	23	28	14
Total	486	608	654	804	940	1,049	1,089	1,111

Source: British Hospitality Association (1997) Contract Catering Survey 1997

try than of any other sector. Of some significance is the continuing slow decline in the share of the total market held by the business and industry sector, with the complementary increase in the share held by most other sectors. Clearly, areas outside the traditional business and industry sector are offering the greatest potential for expansion. In addition to these permanent locations, contract caterers provide catering facilities at a large number of non-permanent events. It should be noted that local authorities catering includes town hall administration, police, fire and welfare; state education includes state schools, further education and higher education; independent schools include all private schools; health care includes NHS, private hospitals, nursing homes and retirement homes.

In 1997 there was a modest growth in the number of meals served by contract caterers. Overall the increase was 2% with an improvement in the number of meals served in state education and health care. The contractors' share of the total number of meals served in business and industry has virtually remained static in 1997 compared with 1996.

Market size and trends

Contract catering in the UK is still focused relatively narrowly on the provision of meals to the private sector, i.e. business and industry. Industry statistics assess the penetration of this market by contract caterers at less than 50%, implying that perhaps more than half of the private sector has yet to explore the possibility of contracting out their catering operations. Gardner Merchant/Sodexho and Compass together account in the UK for some 60% of contracts. The other major competitors in the market are Sutcliffe, accounting for over 20%, and the fourth largest is ARA Services which has approximately 3%. It should be borne in mind that contract caterers are competing not only with other contract caterers but also with self-operated outlets as the marketplace is one of employee feeding. In terms of the total outlets in all private and public sectors, Compass and Gardner Merchant/Sodexho account for a market share of approximately 7%. It is this fact that underpins the view that growth potential in the industry is considerable. In the USA contract caterers operate approximately 80% of outlets in business and industry. In both the health and education markets, contract caterers provide food management services to only 5% or less of the available outlets and between 5% and 10% of the meals served. These areas are likely to come under increasing pressure to adopt a commercial stance: contracting out is one way of reducing cost pressures.

During 1996 there was a clear indication of consolidation within the UK contract catering business. Looking at a sample of the acquisitions that the major companies have made in 1996 it is clear that consolidation has continued on both a national and international basis:

UK acquisitions in 1996	Acquiring group
Northdowns	Granada
CCG	Granada
Bromwich catering	Granada
Wheatsheaf	Gardner Merchant
Russell and Brand	Marriott
Payne and Gunter	Compass
Shaw Catering	Granada
Tillery Foods	Gardner Merchant
Hallmark Executive Catering	High Table

Overseas developments

Fedics (South Africa)	Granada, Expertise sharing agreement
Eurest (France)	Compass, Management and Sodexho shareholdings
PFM (USA)	Compass
Service America (USA)	Compass

The increase in size and concentration of the major contract caterers has enabled several other changes to take place beyond the simple economies of scale that result in better purchasing and lower central charges per contract. The size and scope of players such as Sutcliffe, Sodexho and Compass have meant that the licensing of external concepts and the creation of internal brand share become a realistic possibility. High street favourites such as Burger King and Pizza Hut have been exclusively licensed in contract catering areas. One of the largest pizza brands in the USA is Itza Pizza which was invented by ARA for the contract market. Some of the largest companies are moving away from institutional food service into high street brand management, particularly shopping centre food courts. The UK contract catering market is clearly neither saturated nor mature. There is a continuing trend of companies to contract out non-core activities: facilities management and staff catering in large hotels, and the willingness of companies such as ARAMARK and Marriott to grow within the UK is evidence of this growth.

Turnover

Turnover within the industry is calculated from a combination of wages, management fee and food purchases. Despite the recession of the early 1990s along with low inflation, turnover increased from a figure of £977 million in 1990 to £2227 million in 1997 which represents substantial growth. The trend reflects not only the increased number of outlets but also the increased number of meals served; it shows that food service management is expanding in both volume and value terms.

It is noticeable that turnover from overseas operations of contract catering companies registered and based in the UK rapidly expanded during the early 1990s. During 1997, turnover from overseas operations of food service management companies rose to £2.4 billion; the figure in 1993 was £277 million. This reflects the global nature and strategies of the industry's largest contractors. Most of this turnover comes from EU countries although 1997 also saw an increase in North American turnover.

Employees

Despite an increase in the number of outlets over the period 1990–7, the number of staff per outlet has fallen which is an indication that contractors have been careful to maintain levels of productivity, a point illustrated in Table 9.6.

Further analysis of the employment figures show the recession of the early 1990s affected the number of full-time school-leavers recruited but there was an increase in the number of part-time school-leavers. Recruitment of full-time college-leavers followed the same trend, with part-time recruitment of college-leavers increasing slightly. During 1997 there was a slight reduction in both school-leavers and college-leavers entering employment with contractors.

One important area related to that of employment is the subject of wages and wage control. Total wages reduced marginally in 1997 to 42%: the figure in 1995 was 42.4% which indicates that contract caterers kept a tight control over one of their biggest items of expenditure.

Table 9.6 Number of staff per outlet 1990–7

	1990	1991	1992	1993	1994	1995	1996	1997
Number of outlets	8,583	9,388	10,405	10,552	13,354	14,941	15,632	16,722
Number of staff	74,813	81,500	90,880	91,802	105,436	113,606	115,430	111,875
Number of staff per outlet	8.7	8.7	8.7	8.7	7.9	7.6	7.4	6.7

Source: British Hospitality Association (1997) Contract Catering Survey 1997

Other services

It is noticeable that there has been a significant trend in the recorded number of **vending machines** operated by contract caterers. It is likely that many meals, particularly snacks, are provided from vending machines.

Finally, the **diversification** of food service management companies into other areas such as housekeeping, cleaning, maintenance and others reflects a growing trend for client companies to concentrate on their core activities while letting contractors, whose catering activities are generally perceived as the most skilled part of the contract, provide these additional services as part of a total contract package. It should be noted that several food service management companies have established separate facilities management divisions. Some 20% of contracts are now conditional upon the contractor providing a range of support services apart from catering. This is particularly true of the health-care sector. This trend will continue because clients prefer to deal with one contractor rather than a number. Contractors who can provide these services are at an advantage when tendering for contracts.

Three major companies

Approximately thirty companies in the UK dominate over 90% of the contract catering industry. The three major companies within the industry are Gardner Merchant/Sodexho, Compass and Sutcliffe Catering Group.

Gardner Merchant Services Group

Both 1992 and early 1993 were a period of speculation and rumour within the contract catering industry. The creation of Gardner Merchant originally stems from a merger of Gardner and Merchant in 1966. It was, after a number of months of speculation, finally sold by its parent company Forte plc in January 1993. The purchaser was a management buyout team led by the company's chief executive Garry Hawkes and funded by a consortium led by CINven, the venture capital arm of the British Coal Board pension fund. The new company is now known as Gardner Merchant Services Group. The company was subsequently sold in what Garry Hawkes described as a joint venture to the French group Sodexho.

Compass Group

Compass Group was originally formed to acquire Grand Metropolitan's contract services division. Various companies within Grand Met which had been acquired during the early to mid-1970s and operating in the services sector (including catering, security and building maintenance) were slowly over the course of the next decade developed into what became known as the Compass Group. The group made its first move into health care in 1981. It subsequently acquired Rosser & Russell in 1983 to take it into heating and ventilation in the building industry. Gerry Robinson joined the group from another Grand Met subsidiary in 1984 to rationalise the unprofitable overseas contract services business and became the contract services divisional managing director in 1985. These businesses were subject to a management buyout from Grand Met in 1987 led by Robinson, and the company was subsequently floated on the Stock Market in December 1988. It sold Rosser

& Russell in 1990. Compass is now led by Francis Mackay after Gerry Robinson left to become chief executive of Granada in 1991. At the same time Charles Allen who was managing director of the catering division also left to join Granada.

A trend, developed in late 1992 by Compass, was the purchase of both Travellers Fare and Letherby and Christopher. The acquisition of Travellers Fare will allow it to expand with respect to recognisable brands such as Burger King and Upper Crust. The Letherby and Christopher purchase took Compass into other areas such as racecourse catering where it holds about a 35% market share.

Sutcliffe Catering Group

Sutcliffe Catering Group was owned by the P&O Group, although in terms of size it was very small within the wider parent group. It was sold in March 1993 to Granada for £360 million which gives an indication of size relative to Compass and Gardner Merchant. For Granada, in many ways this was a logical move that brought a cash generating business to a company headed by former Compass directors Gerry Robinson and Charles Allen. Total turnover at Sutcliffe is in excess of £300 million and its style of management is to decentralise management responsibility to a number of regional operating companies. It also owns Fairfield Catering, a specialist in the educational catering market along with Taylorplan Catering Services.

Gardner Merchant and Compass: a comparison

A side-by-side analysis of Compass Catering and Gardner Merchant (GM) is illuminating. While both companies' interests are world-wide, a comparison between GM's UK business and Compass Catering gives the most direct comparison. One issue in such an approach is that there are few definitions in the industry. For example a contract may call for the operation of three catering units on a large site, which may be regarded as one contract or three contracts.

Both companies are broadly comparable in terms of the number of contracts operated, each having a little over 30% of the UK market; however, GM generates significantly more turnover than Compass. This is due to GM operating a larger number of bigger contracts and differences in the way the companies record their turnover.

The fundamental issue is determining what constitutes a sale. The cost of running a typical restaurant include food, labour and the management fee. Offsetting this will be the cash taken at the point of sale. Effectively, turnover is represented by costs incurred by the food service manager including its management fee. Depending on the policy of the employer on staff feeding, however, it is possible that the employer will choose to subsidise the cost of meals to the employee so that the cash at point of sale (a cost to the employee) does not recover the costs of the goods and services provided. This difference (the subsidy) could be construed as an extra cost. There could, however, be a difference in the treatment of this subsidy which has an effect on invoiced turnover. Such a subsidy does not operate in all restaurants and will therefore explain the discrepancy in margins. GM's average contract size is larger and this would contribute to lower margins because the balance of negotiating power between contracted and contractor is different from that at Compass.

There are two other areas where Compass seems considerably more efficient than Gardner Merchant. Compass uses designated suppliers and thus secures greater purchasing discounts. It is also able to retain more of those discounts by virtue of its bargaining power relative to its customers. Purchases as a percentage of sales have always been considerably less at Compass than at GM and would explain the difference in margins between the two companies. At Compass the use of working capital seems to be better so that it has better credit control. As a final point GM's overseas businesses are partly responsible for the reduced UK margin since much of the management and administrative costs are borne in the UK.

Prospects for the contract catering industry

Since 1990 a number of continuing trends have been seen within the contract catering industry. Catering contractors have experienced a period of robust growth; this will probably continue, though not at the historic average rate of some 14% per year as few industries can continue to grow at such a pace. There are a number of reasons for this caution.

Growth in the contractors' main market – business and industry – is slowing down. Employment in industry generally, though rising, is not buoyant and many companies are still endeavouring to reduce staff numbers or to make more efficient use of existing staff in order to contain costs. Where employment is improving, it is doing so slowly; new businesses are mostly small and do not require a catering service. Many of the large industrial complexes have disappeared since the mid-1980s; while new factories are opening, many older factories have closed down. The structural changes which industry has experienced since the early 1980s have had an effect on the contract catering industry and, as a result, the potential growth of catering services in business and industry is more limited than in many other sectors. Despite these changes, contractors have increased their number of outlets in business and industry by some 7% since 1990 and the number of meals by over 40%. Yet it is significant that, even though the number in real terms has increased, the business and industry sector's share of the total contracting market in terms of number of meals has declined from 63% in 1990 (304 million) to 43% (465 million) in 1996, and the share of the total number of outlets has dropped from 83% (7,089) to 48.5% (7,574) during the same period. Business and industry remains a core market for the contracting industry but future expansion in the sector will principally reflect the rate of growth of the UK economy. Higher levels of employment and greater industrial activity should see a greater use of contractors. This will be encouraged by the increasingly favourable view of contracting taken by clients who, by concentrating on their core market, recognise the advantages of outsourcing their key support services. This remains a continuing benefit to the industry. New markets are also opening up: for example, some hotels have begun to contract out their staff feeding arrangements; others are now even managed by contract catering companies. New markets such as these will help contractors to expand in the business and industry sector.

Much of the recent expansion in the contract catering industry has been in the emerging sectors such as education, health care and catering for the public. Education – particularly state education – has seen remarkable growth since 1995 as a small number of companies have entered the sector, winning major local authority school contracts which had been put out to competitive tender. State education now accounts for 37% of contracted outlets and 18.5% of the number of meals served by contractors.

The contracting companies in this sector are necessarily large and some have faced significant difficulties to such an extent that, while wishing to increase their penetration of the sector, they are reluctant to expand further in the immediate future. The problems in this sector have also discouraged other companies from tendering for state school meals contracts. Difficulties have centred on the information provided at the tender stage, which has led to higher than expected labour costs, and other unforeseen factors. Until these problems are resolved, this sector is likely to see little further significant penetration by contract caterers. State education includes state schools, universities and colleges of higher and further education, which are proving to be increasingly attractive to contractors as they provide large sites which can accommodate a number of new catering outlets – some of them High Street branded restaurants – as well as the more traditional counter service facilities. The trend to branded restaurants has also emerged in the healthcare market where large hospitals have a considerable amount of passing traffic in terms of visitors, medical staff, out-patients and ambulant in-patients. At least one large hospital has opened a food court and others will undoubtedly follow.

The number of NHS and trust hospitals which now employ catering contractors has risen from 130 in 1995 to 142 in 1996. As these are frequently large sites, often with as many as 1,000 beds, there is considerable potential for growth in this sector. Ironically, the number of contracted outlets in health care declined in 1996 as a result of a drop in the number of contracted nursing homes; however, the total number of meals provided increased from 77 million to 81 million, reflecting the size of hospital outlets compared to those operated in nursing homes.

Independent schools, far less numerous than the state sector, represent just under 4% by outlets and just over 9% by number of meals. Although their number has remained more or less constant since 1993, the number of meals served in the sector is dropping because, in the present economic climate, the number of boarding pupils at independent schools is declining, thus reducing meal uptake.

Of the other sectors, the most important is commercial catering – that is, catering for members of the public. In 1996 growth was less spectacular than in previous years but the sector represents one of the contract catering industry's potentially biggest – and most profitable – markets. Traditionally, contractors have rarely been involved in commercial catering; it is only since 1991 that they have made significant inroads into this market, initially through local authority leisure centres. In the late 1990s they work in almost every area of commercial catering – in railway stations and airports, theatres and museums, golf clubs and racecourses. This, and the contracting industry's expansion into education and health care, has been the main spur to its growth since the mid-1980s. As contractors see only limited growth in business and industry, and as both the education and health-care sectors are perceived as being vulnerable to political will, commercial catering continues to offer new opportunities. Those companies who take most advantage of them will be those contractors who can best harness their organisational and purchasing techniques to new-found marketing and merchandising retail skills.

Indeed, that is the case with almost all contracts. Clients are increasingly seeking to reduce their catering costs and putting pressure upon the contractor to abandon the traditional cost-plus contract in favour of nil-subsidy catering, in which all the costs of the catering operation – and the caterer's profit – are covered by sales revenue. This is not possible in every location but the trend is certainly apparent and the introduction of branded restaurants – often on a concessionary basis in which the client might share any profit as well as receiving a rent – is one step towards this goal. Higher education and health-care institutions, together with some of the largest business and industry sites, have already adopted this approach, which has been encouraged by the investment that many contract catering companies are now prepared to make in new client catering facilities, always providing there is sufficient return on capital over the length of the contract.

Ironically, it is education and health care, both of which have benefited most from the contractor's expertise since the mid-1980s, which pose the greatest uncertainties for the contractor. The industry will suffer should the present programme of compulsory competitive tendering diminish. Nevertheless, many authorities will have already experienced the advantages which contracting can bring to their catering arrangements and it is likely that they will continue to contract out in order to take advantage of a highly cost-efficient service.

Clearly, the changes which have been wrought in the contract catering industry will increasingly focus the contractor's attention on future expansion.

The strength of the contracting industry's sales and marketing programmes has already had a pronounced effect on the expansion of the market and this will become more pronounced in the future. Added to this is the challenge which faces all contractors to increase food and beverage sales in existing contracts. This is particularly so when catering for members of the public. For many contractors, the need to increase sales and to maximise the use of underused catering facilities is as important as increasing the number of contracts.

The commitment of the Labour government to the social legislation coming from the EU raises further concerns for the industry, particularly in the areas of the minimum wage, equal treatment of full-time and part-time employees, and works councils. If a minimum wage were to be introduced, depending on the level at which it was set, the cost to the contract catering sector could be significant in an industry in which over 25% of the labour force is part-time. Although many companies – primarily those with European interests – have voluntarily introduced works councils, any compulsory requirement to introduce them to the British catering industry would add an extra burden of cost and time to management. Moreover, a stricter judicial interpretation of the TUPE legislation, while clarifying the position, also holds out a serious threat to contractors by placing additional burdens upon their businesses. This threat is felt by contract caterers to reflect the position in respect of much EU legislation.

In spite of these doubts, the contract catering industry is likely to maintain its impressive performance of the 1990s. The industry has adapted successfully to changing circumstances by seeking new markets and new opportunities and this will continue. The business and industry sector remains crucial, and provides the basis of the industry's profitability, but further expansion will come in other areas – and overseas – and by encouraging a higher uptake on the part of existing customers. Marketing, merchandising and promotional retail skills remain crucially important, and there is every sign that contractors are acquiring, and have acquired, these skills and will use them to increasing effect.

Summary

Two key underlying trends in food service management have been discussed in this chapter: the growth of the total food service management market and the reducing share of the total market held by business and industry. Both these trends will continue throughout the 1990s although there is perceived to be great potential for growth in catering in the areas currently self-operated (i.e. non-catering businesses running their own staff catering services). It can be seen that the opportunities presented by the non-traditional sectors of health care, local authorities and education should be sufficient to offer continued growth to contract catering companies in the medium term.

Further reading

● Anon. (1993) *Facilities Management: Business of the Future? Cost Sector Catering*, London: Dewberry Boyes.

- British Hospitality Association (1992) *Wages and Salaries Survey*, London: BHA with Touche Ross and Greene Belfield Smith Division.
- British Hospitality Association (1996) *Contract Catering Survey*, London: BHA.
- British Hospitality Association (1997) *Contract Catering Survey*, London: BHA.
- Hawkes G. (1989) 'An overview of the contract catering industry in the United Kingdom: a view from the industry', in C. Cooper (ed.) *Progress in Tourism Recreation and Hospitality Management*, vol. 1, London: Belhaven Press.
- Hawkes G. (1992) 'Quality in the contract catering industry', in C. Cooper and A. Lockwood (eds) *Progress in Tourism Recreation and Hospitality Management*, vol 4, London: Belhaven Press.
- Housden J. (1984) *Franchising and Other Business Relationships in Hotel and Catering Services*, London: Heinemann.
- Key Note (1993) *Contract Catering Report*, London: Key Note.

Chapter Ten

Brewing Industry

Objectives

After reading this chapter you should be able to

▪ Discuss the background to the brewing industry and set it within the context of the hospitality industry.

▪ Give a brief history of the industry.

▪ Illustrate the twin issues of horizontal and vertical integration within the industry.

▪ Discuss the effects of the Monopolies and Mergers Commission report on the brewing industry.

▪ Illustrate how the major brewers have a substantial interest in the hotel and catering sector.

Historical development

Many breweries were founded in the eighteenth century, with alehouses brewing their own beer on the premises. By the turn of the century a number of these breweries were commercialised enough to enjoy the economies of scale achieved by brewing in one location, and developed as regional companies.

Throughout the nineteenth century, economic and legal changes encouraged the beginnings of a closer relationship between the brewing industry and the pub retailers. By the end of the century, breweries had come to own estates of public houses, and the phenomenon of the **tied house** with its tie on supply between breweries and retailers was developed. The benefits of this integration were immediately felt, as these commercial brewers gained greater control of both sales and quality; this was the beginning of what economists would describe as vertical integration within the industry.

During the early twentieth century a major influence on the industry occurred at the beginning of the First World War when Parliament introduced the Defence of the Realm Act 1914 (DORA), which was in order to ensure that all men were fit for duty and to overcome shortages of materials. These first licensing laws were intended to be temporary measures.

In time, the larger brewers adopted acquisition strategies and diversified into alternative products through the development of soft-drink production plants. By the end of the 1920s the brewers also had extended their product range to wines and spirits. These changes were driven as part of the need to provide the consumer with what they desired within brewery-owned retail outlets.

Restrictions imposed by the government during the Second World War affected the brewers. A shortage in supply of all production materials, from hops to glass for the bottles, long outlasted the war. Consequently there was a temporary pause in the continued development of companies within the industry. By the 1950s, those breweries that had survived began to redevelop their interests. During the 1960s, brewers were interested in penetrating the growth in the leisure market, but the ability to diversify into leisure was dependent on the size and financial position of companies. By the early 1970s, Grand Metropolitan began to expand and Scottish and Newcastle had initiated a new group of hotels to be called Thistle Hotels (which were sold to Mount Charlotte Hotels in 1989, later to be acquired by Brierley Investments Limited and finally floated on the Stock Market). Whitbread expanded into this sector with its interests in Country Club Hotels, Landsbury Hotels and its budget chain, Travel Inns and subsequently Marriott. Bass took a quantum leap forward in this sector with its acquisition in 1988 of Holiday Inns International and extended in 1990 to the purchase of the Holiday Inn chain in North America. Food and drink seem to be a natural combination for hotels and leisure. As had happened over a century previously, when the brewers invested in public houses, throughout the 1970s and 1980s the breweries broadened their interests.

At the end of the 1980s the leisure industry was identified as being one of the most vibrant sectors; despite the economic downturn of the early 1990s, longer term prospects remain good. The larger breweries have had the combinations of foresight and finance to back investments in different leisure areas. Department of Employment figures show that the public houses, bars, night-clubs and licensed clubs sectors accounted for over 450,000 jobs. Of total UK leisure spending in the 1990s, the breweries' interests alone made up 25% with a further 10% accounted for by interests in other markets, such as food and hotels.

The public house

In *The English Pub,* Jackson claims that the public house was once a house, where the public were guests of the host and hostess. This concept holds true in the best of pubs whose success depends on the welcome of the landlord and landlady. The term **public house** has, to a large extent, become a generic term encompassing the inns, taverns and alehouses that date back to about the eleventh century whose once distinct functions have become blurred with the passage of time.

In a social context the pub and church are a traditional part of the English village and their physical proximity evolved from the need to build hospices to provide rest and sustenance during the years it took to build the early churches. Hospitality was traditionally provided to travellers by the abbeys and priories visited by pilgrims like Chaucer's. The close link between the church and the pub was severed by the dissolution of the monasteries in the sixteenth century, when the responsibilities of innkeeping passed to the lord of the manor. England's heritage and history is reflected in the art form of the public house: the inn sign, where ecclesiastical signs gave way to the heraldic emblems of the aristocracy such as The Red Lion, The White Horse and others. An inn was often run by the local squire's estate steward or **landlord** and thus a new word became associated with the public house. As late as 1604, an Act of Parliament recognised inns, taverns and alehouses as places '*for the Receipt, Relief and Lodging of Wayfaring People travelling from Place to Place*'.

The term **public house** appears to have been officially recognised in 1854, in a reference by a House of Commons Select Committee. The importance of the coaching inn was greatly diminished by the advent of the railways in the 1830s and 1840s, but the Victorian era saw the development of the big city pub. The 1890s were their golden age. The pubs then were bigger and brighter, their fittings more sumptuous than they had ever been before or were to be again. In this pub boom, hundreds of city pubs in London,

Manchester and Liverpool were rebuilt or reconstructed with an uninhibited extravagance of style and design that reflected the energy and exuberance of the era.

The original segregation by socio-economic class of tap rooms and saloon bars has largely become redundant. Major brewers have conceptually modernised their pubs with large open bars and now only pubs in the north of England and those outside the main cities still retain the original divisions. History is cyclical, however, and it is interesting to note that there is currently a move to revive the nineteenth-century concept of segregation in pubs in order to meet the diverse needs of the twentieth-century consumer.

Towards the end of the nineteenth century, alcohol was a major moral and political issue and many people believed that public houses were a social nuisance. However, the pub was recognised for its vital contribution to community life by a Central Public House Trust Association, whose main principle was that a public house as a social institution is a public necessity, and that consequently it is desirable to convert it as far as possible from a mere drinking bar into a well-conducted club. A government campaign in 1916 set out to improve pubs through state ownership by serving meals, offering soft drinks and encouraging women and families to accompany their menfolk. After the two world wars, there was a backlash until the 1970s and 1980s when the pub concept was segmented, notably in the development of the modern destination or theme pub. Segmentation was the inevitable marketing response to twentieth-century consumer sophistication, an increasingly competitive environment and the realisation that the traditional British pub could no longer be all things to all people.

There are many types of public houses. The consumer is drawn to the amenities of an individual pub, and is generally unaware of a process of product segmentation. For ease of management, however, pubs are categorised under different banners, defined principally in terms of travel distance. The traditional **local** is described as a community pub and caters to those who live within half a mile of its location. The **destination or venue pub** attracts people from up to thirty miles away, who travel there on a predetermined basis because of the entertainment that is offered. For example, **cask ale houses** are destination pubs that offer traditional beers in response to modern demand. **Sound and light houses** are venue pubs that provide a high technology environment for young people and offer an alternative to other less regulated events. Another important category is the twentieth-century **food and family** concept, described by pub retailers as the pub of the future.

The diversity of modern pubs has developed in response to consumer demand in the face of competitive market forces. Traditionalists object to the destruction or transformation of the traditional British pub and persist in their allegations that the profit motive of the major brewers is the biggest threat to the national institution. Both sides defend their stance, but the historical perspective serves to show that the pub has evolved over the centuries, and that it is by nature, and in more ways than one, a fluid and not a fixed concept.

A unique social institution

The British pub has been at the centre of many social and sporting activities over the centuries. A survey carried out by an unnamed Midland brewery revealed that nearly 3,000 societies or committees held their meetings in pubs, ranging from yacht clubs to anglers' societies, pigeon fanciers to professional rat-catchers. Throughout its history, the pub-goer has joined in (or tolerated) the sound of live entertainment, music or drama, whose current vogue ranges from jazz, to discos or karaoke. The pub, unlike other leisure venues, charges no entrance fee.

Boxing has links with the pub that go back over eight centuries. Archery was the precursor for the popular game of darts. The modern game of cricket was conceived at the Hampshire pub called The Bat and Ball, and many village cricket grounds can be found within a stone's throw of the village local, some named after the sport. This typically English summer scene has its winter counterpart in the traditional stirrup-cup meet of the hunt outside a country inn, although this association may soon be an event of the past.

The pub as an institution cannot be judged in isolation within its community, for, like its fellow constituents, it also forms part of a broader picture. A village is not considered complete without its pub, church and cricket green. Similarly, the image of the traditional rural pub would not be the same without its connections with local sports.

The appeal of the British pub lies in its uniqueness. Different types of pubs satisfy varying needs in different people and, despite the branding attempts of the big brewers, no two pubs are the same: each has its peculiar character and atmosphere, shaped by the local environment, the licensee and the clientele. The pub's unique character lies in its evolution over hundreds of years and this simply cannot be replicated in plain bricks and mortar. The pub, in its many guises, has survived the centuries as a permanent and resilient institution in British community life.

Time will tell whether the pub will emerge leaner and fitter from its current burdens, but history shows that the pub has endured in the face of political opposition and adverse social trends in the past. The majority of houses will have to adapt to changing trends and a more demanding clientele. The pub tradition is hospitality; the traditional pub may be sacrificed in its name. The question, one which pub operators have had to address, is whether a unique but unprofitable pub can be retained. Another question may be whether the modern branded pub will lose the unique appeal accorded to its traditional forebear, and become just another retail outlet. In evolving in this way, will the pub, one of the many faces of Britain, lose its tourist appeal? As major employers and contributors to the economy, brewers must carefully review their strategy towards their pub outlets.

Leisure trends

The second half of the twentieth century has witnessed a tremendous leap in the evolution of tourism and hospitality. Advances in travel and technology in an ever-changing world ensure that tourism will always be dynamic, responding to economic, social and environmental stimuli and part of the lifestyle of a large and growing number of people. The trends indicate that all European countries are becoming more leisure-based societies. Time spent at work is decreasing while leisure time is increasing. Trends also show that the population in the western world is growing older and there are more working women, important demographic changes for both tourism and hospitality. In the context of these changes, the image of the pub itself is undergoing a transformation.

Since the mid-1950s there has been a gradual erosion of the pub as a predominantly male enclave in the wake of changing social and demographic trends, particularly in the role of women and the family. An examination of leisure trends published in 1951 serves to highlight the differences between then and now. The public house was then described as a place of relaxation and sociability in which predominantly working-class or lower-middle-class males met to discuss sport and local matters; it was noted that a large proportion of women of all classes of society never entered public houses for the fact remained that they existed for the sole purpose of retailing alcoholic liquor. In the 1990s pubs are diversifying into catering as a means of attracting the family and efforts are being made to enhance their appeal to women.

The 1951 study also differentiated between the impersonal, cold, and often rather sordid city pub and the rural pubs which were social institutions of considerable importance to the communal life of the neighbourhood. Both the city pub and the village local are now under threat while the theme or destination pubs are proving their success. It is obvious that there is a need for diversity within the pub scene.

The leisure retailing trade has experienced considerable change and it is useful to analyse the data on trends and forecasts for the public house of the future. The leading market research companies such as Mintel Marketline International, Keynote, Henley Forecasting Centre, Marketpower, Euromonitor and the Economist Intelligence Unit (EIU), among others, provide some of the most up-to-date information on the leisure market, covering key industry issues and trends in consumer behaviour.

Analysis of the market

The Euromonitor report, *Catering in the 1990's*, claims that the growth and changes in the pattern of eating out constitute one of the four most significant changes in British leisure habits since 1945, the others being television, increased car usership and foreign travel. Going out for a meal comes second only to going out for a drink according to a ranked table of leisure pursuits carried out by the government's *General Household Survey* (1986).

The Euromonitor report examines pub catering in the wider context of fast food and take-away, restaurants and café's, hotels and vending. The report includes branded restaurants that are attached to pubs, such as Whitbread's Beefeater. By turnover, pubs now constitute the biggest sector of catering businesses (as reported by the government's Business Monitor series); in the early 1990s, pubs accounted for one in three of all catering businesses. Alcoholic drinks account for about 70% of the business, but food is on the increase and is seen as one of the biggest changes in British catering since the mid-1950s. Figures from the Brewers and Licensed Retailers' Association (BLRA) show that public house meals now account for 15% of the total eating-out market. Key Note and Euromonitor both identify the extension in licensing hours in 1988 as a significant contributory factor in the growth of food provision at lunchtime and in the evenings in pubs.

BLRA found that the pub is the preferred location for lunchtime eating, which is why an estimated 96% of public houses now serve food at this time. Pubs have undoubtedly benefited from the consumer trend of trading down when times are hard and the recession has given many the opportunity to promote an all-round value-for-money image for the family. Euromonitor subsequently predicts a brighter outlook for the pub than other industry sectors.

Food sales differ sharply between managed and tenanted public houses, according to Key Note. Food sales in a managed pub are around 75% higher than its tenanted counterpart, reflecting the level of investment by the brewer. Tenants may not have the capital to expand a catering operation; a separate Marketpower survey suggests that food accounts for only about 19% of turnover for independent or small multiple operators. However, catering in all types of pubs was greatly facilitated by the advent of the microwave and the catering pack. All pubs have access to a universal range of pre-prepared meals to offer their clientele, a development that has provoked a backlash from the traditionalists and connoisseurs who complain that pubs have the same menu nation-wide.

Both pubs and consumer demand are witnessing a swing back to home-made pub food. According to Jeremy Spencer, director of catering at Bass Taverns, it is a question of economics. In-house dishes involve more preparation which means longer hours and extra pay for staff. Buying in frozen dishes is more cost-effective. Bass looks for 55–60% profit after VAT on food and is committed to the idea of serving food in its managed pubs.

The **Campaign for Real Ale (CAMRA)** successfully reawakened an awareness of British brews. In the late 1950s and early 1960s, there was a major change in the brewing industry which had a sharp impact on the production of traditional beers. It was found that **bright beer** could be produced in new factories more cheaply and on a larger scale than **cloudy beer**. The major brewers moved to more modernised brewing techniques consistent with the growth of lager and all capacity was concentrated on the more profitable product. As a result, the ineffective smaller breweries were closed, and production of cask ale beer virtually ceased. CAMRA's purpose was to prevent the national beers from dying out, and their active promotion saved many small breweries from demise. After twenty years' absence, cask ale is now enjoying a revival among young people and is famed for its range and diversity. It is an example of a revived tradition which fits in with the contemporary preoccupation with heritage issues.

For its special report, Mintel commissioned exclusive consumer research into a number of different aspects influencing the eating-out market. It notes that changing consumer behaviour and drinking habits have resulted in a dynamic growth in soft drinks, light and non-alcoholic beers and wines, which now contribute significantly to pub turnover along with alcohol, catering and entertainment. Pubs are having to reposition themselves as family leisure venues, which often entails substantial restructure or refurbishment and the upgrading of catering facilities. In order to compete with other leisure outlets, pubs may also offer amusement machines, which generate a considerable amount of profit. Industry-wide, 25% of profits from pubs come from amusement machines; in some cases, they constitute the lifeblood of a pub. Other options are video games, pool tables, discos and live entertainment. Around 90% of pubs offer darts, dominoes, cribbage or shove ha'penny, according to Mintel. Quiz nights and karaoke are other types of entertainment that have sprung up in recent years. Although karaoke is imported from Japan, it is really only the latest trend in a long tradition of raucous singing in pubs that goes back to the times of Chaucer.

The Mintel consumer research aimed to find out the type of people who visit a pub as opposed to other establishments. The findings showed that the appeal of the pub is universal. However, a comparison of pub visitors with the sample population showed that there are more men than women, more people aged under 45 and more in socio-economic group C. If publicans are to increase their profits, more needs to be done in response to demographic changes to attract women and older age groups; hence the development of the **pub-restaurant**, which offers a more attractive atmosphere for women, especially those with children. There is also a need for more family rooms and play areas. The research may be UK-based, but the findings have important implications for the development of tourism in the UK. In Europe especially, children are very much part of the eating-out trend; more venues offering facilities for children would be very attractive to overseas tourists.

Choice of pub is predominantly for its **location** – preferably within walking distance – which reflects the impact of drink-driving campaigns and legislation. The availability of food, atmosphere and good service were followed by a good range of beer and a non-smoking area. Being alive, bustling and a smart or modern décor was not important, nor was whether the pub was open for longer hours. Choice of pub also varied between the sexes: women were interested in location and availability of food; men were more concerned about real ale and a selection of good beer. Among those with children, 40% thought the facility of a children's area was an important reason for choosing one pub in preference over another. These findings are based on the priorities of the home market; their relative importance may vary among overseas visitors which is an important point that tourism marketers should take into account.

Young people visit a pub because of its choice of beers and because of its image, according to the Mintel survey. A report into drinking and eating out, carried out by the Henley Centre for Forecasting, emphasises the different attitudes to alcohol drinking between older and younger people in the wake of drink-driving legislation and drug-awareness campaigns. Young people drink less in the 1990s than their predecessors in the 1980s, and the trend for responsible drinking looks set to continue. Between 1987 and 1991 the number of pub visits declined by 11%. The Henley Centre expected the 1997 figure to be 20%, which correlates with the projected 9% decline in the number of 16–24 year olds during the late 1990s. This age group takes part in a greater variety of leisure activities, including pub visits, than any other. Understandably, it is a major area of concern for pub operators.

Despite a change in behavioural patterns since the late 1980s, the Henley Centre research finds that the pub still appeals to young people as a companionable meeting place. What is significant here is that the pub continues to play an important social role for the 16–24 age group, for whom the vast majority are looking for a friendly place to meet rather than somewhere in which to indulge in excessive drinking. The report warns the brewing and pub industries that 'the pull of exclusively youth-oriented venues (like discos) has not replaced the traditional atmosphere of the pub', but alongside this apparent conformity, there are signs that the trend towards drugs and rave parties is taking over among more fashionable and affluent young people.

Respondents to the Mintel survey, *Eating out in the UK,* were also asked about the type of restaurant or food they would like to see; this is an area of key concern to operators planning future business development. Despite the proliferation of international cuisine available since the 1970s, the overwhelming response, particularly from the age of 35 onwards, was a demand for more traditional British cuisine.

The survey concludes that the long-term future for the eating-out market looks buoyant, with pubs focusing on food as a greater source of revenue, and the pub-restaurant taking the fore as one of the fastest growing sectors and a promising source of future profits. The pub is one of the many alternatives in the mid-priced leisure market and faces competition from café bars and themed restaurants, in addition to the off-trade. In socio-economic terms, the research found that availability of food is far more important to the more affluent respondents, with over half of all pub visitors from the highest earning AB group citing this as a reason for visiting a particular pub.

The historical perspective of the pub revealed its origins as an inn, where travellers would seek refreshment and a room for the night. The pub or inn is no longer associated with accommodation, either because it is inappropriate or the opportunity is under-developed. Each year, the BTA produces a booklet entitled *Stay at an Inn,* which includes entries from all over the country. However, the percentage of visitors who do so is negligible. In 1993, less than 0.5% of total respondents stayed at an inn.

Future implications for the market

In order to survive in an ever-crowded marketplace, pubs will have to become more like family centres within close proximity of diverse leisure pursuits. Even in the more isolated rural pubs, time is being called. The traditional pubs may be in decline, but Mintel antici-pates that there will be an improvement in the quality of pubs and choice, as operators exploit niche markets. This trend can already be seen in the cask ale houses and the pubs that offer ten pin bowling. Whitbread's Brewers Fayre chain have also introduced Charlie Chalk fun factories for children's entertainment as part of their commitment to creating public houses for the whole family.

The 1994 report by Marketline International, *Public Houses in the UK,* looks at devel-opments over the period 1994–7. It anticipated that pubs would continue to be branded to target particular customer groups in response to consumer demand for improved cater-ing services, comfort and range of family facilities and entertainment. The introduction of children's certificates and the extension of Sunday licensing hours should provide a wel-come boost to revenues for a number of pubs.

For its research, Key Note asked several major pub operators for their views on trading conditions. A common theme in all the responses was a commitment to quality and stan-dards in all areas of the business. Investment in systems technology and training and de-velopment were shared concerns. Bass, for example, has trained 43,000 staff in the use of its Retail System now installed in all its managed houses. Whitbread, followed by Greenalls, have developed National Vocational Qualifications which link pay to training. Having cut costs during the recession, a better quality of service is universally recognised as the key to competitive advantage.

Key Note reveals that Bass's plans for a pub of the future will take advantage of progress in modern communications. Among other innovations, there will be inter-pub games using multimedia video networks and the use of smart cards to access entertain-ment facilities and refreshments.

Profile of the brewing industry

Public houses, through which a major part of the sale of liquor and associated products is effected in the UK, are a significant component of the hotel and catering industry. They represent many thousands of outlets at which consumers may purchase food, drink and entertainment (in its broadest sense). The majority of them are owned by a handful of companies, whose interests extend to a number of fields of activity.

Most breweries have a long history of operations; many have tended to be family-owned concerns, centred in one locality or region. With the trend towards amalgama-tions, many breweries have moved away from dynastic ownership and become instead part of large conglomerate companies, with a more evenly spread national distribution.

In 1967, a total of 117 companies operated 243 breweries; in 1982, there were 80 companies operating 138 breweries. Brewery companies, in total, currently own some 43,000 on-licensed premises in the UK; there are also over 27,000 free houses owned by individuals and non-brewery companies.

Four brewery companies dominate the industry: Carlsberg/Tetley; Bass; Courage/Scottish and Newcastle; and Whitbread. Between them they own some 20,000 tenanted and managed premises and each is involved in the production, distribution and sale of a wide range of products. Together the **Big Four** own a high percentage of all outlets which are under brewery ownership and over one-quarter of all licensed outlets. Their actions and policies must inevitably greatly influence any assessment of brewery companies as a whole. The big four are responsible for approximately 75% of the UK's beer.

The remaining sixty breweries (apart from the Guinness brewery which owns no licensed premises) include a handful of medium sized companies, with the balance being relatively small concerns each centred in one locality or region. Such companies tend to reveal characteristics of a paternalistic nature in their relationship with their tenants and employees, characteristics which are no longer evidenced by the major companies.

Policy towards tenancies

The policy of breweries towards their tied-house estate has varied over the years. The inherited situation, resulting from historical actions of mutual benefit to both brewer and licensee, was a predominant factor in determining the ratio of directly managed to tenanted houses. In the recent past, almost all breweries indulged in a move towards decreasing tenanted outlets in favour of directly managed public houses. The main reason for such a move was the relatively less beneficial return on tenanted houses, compared with the wholesale plus retail margins derived from managed houses. There was also a need to build larger public houses than had previously been customary in order to provide the public with more extensive catering and entertainment facilities and to ensure a more economic system of distribution (i.e. fewer but larger deliveries). These large public houses required considerable capital investment which, the brewers maintained, could be serviced only by a combination of wholesale and retail margins; an economic rental for such premises was beyond the capacity of any tenant.

However, during the late 1970s some changes in policy occurred. The breweries found that managed houses were no longer providing such a good return as a result of increased salaries to public house managers and the general rise in cost of supplies and fixed expenses. Head office and regional administration costs borne by brewery companies also considerably increased with a resultant rise in supervisory costs per managed house. Thus most breweries have a current policy of selectively discarding those managed houses which are making a loss, are only marginally profitable or are widely dispersed (thus involving a disproportionately high element of administrative time and cost). These houses are either sold on the open market or offered as tenancies, in which latter state the breweries reckon that they can be operated profitably by the licensee.

Where other public houses are bought and substantially renovated, or newly built either to replace such losses or to enter a new market (such as new towns or redeveloped areas), these houses are put to direct management.

A number of breweries have embarked on a policy of issuing tenants with long leases of up to twenty years, at an agreed rent and on agreed conditions. Under these conditions, the tenant accepts total financial and operational responsibility for the upkeep of the premises but gets supplies of liquor at better rates than normal tied-trade tenants. Such arrangements have been stimulated by the escalating costs of renovations and redecoration. These were making both brewer and tenant less ready to undergo capital investment, the former because of the difficulty of recouping such costs through rent increases and the latter because of insecurity of tenure.

In addition to various changes in type of tenancies, and in ratios of tenanted houses to the total estate, there is a general tendency among all breweries of raising rents payable by tenants to a more realistic level. Although tenants in general may prefer to be completely independent of their brewery, in practice the majority of them have insufficient capital to buy a licensed free house, equip it, and keep it in a good state of repair. Their initial investment in a tenancy includes ingoings (covering fixtures, fittings and equipment) plus stock and a security deposit. The sum required is normally a relatively modest one, varying according to the amount of liquor stocks and other supplies, equipment and furniture.

The enormous variation in the annual turnover and retained net profit for tenants is the result of a number of reasons. This obviously varies according to the size, type and location of licensed premises, as well as according to the skills and efforts of individual licensees. Bearing in mind the widespread practice of tenants drawing directly from their takings some pocket money for themselves and for working members of their families, any precise indication of the range of earnings would be unwise. What is clear, however, is that some achieve a very substantial gross revenue and net profit, while others (although benefiting from having a roof over their heads) barely scrape a living.

Payments to the brewery

In addition to an initial capital investment, tenants must make continuing payments to their brewery. These are made by a traditionally accepted dual method: a fixed rental sum, the **dry rent**, and a sum calculated as a premium on supplies, the **wet rent**, which varies with the size of orders placed. However, no specific mention of the latter form of payment is generally found in tenancy agreements. Wording relating to prices of supplies tend to be such as prices equivalent to those charged to other tenants in the area.

The amount of dry rental payments and terms concerning the timing of such payments (varying from one month in advance to quarterly in arrears) is included either within the contract or in a separate agreement. Tenants are usually unaware of the specific basis upon which rental calculations are made. Different brewers vary, but normally use one or more of the following criteria:

- required return on capital value of property
- repayment for cost of maintenance and repairs
- reasonable rental for tenant's quarters
- rental linked to rateable value of premises
- standard percentage on estimated gross turnover
- standard percentage on estimated pre-tax profit (before rent).

Even where a formula is specified, at least one imprecise factor (such as capital employed, estimated revenue or pre-tax profit) usually permits latitude of decision and thus allows some negotiating scope on the part of the tenants. It has been known for tenants to obtain substantial rent reductions, either through submitting evidence or through misleading their brewery representative as to their actual or potential financial hardship. Breweries acknowledge that they take into account the fact that tenants often understate their gross revenue and pre-tax profits, or overstate their costs, and make their calculations accordingly using their managed houses as indicators of current levels of trading.

The calculation of a dry rent payment needs very fine judgement in order to ensure a reasonable return to tenants for their labour without reducing motivation to sell the product. Whether or not a wet rent is paid by tenants on liquor supplies is an issue that is difficult to determine. Most tenants suggest that a wet rent is retained in all but name and believe that they are charged a premium over and above free trade prices. However, most brewers claim that no premiums are charged to tenants on wines and spirits and many state that beer is sold to tenants at free trade prices.

The probable explanation is that a different interpretation is put on **free trade prices** by the two parties. In respect of prices charged to tenants for wines and spirits, a number of brewery contracts include reference to local market prices or prices of leading wine merchants in the area. Tenants tend to interpret free trade prices as the lowest price at which supplies are available (for instance, including a loss leader offer on a branded liquor product at a discount store or supermarket).

Tenancy contracts normally include provisions concerning the frequency and timing required for payments for supplies, with harsh terms against those tenants who do not comply. Most brewers require a deposit from tenants, usually equivalent to one or two weeks' supplies of liquor.

Monopolies and Mergers Commission Report

Since the mid-1960s breweries have expanded away from their core business of beer production into a range of related fields. Control of the industry is vested in a few large companies and so the government asked the Monopolies and Mergers Commission to investigate.

The MMC report was the result of a two-and-a-half year investigation into the supply of beer. When its results were published, on 21 March 1989, the brewers realised that this was a sign of worse things to come. The MMC's examination was a thorough and comprehensive look into the operations of the brewers with regard to their relationships with the on-licensed, **tied premises** they own, both managed and tenanted, and the offering of low interest loans to the **free trade**. It was concluded that this complex monopoly acted against the public's interest. The MMC reported that there were two major ways that the brewers restricted competition:

● Brewers restricted the supply of drinks by other competing brewers and wholesalers to the pubs they owned. With the Big Six companies (in 1989) producing a high percentage of all beer brewed in the UK, and owning 22,000 tenanted and 10,0000 managed houses out of a total of 60,000, this was deemed to be an extremely unfair weighting of business.

● The brewers apparently had captured about half of the free houses by offering 'sweeteners' in the form of low interest loans if licensees agreed to sell only their products.

The overall effect of these conditions was that both wholesale and retail prices were higher than necessary, thereby ultimately harming the consumer. Various recommendations were made to try to remedy the situation by preserving the good features of the present system while making the market more open to competition. For the regional brewers this meant the chance to feature a **guest beer** in tied houses thus gaining a broader market share, while allowing the pub tenants a wider choice in what products they supplied and how they financed their pub.

The brewers' worst fears in reaction to MMC are in one respect coming true. The forced sale of many pubs belonging to the Big Six (in 1997 the Big Four) has created an excessive number on the market, thus reducing market prices. A number of these have been acquired by the up-and-coming breweries.

Even though November 1992 was the time when the breweries had to conform to all the requirements of the report and the subsequent Department of Trade and Industry orders, it was another four or five years before the true effects were felt.

The MMC tried to weaken the brewers' control over the retail end of the beer market and recommended that the number of outlets that the brewers control should be limited and that the tie should cover only beer. While the key principles of the report have now come into effect certain parts have been watered down and in many cases the brewers have circumvented the spirit of the rulings.

The government thought that the MMC report would promote competition and protect diversity of ownership. It did not happen that way. Some of the smaller regional breweries such as Greenalls, Boddingtons and Devenish immediately abandoned brewing, judging correctly that it was more profitable to be pub retailers. The nationals also set about restructuring. Most of the major brewers restructured their operations to separate brewing (production) from retailing (public houses). The most significant response to the MMC came from a deal between Grand Metropolitan and Courage. This involved the former selling its brewing interests to Courage, with a supply agreement for Grand Metropolitan's public houses and restaurants. In return, all the tenanted estate of the two companies were merged into a jointly owned company called Inntrepreneur Estates Limited. In 1997, the pub estate of Inntrepreneur was sold to Japanese investment company Nomura.

While the original ten year supply agreement was reduced to seven years after discussions with the Office of Fair Trading, the result meant that Courage (at that time in 1992) was the UK's second largest brewer. This agreement shows the likely pattern of the UK brewing industry for the 1990s. The forced sale of public houses by the report has cut both property values and sale prices, and effected the asset values of brewers' company accounts.

Carlsberg/Tetley was formed by the merger of Allied's interests with those of the Danish brewer in 1992. In 1995 this consolidation process culminated in Scottish and Newcastle's takeover of Courage, a north–south combination that meant for the first time Bass was no longer the UK's biggest brewer. Bass has 23% market share, while Scottish and Newcastle have 28%. Since the MMC report, the six main brewers have now become four controlling three-quarters of the market. It would seem that the MMC report and the subsequent beer orders have shifted the balance of power to the pub retailers. Further consolidation of the brewing industry was blocked in June 1997 with the Department of Trade and Industry not allowing the merger between Carlsberg/Tetley and Bass which would have created the Big Three. The winner so far in this industry restructuring is Whitbread with a market share of between 13 and 15%, and concentrating on a handful of brands – Heineken, Boddington's, Murphy's and Stella Artois. Further concentration would have severely affected the profitability of Whitbread's operation. It is however hard to see for how long the big four will remain: it is perhaps when rather than if the big four become three.

The MMC report has resulted in three major developments:

- development of new tenancy agreements
- sale of the least profitable public houses
- shift from tenanted to managed public houses.

In terms of public house sales, the brewers are keeping their most profitable pubs and offering for sale their least viable outlets. The brewers have also been forcing the more successful pubs to be handed over to managers employed by the brewers, thus maximising profits and reducing the effect of the guest beer ruling. The introduction of new long-term leases has many benefits in that they give tenants a great deal of freedom from the landlord, but these benefits have come with much higher rents, rising by as much as 50%.

Apart from the stronger small breweries, the brewing industry seems to have lost from all sides. Some small breweries have managed to enter agreements with the nationals concerning the **guest beer ruling**. For those that have not, the cost of delivery to a dispersed selection of pubs is prohibitive, and therefore this ruling does not help them. The bene-fits of economies of scale achieved in running the larger estates have been lost as have many of the long-established advantages of the **vertical integration** for these companies.

The original point for the MMC investigation was the dominance of the Big Six brew-eries in the supply of beer, and the high and regionally variable price of beer. These are two areas where no benefits have resulted so far. The price of beer has continued to rise and the uniqueness of the regional brewers has slowly decreased as they fight for sur-vival in conditions where the brewing industry seems to be carved up between giant retailing chains and increasingly large brewers.

The takeover by Scottish and Newcastle of Courage means that there are only four major brewing companies against the Big Six in 1989. Furthermore Bass expressed an interest in purchasing Carlsberg/Tetley from Allied Domecq (subsequently blocked) which would have left three major brewers. This increasing concentration of the supply market may well lead to a similar situation as the US market where only two major pro-ducers dominate the market, competing more heavily with each other and placing even more emphasis on pricing strategies and reduced choice for consumers. There will also be continued pressure of cheap imports from Europe. Given that sales of beer products are predicted to decline by about 5% by the year 2000 which will be more pronounced in the free houses and lesser quality outlets, the brewers will continue their discount poli-cies. The pubs themselves will continue to develop non-wet sales, particularly food and entertainment. The pub companies will be driven to actively marketing their food brands to maintain their position in the marketplace. One possible consequence of all this polar-isation would be that the medium sized brewers would be squeezed out of the market, being too small to compete for national supply agreements with the retailers and too large for the small niche markets of the independents.

An indication of the change in the structure of pub ownership before and after the MMC report is illustrated in Table 10.1.

Industry supply

There are over sixty sizeable brewers' pub retailers in the UK, of which six are national companies with very wide portfolios of beverage, leisure and food products. Others in-

	Pre-MMC 1989	Post-MMC 1992	% change
Big Five Nationals			
Tenanted	22,000	9,700	−56
Managed	10,000	9,500	− 5
Regionals			
Tenanted	9,000	10,000	11
Managed	3,000	5,000	66
Independents			
Single outlets	16,000	15,800	− 1
Multiples	–	8,000	–
Total	60,000	58,000	− 3

Table 10.1 The structure of public house ownership 1989–92

Source: *Economist Intelligence Unit (1993) Eating Out in the UK: Special Report 2169*

clude a wide range of local brewers. Expansion into overseas interests has led larger groups to import new concepts into the UK. In contrast to the large national companies, the balance of breweries have focused their interests on the traditional brewing business. They are mainly associated with a local or regional area in which the beer is both produced and sold.

The size of the larger brewers can perhaps be put into perspective if one considers their contribution to the total beer market. The Big Four own less than half of UK on-licensed premises. Thus a substantial part of the market is available to the regional and local brewers. The Big Four produce 75% of all British beer, which admittedly is an enormous proportion of the market, but it still leaves 25% of the total to be produced by the smaller breweries.

This market share and distribution has changed quite considerably during the 1990s, when all the necessary changes have been made in accordance with the orders of the DTI, resulting from the MMC report (see Table 10.1).

Four major operators

Four companies in the brewers and distillers sector can be identified as having significant exposure to the UK hotel industry:

- Bass
- Greenalls Group
- Vaux
- Whitbread

Bass

As the second largest UK brewer with all its brands owned, Bass is in a strong position (post-MMC) to gain market share in the free trade. Prior to the creation of Inntrepreneur Estates Ltd and the Scottish and Newcastle/Courage takeover, Bass was the UK's largest publican and brewer as well. Because the company intends to remain both a brewer and a retailer of beer, it was forced to sell outlets in order to comply with the MMC ruling.

Bass Brewers represented about 34% of the company's total profits. Bass is the UK's no. 1 beer company with a 23% market share and owns the two leading brands, Carling Black Label and the Tennants range, both selling over 2 million barrels annually. Its ales include Stones, Bass, Toby and Worthington. Bass Inns and Taverns contribute about 28% of trading profits of which some are managed and others are leased or tenanted.

In addition to brewing and pub retailing the company also has its hotel division, Holiday Inn. Within the USA there are about 1,700 Holiday Inns of which 90% are franchised. Outside the Americas there are around 600 Holiday Inns of which 60% are franchised.

The final two divisions of Bass plc are leisure activities and interests in soft drinks. Coral Racing is the UK's third largest bookmaker with approximately 890 outlets. The company also has interests in bingo clubs, one-armed bandit machines and bowling alleys. They acquired ten Hollywood Bowl bowling alleys in 1992. It has a partial equity interest (45%) in the UK's no. 2 soft drinks company, Britvic Corona, with its 15% market share.

The company's strategy is to maintain and improve upon its market share through the use of free trade loans and discounts. Bass's strength is heavily concentrated within the

Midlands and the North; there will probably be a shift in emphasis to larger outlets in the South. Its hotel division over the longer term will look towards developing its franchise system in Europe and the Far East.

Greenall Group

Following the closure of its brewing operations based in Warrington, Greenalls is the largest customer of both Carlsberg/Tetley and Bass in the beer market. It can be regarded as a pure retailer and hotelier. Its pubs division, Greenall Inns, represents about 59% of the company's trading profits. Its Premier House division consists of the top managed pubs including the restaurant brands, Miller Kitchens and Hudsons. The company's major hotel division is De Vere hotels which operates thirty-three mainly four star hotels including the Belfry, which hosts the Ryder Cup golfing tournament, and the Grand at Brighton. The development of several hotels as leisure resorts has compensated for their poor location relative to the main UK markets and their low exposure to overseas business.

Other divisions within the company include its wine and spirits business, G&J Greenalls Direct, Cambrian soft drinks, off-licences and its one-armed bandit machine company, Stretton Leisure.

Vaux

Based in the North of England Vaux has its beer, brewing and wholesaling division of Vaux Breweries which produces some 48% of trading profits. Vaux is second in the north-east of England with volume of about half a million barrels from its two breweries, Sunderland (Vaux) and Sheffield (Wards).

Vaux owns Swallow Hotels, a three and four star hotelier which has thirty-four hotels, a high percentage of which have leisure facilities and are based in the UK. Swallow has a high exposure to UK demand, with overseas demand concentrated in its hotels in London, Edinburgh and York. The company also operates nursing and residential homes. The major thrust of the company's strategy is to improve brewing margins by the purchase of tenanted pubs. Vaux Inns and the St Andrews nursing homes will be expanded more selectively while any further expansion of Swallow Hotels is likely to take place by acquisition.

Whitbread

A major problem at Whitbread in the past has been lack of clear focus with its strategic thinking. For many years it has been difficult to say in simple terms what Whitbread's business was about. The philosophy changed quite definitively in 1989. Whitbread decided on a three-pronged strategy in business terms:

- **Brewing and beer**. Following the purchase of Boddington's beer and breweries its market share is approximately 13–15%, making it the UK's third largest brewer.

- **Pub ownership and operations**. Management of the managed pubs within Whitbread Inns division, business relations with the tenancy in Whitbread pub partnerships and an element of cross-fertilisation within the two.

● **Chain retailing**. This activity covers specialist retailing concepts starting where managed house leave off with restaurants and spreading into hotels and off-licences. The retail division is split into Whitbread Leisure managing hotels, off-licences and café bars and Whitbread Restaurants.

One main feature of the company is that it does not own its major lager brands, Heineken or Stella Artois, other beer brands on which it relies such as Murphy's Stout and Marston's Pedigree and such retail concepts as Pizza Hut and TGI Friday's. In all of these Whitbread relies on long-term agreements, licences or joint ventures to secure its share of control of the brand. Clearly such agreements are finite and may not necessarily be renewed and therein lies a potential vulnerability. Equally it is wrong to claim that such agreements do not offer advantages to Whitbread which help counter-balance such vulnerabilities. However, in simplistic terms a comparison between the cost of developing a national lager brand in the UK with full international credibility like Heineken would be virtually prohibitive. One of the key values in licensing brands lies in the education of Whitbread; Heineken taught Whitbread how to brew lager; Pizza Hut taught the company about branding retail outlets; TGI Friday's has taught the company a great deal about customer service and training. None of this expertise would be so accessible or available to Whitbread without licensing. Indeed not only would it have taken years for Whitbread to reach the same stage, but also it is possible that it would never have got there at all. Another key advantage is that it is a low risk, low cost entry into markets where the cost of entry and risk of failure has accelerated massively in recent years. Launching a brand from scratch is now a hugely expensive process and is far from guaranteed of success. Indeed where Whitbread has tried to launch home-grown brands from scratch it has not been uniformly successful. Furthermore increasingly mature markets mean that the cost of entry rises.

Perhaps the most critical point is that successful ventures of this kind are not just licences but partnerships. Being the licensee for Heineken or Pizza Hut involves working very closely with the brand owner: it is most unlikely that such a relationship would be broken even at the end of the contract. Indeed the closer the working relationship, the more probable it is that the partnership will continue. In the final resort the brand owner is unlikely to destroy a partnership that is successful. If Whitbread continues to do well with Heineken, Stella Artois, Pizza Hut, TGI Friday's, and other licensed brands there is no obvious reason to change the relationship. In an ideal world, Whitbread would own all of its brands; in such an event it is unlikely that Whitbread would have anything to rival the success of brands such as those which are currently licences: no mainstream lager with the international cachet of Heineken, no restaurant chain with the system and marketing skills of Pizza Hut nor with the extraordinary concept and service quality of TGI Friday's. The company is made up of a blend of home-developed and licensed bought-in brands. Its beers owned include Whitbread Best, Boddington's and White Label. Its retail operations owned include Marriott, Travel Inns, Beefeater and Threshers off-licences.

Prospects for the brewing industry

What does the future hold for the breweries and indeed the whole hospitality industry? A number of themes can be identified in the continuing development and evolution of the brewing industry.

An area of direct concern for breweries is the trend towards healthier lifestyles and away from alcohol. All of the major brewers and many of the regional brewers now produce at least one low/no-alcohol beer, lager and/or bitter. This relatively new market has enjoyed spectacular growth since the early 1990s. The market prospects for this segment of the market look promising, as consumer attitudes continue to change with regard to social responsibility and the detrimental effects of alcohol. Presently brewers are investing time, expertise and money in an attempt to reproduce the authentic taste character of these products. The possible adjustment of the present legal limit of alcohol in the blood for driving may well encourage further development in no-alcohol beers.

Along with changes in consumer preferences and leisure options, there is the increased choice by many to stay at home. The drinks sector has traditionally been reliant on two sorts of drinking trips: the high volume consuming male and the individual who makes unplanned trips to the local pub. A number of social trends suggest that these types of trips may decline in the late 1990s and beyond. There is a wider variety of leisure options and the growing affluence of individuals. Increasingly the decision to go to the pub will be for a clear reason rather than by default. Consumers will make comparisons between the pub and other leisure venues they may visit. Changes in demographics will require the pub to provide an atmosphere more suitable to women and families and less to their traditional male clientele. Understanding the nature of people's drinking trips and the way in which this influences what they drink will be a powerful indicator of behaviour.

A change in the licensing laws in 1988 saw the introduction of 11 a.m. to 11 p.m. opening times. As a direct result, catering in pubs was developed by all the brewers. An increased number of choices have been available to pubs when determining plans for the future. Promotion of the pub as a family centre has increased, with brewers such as Bass improving facilities for families in many pubs, and Whitbread focusing on the **community pub concept**, with each operation offering a games/family room. It is likely that these themes will continue, yet it is also crucial that a proportion of traditional pubs are maintained. With the opening of so many themed restaurants and café-bars, preservation of the pub is necessary for maintaining a choice for consumers as well as for the tourist trade. Many tourists place a visit to a British Pub high on their list of things to do.

The trend towards a shorter working week and an increase in holiday entitlement will result in more leisure for many people. Brewing companies have taken a keen interest in the wider leisure market and there is evidence of diversification into this area. With the development of chains such as Scottish and Newcastle's Center Parcs, people will find it just as enjoyable to holiday in the UK in the winter as to go abroad for a couple of weeks. In addition many British hotel chains now offer very good leisure facilities, for example Whitbread's Marriott brand, thus positioning themselves for the weekend break market. Bass with their Holiday Inn chain of hotels are also well placed to exploit this market.

The tourism and hospitality industry constitutes an essential part of the European economy and is expected to grow considerably by the year 2000. The establishment of the single European market has stimulated many mergers and take-overs, not least within the brewing companies. A consideration of present movements within the tourism and hospitality industry shows that multinational companies are at present the most active, in restaurant chains, hotel chains, food manufacturers and brewers. The constant mergers and acquisitions that allow these large multinationals to dominate the arena must have an effect on small and medium-sized operations. Once established these mega-chains enjoy economies of scale and consequent cost benefits. A combination of cost benefits and market share help to position such companies very positively within the market.

The VAT issue is perhaps the most important problem area that faces the hospitality industry, since the single European market in 1992. In all member states, VAT is levied at each stage of the process of production and marketing and is then collected by the government at the point of sale. The purpose of this tax is the same in all countries but the rate varies. In mainland Europe, cross-border eating out and drinking may be influenced by the variation in VAT levels. If VAT harmonisation within stipulated bands leads to governments agreeing to adopt a policy of placing accommodation, food and beverages in the higher VAT rate band, this will increase costs and affect competitiveness in the provision of hospitality services.

Another important area of taxation legislation is related to duty-free goods and excise duty. Of interest to the brewers is the amount of money they earn from duty-free sales. The EU may abolish the duty-free market as part of its harmonisation policy. This could lead to a loss of revenue for the brewers and increase airport and ferry-port costs due to a loss of duty-free outlet rentals.

Summary

This chapter has mapped out the development of the brewing industry within the UK. The MMC's recommendations have seriously affected the profile and nature of the industry. It has caused a period of great uncertainty for all brewing companies and, contrary to the original intention of the investigation and subsequent rulings, has been partly responsible for the demise of the regional brewers. For much of its history the industry has been divided into two main sectors – brewing and pub retailing. The hospitality industry has been the area of diversification for brewing companies with many investing heavily in it throughout the 1980s and 1990s. Since the early 1990s the rationalisation of each brewer's interests has resulted in some determining to focus increasingly on hotels and leisure as a major part of their future activities. Others, noticeably the large brewers, have decided to leave this sector.

There is much more to the success of the UK brewers than the brewing and retailing of their beer products. These beer, food and leisure companies are capable of having a significant impact on the hospitality and leisure industry not only in the UK but throughout mainland Europe.

The comments on leisure trends present an overview of the major social and demographic factors that affect the pub and are set within the role and history of the public house. The findings illustrate the diversity of factors that must be taken into consideration when analysing the pub market. They also indicate the likely future development of the pub in the face of current trends. The comments were made on a national basis for the domestic market. In this respect, consumer behaviour patterns may be representative of Britain but will not necessarily reflect those of visitors to this country. The tourist market for the pub must therefore be regarded as a separate segment.

Further reading

- Aird A. (1993) *The 1994 Good Pub Guide*, London: Vermilion.
- Brewers and Licensed Retailers' Association (1992) *Pubs – 'The Best of British' – Foreign Visitors' Views of Pubs*, London: BLRA.
- Brewers and Licensed Retailers' Association (1993a) *An Industry at Risk: Memorandum to H.M. Treasury*, London: BLRA.
- Brewers and Licensed Retailers' Association (l993b) *Pubs are Best*, London: BLRA.
- Brewers and Licensed Retailers' Association (1994) *A Real Alternative*, London: BLRA.
- Capel J. (1990) *Whitbread: The Beer Food and Leisure Group*, London: James Capel.
- Economist Intelligence Unit (1993) *Special Report: Eating Out in the UK* (Introduction and Market by Sector, the Consumer and Prospects), London: EIU.

- Elwood Williams C. and Lincoln G. (1996) 'New directions for the licensed trade: a structural analysis', *International Journal of Wine Marketing*, 8(1).
- Euromonitor (1993) *Special Report: Catering in the 1990s* (Introduction and Overview, Market Sectors), London: Euromonitor.
- Gilbert D.C. (1994) 'The European Community and leisure lifestyles', in C. Cooper (ed.) *Progress in Tourism, Recreation and Hospitality Management,* vol. 5, London: Belhaven Press, pp. 116–32.
- Gilbert D.C. and Smith R. (1992) 'The UK brewing industry: past, present and future', *International Journal of Wine Marketing* 4(1).
- Girouard M. (1975) *Victorian Pubs,* London: Studio Vista.
- Gourvish T.R. and Wilson R.G. (1994) *The British Brewing Industry 1830–1980,* Cambridge: Press Syndicate of the University of Cambridge.
- Henley Centre (1993) 'Drinking and eating out; Generation X: an army of ageing Bart Simpsons or the wave of the future?' in *Leisure Futures,* vol. 3, London: Henley Centre for Forecasting.
- Housden J. (1984) *Franchising and Other Business Relationships in Hotel and Catering Services,* London: Heinemann.
- Hyam J. (1993) 'Pub food's new order', *Caterer and Hotelkeeper* 186 (3780): 48–50.
- Jackson J. (1976) *The English Pub,* London: Jackson Morley.
- Key Note (1991) *Public Houses,* London: Key Note.
- Key Note (1994) *Public Houses in the UK,* London: Key Note.
- Knowles T. (1993) 'The UK Brewers: their links with hotels, consumer catering and leisure markets', *International Journal of Wine Marketing,* 5(4): 42–56.
- Knowles T. and Dingle A. (1996a) 'The role and history of the pub', *International Journal of Wine Marketing* 8(1).
- Knowles T. and Dingle A. (1996b) 'The pub within the tourist product', *International Journal of Wine Marketing* 8(2).
- Knowles T. and Dingle A. (1997) 'The preservation and marketing of the pub experience: an integral part of the tourist product for overseas visitors?', *International Journal of Wine Marketing* 8(3).
- Marketline International (1994) *Public Houses in the UK,* London: Marketline International.
- Mintel (1988) *The On Trade Revolution: The Brewing Industry's Response to Change,* London: Mintel.
- Mintel (1992a) *Special Report: Eating Out 1992* (Executive Summary, Pub Catering, The Consumer), London: Mintel.
- Mintel (1992b) 'Pub visiting in the UK', *Leisure Intelligence,* vol. 1., London: Mintel.
- Rowntree B.S. and Lavers G.R. (1951) *English Life and Leisure,* London: Longmans, Green.
- Spiller B. (1972) *Victorian Public Houses,* Newton Abbot: David and Charles.
- Woods R (ed.) (1992) *Leisure Futures,* London: Henley Forecasting Centre.

Chapter Eleven

Leisure Industry

Objectives

After reading this chapter you should be able to

▪ Identify the main reasons for the establishment and development of hotel leisure facilities.

▪ Describe the benefits of leisure to hotels.

▪ Discuss the extent of provision and types of facilities in hotels.

▪ Review the importance and structure of the theme parks industry as a component within tourism and leisure.

Background

In the early 1980s the UK was in mid-recession, and prospects for the hotel industry were not good. The dollar was weak against the pound, causing a substantial drop in the number of visitors from the USA. The rest of the world was suffering from an economic downturn, and international tourist spending in general was severely reduced. The pound, however, was strong against a number of currencies, and many more British people took holidays abroad.

This massive swing towards foreign package holidays had a devastating effect on UK hoteliers, who in turn had to start reassessing their service and the products that they offered. The short break and conference markets were the two sources of business picked, almost universally, by hotels. In the USA it was becoming clear that fitness was big business, and while the 'North American concept of an exclusive club, high on snob value, heavily dependent on outside members and closed to the public has not yet caught on in the UK', hotel fitness centres have become a widespread panacea for the UK hotel industry.

In the early 1990s, the UK was faced with a similar set of economic circumstances to those of the early 1980s. However, by then the hotel industry had changed considerably, in terms of both products and markets, and the UK hotel was nearing the maturity stage of the life cycle. The first years of the next millennium will be characterised by only marginal growth in total supply, according to industry analysts.

To combat this new set of circumstances, hotels will probably upgrade their existing facilities in order to add value to the product. According to a Horwath and Horwath report, *Hotels of the Future*, 'the emphasis of the future hotel will be on quality, *vis-à-vis* value for money, of both product and service. In terms of overall standard, the "high" of today will become the "minimum" of the future.' An integral part of these developments will be to offer improved leisure facilities, to increase room sales and to meet enhanced customer expectations. However, a pitfall for many managers in the past has been jumping on the bandwagon of other hotels and treating the leisure operation as a mere add-on, not considering the full financial and operational impacts of such a major change. A leisure centre should be considered only within the context of the whole hotel. It should not be a half-hearted 'sports shed' tacked on at the back.

There have been problems. Country House Hotels in the UK paid heavily for investing in leisure centres during the 1980s. It was not the actual facilities themselves, but the timing of the purchase that created problems i.e. the boom times of rising property prices in the late 1980s. Even in the late 1990s, there are many small independent hoteliers, making up the majority of the UK hotel industry, who are still desperate to invest in even the most basic facilities. It is predicted that by the year 2000 nearly 70% of hotels will provide indoor or outdoor facilities.

Trends in leisure consumption

The leisure industry has been developing rapidly, influenced by a number of economic, social, demographic and environmental trends which will be identified in this section. The majority of developments have been favourable, although they have made the industry as a whole more complex and unpredictable. The challenge for all leisure companies and providers is to maintain their competitive edge, while the number of products available increases and diversifies.

Success in this, as in any field, is heavily reliant on researching and responding to consumer changes. Managers need to take the long-term view, instead of focusing solely on current trading issues. Such a proactive approach will require looking beyond the current requirements of the leisure spender. It will become essential to assess and review the changes in consumers' attitudes and circumstances (both economic and social), even if sometimes they are barely perceptible. It is these factors that will transform the leisure market, creating new product opportunities and taking it forward into the twenty-first century. The questions that managers must address are:

● What will leisure mean to consumers in the year 2010?
● Who will want it?
● What purpose will they want it for?

Economic trends

Most leisure chiefs agree that the 1980s were the most successful years that the industry has seen. However, in the early 1990s recession hit the UK, and much of the industrialised world, with conditions generally as bad as those experienced at the beginning of the 1980s. Recovery in the industry was a slow process, with operators struggling hard to regain their previous peak levels of trading, finally achieved in 1995. From a historical perspective, the overall trend in leisure spending saw a fall of 3%, in real terms in the size of the total leisure market in 1991, compared with a 1% decline in both 1980 and 1981.

Part of this fall can be attributed to the drop in international tourist arrivals in 1991: there were 16.7 million arrivals, a decrease of 7.5%. Receipts were $12.7 billion – a decrease of 8.8%. Other factors include a drop in both GDP and consumers' disposable income. It seems unlikely that the boom conditions of the Thatcher years will be seen again although the recovery began in 1994–5 with retail sales picking up. Consumer borrowing increased slightly and sustained cuts in interest rates following the departure of the UK from the Exchange Rate Mechanism in September 1992 continued through until

1996–7. Leisure markets depend on consumers who are willing and able to spend freely on their enjoyment and are particularly affected by the economic cycle.

The mid to late 1990s was a period of slow but steady expansion in the economy, with leisure operators noting an upturn in consumer confidence, thus influencing demand. The 1990s have proved to be a time of caution with greater thoughtfulness on the part of consumers. People seem to prioritise their expenditure, and value for money is of prime importance. It will take several years of greater prosperity and more favourable credit conditions before these cautious attitudes are relaxed.

Demographic and social trends

During the 1990s the leisure sector has had to adapt to some fundamental demographic and social changes. The 1980s saw developments such as the fitness boom, the fibre revolution, the slump in smoking and the rapid rise of low alcohol alternatives. The 1990s has augmented this process. In terms of demographics the physically active sector has remained the most dynamic leisure grouping in terms of volume growth. Much of this growth is expected to be a result of the continued expansion of the A, B and C1 socio-economic groups.

As people have become wealthier, expectations have changed. It is now the norm that leisure pursuits such as holidays are integral to most people's lives and will not be given up lightly. Leisure options outside the home compete with home-centred leisure activities such as wider television choice, electronic games and videos. Forecasts show that the number of adults taking part in outdoor sports is set to increase.

Despite the improved economic climate in the mid to late 1990s, different levels of spending mean that leisure opportunities need to be found and taken. Increased marketing to the correct segment from the leisure industry could stimulate people to take up a new leisure activity. Six key themes can be identified in relation to the leisure industry:

- time and money
- young people
- women
- families
- middle aged and ageing people.
- environmental issues

Time and money

During the 1980s real disposable incomes rose by an average of 25%, yet this was often at the cost of total leisure time. Against this increase in wealth, leisure time reduced and people were finding it hard to make time available for themselves to enjoy leisure pursuits. As people continue to work longer hours, commute further distances and juggle families, careers and friends, the time element in the 1980s and 1990s has become increasingly important for leisure providers who wish to gain a competitive edge in offering quality of leisure time at their facilities.

Longer opening hours at leisure facilities will be a particular benefit (many hotels are ideal for this with their 24 hour service), as will those services which free up time for people, for example crèche facilities. In the 1980s working hard and succeeding were heavily emphasised. In the 1990s there has been less emphasis on the work ethic and greater emphasis on leisure and self-fulfilment. For many the retirement age is reducing, as is the number of working hours per week. Leisure time will be come to be seen as status enhancing, particularly with the growth, in the UK, of 'one on one fitness programmes', following the trend in the USA.

Young people

Predictions in the mid-1990s have forecasted that as a whole Britain's population growth would be minimal; however, there would be some significant changes in the distribution of the population.

One of the areas of greatest importance to the leisure industry is the decline in young adults between 16 and 24 years old. This age group represented 14% of the population in 1989, but according to national demographic indices, the proportion fell to 11% by the mid-1990s. However this segment still forms a significant part of the market, particularly when looking at the numbers participating in activity holidays. Such a segment is more likely to be young and male from A, B or C1 social backgrounds. It is young people who have set the trends in leisure in the past. With this shift in demographics, leisure markets seeking young people are finding competition increasingly difficult and are now having to look to other segments of the population.

Women

During the 1980s female participation in sport and fitness increased, in part due to the influence of Jane Fonda and others with their fitness videos. The 1990s have been heralded as the decade for women, who can now have both a successful career and a family. From a leisure industry perspective one must ask how much extra income, confidence and status women will really enjoy, and how will they develop as consumers of leisure services?

Families

The nuclear family of the past is disappearing, although it still forms a substantial part of the market. Parents are looking for leisure facilities which will suit the needs of themselves and their children. Family structures are changing through such factors as the divorce rate, which affects approximately one in three marriages in the UK, but leisure providers and other sectors have been slow to react to this ever growing body of consumers.

Middle aged and ageing people

The so-called 'grey market' is much talked about by all those forecasting leisure into the future. This is not because numbers of people in the over 65 age group are growing particularly fast at the moment. Instead it is in the 45–64 age group that increases are showing, with obvious impacts for the older group in the future.

Meanwhile affluent middle-aged people are a key leisure market segment, as they have the time and money to enjoy leisure activities. The 'inheritance phenomenon' is giving these people extra indulgence money. However, having extra disposable income does not mean that they will be willing to spend it. This is borne out by the statistics which show that people over 65 years of age are better off in terms of disposable income, but tend to indulge in treats less frequently than others: only 63% of the over 65 age group eat out regularly, compared with 71% of the 35–54 age group; only 29% of the over 65 category took a short break holiday, a smaller percentage than all other groups.

Obviously this key group is not being attracted to some leisure activities. Those leisure managers who are doing nothing about this will be left behind as older people are the market of the future.

Environmental trends

During the late 1980s concern about the environment grew, and this concern became more pronounced during the 1990s. Both producers and consumers have become more acutely aware of how they as individuals have a role in preventing further environmental damage to the planet. This will influence not only our day-to-day retail product choices, but also those activities pursued for leisure. In 1988 a poll conducted by MORI asked whether people had 'selected one product over another because of its environmentally friendly packaging, formulation or advertising. 19% said that they had. By May 1989 this figure had risen to 42%'. MORI concluded that 'the Green Consumer is here in seven league boots'. People will continue to use their purchasing power to express their approval or disapproval; there could come a point where they choose hotels or restaurants on the basis of their green factor.

Leisure operators will have to think 'green' to survive. Activities such as walking, bird-watching and cycling will probably become more popular. However, skiing could become socially unacceptable, due to the way it scars the landscape. Changes in preferences may show a shift away from the mass package tour, with increased demand for environmentally sensitive vacations. This has already started with the popularity of holiday villages, in natural and tranquil settings. For those who have plastic or artificial developments, which are environmentally hostile, alarm bells are ringing, as there is a definite shift towards the countryside for leisure purposes with a more natural appeal.

Provision of leisure facilities in hotels

In order to survive in ever competitive markets, all managers must constantly evolve their products. Two strategies can be identified to stimulate constant consumer interest. These are product innovation and product augmentation. They can be applied to any business, but will be specifically applied to hotels for the purposes of this chapter.

Product innovation

Basically this is the systematic development of new products and services, and is based on the idea that no business can exist for long without an innovative element, within its total product offering. Currently innovations such as voice mail, electronic checkouts and credit card keys have become standard in many hotels. Leisure facilities in European hotels were very much an innovation of the 1980s, but are an area which is constantly changing and must be closely monitored to retain the hotel's competitive advantage and subsequent market share. With any change there is an element of risk involved, but in order to stay ahead, the pressure on hotel managers to innovate is strong.

Product augmentation

This concept is based on the way in which the consumer views the total consumption package – both tangible and intangible elements. By extending the core product, in the case of a hotel – the bedroom – with other facilities and services, and emphasising these additions in marketing and promotional literature, the hotel can become a unique selling proposition, hopefully achieving a competitive edge through increased sales. Leisure facilities are now seen by customers to be a crucial part of this augmented hotel product, and are becoming an integral part of the expected product bundle.

Definition of leisure facilities

A hotel's basic leisure facilities consist of a small indoor swimming pool, sauna, steam room, solarium and fitness room. From these basic requirements there are many add-ons up to what could be termed a mega-resort with golf, tennis, riding, watersports, etc. Virtual reality could add a whole new dimension to these advanced resorts.

During the late 1980s in the UK a total of £72.3 million was invested by hotels installing new health and leisure facilities, and updating existing facilities. This investment indicates how convinced hoteliers are of the benefits accruing to leisure facilities.

Benefits of leisure facilities

The major reason for any hotel to invest in leisure facilities is the profit motive. However, it is frequently difficult to make an exact correlation between increased trading profits and installation of leisure facilities. Leisure facilities do benefit the following seven areas, thus creating extra revenue and profits, particularly if using previously under-utilised space:

- increased room occupancy
- competitive advantage
- business users
- membership fees
- increased room rates
- marketing asset
- positive image.

Increased room occupancy

For any hotel its biggest source of profit is its room revenue; it is the room that the hotel is really selling. This increase in room occupancy is the single most commonly cited reason for the addition of leisure facilities. How much the rate will increase is difficult to determine, but one can assume that the majority of guests would rather stay at a hotel with such facilities than without. A high percentage of hoteliers directly attribute an increase in room sales to the provision of extra leisure facilities. In addition approximately 50% of mid-spend guests expect facilities, and this percentage increases with spend. However, there is little correlation between expectation and usage as is shown in Table 11.1. The main areas suggested by Knutson for increased occupancy was the short break

	Economy		Mid level		Luxury	
	E	U	E	U	E	U
Swimming pool	30	64	83	65	92	67
Fitness room	*	*	32	32	83	39

Source: Knutson B. (1988) Cornell Hotel and Restaurant Association Quarterly 28: 83–7

Notes: E = Expectation U = Usage

Table 11.1 Hotel leisure facilities: their role in product expectations and usage levels (%)

weekend market, with free use of the leisure facilities offered as one of the bonuses of the weekend rate.

Competitive advantage

A second benefit for hotels is that a leisure centre will give the business a competitive advantage or help it retain a competitive edge. For instance hotels targeting the conference market can no longer afford to be without leisure facilities. The fact that a hotel has the facilities simply makes it a more attractive proposition to conference organisers.

Business users

In the past many business travellers would have relaxed in the hotel bar. With the fitness boom of the 1980s more people work out than ever before, to relieve stress and to stay healthy. Many will therefore simply not stay at a hotel unless it has leisure facilities. It is for this reason that the Savoy Hotel have created Fitness Gallery because it was felt that some guests had defected to other hotels due to the lack of leisure facilities.

Membership fees

This is probably the only direct correlation between leisure facilities and the profit and loss account. Raising revenue from creating a club for non-hotel residents can directly offset not only the investment costs of the facilities, but also the day-to-day running costs associated with heating, lighting and laundry. This has an indirect effect of boosting sales in other areas, particularly restaurants and bars, and may attract local custom for functions such as weddings.

Increased room rates

This is a debatable point but the argument here is that over time the hotelier will be able to increase room rates or alter the room rate structure in order to account for the new facilities. However, any immediate rise in rates will be seen by customers in a negative light. This is due to the fact that customers now expect leisure facilities, particularly in four and five star hotels, as part of the package, and do not wish to pay more because of them.

Marketing asset

Leisure facilities will become a valuable asset for sales staff, increasing the chance of repeat business and in targeting specific new markets. Sales people will always prefer to have such an amenity to use as a sales tool. However, the facilities will be of marketing value only if the hotel is marketed well to begin with. For consumers the choice of hotel may be based solely on promotional literature from which they can only assess the tangible elements of the hotel product. Frequently therefore the decision is made on a hotel that is perceived to have the 'best fit' bundle of tangible attributes. The more attributes there are, the more perceived value for money the customer will have, and the more likely it is that these attributes will produce benefits leading to ultimate customer satisfaction. This is the basis of benefit segmentation which relies on the casual factors of consumer behaviour and values, rather than traditional market segmentation which is based on social and demographic factors. If hotels can successfully identify consumer behaviour and values, it can develop new ways to position and market the hotel in order to maximise sales. If consumers highly value health and relaxation, the leisure facilities provided can enhance the perception of value from the total hotel product.

Positive image

This is an indirect and yet very important aspect of leisure facility provision. Having such an amenity will no doubt improve the perception that customers have about the hotel. It states that the property is up to date and that the management and staff are concerned about their guests and their health. In addition to this a leisure facility can also push up the perceived quality of other amenities within the hotel; if it is part of a chain, stronger branding for the hotel as a whole can be the result. A positive image can result only if the facility is integrated along the same lines as the rest of the hotel. A four star hotel cannot expect positive results if it installs only one star facilities. The facilities must not be left to go stagnant, as this will damage any positive impacts created by them.

Approaches to providing hotel leisure facilities

There are several varying approaches that hotels can adopt in order to provide leisure facilities, from the most basic of provision to the ultimate health experience at a spa. All are the result of hotels needing to market fitness facilities like any other guest service.

A health and fitness facility within a hotel can produce many benefits as described. However, with so many different types of activities and facilities on offer, the hotelier has serious decisions and choices to make about the pros and cons of each, and how they relate to the particular market of the hotel. Many make the mistake of just filling a room with some equipment and calling it a fitness room with the result that the customer is not fooled and the facilities are under-utilised. The key to making the correct choice in the provision of facilities, whatever they are, is to offer the selection and the service that the guest is asking for. Six types of provision can be identified.

- referral option
- health suites
- basic facility provision
- health and fitness resort
- holiday villages
- spa concept

Referral option

This is becoming a popular choice for those hotels without the time, space or budget to provide effective leisure services themselves. Small hotels (those with fewer than thirty rooms) could find this a viable option. Instead of converting a conference room, which could lead to a loss of business, referral of guests to a local reputable fitness facility means that fitness-conscious guests are still catered for. Guests who are serious about their fitness regime will not mind leaving the hotel if they are presented with a well-equipped facility. In fact this approach would be preferable to any minimal provision that the hotel could make. Many city centre hotels have adopted this concept. The hotel may pay a fee to the club, or in some cases the referral approach may be seen as mutually beneficial, as clients could pay the club for additional classes and treatments, thus creating extra revenue.

Referral options do not have to be limited to fitness facilities. A hotel can utilise the many resources available within a few miles to provide clay pigeon shooting, horse riding, fishing, tennis and golf. Such facilities may be mentioned in any promotional litera-ture about the hotel, which is beneficial to both the hotel and the club in question.

Health suites

A current trend in hotels is to place an exercise bike or stair climbing machine in a guest room, calling it a health suite. This can bring in extra revenue for hotels, particularly be-cause some people are not comfortable working out in unfamiliar surroundings. Women, in particular, prefer to exercise in private. The equipment should be located in an area specially designed to accommodate it. Some hotels remove the equipment from the room, installing it only when a 'health suite' is requested. Others leave the equipment there all the time. More permanent fixtures to some rooms are full length mirrors and dance bars. Some hotels can offer video cassette recorders with exercise tapes.

Embassy Suites have been the pioneer of this concept in the USA. Normal leisure facilities were already found in the hotels, but since the introduction of the concept, 'participating hotels have an average of five "Cycle Suites" and in a survey almost two thirds of respondents – former guests and non-guests – said they would be very likely to request a cycle suite'. This is a low-cost alternative to providing a full leisure facility.

Basic facility provision

Many hotels consider a basic level of facility provision to be a swimming pool, sauna solarium and exercise room. However, despite the fact that 'swimming pools are the most requested facility in hotels for leisure guests ... 90% of all guests ask for one, only 10% use them'.

Therefore it must be stressed that a fitness facility does not have to be extensive to serve its purpose. Even a space of 500 square feet, if planned properly, can be effective with the right equipment. It is unlikely that in such a small space staff would be required but safety in this situation is important: only adults should be allowed; access should be through a guest's room key or a key borrowed from the front desk; freeweights should not be used as injuries are more prevalent due to misuse, so machines should be simple to use, with clear instructions in a prominent place. Such a level of provision would be suitable for a short stay business guest or conference user.

Health and fitness resort

This is a hotel with leisure facilities designed for maximum market penetration. It would include the provision of a pool, sauna, solarium and fitness room along with a combi-nation of other activities such as golf, tennis and squash.

The pioneer of this concept in the UK has been Whitbread's Country Club Hotels (now branded Marriott), which provide a fully integrated selection of facilities. Their standard formula is based around the central feature, a golf course, of which there may be one or two, a good sized leisure complex including the facilities listed above, alongside a luxury hotel. The hotels are geared to mid-week conference visitors and short break family weekends.

Holiday villages

This is the next step up from a resort. The pioneer of holiday villages is a Dutch company – Sporthuis Centrum Recreatie NV – who have introduced the Center Parcs concept to the UK, following success in the Netherlands, France and Belgium. Scottish and Newcastle Breweries subsequently bought the UK resorts. These villages are successful at integrating conservation into a commercial development, against a backdrop of growing concern about the environmental impacts of just such developments. Creating an attractive natural environment is an objective of Center Parcs: a visitor's first impression is one of peace, tranquillity and a sense of being at one with nature.

The concept is to cater for a year-round market including short breaks and winter holidays which appeal to the growing interest in healthy lifestyles, offering a resort in a woodland setting within a couple of hours' driving time from large population centres. The centre of the village is covered with a transparent all-weather dome which slides open in good weather. This encloses a tropical atmosphere with the temperature at 25°C where tropical flora flourish, around an extensive leisure pool. Additional facilities include squash, tennis, badminton, bowls, miniature golf, a bowling alley, lake fishing, windsurfing, boating, walking, cycling and horse riding, as well as a number of beauty treatments all of which are based around a hotel, villas, shops, restaurants and bars.

Ecological aspects are paramount in site selection, and woodland settings are always chosen, to which the company adds artificial streams and lakes. Normally the company undertakes a large degree of tree planting and introduces numerous plants. A team of rangers and ecologists maintain the flora and fauna. Many wild flowers have returned under their care. With the advent of the green consumer age, this unique combination of superb leisure facilities in a natural setting is one that many people enjoy and many more will start to demand.

Spa concept

The British have been slow to accept that relaxation and personal fitness programmes, along with a little pampering, can result in improved performance at work.

There has been no definitive research into the potential size of the market for health-related tourism in Britain. However, there has been 'a growing emphasis particularly in the USA on "wellness" treatments to enhance overall well being rather than development of the physique'; such activities are popular with both men and women. The UK is experiencing similar patterns of growth and when coupled with the growing over 55 market, there is a great deal of potential for development.

The Spa Resort must not be confused with the Spa within a Resort, which is the concept being considered here. A Spa Resort is where people go for a week of total immersion in a strict regime, normally to detoxify or lose weight. A Spa within a Resort is normally an amenity to the resort in addition to other social and recreational activities. An example of such a concept in the UK is the hotel Chewton Glen. In planning the extensive leisure facilities, the company allowed for six therapy rooms, encompassing treatments from reflexology to acupuncture.

In order to promote the total resort concept, spa activities will have to be available on a selective rather than intensive basis. They can become a significant revenue generator for the resort and can provide a certain amount of prestige for the hotel.

Types of leisure facilities

A wide range of leisure facilities can be identified within the industry.

Fitness centre/exercise room

This is one of the most commonly found amenities in a hotel health club. In fact it is the major aspect, and many believe that one cannot have a health club without an exercise area. The space for exercise rooms varies from 400 to 2,000 square feet depending on the property, with the average closer to 600 square feet for non-staffed facilities.

Indoor swimming pool

This is frequently the initial foundation of a health club. However, many pools have been criticised for not being adequate in size and shape, negative factors for guests who like to swim seriously. A minimum size for a pool is 30 × 20 feet. In the UK indoor pools are essential; in warmer climates outdoor pools are more frequently found.

Whirlpools

There are two types – fibreglass and gunite cement. Fibreglass units are less expensive but do not have the durability to maintain a quality appearance over longer periods. Gunite units cost about 50% more, but have enhanced qualities.

Saunas

These are a popular addition to any health club, as some form of relaxation area involving heat is needed – a sauna, steam bath or whirlpool. Due to cost and space requirements, along with minimal maintenance, saunas have become one of the most widely used relaxed amenities.

Steam bath

Although certain market segments use these, there are those who feel very uncomfortable in a steam bath. For this reason, along with higher maintenance and installation costs, saunas will always be the choice over steam baths.

For the above three facilities a management question arises about whether to offer such facilities to both sexes or have single sex units. Usually whirlpools are for both sexes, with separate single sex saunas and steam baths for privacy reasons.

Solarium

An area with tanning beds is a popular addition to a leisure centre – particularly in commercial fitness clubs – where part of having the 'body beautiful' included having a permanent tan. Usually one bed is sufficient in a hotel, and as concerns about skin cancer rise, fewer people will use such facilities; therefore doubts remain as to their necessity in a hotel health facility.

Massage facilities

The larger the property, the more feasible it is to have a massage room. They are therefore more commonly found in resorts. With the advent of spa amenities in resorts, a masseuse has become increasingly important, along with other treatments such as reflexology, hydrotherapy, floatariums, thalassotherapy, herbal wraps and aromatherapy. Such facilities need experienced and qualified staff.

Racket sports

For this type of facility space is one of the prime concerns. With tennis courts a decision must be made as to whether they should be indoor or outdoor. In the UK better usage rates will result from indoor facilities.

Outdoor exercise courses and jogging trails

These have become popular in recent years. Exercise courses involve running round a predetermined course with exercise stations placed every so often. Climate is once again a consideration for such an amenity. Jogging trails are popular, particularly in city centres where hotels can offer a mapped-out route, through a park for example.

Golf

There has been a huge increase in the popularity of golf in recent years. It has been seen as a means of enhancing the image and facilities of a hotel when golf is offered as an additional facility to the hotel's leisure profile. Golf hotels are generally at the quality end of the market, as shown in Table 11.2. The major markets for golf are the AB socio-economic groups, which in turn fall into the business/conference markets and the short break markets. A golf course can add a great deal of value to the property's land value. For those properties that do not have available land to construct a golf course, a referral

Table 11.2 Hotels with golf facilities

	No of hotels	Offering golf	%
1 CROWN	266	21	8%
2 CROWN	1,858	145	8%
3 CROWN	2,290	414	18%
4 CROWN	1,624	598	37%
5 CROWN	246	124	50%

Source: Wooder S. (1991) Leisure Management February: 54–6

deal with a local golf club could be the answer. The expansion of the number of golf courses in the UK is not limited by demand, but by planning legislation.

Other facilities

Watersports such as fishing, sailing and windsurfing can be found in lakeside or seaside hotels. Cycling and horse riding are also popular pursuits, particularly in the countryside. Some traditional activities such as croquet, crazy golf and bowling are also found at some properties. Bowling is experiencing somewhat of a resurgence and is expanding rapidly as an important facility for the over 55 age group.

Considerations in implementing hotel leisure facilities

For the hotel that is looking to invest in leisure only a well-planned, well-resourced facility will give a real increase in business. Any design must be in keeping with the rest of the property, a particular concern for older hotels. It is therefore important that some form of market and financial feasibility study should be undertaken.

The most important factor in creating an effective fitness facility is to determine its overall purpose in relation to the hotel. Managers must define their ultimate goals as to whether the fitness facility is to be an additional amenity or part of a comprehensive total resort concept. A number of aspects will now be considered.

- space vs cost
- design considerations
- construction considerations
- consultancies
- equipment
- health and safety
- staffing
- memberships
- marketing

Space vs cost

The feasibility study must determine the usage level of any proposed facility, based on the number of guest rooms, and whether an outside membership is proposed. A facility must not be too small; however, space is always at a premium in hotels. Managers must not be tempted to install an undersized facility, as that could undermine the success of the venture; 5,000 square feet may be about right for a health club with 200–300 members, while a compact pool could be introduced in a space of about 8,000 square feet for a similar size membership. The cost for a typical hotel leisure complex is between £400,000 and £1 million. Swimming pools are the most costly facilities; however, if cost or space are limiting factors, an alternative such as a jacuzzi could be installed. Before any facility is built a comprehensive financial forecast of capital costs, operating costs and revenue should be undertaken. Table 11.3 illustrates the costs of various facilities and the space required.

	Average space (M)	Average cost (M)
Indoor tennis courts	2,610	250
Gymnasium	760	560
Squash court building	595	545
Leisure centre	2,825	650
25 metre pool	1,375	1,015

Source: Vierich W. and Calver S. (1991) *International Journal of Contemporary Hospitality Management* 3(3): 10–15.

Table 11.3
Approximate costs based on a sample of completed projects

Design considerations

The location of a fitness centre is important. For guests it should be close to their rooms, but away from public areas, as they require some privacy when walking to the centre. For outside members the facilities must have easy access from the car park, to avoid additional congestion in the lobby.

A particular concern in leisure facilities is the wet and dry aspect, which has serious implications for the types of materials used in construction. Fixtures and fittings must be robust and functional, easily cleaned and attractive to make the environment as pleasant as possible. Ceramic tiles should be used in changing areas on the floors and the walls. For wet areas tiles with a slip-resistant grip can be used. Other preferred materials are stainless steel, which can be coated, or polished alloys, toughened glass or solid melamine. Changing rooms need good drainage, and humidity and air controls. Many hotels chose a luxury design incorporating marble and granite, but such materials add to the expense. The aim should be to ensure consistency with the hotel; images can therefore range from the luxurious to the spartan.

Construction considerations

Once construction of the proposed facilities begins it could create substantial disruption to guests. Proper arrangements must be made to ensure that guests are not overly disturbed, and that they are informed of what is going on both from front desk staff, and possibly by posters, giving an indication of how the project will look once completed.

Consultancies

The scope of choice in facilities and implications for the design and construction is large. Hotel managers are therefore frequently turning to outside leisure consultants to come up with a feasibility plan for their proposed facilities.

Consultants need a description of the proposed scheme, an indication of the scale of provision, details of the proposed location, an indication of the budget available, a timetable for the work and what the hotel intends to use the feasibility study for. It can be useful to choose an accountancy based company as they can offer other services, such as project management, property expertise, financial advice and detailed market knowledge.

The most important message in a brief is the end result, namely the leisure facility. This can be the end of participation for some consultants. However, others remain involved from the design process, through to selecting and training the staff and providing a specialist management service once the operation is up and running.

Equipment

Fitness equipment is a large industry all of its own. There is a vast array of products to suit different facilities. From the hotel industry's point of view, the point has been made in comments about the demographic profile that when selecting fitness equipment it is the 45–65 age group that should be targeted. To this end, the equipment must be non-intimidatory, attractive, safe, durable, easy to maintain and fun to use. There are ten major muscle groups in the human body that need looking after in order to stay fit and well. So a gym needs at least ten types of resistance equipment.

Factors affecting equipment selection are

- size of the exercise room
- whether it will be staffed or unstaffed
- demographics of the target market
- financial budget.

Frequently it will be necessary to use more than one manufacturer when completely equipping a fitness room. The broader the choice of machines, the more interest will be generated by prospective users. Currently the most popular fitness trend is cardiovascular exercise, thus more floor space should be devoted to this. Exercise equipment is available in either single station or multi-station units. Equipment should be designed with women in mind, for example the first 100 kg of weight stack should be in 10 kg increments to accommodate women. A balance must be struck between cardiovascular machines and weight training machines.

Cardiovascular machines exercise the heart and the circulatory system. The most popular items are treadmills, stationary cycles, stair climbing machines and rowing machines. These have now become high tech: the machines are computerised and have digital readouts which provide information such as heart rate, speed, distance and calories expended. However they are very costly to purchase and maintain.

Weight training machines can include multigyms, which are designed to allow one person to do a variety of exercises; individual exercise machines, where one machine exercises one part of the body; free weights, including dumbbells and barbells. In general machines are safer because they restrict movements, reducing the chance of injury.

Installing all of this can be very expensive, therefore it may be worthwhile considering purchasing reconditioned equipment, at about 50%. Finally a reputable supplier should be chosen who will provide a guarantee and maintenance programme for the machines.

Health and safety

There has been a rapid increase in the number of hotel leisure clubs, and as a result an increase in the number of inexperienced people in charge of pool management. Safety is of paramount importance both in terms of the cleanliness of the water and avoidance of potential fatalities through drowning.

Provision of a large shallow end, lifeguards, safety signs and emergency lighting, along with forbidding diving and unruly behaviour, can help to prevent fatalities. If the pool is used infrequently it may be enough to have a reception desk which looks directly on to the pool, instead of a lifeguard.

UK swimming pools tend not to be diluted with enough fresh water to cope with pollution from heavy numbers of bathers. Frequently there is inappropriate use of chemicals such as chlorine, which this could cause an outbreak of bacteria if underused or create the unpleasant smells associated with over-chlorinating. Some hotels are now turning to an ozone system for treating their pools, whereby ozone gas is passed through the water to keep it clean and fresh.

Spas have particular problems because of their intensive usage and relatively low volume of water. Microbial contamination from the air and users can cause organisms in the water to multiply, in some cases to very high numbers. Frequently they will grow as a biofilm over the walls as well as growing in the liquid itself. Once in place these films are difficult to eliminate completely and will always present a potential risk. Good practices such as water changing and backwashing can keep the level low and ensure that any organisms released from it are rapidly inactivated. Local enforcement officers do make checks on swimming pools and they can put businesses out of operation if they do not meet the required standards. These are obviously important considerations for any hotel manager.

Staffing

The initial question in the feasibility study that must be asked is whether the health club is going to be staffed. The larger the facility, the greater the need for staff will be. The only reason not to have staff is cost; however, staffing has several benefits including safety, security, less wear and tear to equipment and provision of good guest service.

Staff should be selected who have prior experience in health clubs and preferably a related degree or qualification. The employment of specialist staff is a problem, as frequently they are costly and under-utilised. They should be employed only in clubs where a high volume of clients are expected.

Training should cover a hotel orientation so that staff can learn how to deal with hotel guests and what they expect. It should also include training in the proper use of equipment. Employees should understand the basics of fitness and revenue control, and that they are kept up to date on current trends. Training in first aid and basic resuscitation techniques is another essential.

Staff are an integral part of the facility and good training is absolutely essential; this should be carried out while the facility is during its final stage of construction, so that they can be fully prepared for the opening day.

Memberships

The concept of selling outside memberships has been gaining in popularity to offset operating expenses and create a profit. Membership can be either individual or corporate. However, hotels have to be careful about saturating the health club, and maintaining a balance between guests and members. It has proved useful at some properties to start of with a low number of members, increasing this up to a suitable point once the club is up and running.

Staffing is essential for a membership club, as is a well-planned facility with good equipment. It is useful to have a computer system to handle administration and increase efficiency, by producing a membership list and database of users, thus enabling cash to be handled effectively. Memberships can be the lifeblood of a hotel health club and must therefore be handled with care.

Marketing

Marketing is the key to a successful fitness facility. This should start before the facility is built, with research into whether there is any demand for it and into the markets that will be the end users of it. Additionally such research will give information concerning competitors and what prices can realistically be charged for memberships.

The facilities should be described in any promotional literature so that the consumer is aware before the decision to purchase. Reservation clerks should remind guests about the facilities, so that they remember to bring their sportswear and the concierge should give the guest any pertinent information about the club on check in. Finally this can be reinforced by proper signage to pinpoint the location of the club and information in guest rooms with tent cards, guest information folders and a spot on the in-house promotional video.

The opening of the facility provides an ideal public relations opportunity for the hotel and its new facility. This should help to boost initial sales of club memberships. A final marketing initiative can be in the form of merchandise supporting the hotel's logo, but this is probably applicable only in larger operations.

Theme park industry

One major sector within the context of leisure is the theme park industry. Many of the major companies that invest in the hospitality industry also invest in both leisure and specifically theme parks. The theme park industry will now be analysed in terms of

- markets
- ownership and investment
- diversification and destinations
- economic performance

The theme park industry was born in 1955 with the opening near Los Angeles in California of Disneyland. Since then the industry has grown rapidly with the market world-wide currently representing a multi-billion pound industry. Since 1990 the world-wide sales within the industry has grown by over 40% with much of this growth being in Europe and the Far East. There are nearly 300 parks world-wide attracting some 400 million visits. Overall the industry, like many others, is mature in many western and North American countries. Growth in the industry is occurring in developing countries and in the Far East, where an emerging middle class with a rising disposable income is fuelling demand.

Markets

Since 1955 North America has led the world in theme park design and operation. It accounts for one-third of the world's theme parks and approximately 50% of turnover; it is now in the mature stage of the product life cycle with minimal growth rates. Parks in North America exhibit strong patterns of pricing, attendance and overall performance. As would be expected from a relatively homogenous, mature market, parks operate similar pricing policies and within a similar pricing structure. While park size varies considerably, most parks have comparable numbers of rides, shows, catering and merchandising outlets.

Most North American parks open during the summer period between May and September and draw most visitors during the July and August school holiday periods. The majority of visitors come from the local marketplace within two hours' drive, although those in resort areas such as Florida and California attract significant numbers of international tourists. One measure of theme park attractiveness is market penetration: this is described in a case study of the theme park industry in the USA, including comparisons world-wide.

Case Study: Market penetration in the theme park industry

Theme parks in the USA

A key measure of the success of a given recreational attraction is its rate of penetration within the available markets. Market penetration rates for major and moderate-scale theme parks in the USA are displayed in Table 11.4. Large-scale theme parks are located in main metropolitan areas, attract attendances of over 1 million people and have an investment value in excess of $100 million. Moderately sized parks are typically located in smaller metropolitan areas and attract attendances of fewer than 1 million. Accordingly, large-scale parks are able to achieve greater market penetration rates than moderate parks.

The primary resident market typically includes people living within a 100 km radius or within an hour's driving time; the secondary market, generally a 100–200 km radius or between one and two hours' driving time; and the tertiary market, 200–300 km or more, or a driving time of over two hours. The tourist market is comprised of an out-of-area or an out-of state visitor market, depending on the size of the resident market designation, although tourists will generally stay within 30–60 minutes of the attraction.

Market penetration rates for major parks in the primary resident market area range from 25 to 45% as indicated in Table 11.4. The upper limits of this range are experienced at the Disney parks and other very successful parks. The majority of non-Disney facilities experience primary resident market penetration in the range 25–35%. Secondary resident market penetrations for this group range between 8 and 17%, and tertiary penetrations typically vary from 3 to 10%. A wide variation in penetration is shown for the tourist market for major parks, due to the influence of the Disney parks and other destination market parks at the upper limits of the indicated range. Excluding the Disney parks, typical tourist market penetration for major parks ranges from 2 to 10%, depending on the market area in question.

In contrast, parks with a moderate investment level realise market penetration rates in the range 15–28% of the primary resident market area. Secondary and tertiary resident market penetration rates are also lower than those exhibited by the major parks. This is

case study continues ▶

case study continues

Table 11.4
Penetration rates
US theme park

	Range of penetration rates (%)	
	Major park[1]	*Moderate park[2]*
Resident market[3]		
Primary market area[4]	25–45	15–28
Secondary market area[5]	8–17	6–11
Tertiary market area[6]	3–10	2–6
Tourist market	2–31	1–15

Notes:

1 By major theme park it is meant an initial investment in excess of $100 million

2 Initial investment of less than $100 million

3 Percentage of persons in each market category who attend the park one time per year (or equivalent person visit)

4 Typically 0–1 hour's driving time

5 Typically 1–2 hour's driving time

6 Typically 2–3 hour's driving time

indicative of the lower investment levels and thus the lower drawing power of these attractions. Tourist market penetrations for moderate-scale parks range between 1 and 15% depending upon location and market emphasis.

It is important to note that market penetration rates are reflective of the concept and appeal of a park, the level of investment, and the level of competition more than the absolute size of the catchment population.

Theme parks in Europe

In Europe the picture is somewhat different from that in North America. Having developed from family owned or municipal gardens, most European theme parks are still evolving. In relation to North America, Europe is still relatively immature and in a growth phase with some seventy-five parks in all. The effect of the opening of Disneyland Paris in 1992 (which set new standards in quality, operation, marketing and price) was significant. Between 1990 and the mid-1990s, the number of theme parks in Europe with attendances of 500,000 or more grew by almost 20%, while attendances grew by over 30%. In Europe in 1996, the theme park business was worth some $1.5 billion, which is over 50% more than in 1990.

Unlike North America, the industry in Europe has not grown through a typical product life cycle curve, but rather in steps, with development spurts occurring in the late 1960s, late 1970s and late 1980s. This is due to a combination of factors, including the variation in the economic welfare of different European countries. This variance can be seen in the admission pricing levels at parks in Europe. Parks in Europe typically operate under greater competitive conditions than those in North America as European cities are generally more densely populated and closer together. While North American parks often have a monopoly within a marketplace, European parks compete with one or more other parks

case study continues ▶

for the same customers. As a result, European parks do not achieve the levels of attendance or market penetration achieved by those in North America.

The design, layout and performance of European theme parks follows that of parks in North America, although in many cases, European parks do not possess the level of retail and catering provision provided within North American parks. As a result, the total revenue generated in European parks is typically lower than that achieved in North American parks.

Theme parks in Japan and the Far East

Japan and the Far East have seen the greatest development of theme parks in recent years. In the mid-1990s, the Far East theme park market generated $3.3 billion in revenues – one-third of the world-wide total, and more than double that of European theme parks.

The two largest Far Eastern markets are currently Japan and Korea. Japan is at a similar stage of development as North America. With a total of around sixty parks in Japan, the 80 million visits from a population of 125 million represents a visitation rate of just over 0.6 visits per person. This demonstrates that Japan is nearing maturity, and with the scarcity of land in Japan, developers are looking to create smaller parks both indoors and outdoors.

Elsewhere in the Far East, major outdoor theme parks are being developed. China is the country with the most activity at present, with seven parks, each with an investment value in excess of $100 million, being planned or under construction.

As in Europe, there are considerable variations in admission pricing and spending patterns within the different countries of the Far East. Japan leads the way, and Tokyo Disneyland is the most expensive theme park in the world, with an admission price of approximately $50 per person. It is also the most visited park in the world attracting over 16 million visits.

Theme parks in Australia

Australia has eleven parks serving a resident population of 17 million people. The market there is relatively mature and the 9 million annual visits represent 0.5 visits per person. While the opening of Warner Bros Movie World in 1991 expanded the total market, it had a detrimental impact on some of the smaller parks.

South and Central America

South and Central America is another area of considerable development interest although the political and economic instability in many countries is preventing rapid development. Brazil and Mexico host the main attractions, and there are plans for more parks in Brazil as well as in other countries in the region.

Ownership and investment

Investment in theme parks in the mature markets is expanding and moving into the 'third wave' of ownership. The 'first wave' of ownership was through family businesses; the 'second wave' occurred as family assets were bought up by larger corporations; and the 'third wave' is happening now where investment banks, venture capitalists and other investor groups are purchasing leisure facilities and companies.

In North America the 'second wave' led to a consolidation of ownership with five companies – Disney, Time Warner, Anheuser-Busch, Paramount and MCA/Universal – controlling thirty-two of North America's top forty parks. The 'third wave' is just now occurring with some of these park groups trading partially or fully into investors' hands, such as in the recent purchase of MCA/Universal by Seagrams. In Europe, which is slightly behind North America in ownership trends, the 'second wave' has seen Pearsons/The Tussauds Group and Walibi Group emerge as two leading operators.

Most leading operators are media companies with wide-ranging interests, and theme parks offer them opportunities to capitalise on their intellectual property rights. Combining theme parks with off-site merchandising, licensing rights and associated property development can generate significantly greater returns than from the theme park alone; through such measures, the value of the whole company can be increased.

Diversification and destinations

Theme parks are targeted at middle-income family markets, and as the industry has matured operators have sought to diversify from the standard theme park product to provide a number of products targeted at different niche markets. Examples of these include Universal Studios, which is targeted at an adult audience, Legoland, which is targeted specifically at children, and Silver Dollar City, which is targeted at an older, more culturally minded audience.

This diversification is having an influence outside theme parks in indoor family entertainment centres, urban leisure developments and other attractions. Operators are looking to take the experience learned from theme park operations and incorporate the latest technology innovations into specialised leisure environments targeted at specific market segments.

While the majority of theme parks are targeted at the local resident market, the development of The Magic Kingdom at Walt Disney World in 1971 saw the birth of a new brand of theme park – the destination park. These destination parks, typically in resort areas such as Florida and California, generate significant numbers of visitors from tourist markets and the rapid growth in Orlando's tourism in the 1970s and 1980s following Disney's development testifies to the appeal and impact of such parks.

The ongoing development in Florida, where both Disney and MCA/Universal are planning new attractions, reveals the importance of destination parks to some of the major operators and in many resort developments around the world.

Economic performance

The economics of theme parks are similar throughout the world. Theme park revenues are driven by a combination of attendance and per capita expenditures, which in turn are affected by other factors. Attendance is a function of the total park investment, the level of competition, the quality of the site and attraction, the appeal of the concept, the climate and, most importantly, the size and characteristics of the market. Per capita spending levels are a function of length of stay in the park, pricing and the appeal and availability of purchase points for secondary spending inside the park.

Theme parks in North America generate between $25 and $40 from each visitor. Typically between 50 and 60% of this revenue is generated from admissions, with the rest being spent on food and drink, merchandise and games within the park. In other countries, the total revenue generated varies considerably, but the split between admissions and in-park revenues is common.

The operation of a theme park is very labour intensive. Typically staff account for between 45 and 60% of total costs. Advertising, promotion and an allocation for improvements and new attractions are other important expenditure items. Well-run parks seek to generate pre-tax profits in the order of 20–30% of turnover.

While the key factor in attendance is the size of the catchment markets, there is a strong correlation between the amount invested in the development of the park and the total number of visits attracted annually. Generally, successful parks spend between $70 and $100 per attendee on developing the park.

Prospects for theme parks

Strong socio-economic growth in developing countries will lead to the continued development of theme parks which follow the standard theme park format in those locations. In more mature markets, however, theme park developments will follow a pattern of diversification towards niche markets as has been seen in North America.

As markets around the world mature, the leading operators will seek to develop world-wide brands and groups of theme parks. Disney led the way with Tokyo Disneyland and Disneyland Paris, and interest is increasing with Warner Bros Movie World parks in Australia and Germany, and Anheuser-Busch's and Tussaud's stake in Port Aventura in Spain.

Other operators are looking to combine theme parks with retail and entertainment in urban settings as the next step in the development of the industry, and the use of technology breakthroughs such as simulators and virtual reality will enable theme park experiences to be offered in locations which could not previously support a theme park.

The world-wide theme park industry grew from nothing to a $10 billion industry in forty years. In the late 1990s, only one-third of the world's population have access to a theme park. With more parks planned, and market areas expanding around the world, it is possible to foresee sustained growth in the number of parks and the size of the industry world-wide to the year 2010.

Summary

By the year 2010 leisure consumers will be increasingly sophisticated, and far more discerning and knowledgeable than their 1980 counterparts. Leisure providers will have to look more closely at the demands and wishes of social groups, bearing in mind the economic conditions of the time. It is hoped that free time will increase; however, it is probable that time will become more pressured, causing people to select narrower leisure portfolios. In turn their expectations for good service will increase, along with their personal expertise.

The provision of leisure facilities is given a high rating by hotel guests and is a major reason for initial and repeat bookings. The increasing awareness of leisure facilities as part of the hotel's benefit bundle makes provision of them a very important consideration for all hotels.

There are many reasons to consider leisure in hotels. To be a success, as in any business, hotels will get out what they put in. Those managers who invest half-heartedly, and install a health club as a token gesture, will not be able to maximise the possible bene-fits. The general public have an increased consciousness, sophistication and level of par-ticipation in self-improvement activities, know when a minimal attempt has been made, and will react negatively to the hotel in question. Leisure is more than just a trend, to be copied in order to keep up with the market. If planned, designed, implemented and mar-keted properly it can provide substantial benefits to a hotel, as well as being a viable financial investment, from which the hotel can reap considerable rewards. An extensive range of facilities is available to a hotel, in ever varying combinations to match the par-ticular market needs of the hotel. Many can be installed with little or no cost, such as jog-ging trails and exercise bikes. Packages with local leisure establishments are popular and can extend the scope of provision further. Whatever facilities are planned, a range of activities within easy reach of the hotel will create more appeal. The opportunities for growth are excellent, but the industry will have to re-tailor its marketing strategies to meet the consumer's ever changing and evolving needs.

An allied area to both the leisure and hospitality industry is the theme park industry. Theme parks are usually outside attractions which charge a one-price admission fee to visitors. The history and development of the industry was described along with demand and supply characteristics in a number of regions of the world.

Further reading

- Algar R. (1992) 'What equipment?, *Leisure Management* September: 8.
- Ash N. (1993) 'Getting on the network', *Leisure Management* May: 65–6.
- Barr C. and Wynter C. (1989) 'The changing challenge', *Leisure Management*, 9(9): 54–9.
- Bergsman S. (1990) 'Company sees profit on resort golf greens', *Hotel and Motel Management* 5 November: 118–19.
- Breen T. (1987) 'Marketing is the key to a successful fitness facility', *Hotel and Motel Management* March: 22–3.
- Carter B. (1986) 'Tailor a fitness facility to your market', *Lodging* June: 19–25.
- Chitty G. (1986) 'Hotels splash out £20 million on leisure', *Caterer and Hotelkeeper* 2 January: 22–5.
- Collings R. (1990) 'Active duty', *Caterer and Hotelkeeper* 18 October: 66–8.
- Cooper C. and Latham J. (1993) '1991 – a year of decline', *Leisure Management* March: 26–9.
- Crutchley-Macleay D. (1991) 'Swimming pool safety', *British Hotelier and Restaurateur* November/December: 13–15.
- Culligan K. (1990) 'A less harried future', *Leisure Management* February: 28–30.
- Dane J. (1987) 'One man and his leisure centre', *Hospitality* July/August: 14–15.
- Drummond G. (1992) 'Fighting fit', *Caterer and Hotelkeeper* 19 March: 78–83.
- Fache W. (1990) 'Splash out', *Leisure Management* September: 26–7.
- Feature 1 (1991) 'Taking leisure seriously', *Hotel and Catering Review* June: 17, 29.
- Feature 2 (1990) 'Green leisure dare the industry ignore the warnings', *Leisure Business* February: 32–3.
- Feature 3 (1990) 'Leisure into the 1990's … a very exciting prospect', *Leisure Business* May: 78–80.
- Feature 4 (1989) 'Country Club Hotels', *Leisure Business* May: 56–7.
- Foley F. (1991) 'Wise pool usage yields profits plus satisfaction', *Hotel and Motel Management* 8 April: 44, 46.
- Gassor E. (1991) 'Whirlpool appeal', *Leisure Management* January 66–7.
- Guthrie B. (1991) 'Pool perils', *Leisure Management* August: 53–5.

- Hales C. and Collins P. (1988) 'A leap in the dark', *Hospitality* November: 18–20.
- Harmer J. (1991) 'Height of activity', *Caterer and Hotelkeeper* 21 February: 36–8.
- Harmsworth S. (1991) 'Body and soul', *Leisure Management* September: 31–2.
- Harris V. (1992) 'Differentiation or expectation? A discussion of the role of the indoor leisure complex as part of the hotel product', Leeds Polytechnic.
- Insight (1990) 'The industry should reassess its attitudes to green leisure as the power of the consumer grows', *Leisure Business* February: 32.
- Jones W. (1992) 'Come on in?', *Caterer and Hotelkeeper* 3 September: 38–9.
- Knutson B. (1988) 'Hotel leisure facilities', *Cornell Hotel and Restaurant Association Quarterly* 28: 83–7.
- Leisure Feature (1989) 'Body talk', *Caterer and Hotelkeeper* 27 April: 94–5.
- Lyons V. (1992) 'Health benefits', *Caterer and Hotelkeeper* 9 July: 59–61.
- Lyons V. (1994) 'The fitness factor', *Caterer and Hotelkeeper* 17 February: 60–2.
- Martin B. and Mason S. (1992a) 'Holiday action', *Leisure Management* September: 24–5.
- Martin B. and Mason S. (1992b) 'Recovering lost ground', *Leisure Management* January: 26–8.
- Martin B. & Mason S. (1993) 'Cautious customers', *Leisure Management* January: 26–9.
- Monteson P.A. and Singer J.L. (1992) 'The spa who loved me', *Lodging Hospitality* February: 46–8.
- Morse S. and Lanier P. (1992) 'Golf resorts – driving into the nineties', *Cornell Hotel and Restaurant Association Quarterly* August: 44–8.
- Murray J. (1992) 'Computer applications', *Leisure Management* August: 47–8.
- Rowe M. (1990) 'The health club edge', *Lodging Hospitality* March: 94–6.
- Satchell A. (1992) 'A leisurely lease of life', *British Hotelier and Restaurateur*, October: 16–19.
- Sinden N. and Jones G. (1992) 'Face to face – do holiday villages damage the environment?', *Leisure Opportunities*, October: 30–1.
- Stanton L. (1992) 'Down on the health farm', *Leisure Management* July: 6.
- Stewart R. (1990) 'Aiming for growth', *Leisure Management* July: 23–5.
- Tibbot R. and Dodds M. (1991) 'Leisure 2000', *Leisure Management* April: 46–52.
- Tilley C. (1989) 'Expert advice', *Leisure Management* 9(8): 57–62.
- Tyrell B. (1990) 'Leisure trends', *British Hotelier and Restaurateur* March: 22–3.
- Vierich W. and Calver S. (1991) 'Hotels and the leisure sector', *International Journal of Contemporary Hospitality Management* 3(3): 10–15.
- Ward P. (1988) 'Country club get in the swing', *Caterer and Hotelkeeper* 10 March: 34–6.
- Wason G. (1992) 'Euro Golf', *Leisure Management* October: 52–4.
- Whelihan III W.P. and Chan K.S. (1991) 'Resort marketing trends of the 1990's', *Cornell Hotel and Restaurant Association Quarterly* August: 56–9.
- Wyatt T. (1992) 'Germ busters', *Leisure Management* November: 59–60.

Chapter Twelve

Trends to the Year 2000 and Beyond

Objectives

After reading this chapter you should be able to

■ Assess the development, history and relevance of environmental issues within both the tourism and hospitality industry.

■ Discuss the evolution and effects of technology on both the structure and marketing practices of hotel firms.

■ Investigate the meaning and relevance of quality assurance within the hospitality industry.

Environmental problems: the context

The environmental problems arising from the hotel industry are well known and the need is to identify the specific policy options to deal with these problems. A major distinction between the hotel industry and other industries is that the consumers travel to the places they visit for the hotel product they wish to buy. It is an inevitable consequence that a destination approach must be increasingly taken in environmental issues within the hospitality industry. The greater the pressure for visitor numbers the more comprehensive the management influences must be. The tourism industry as a whole moves and accommodates hundreds of millions of people around the world every year and therefore a good environment is at the core of the business. This good environment includes protecting the air, water, landscape and heritage.

In 1996, in an impassioned plea to the industry, the Prince of Wales called for hoteliers to respond to environmental concerns by addressing the issue of sensitive design and construction. A critic in the *Independent* pointed out that Prince Charles seemed to have realised that 'when many start to do the things that once only tiny elites could do, then these things become transformed, become ugly'. Prince Charles recommended designs that are able 'to enhance local culture and traditions, to preserve a "sense of place" and to minimise disturbance of the environment', which echoes his earlier support for the International Hotels Environment Initiative (IHEI) guide in which he commended those who were making environmental responsibility integral to their overall corporate strategy.

The IHEI guide is one of many books, articles and other sources which describe the actions that hotels can take to improve their environmental performance. Examples of these measures include

● reducing consumption of energy and water

- limiting use of hazardous materials
- using environmental criteria as part of their purchasing policy
- reducing, reusing and/or recycling packaging
- cutting their use of transport.

Energy conservation

Although concern over the environment appears a relatively new phenomenon – one to have emerged largely since the mid-1980s – some of the issues have been the focus of action by the hospitality industry over a much longer timescale. Energy is probably the most obvious of these.

Concern for energy conservation can be traced back at least as far as the 1973 oil crisis, when the cost of energy increased dramatically. Individual responses were immediate. The Hilton International chain, for example, quickly developed two programmes in its hotels to identify and implement good management practices and efficient technologies across the whole chain. The European Division of Hilton International introduced a European Award for Best Environmental Practices within a Hilton International Hotel in the early 1980s, which was won by the Munich Park Hilton in 1984; this hotel continues to exemplify good practice.

During the early 1980s early **building energy management systems** (BEMS), in which computer software is used to control the building's heating, lighting and ventilation, were pioneered in hotels – with the UK government support under the Energy Efficiency Office's Energy Demonstration Scheme. Hotels also piloted monitoring and targeting systems, using computer software to check consumption levels against weather conditions and occupancy levels. Forte (then Trust House Forte) experimented with **combined heat and power** (CHP) systems, in which an engine in the boiler room burns gas to generate electricity on-site but with the heat from the process also being utilised, thereby avoiding wasting this heat as happens in central power stations. At least 150 hotels now have CHP systems, which are suited only to buildings that have all-year-round need for heat (or hot water). **Occupancy-linked controls** were introduced in larger hotels, sometimes connected to room-booking systems. All these technologies received UK government support in their early stages, and are now continuing to mature, often reducing in capital cost, becoming increasingly more reliable, and therefore more widespread.

Catering has also been a focus for energy conservation. Government-funded studies during the 1980s included surveys of current practices undertaken by the University of Surrey. Manufacturers partly supported the work of Cranfield University: laboratory work on individual items of equipment, and case studies of individual premises. The resulting findings and recommendations were published by Sutcliffe Catering, now part of Granada plc.

Environmental management is, however, a broader topic than energy efficiency, embracing a range of issues including water conservation, waste management, hazardous materials, purchasing policies, noise, and other concerns. As these issues became more widespread, the hotel industry or rather the major international hotel chains responded. The Inter-Continental Hotel Group agreed to make its own in-house environmental manual available to other companies. Chief executives from a number of top international hotel chains formed a working committee, co-ordinated by The Prince of Wales Business Leaders Forum, to promote responsible environmental management throughout the industry. In 1993 they formed the International Hotels Environment Initiative, drew up the

Charter for Environmental Action in the International Hotel Industry and pooled their experience to turn the Inter-Continental manual into an international guide to best practice.

The second edition of this manual was published in 1996, with the intention of ensuring that the guide continued to reflect the growing scientific understanding of our impact on the environment – globally, regionally and locally. It adopted the new terminology of **environmental management** and **sustainable development** emerging in national and international standards and codes of practice. The new edition also introduces a simple method for benchmarking environmental performance in hotels against 100 key criteria.

The UK's *Green Hotelier* was launched in autumn 1995. This quarterly magazine contains a range of articles about the actions available to the industry to improve environmental performance, together with international case study examples of what some innovative hotels have achieved. It can thus be seen that a very wide range of information exists about environmental issues.

Corporate policies

It appears that with a few exceptions, most corporate attitudes to the environment originated in the late 1980s and early 1990s. An essential ingredient of these policies is environmental commitment which should start with the full support of the chief executive and be an integral part of management practice communicated to all personnel. Once they have been agreed, corporate policies can be implemented and assessed only through management techniques such as **environmental audits**. Audits are increasingly seen as an essential first tool in setting environmental targets as well as a framework for monitoring achievements. Environmental problems arising from business operations can be identified effectively through a formal monitoring system such as the auditing of projects and major developments. **Environmental impact assessments** are the internationally recommended methodology to determine the likely impact of a project on the environment, an example being the Channel Tunnel. Increasingly this is an area subject to regulation and legislation throughout the EU.

Influence of the EU

Since 1991 there have been a number of government or government-related initiatives in the area of environmental matters.

Towards the end of 1991 the European Commission approved a proposal for a council regulation to establish a **European Union Eco Audit Scheme** open for company participation by industrial companies. The objective of the scheme is to promote improvements in the environmental performance of industry by encouraging companies to achieve three points:

- establish and implement environmental protection systems
- carry out a systematic and objective evaluation of the environmental performance of the systems
- provide information about the environmental performance of the operation to the public.

The purpose of this scheme is not to indicate compliance with legislative requirements but provide the means for recognising efforts made to improve environmental performance whatever the starting point. There are various steps in the process, from an initial environmental review of the activities on a site through the development of corporate and site environmental policies, objectives and their action plan. This approach will underpin the environmental protection system, its establishment, implementation and auditing. The final stage is a revision of the whole system.

European member states are expected by the EC to establish voluntary Eco Audit Schemes, which will operate with European standards to be developed on environmental management systems and related certification activities. It will be possible for companies who meet the requirements to be registered and use an official EC logo.

After setting up the system there should be an evaluation or audit carried out with a particular focus on the system's performance. Following on from this evaluation, an external environmental statement would be prepared and validated. Finally the statement would be submitted to a competent body.

In March 1992 the EC adopted the fifth of its environmental programmes, which is designed to protect and enhance the quality of the environment in the EU and runs to the year 2000.

The programme, **Towards Sustainability,** is a departure from the four previous programmes. The Single European Act has for the first time given the EU a constitutional mandate to consider environmental protection; unlike previous programmes which were very much reactive, the fifth programme is much more proactive and is based on the thesis of sustainable development as put forward by the 1987 Brundtland Report. This is whereby the route causes of environmental degradation are addressed before the problems become so pressing that they can no longer be ignored. The programme is in three volumes, the two most prominent being volumes 1 and 2.

- **Volume 1** allows the European Council of Ministers to administer, approve and support the commission in the strategy outlined, and give the EC the go ahead to come forward with further proposals, to put the programme into effect.

- **Volume 2** contains the EC's suggestions for action and contains three main sections. The first section concentrates on the need for change and the strategy to achieve this. The second section looks at the EU's role in the wider international arena. The third section briefly assesses priorities, costs and review processes. One selected target sector is the tourism industry.

Tourism has a great and growing significance in the economy of the EU. With increasing affluence, more people are taking holidays further afield and taking more holidays each year. Certain areas of the EU, notably the Mediterranean coast and the Alpine zones, have been disproportionately affected by the increase in tourism and the attendant environmental impacts. Such impacts include destruction of natural habitats through hotel development and transport infrastructure; greatly increased use of water often in areas where water is already in short supply; increased output of waste water and sewage.

Energy management in hotels

Within the hotel industry one area of particular interest in environmental matters is energy management. There are approximately half a million rooms within the UK hotel industry, with the thirty largest hotel companies owning approximately 20% of the stock while a further 10% of the stock are affiliated to consortia. So in theory 30% of the stock can be accessed through only forty organisations. This degree of centralisation gives an opportunity to promote the adoption of a company-wide energy policy in hotel chains.

Energy use in the hotel sector lies between 22% electricity and 78% fossil fuels. Energy costs (including water) average some £828 per available room per year representing approximately 2.5% of total revenue. A comparison with the figures for the period 1990–3 shows that spending on energy in hotels rose by approximately 10% at the same time as occupancy rates dropped. Changes in fuel prices during this period were minimal. Space heating and hot water are responsible for 60% of consumption, catering for 18% and lighting for 9%. If a comparison is made across hotels, there is revealed wide variations in consumption, implying scope for saving of energy consumed.

Hotels are associated with luxury, particularly at the four and five star level; the primary concern of hotel management is towards customer service and the comfort and well-being of guests, even if these have to be achieved at higher cost. Internal temperatures and lighting levels are typically high and hot water is constantly available to guests. In some hotels conspicuous consumption of energy may be a way of demonstrating a commitment to luxury. While occupancy averages around 65–80% there is evidence of limited correlation between consumption and occupancy rates implying a lack of energy controls. These factors make hotels an energy-intensive building type by comparison with other industry sectors.

However, hotels are not necessarily perceived by management as energy intensive. Energy may receive relatively little attention for it is considered to be a small percentage of operating costs. By contrast staff costs are large so priority is towards using staff efficiently and it may be seen as more efficient to waste energy in order to improve staff performance. On this basis, the measures most likely to be taken up are those which will improve customers' perception of comfort and reduce staff and other operating costs.

In catering, current practices are frequently wasteful of energy. There is some scope for promoting good practices in training courses and also for rationalisation, maintenance and good housekeeping. Technological improvements in appliance design also offer potential. The hotel sector, dealing with residential accommodations has among all building types one of the highest fuel consumption figures per square metre: even modest percentage savings are likely to be substantial in absolute terms.

Five main ways in which energy savings can be made are listed below, with the measures requiring the largest investment and having the longest payback period listed first. Most measures have payback periods of between one and three years. If the figure of half a million rooms is multiplied by the average expenditure cost per room of £796 it would appear that energy costs within the UK are in the region of £400 million per year for the industry. If one translates the potential savings into practical opportunities, the five areas are

- converting boilers from oil to natural gas
- changing to energy-efficient lamps in all working areas
- experimenting with new technology in building management systems
- fitting thermostats and timers
- insulating hot water systems and roof spaces.

There appear to be a number of technical barriers to energy efficiency within the hotel sector. It is important that the level of disruption must be minimised if the measures are to be adopted. Systems must be reliable and offer minimum risk in the day-to-day provision of heating and cooking, hot water and lighting to customers. It is often the case that technology perceived as too novel, particularly if novelty is associated with attendant risk and reliability, is unlikely to be acceptable. Finally in terms of quality, lighting in particular should be considered as there is some evidence to suggest that some forms of low energy lighting are not considered to offer the same quality of light as traditional tungsten lighting.

Company priorities tend to focus on least cost, short payback period and low levels of disruption. The Ladbroke chain has a remote energy management system installed in a number of its hotels. Its centralised control is based in London and was part of a demonstration scheme in the 1980s partly funded by the Department of Energy. Subsequently other companies have obtained contracts to manage energy in a number of hotels including the Swallow chain on the basis of a management fee. In terms of investment criteria some hotels have a mechanism for considering investment in energy efficiency. For example, Hilton Hotels have established an energy fund for investing in energy efficiency measures and will consider measures which will have a payback period of less than three years. Other companies look for a period of one to two years.

There seems to be a considerable variety in the level and extent to which energy management forms part of management policies. At best the hotel chain has an energy policy which is agreed at board level and is the responsibility of one of the directors. The best known example of this is Forte, the largest hotel operator in the UK, whose energy costs including water charges are some £30 million a year. At group level there is an energy manager providing co-ordination throughout Forte. This manager also initiates and monitors trials for new products and services, technologies and methods which make the best possible use of the energy commodity. However in other companies, while energy tariffs are negotiated centrally within the chain, energy policy and expenditure remains the responsibility of the hotel manager. In many cases energy costs are not distinguished by department nor can they be directly related to income or comfort.

Barriers to energy efficiency within the hotel industry include apathy, failure to identify energy as controllable, and lack of awareness of the availability and cost-effectiveness of measures. However, management is becoming much more aware of detailed operating information. The development of information systems that operate to facilitate bookings, produce accounting records and compile marketing information, also incorporate maintenance and monitoring facilities as an integrated package. Such systems have the potential to make managers aware of energy costs.

The late 1990s will see pressure exerted by the major hotel companies directed towards both the suppliers of the industry and the management of energy. The view of industry is that suppliers will be expected to assist in providing environmentally friendly products, equipment and services.

Case Study: Environmental initiatives in London hotels

Having considered environmental matters in the tourism and hospitality industry the purpose of this case study is to establish what hotels are doing in practice within the London hotel market.

The survey

The research involved a self-assessment questionnaire that was sent to 150 London hotels – both chain and independent, large and small – to enquire about their environmental actions. The survey asked questions including

- Has the hotel taken any action to reduce the effect it has on the local or global environment? If so, how?

case study continues ▶

case study continues

- Does the hotel include environmental criteria in negotiations with suppliers?
- Is the hotel a member of any environmental organisations, forums or initiatives?
- Has the hotel had an environmental review or audit carried out?
- Does the hotel have an environmental policy or statement?

Hotels responding to the questionnaire comprised 28% of the sample, which is an excellent response rate for an unsolicited survey, although as a proportion of the total number of UK hotels (around 18,000) it is only some 0.2%.

The results

Out of the 150 London hotels who were sent the questionnaire 42 responded, of which 28 categorised themselves as part of a hotel chain and 14 were independent hotels (see Figure 12.1). Even in a mature hotel industry like the UK only some 20% of hotels are part of a chain – the rest being independent. The purpose of looking and the breakdown in this way is to investigate if there are any differences in response between the two hotel categories.

However, by nature of their size and the need to generate all-year-round demand, chain hotels are usually located in the major cities. It is therefore to be expected that the sample is biased towards the hotel chains.

The first question asked whether the hotel had taken any action to reduce its effect on the local or global environment. Over 90% of the sample said yes (Figure 12.2) and many had focused their efforts on recycling (38%).

In considering differences between the hotel categories only two chain and two inde-

Figure 12.1 Hotel categories

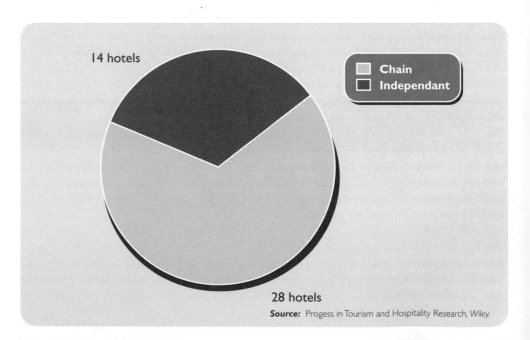

14 hotels

Chain
Independant

28 hotels

Source: Progess in Tourism and Hospitality Research, *Wiley.*

case study continues ▶

case study continues

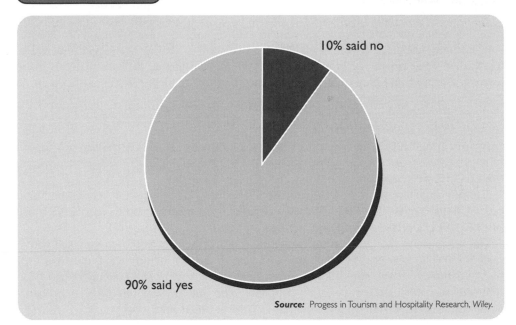

Figure 12.2
Environmental
initiatives in hotels

10% said no

90% said yes

Source: Progress in Tourism and Hospitality Research, *Wiley.*

pendent hotels responded by saying that they had not taken any action to reduce their effect on the local and global environment. It is positive to report that such a high percentage have started the process of incorporating green policies within their firm: it would seem that green policies are becoming an integral part of business policies. It is also important to note that the implementation of such policies is consistent across a wide spectrum of the London hotel industry. The size of hotels in the sample ranged from 27 to 850 rooms reflecting the diversity of the industry not only in London but also throughout the UK.

Having established that a high percentage had taken environmental action the questionnaire sought to identify specific initiatives being undertaken by hotels in London. These possible initiatives were identified under seven areas and from the results presented in Table 12.1 a diversity of responses can be noted.

	Yes	*No*
Have you taken action to reduce the consumption of resources?	61.9	33.3
Have you taken action to exploit renewable resources?	4.8	95.2
Have you taken action to reduce pollution or emissions?	57.1	42.9
Have you taken action to exploit reusable items?	52.4	47.6
Have you taken action to recycle materials?	71.4	28.6
Have you taken action to protect bio-diversity?	9.5	90.5
Have you taken action to reduce social inequality?	61.9	33.3

Table 12.1
Environmental
initiatives taken by
London hotels (%)

Note: Percentage figures may not add up to 100 where hotels did not respond
Source: Progress in Tourism and Hospitality Research, Wiley.

case study continues ▶

case study continues

Some 62% said their actions were intended to reduce consumption of resources and many identified the utilities of gas, electricity and lighting as areas for attention. This result illustrates the importance hotels attach to this area. Further analysis of the results show that while many gave emphasis to the major utilities, only two hotels were interested in tropical hardwoods and none identified the management of fresh water. As this area can offer substantial cost savings to the hotel it was perhaps surprising that the percentage who said yes was not higher. The independent hotels formed a higher percentage of the sample who said no.

In answering the next question the responses indicated that some 95% did not exploit renewable resources. Of the hotels who said yes, two highlighted the use of daylight; both had between 200 and 300 rooms and were hotel chains.

The questionnaire went on to identify hotels that had taken action to reduce pollution or emissions: 57% said yes and of these, 20 hotels had taken action to reduce their use of CFCs (14 chain hotels and 6 independent).

The response to the question on exploiting reusable items was more equivocal with a near 50/50 split. Even for the hotels that said yes, 26 did not identify what initiatives they had undertaken. It was noted in the responses that packaging and containers had been reduced over the past few years by suppliers. The initiative on this issue is probably coming from manufacturers in an attempt to control prices and costs.

In contrast 71% of the sample had taken action to recycle materials with 26 hotels implementing initiatives concerning glass, paper, etc. The percentage that said no was biased towards the independent hotels. Of those independent hotels that said yes, 8 did not specify what initiatives they were undertaking.

The protection of bio-diversity was clearly not a priority for hotels with over 90% saying they had not implemented any initiatives. Many international conferences on the environment have tended to stress this aspect yet it is clearly not regarded as an important issue within London hotels, which may be due to the city-based location of the sample. It would be interesting to investigate if this London-based view is reflected within the whole UK hotel industry.

Reduction in social inequality was regarded as important by 62% of the sample with 24 hotels (18 chain and 6 independent) implementing fair employment practices. No other issues concerning social inequality were noted and a significant element of the 62% who said yes gave no response.

Although it is clear from the data that environmental matters are a matter of concern for the hotels surveyed, it was surprising that 32 hotels (76%), did not have an environmental policy or statement. Many that said they had such a policy were unwilling to provide a copy for analysis; only 2 hotels (4.8%) did so (a notable exception was the Inter-Continental Hotel Group). In the sample 71% did not have staff belonging to trade associations or professional institutions which have environmental policies; of those who said yes only 2 hotels said that copies of such a policy are held in the management's office.

Given the publicity surrounding environmental matters it was surprising that only 47% of the hotels brought their initiatives to the attention of guests. Some managers see environmental matters as rich in marketing opportunities yet this research indicates that hotels are not deriving full benefit on this front.

One question asked about environmental audits. Some 60% of respondents had not

case study continues ▶

case study continues

carried out an environmental audit of both the hotel and its operating procedures. This suggests that many hotels take an informal approach, stressing the importance of action rather than bureaucracy, but as few hotels have an environmental policy, the research suggests that environmental matters in London hotels could benefit from a more systematic approach.

When asked if environmental criteria was included in negotiations with suppliers, 28% said yes. Answers to this question were typified by one respondent who said 'no we are only interested in price'.

A total of 18 hotels said they were part of an environmental initiative with 14 citing the support of the Westminster City Council. Asked if the hotel used published information on environmental matters, 20 said yes. Sources identified in the responses included BRESCU, Energy Efficiency Office, *Green Hotelier* and Westminster City Council. Finally respondents were asked if they knew where to look for information on environmental matters, when 26 hotels responded by saying yes and identified the same sources. It would seem that the many sources of excellent information on environmental initiatives, publicly available, are well known to the respondents. Another positive issue coming out of this is the support and co-ordinating role of Westminster City Council.

Concluding remarks

The hotel industry does face some pressure to improve its environmental performance, not least from consumers and the legislators. In this case study, we have made an assessment of what the UK hotel industry is doing to improve environmental performance, based on a detailed survey of environmental management practices in 42 London hotels.

This research found that environmental matters are a concern to 90% of the sample, although only 47% had drawn this concern to the attention of their guests; 43% were part of a local-authority-led environmental initiative and 38% had had an environmental audit carried out. Against this, only 19% had prepared an environmental policy or statement and only 28% included environmental criteria in negotiations with suppliers of goods and services. The hotel sector clearly exhibits a gap between environmental 'good' intention and action. However, a high percentage of respondents expressed concern about environmental matters and it is hoped that over time a greater number will implement specific environmental initiatives. Hotels can act to reduce their environmental impacts and, collectively, could make a substantial contribution to improving the quality of the environment. The respondents were aware of the wide range of publications offering guidance and advice on the actions that hoteliers could take to alter their practices and so address environmental issues. The results show that a proportion of hotels are applying this guidance, and that some actions, such as recycling, are more common than others, e.g. bio-diversity. In terms of specific initiatives a more positive approach was detected by the chain hotels as opposed to the independents.

In the industry there seems to be widespread awareness of environmental issues among hoteliers, but it is not always translated into action. These hoteliers are responsive or reactive to market forces and collaborate with others when opportunities arise to take action. Only a proportion, however, appear to be socially responsible enough to be proactive and take actions in advance of customer and commercial pressures to reduce

case study continues ▶

case study continues

their impact on the environment. The work of the Inter-Continental Hotels Group is a positive case in point.

Taking a wider perspective the examples above may suggest that the industry's response has been active and effective at responding to and mobilising the environmental concerns of their stakeholders (customers and employees) in order to create a competitive advantage. There is no suggestion that these programmes are conducted for philanthropic motives. The leading companies adopt initiatives that are right for them, in terms of a strategic fit, whether it is donations, links with education and training, recycling of materials, or the use of unleaded (and cheaper) fuel for a large fleet of cars. It would seem that environmental opportunities allied with the core business seem to be the most successful. As has also been demonstrated, many of these initiatives have considerable financial benefits for companies whatever their additional benefits for the community.

If social responsiveness is about meeting consumer expectations, then social responsibility is about the ethics and values that lie behind corporate social policies. It is less clear what values, beyond commercial expediency, underlie the industry's attitudes to the environment, let alone what corporate values should be. At one extreme, it could be that there is only one social responsibility of business and that is to engage in activities to increase its profits as long as it stays within the rules of the game.

London hotel managers may increasingly recognise the need to protect the environment, but it seems likely that most continue to take a pragmatic approach and will take the actions that are most likely to advance the company's objectives. While this attitude may seem far from ideal, the approach of many of the hotels in London can be regarded as positive.

Computer reservation systems (CRS)

In the hotel industry there will be continued development of technology with a special emphasis on computer reservation systems. The background to this trend has come initially from the airline industry.

The 1970s and 1980s saw the development and consolidation of powerful CRS mostly initiated by airlines and concerned primarily with air transport. Initially concerned with the reservation of seats on airlines, they now incorporate accommodation, car rental and even visitor attractions and reservations. They therefore offer a global means of travel product distribution including the element of accommodation. These systems have mainly been directed at the business or frequent travel markets but there are indications that this sector is getting saturated and attention is turning towards the leisure market. The availability of communications and networking technology will make possible the creation and management of destination databases.

Airline CRS

The first CRS, Sabre from American Airlines, started in 1959 as a way of using the emerging tools of technology to keep track of seats sold, and in 1976 it began to be used by travel agents world-wide. The emergence of airline deregulation and the need to respond to US airlines spurred Europe into the creation of two CRS – Amadeus and Galileo.

In 1985 Sabre introduced Tourfinder, a tour availability and reservation system, and the

Sabre travel guide and information system for tourist offices. The European systems have become a huge business in their own right with profits of over $200 million in the mid-1990s. All the systems now emphasise that their information is presented in a totally neutral and unbiased way, partly as a result of regulatory and consumer pressures. In the short term, the ability to provide the consumer with a greater range of services and fares than ever before through the mega-systems is likely to provide intermediaries such as airlines, travel agents and corporate travel offices with greater control of the market. Within the system, such intermediaries will have their own list of preferred properties and hotel groups with whom advantageous arrangements, commissions or discounts have been negotiated. The strength of any global CRS will be the number of terminals linked to it in travel agencies at the point of sale and its geographical coverage. The key technical factors are speed, capability, flexibility and simplicity of use.

Servicing travel agencies is very expensive for airlines and in order to defray costs, other services have been invited to join the system such as hotels or car hire. Hotels looking at the CRS options available to them should remain aware however that the airlines regard hotel bookings as an ancillary service and that their marketing objectives differ quite significantly from those of the hotel. Hotels always strive to project their own identity and the uniqueness of their product. However, economies of scale mean that CRS use a standard display and include as many properties as possible in order to maximise transaction revenue.

Destination database

The required technology is available for destination databases to the operators of the large CRS but it is notoriously absent in the communications infrastructure of medium and small tourist destinations. It is these destinations that a national tourist organisation would be more interested in promoting. It is therefore the expansion of CRS and the creation of destination databases to small and medium size tourism enterprises, which may be the trend over the next few years.

Such a destination database would be in its simplest form a collection of computerised and accessible information about a destination; it could also include information on accommodation and attractions, text and pictures. However, the large investment required by these sophisticated systems cannot be justified unless the system can take reservations and bookings. One particular concern of hotels is that they will need to balance potential gains in revenue against the increased investment in hardware, software and communications as well as the additional booking commission. Areas of conflict may include the lack of agreed standards for the network and the interface. The required information and transaction ratio and the degree of activity for inclusion in the database will also be of concern. It is clear that these systems could assist in marketing and distribution of tourism products, including accommodation and air travel.

Cost of using CRS

The use of such CRS will inevitably mean an increase in the published tariffs of participating hotels, and costs may rise by as much as 25 or 30%. With commissions payable to the CRS, in some cases the travel agent and perhaps a credit card company, the true cost of making a hotel room easy to buy can be high. As new systems are developed it is important that hotels do not commit themselves to long-term contracts. Global CRS provide the consumer with a one-stop booking opportunity and consequently make the hotel product more easily accessible. In the USA about 40% of the major chains' reservations and a lower proportion of all hotel bookings are made by this route.

The costs of international promotion are frequently beyond the resources of smaller groups and independent hotels. Representative companies and consortia spread these costs by providing sales expertise and reservation facilities on a shared basis in different countries to large numbers of hotels located elsewhere. Several of these representation companies have developed their own CRS. Such companies include Best Western International, Leading Hotels of the World and Utell International.

Extensions to CRS

One extension to CRS is to give travel agents local maps and reviews of many European hotels. It is possible for travel agents to have direct connections with hotels for instantaneous confirmations and negotiated rates on a confidential basis. Added value features include credit card processing, links to travel agents' networks and marketing programmes. Further improvements are possible. These include improved travel agent commission tracking and payment systems and additional links to travel agents' networks beside Sabre and Apollo around the world. A programme has been introduced which updates rate information in the airline databases and changes can be made in the hotel's CRS. It can also offer a bulk booking information source which shows hoteliers where they are getting their business from and which agencies are not generating any business.

Future of CRS

In terms of the future the central question is how can hoteliers get travel agents to sell more rooms? Automation is the daily link between hoteliers and travel agents. For both travel agents and hotels, the key part of travel technology is the computer reservation service. The CRS has substantial impact to go along with its sometimes substantial fee, and it is often a first step in travel planning. Travel agents are consumers and to get their business, hoteliers must give them what they want. Updated information should be a priority especially when the range of hotel products has grown constantly and tariffs have changed quickly. Computerised reservation systems are important and for many hoteliers essential, but they often require monitoring. However, the concern to the hotel industry is that CRS can drive the business if the industry does not participate actively in their development. They are costly to operate, and the hotel industry have to keep up with technology. In doing so equipment may become obsolete as the system is updated. These points about computer reservation systems will become key issues over the next few years and will be expanded in two technology related case studies. The first case study explores the subject of relationship marketing and the second gives an in-depth analysis of an organisation known as THISCO, The Hotel Industry Switch Company.

Case Study: Development of relationship marketing in hotels

Database marketing and customer loyalty programmes are major trends within the hotel industry. Originally developed by the airlines they are now being adopted by the chain hotel companies and are regarded as major assets. The purpose of this case study is to investigate the results of loyalty programmes, the main one being a more distinct marketing focus.

Customer loyalty programmes build business by

- maintaining current customer loyalty
- building awareness among, and targeting, new travellers
- taking share from competitors via a clear competitive advantage.

The programme works by creating individual one-to-one relationships with customers, and in doing so personalising the brand and making it relevant to the individual. In developing a form of frequent stay programme, a relationship is developed between customers and their preference for individual product lines and hotels. This focus on the frequent guest recognises and rewards the firm's best customers. Some of the rewards from the Hilton International's programme are as follows:

- free weekday newspaper
- separate member check-in (pre-registration)
- late check-out on request
- spouse stays free
- space available upgrades for diamond and gold VIP members.

Measurement of success in such a programme is essential and at Hilton International it consists of member surveys, member activity, preference polls and market share reports. The results of the Hilton honours programme are spectacular with the membership profile showing

- members earn more than $75,000 per year
- members take 30 or more trips per year
- 65% take 4.3 leisure trips per year
- 27% take incremental stays
- 32% of members viewed the programme as an important factor in stay decision
- Hilton honours members spend 10.5% more

Figure 12.3 shows that is clear that in comparison with the other major hotel chains there is a clear preference for the Hilton programme.

The honours programme allows Hilton to increase awareness of its product among its high spending and frequent customers and through the database created allows the firm to trail and ultimately monitor the spending patterns of individuals. It is this creation of an integrated relationship management database that has allowed Hilton to capture market share from its competitors and build a loyalty base for its product.

Within the hotel industry the best way to build business is to target the right customer

case study continues ▶

case study continues

Figure 12.3 Share of preference with competing firms

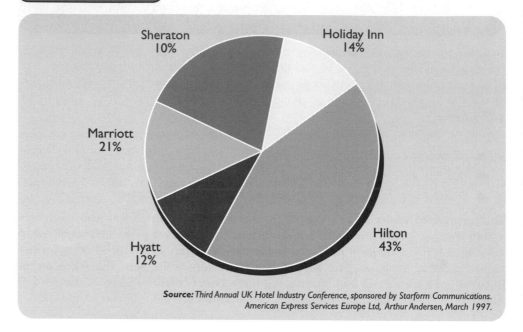

Sheraton 10%
Holiday Inn 14%
Marriott 21%
Hilton 43%
Hyatt 12%

Source: Third Annual UK Hotel Industry Conference, sponsored by Starform Communications. American Express Services Europe Ltd, Arthur Andersen, March 1997.

via the most efficient communication vehicle with a compelling incentive. Such targeting can be based on past users (frequency), profiling respondents (sometimes through what is known as data mining) and source markets (streets, cities, countries). By monitoring for instance credit card usage the programme allows the firm to track customer frequency, usage and value. The benefit comes from being able to market directly to the firm's target audiences. Compared with other forms of sales promotion a loyalty programme is more efficient and the data collected can be used at both the hotel unit or at corporate level. The distinction between unit and corporate level is important because at Hilton, turnkey direct mail programme and marketing tool kits are available to all hotel units, with more than 220 individual and co-operative hotel unit promotions supported in order to attract the best customers and those all-important new prospects. In devolving the programme to unit level it is of course important to ensure that staff are well versed in identifying and processing member transactions for peak satisfaction; indeed they must be familiar with current and partner promotions. The benefit for the unit is that the programme helps identify its most valuable customers to front-line staff and involves them in the delivery of service extensions. The programme also empowers customers to seek superior service.

Case Study: The Hotel Industry Switch Company (THISCO)

THISCO was founded in 1989 by the hotel industry with a mission to develop a universal electronic switch to connect hotel reservation systems to major distribution systems selling the hotel product to the travel agency industry and consumers around the world. In 1997, THISCO consisted of 22 hotel companies with 70 hotel brands, a total of 19,000 properties and more than 2.3 million rooms.

No hotel company can afford to ignore the explosive growth of electronic bookings from travel agencies around the world or avoid the rapidly growing consumer demand for direct electronic access to the hotel product. THISCO connects hotels to every major global distribution system and alternative distribution systems including the Internet's World Wide Web through Pegasus systems' TravelWeb. In doing so it has brought a substantial level of growth and profitability to its hotel members.

Focusing specifically on travel and the Internet, it is predicted that travel booking on the World Wide Web, in 1997 at $400 million a year, will hit $4 billion by the year 2000. It is estimated that 4.4 million people in the USA bought travel-related services on line in 1996 and 11.3 million are very interested in booking on-line. The American Society of Travel Agents show that 38% of agents have an Internet connection or are connected to another on-line system such as CompuServe. Some 47% of frequent business travellers and 32% of frequent pleasure travellers use on-line services according to the Travel Industry Association of America.

Growth in this form of electronic booking has been exceptional over the past few years. Hotel bookings via Global Distribution Systems (GDS) grew by 21.2% during 1996, based on a survey of the major GDS, including Amadeus, Galileo, Sabre, Sahara, System One and WorldSpan/Abacus. GDS hotel bookings in 1996 totalled more than 30 million, representing about 60 million room nights, compared to 25 million bookings in 1995, 20 million in 1994 and 16 million in 1993. The number of hotel bookings made through the GDS rose nearly 84% between 1993 and 1996.

At a unit level an example of how technology has helped can be seen at the Hyatt Regency, Chicago. Ranked one of the largest luxury conference/exhibition hotels in the world and the largest Hyatt property in the chain, the hotel handles more than 600,000 bookings from the conference business each year. The 36-storey 2,019 room hotel frequently works in conjunction with International Travel Service Inc (ITS), a conference placement agency, in arranging accommodation for delegates attending conferences in Chicago. For the hotel an average city-wide conference represents approximately 1,500 guest reservations.

Traditionally, the preliminary reservation list (100–200 pages) is sent four weeks prior to the event by fax from ITS to the hotel. Upon receipt hotel staff manually enter the information into the property's reservation system. This necessitates two or three people's time for seven days to enter just one list.

To improve the transmission of data from ITS to the hotel, the latter approached THISCO. Utilising THISCO's Ultra Res technology, ITS and Hyatt have automated the transfer of guest reservations, reducing seven days of manual labour to one hour for automated data transfer. ITS electronically transfers the reservations list to THISCO, which formats the information to fit the Hyatt computer reservation system. THISCO then elec-

case study continues ▶

case study continues

tronically sends the information to Hyatt's main CRS, where it is automatically recognised at the property level, thus eliminating the manual entry of guest reservations at the hotel. With this approach the hotel is able to control the level of over and under bookings, while at the same time significantly cutting costs associated with staff time manually entering the reservations data.

Quality assurance

In order to apply the concept of quality assurance to the hospitality industry, it is important to define what is meant by quality and how it can be related to a service industry such as hospitality.

Definition

The notion of quality in service industries is largely tied to the understanding of the service phenomenon. Four points can be identified as the characteristics of service:

- Services are intangible.
- Services are activities (performances) rather than things.
- Services are produced and consumed simultaneously.
- The consumer participates in the production process to some extent.

Two definitions of service quality can be identified. First, the notion of quality is the difference between what the consumer expects and what the consumer *perceives* to have received. Service quality is therefore conformance to customer specifications. In essence this suggests a user-based definition and that it is the customer who defines the quality. The second view is the value-based approach, where quality is defined in terms of costs and prices. Accordingly, a quality service is one which provides performance at an acceptable price or conformance at an acceptable price. This hybrid approach still has the consumer focusing on perceiving value. It is useful since it links quality relative to price and has some basis in economic pricing theory, i.e. price can in the absence of other information signal quality.

The nature of service

This analysis of quality assurance points to three underlying themes.

- Service quality is more difficult for the customer to evaluate than goods quality.
- Service quality perception results from a comparison of consumer expectations with actual performance.
- Quality evaluations are not made solely on the outcome results but an evolved evaluation of the process of service delivery.

The separation of the result and the process in the consumer's perception of quality is fundamental in the design and implementation of quality management systems. Within these two aspects, there is a differentiation between technical quality, i.e. what is delivered, and functional quality, the manner in which it is delivered. The nature of services, i.e. their intangibility, heterogeneity and inseparability, leads to the conclusion that there is an interactive process. The fact that services are produced through the human medium means that errors are inevitable as employee performance cannot be standardised. The result can thus have major implications for the organisation's profitability and competitive position.

This issue of impact on the company's bottom line is illustrated by viewing the service encounter as a series of trade-offs between the company and the consumer, and encompasses a number of elements.

- The quality of the service and customer satisfaction equals service quality delivered minus service quality expected.
- The value of a service to a consumer equals service quality, both technical and functional, divided by the price and other costs of acquiring the service.

The potential profit lies in providing a service which is of value to the consumer, minus the cost of providing the service. Most managers are aware of these trade-offs, but conventional accounting methods do not take into consideration the way that consumers assess the value of quality services. In short, understanding customer value, quality, and ways of leveraging the value over costs can increase margins by providing the company with an opportunity for raising prices and selling more.

This subject can be further expanded by the topic of zero defects. In taking this approach, the focus is also that continuous improvement in service quality is not a cost but an investment in a customer who will generate more profit on a long-term basis than a one-off sale. The premise is based on research which indicates that the cost of acquiring a new customer is five times higher than retaining an existing customer through providing quality service. Such a conclusion is based on three non-traditional accounting factors:

- Long-term customers will often pay a premium for service quality which they have experienced and liked.
- They provide free advertising through word of mouth.
- Traditional accounting practice does not separate the cost of acquiring a replacement customer.

As suggested, the value of a long-term customer exceeds that of a one-off in net present value terms by a factor of five. To the cost side we may add that poor service quality will lead to bad publicity in the ratio of four to one. Similarly a quality service programme can ensure good service recovery and in general greater loyalty at a relatively small recovery cost in relation to adverse publicity for failure. The essence of these arguments is that in cost-benefit analysis, good service quality increases revenues and reduces long-run costs. Examples of organisations who have benefited from such strategies are numerous and include the Marriott Corporation, Club Méditerranée and McDonald's.

Five gap model

One framework approach to quality assurance within the service industry can be illustrated by consideration of the five gap model. The basis of this framework is that the quality of services is defined by the consumer. The model identifies five areas from the marketer's side of the perception/expectation equation where service quality has to be managed by the provider.

Gap 1: gap between management perceptions and consumer expectations

The proposition is that a gap exists between consumer expectations and management perceptions of those expectations which impact on the consumer's evaluation of the service quality. This aspect essentially examines the premise of the service strategy of the company and how well they understand the consumer's requirements. This approach requires the company to fully understand the nature of the consumer being served and hence the service segment in which they are operating. Without a focused strategy the company will not know who its customers are and thus cannot begin to evaluate their expectations.

Gap 2: gap between management perception and service specification

The proposition is that the gap between the management's perception of consumer expectations and the company's service quality specification will affect the service quality from the consumer's point of view. There exists a potential gap because the service provider emphasises variables such as cost reduction and short-term profit in the preparation of the service specification and omits due consideration of the service quality which is harder to measure and evaluate. The key issue for management is that in attempting to meet or exceed the consumer's expectations the knowledge of the expectations exist but the perceived means do not.

Gap 3: gap between service quality specification and service delivery

The gap between service quality specification and service delivery will affect service quality from the consumer's standpoint. In this instance the company has a quality specification which matches or exceeds the consumer's expectation but the company fails to deliver the service quality. This issue primarily relates to human resource management in the delivery of the service. Good training is paramount to good service recovery and good service recovery can turn angry frustrated customers into long-term loyal ones.

Gap 4: gap between service delivery and external communications

The gap between the actual service delivery and the external communications about the service will affect the service quality perception of the consumer. Essentially since the external communication of the service will influence the expectations of the consumer, the company must be certain not to promise more in its communications than it can deliver in reality. The converse is also true. If a company builds a strategy of service delivery which entails capacity for exceeding customer expectations, then on receipt of the service the customer perception of the service will be high.

Gap 5: gap between expectations and perceptions

The quality that a consumer perceives in a service is a function of the magnitude and direction of the gap between expected service and perceived service. Essentially this is the culmination of the total service delivery, i.e. the technical and functional elements of good quality service will match or exceed consumer expectations.

Attributes of service quality

Having examined the conceptual nature of service quality consideration will now be given to the attributes that have been associated with service quality. Ten categories can be labelled as service quality determinants and these can be listed under five headings.

Tangibles

Tangibles include the physical evidence of the service, i.e. physical facilities, appearance of personnel, tools or equipment used to provide the service, physical representation of the service and other customers in the service facility.

Reliability

Reliability involves consistency of performance and dependability, which means that the company performs a service right the first time. It also means that the company honours what it promises in delivering the right product at the right time. Specifically it means accuracy in billing, keeping records correctly and performing a service at a designated time.

Responsiveness

Responsiveness concerns the willingness or readiness of employees to provide service. It involves timeliness of service, i.e. mailing a transaction slip immediately, calling a customer back quickly and giving prompt service, e.g. setting up appointments.

Assurance

Assurance concerns the knowledge and courtesy of employees and their ability to convey trust and confidence. It involves knowledge and skill of the contact personnel, knowledge and skill of the support staff, explaining the service itself, company reputation, personnel characteristics of the contact personnel, confidentiality, and financial and personal security.

Empathy

Empathy concerns the provision of caring individualised attention to customers, i.e. recognising regular customers, learning the customer's specific requirements and providing individualised or customised service.

The winning service position has two elements which uniquely distinguishes a company from its competition and leads customers to expect slightly less than what the company can actually deliver. The understanding of the priorities that consumers place on the various dimensions of service quality can help the company gain a competitive advantage. Once the standards are established leadership must continue to communicate and reinforce these at every opportunity i.e. at meetings, in the training programmes, through internal marketing and most importantly they must be incorporated in the performance measurement, recruitment and appraisal system of the organisation's human resource management.

ISO 9000 Series

One element of quality assurance is systems and methods and this can be achieved through certification to ISO 9000 (previously BS 5750). The British Standard (BS) scheme was first introduced in 1979. Its purpose was to allow organisations to adopt a single method when assessing the suitability of a supplier's product: in this case **product** is a key word. The continuing scheme was amended in 1987 to conform with the International Standards Organisation (ISO) 9000 series to take account of services as well as products.

In short ISO 9000 series (particularly Part 2) sets out to demonstrate to customers that a company not only can establish, document and maintain an effective multisystem which proves its commitment to quality but also can meet their requirements. In order to have the quality management system accredited or certified it must have been documented and been in operation for six months before assessment takes place. The requirements of defining the quality standard fall on the individual organisations. This effectively means that the company must be able to deliver the quality that it plans to deliver.

The standard was first introduced to target broadly manufacturing industries and therefore to a large extent concentrated on goods rather than their associated or related services. A number of other industry groupings have realised that there are benefits to be derived from the direct demonstration of quality. Consequently they have sought to establish an interpretation of the standard that more closely fits their business.

In the hotel and catering industry in particular, a number of companies, especially those involved in contract catering in one form or another, see the benefits of being able to provide both existing and potential clients with evidence that they can and do provide quality goods and services.

Application to the hospitality industry

The standard, in addition to defining management responsibility in terms of the quality policy, organisation and review, and the documentation of the quality system, includes a number of specifics for the industry:

- In terms of the contract review, are the purchaser's needs specified? Can the supplier meet them? This can apply to all sorts of requests, e.g. for accommodation, meals or a wedding reception.
- Document control looks at a range of things such as approved suppliers lists, dish and raw material specifications.
- Purchasing considers everyone who provides an incoming delivery or service and will include laundry and hygiene services.

Other areas included are kitchens and bars for example, and procedures will have to be in place to ensure the proper use and maintenance of all equipment. Food hygiene regulations will be key in this area. Procedures have to be put in place to test and inspect everything from bedrooms to bar optics. Staff have to know how to deal with every product or service that does not meet specification, how to establish what went wrong, agree timescales in which to put it right and take action to ensure that it does not happen again.

The list is extensive; it takes time, effort and commitment and therefore money to achieve the required standard, even though the company will have its own definition of quality. Many companies are already doing this, so all it takes is some formalisation of the process and perhaps the filling in of a number of missing links. There are a number of clear benefits to third party accreditation through ISO 9000. The two main benefits from the customer's point of view are:

- An independent and external assessment or audit has been made of the quality management system, so the customer can confidently expect a professionally produced product of a high standard.
- Because of the investment made by the company in developing the system it should be consistent in delivering the right product at the right time.

Total quality management (TQM)

Philosophy

The introduction of any service quality management system to the hospitality industry must by definition from the analysis be total and this has provided the impetus towards total quality management (TQM). Quality management systems by themselves will fail unless they are part of a planned process of introduction involving the whole organisation. TQM is not just a system but a state of mind that must become corporate culture if it is to succeed. The emphasis here is that TQM within the hospitality industry must shift the focus of management to satisfying the customers' needs and holds that change is inevitable within the organisation. Characteristics of the TQM system include the understanding that quality is neither a technical function nor a department but a systematic process extending throughout an organisation.

Quality should be the concern of everyone and must be correctly structured within an organisation to create these conditions. The emphasis on improving quality must take place throughout all phases of the business and is not just in the operational side, i.e. marketing design, development, delivery, purchasing and service support. The quality achievement must be externally customer and not internally company driven, and be supported by the appropriate use of technology, quality measurement and control processes.

The sustaining of quality improvements needs to be based on the participation and contribution of the whole workhorse, not just a group of specialists. Organisations must establish clear customer orientated quality management systems, the understanding, ownership and development of which should be vested in everyone concerned. The management system must make it simple for customers to give feedback and quality improvements must close the loop.

Elements of TQM

The philosophy of TQM requires consideration of six major interrelated elements, all of which should be developed together to form an integral whole:

- recognition reward
- education and training
- communication
- attitude and commitment
- systems and methods
- targets and goals.

Recognition reward
Every company operates some form of recognition and reward system, usually consisting

of a bonus for the achievement of financial goals set by management. Rarely is there any form of bonus or recognition for the service staff or if there is a financial reward, the amounts involved are so small that they fail to be an incentive. Furthermore typically existing recognition and reward systems fail to support improvement in methods of working or quality; they address only results. In other words they do not encourage staff to improve how they do their task. It is important to remember that recognition and reward systems do not have to be financially based to be effective: it can be as simple as a pat on the back, a staff employee of the month award or a holiday, but it must be designed to reflect the staff and the role at which it is targeted.

Education and training

Although many companies believe that education and training is vital for the development of the business there are many cases where the correct training for the individual is not carried out. Managers are often assumed to have the full qualifications for the job and will look after their own development. Also because of the pressure of work, courses are often cancelled or managers are unable to attend. Usually a TQM programme will include a broad programme of education aimed at improving the basic management skills, the development of managers and staff to improve personal performance and provide knowledge and understanding of the techniques used for service improvement. In the main, the skills are linked with workplace skills, not external formal qualifications. Investment in the people within the organisation is then often safer than may otherwise be the case. The objective is that through TQM all the people in the business can be given the foundations for success upon which their future in the company depends.

Communication

In hospitality organisational cultures, communication with staff and guests is vital but so often it is on a need-to-know philosophy with members of staff being asked to contribute to the overall effort without being told why or shown the results. Also sideways communication between departments fails so the guest is left out in the cold, not getting what was requested. In most organisations the official channels of communication are downward through the company hierarchy. In a TQM-orientated company, vertical communication (both up and down) and horizontal communication flow through direct and simple official channels. Managers should think about encouraging their staff to communicate with them, as true communication can exist only on a face-to-face basis. Usually a TQM programme contains elements designed to break down the physical and personal barriers to communication, and to open new channels.

Attitude and commitment

It is the development of a working environment in which every manager and staff member feels that they are on the same side that creates improved results. Management must demonstrate its own commitment by actually practising what it has preached and encouraging the desire for overall continual improvement. Every member of the management and staff should develop the attitude of constantly seeking to improve what they are doing. This change in attitude comes from education, e.g. an application of systems and methods which support rather than stifle innovation.

Systems and methods

Corporate improvement can occur only if the processes used to achieve it are well documented, so that the improvements are recognised and remain consistent. Causes of poor performance should be systematically identified, analysed and eliminated. The methodology of achieving this is often called the quality system and maybe certification to ISO 9000 can be one of the goals within the TQM programme. If developed incorrectly and independently systems and methods document can become large and complex, rarely used and can have a negative effect on people and profits. If built properly into a quality management programme, it can form the building blocks for other elements of the system.

Targets and goals

Once the company has clearly defined objectives and a strategy for their achievement these need to be continually reviewed or it will eventually stagnate and drift out of control. Equally unless the people in the hotel know where the company is going they will all be pushing in different directions. It is important to remember that if the targets are so great that management and staff lose sight of them, they will become demotivated. Realistic targets should be set against realistic timescales.

If TQM is properly implemented it can lead to an extraordinary return on capital, providing a framework for ongoing growth and continual quality improvement; in some instances (most recently the Japanese) it can lead to market domination. If TQM is to be properly implemented and for the company to gain maximum benefit, there must be commitment from senior management. Furthermore a TQM programme should be tailored to the company's style and culture. There are no simple and effective off-the-shelf solutions.

Summary

The purpose of this chapter has been to identify three key themes which will be of increasing importance to the hospitality industry. In terms of both national and international companies the three topics of environmental issues, technology (especially CRS) and quality assurance will help determine the success of companies over the next few years.

Further reading

- Aaronovitch D. (1996) 'Cheeky Charlie: his hotels are "sensitive" and hugely expensive; ours are "eyesores"', *The Independent* 14 November p. 12.
- Abrahams G. (1990) 'EC airs its reservations over booking systems', *Financial Times* 5 October.
- Anon. (1989) 'How Sam the Hammer could nail the airlines', *Business Week* 26 June: 126.
- Archdale G. (1990) 'Computer reservation systems – the international scene', *Insights* November: D18–D24.
- Bertelsen J. (1990) 'Asian airlines fret over new treat: US computer reservation systems', *Wall Street Journal* 22 January: B7A.
- Boberg K.B. and Collision F.M. (1985) 'Computer reservations systems and airline competition', *Tourism Management* 6(3): 174–83.
- Boerr H. (1992) 'Hotels check out green credentials', *Financial Times* 3 June.
- Boo E. (1992) *Ecotourism: The Potentials and Pitfalls* (2 vols), Washington, DC: World Wildlife Fund.
- Braham B. (1988) *Computer Systems in the Hotel and Catering Industry*, London: Cassell.
- Bramwell B. and Lane B. (1993) 'Sustainable tourism: an evolving global approach', *Journal of Sustainable Tourism* 1: 1–5.
- BRECSU (1996a) *Energy Efficiency in the Catering and Hospitality Industry – Bibliography*

and Commentary for Lecturers and Students (2 vols), London: DoE Energy Efficiency Best Practice programme.

● BRECSU (1996b) *The Munich Park Hilton Hotel*, Case Study 296, London: DoE Energy Efficiency Best Practice programme.

● British Standards Institute (1992) 'BS 7750 published', *Environmental News*, British Standards Institute, June: 1.

● Buhalis D. and Fletcher J. (1992) 'Environmental impacts on tourist destinations: an economic analysis', *International Conference on Tourism and the Environment Proceedings*, Mytilini, Greece.

● Butler R. (1992) 'Alternative tourism: the thin edge of the wedge', in V.L. Smith and W.R. Eadington (eds) *Tourism Alternatives: Potentials and Problems in the Development of Tourism*, Chichester: John Wiley, pp. 31–46.

● Copeland D.G. (1990) 'So you want to build the next SABRE?', *Business Quarterly* 55(3): 56–60.

● D'Aquino N. (1992a) 'The E.C.'s green guru, Carlo Ripa di Meana', *Europe* June: 6–7.

● D'Aquino N. (1992b) 'The new green Europe', *Europe* June: 8–10.

● Davis K. (1973) 'The case for and against business assumption of social responsibilities', *Academy of Management Journal* 16: 312–22.

● De Kardt E. (1992) 'Making the alternative sustainable: lessons from development for tourism', in V.L. Smith and W.R. Eadington (eds) *Tourism Alternatives: Potentials and Problems in the Development of Tourism*, Chichester: John Wiley, pp. 47–75.

● Dowling R.K. (1992) 'Tourism and environmental integration: the journey from idealism to realism', in C. Cooper and A. Lockwood (eds) *Progress in Tourism Recreation and Hospitality Management*, vol. 4, London: Belhaven Press.

● Eadington W.R. and Smith V.L. (1992) 'Introduction: the emergence of alternative forms of tourism', in V.L. Smith and W.R. Eadington (eds) *Tourism Alternatives: Potentials and Problems in the Development of Tourism*, Chichester: John Wiley, pp. 1–12.

● Eber S. (1992) *Beyond the Green Horizon: Principles for Sustainable Tourism*, discussion paper commissioned from Tourism Concern by WWF UK, Godalming: WWF UK.

● Farrell B.H. (1995) 'Sustainable tourism is ecotourism: ecotourism is sustainable tourism?' *TRINET* 21 September.

● Farrell B.H. and Runyan D. (1991) 'Ecology and tourism', *Annals of Tourism Research* 18(1): 26–40.

● Feldman J. (1987) 'Regional airlines in the USA', *Travel and Tourism Analyst* May: 15–18.

● Forte J. (1992) 'Reaping a green dividend', *Voice of the British Hospitality Association* 1(6): 10–11.

● Friedman M. (1989) 'The social responsibility of business is to increase profits', *New York Times Magazine* 13 September: 30.

● Gamble P.R. (1991) 'Developing effective computer systems for tourism', in S. Medlik (ed.) *Managing Tourism*, London: Butterworth Heinemann.

● Gold H. (1985) 'Sabre dancing', *Forbes* 30 December: 88.

● Goodall B. (1992) 'Environmental auditing for tourism', in C.P. Cooper and A. Lockwood (eds) *Progress in Tourism: Recreation and Hospitality Management*, vol. 4, London: Belhaven Press, pp. 60–74.

● Goodwin N. (1989) 'Global connections', *Travel Weekly's Focus on Automation* 7 September: 7.

● Green D. (1992) 'Airline ticket shops bridge the Atlantic', *Financial Times* 9 March.

● Hewson D. (1993) 'Galileo will get you there', *Sunday Times Business Travel* 21 November.

- Hunt C. and Auster E. (1990) 'Proactive environmental management: avoiding the toxic trap', *Sloan Management Review* Winter: 7–17.
- Hunter C. and Green H. (1995) 'Introduction', in C. Hunter and H. Green (eds) *Tourism and the Environment: A Sustainable Relationship?*, London: Routledge, pp. 1–6.
- Hunter C. and Green H. (1995) 'The environmental impacts of tourism', in C. Hunter and H. Green (eds) *Tourism and the Environment: A Sustainable Relationship?*, London: Routledge, pp. 10–51.
- IHA, IHEI & UNEP (1995) *Environmental Action Pack for Hotels*, London.
- Inskeep E. (1991) *Tourism Planning: An Integrated and Sustainable Development Approach*, New York: Van Nostrand.
- Iwand, W.M. (1995) 'Better environment – better business', *Friends of the Earth Seminar*, 24 November, North London University, London.
- Jordan B. (1989) 'Amadeus gains capacity', *Airline Executive* October: 6.
- Knowles T. and Guerrier Y. (1993) Industry responses to environmental issues – examples from the hotel catering and retail industries, Values in the Environment Conference, University of Surrey, September, Conference Proceedings.
- Knowles T., Macmillan S. and Palmer J. (1997) Environmental Initiatives in the UK; a survey of London hotels, Environmental Matters Conference, Glasgow Caledonian University, 29 April–2 May, Conference Proceedings.
- Knowles T., Macmillan S. and Palmer J. (1998) Environmental Initiatives: Responses from a Tourism Sector, Environment Papers Series Vol. 1 No. 1, Glasgow Caledonian University, Glasgow.
- Knowles T., Macmillan S., Palmer J. and Graboswki P., (1999) Environmental Initiatives: reponse from the London Hotel sector, Progress in Tourism and Hospitality Research, John Wiley (forthcoming).
- Kraft K. (1991) 'The relative importance of social responsibility in determining organisational effectiveness: managers from two service industries', *Journal of Business Ethics* 10: 485–91.
- Krippendorf J. (1991) 'Towards new tourism policies' in S. Medlik (ed.) *Managing Tourism*, London: Butterworth Heinemann.
- Lanfant M.F. and Graburn N.H.H. (1992) 'International tourism reconsidered: the principle of the alternative', in V.L. Smith and W. R. Eadington (eds) *Tourism Alternatives: Potentials and Problems in the Development of Tourism*, Chichester: John Wiley, pp. 88–112.
- Lean G., Hinrichsen D. and Markham A. (1990) *WWF Atlas of the Environment*, London: Arrow Books.
- Lee N. (1991) 'Abacus', *PATA Destination Database Conference*, Singapore.
- Lindsey P. (1992) 'CRS supply and demand', *Tourism Management* March.
- Lockwood A. (1993) 'Quality management in hotels', in S.F. Witt and L. Montinho (eds) *Tourism Marketing and Management Handbook*, 2nd edn, London: Prentice Hall.
- Lockwood A. *et al.* (1992) 'Developing and maintaining a strategy for service quality' in R. Teare and M. Olsen (eds) *International Hospitality Management: Corporate Strategy in Practice*, London: Pitman.
- Lyle C. (1988) 'Computer-age in the international airline industry', *Journal of Air, Law and Commerce* 54(1): 162.
- Markillie P. (1993) 'Survey of airlines (6): by the seats of their pants – the handfull of dollars will make or break the industry', *Economist* 327 (12 June).
- Mathieson A. and Wall G. (1987) *Tourism: Economic, Physical and Social Impacts*, London: Longman.
- McDermid K. (1993) 'Going green', *Hospitality* 137: 14–18.

- McGuffie J. (1990) *CRS Development and the Hotel Sector – Parts I and II in Travel and Tourism Analyst no. 1*, London: Economist Intelligence Unit.
- Mitchell T. and Scott W. (1990) 'America's problems and needed reforms: confronting the ethic of personal advantage', *Academy of Management Executive* 4(3): 23–35.
- Mori T. (1992) *Tokyo Business Today* 60(6): 41–2.
- Mowforth M. (1995) 'Focused workshops: environmental issues', *Managing Tourism: Education and Regulation for Sustainability Symposium*, 16 November, Commonwealth Institute, London.
- Nash, D. (1979) 'The rise and fall of an aristocratic tourist culture – Nice, 1763–1936', *Annals of Tourism Research* 6: 61–75.
- Newman J. and Breeden K. (1992) 'Managing in the environmental era: lessons from environmental leaders', *Columbian Journal of World Business* Fall/Winter: 210–21.
- O'Brien K. (1993) 'The western European business travel market 1993–1997', *Financial Times Business Information* pp. 29–42.
- Odell M. (1993) 'Rules and reservations', *Airline Business* August: 34–7.
- O'Reilly M.A. (1986) 'Tourism carrying capacity: concept and issues', *Tourism Management* 7(4): 254–8.
- Pearce D.G. (1992) 'Alternative tourism: concepts, classifications, and questions', in V.L. Smith and W.R. Eadington (eds) *Tourism Alternatives: Potentials and Problems in the Development of Tourism*, Chichester: John Wiley, pp. 15–30.
- Pigram J. (1992) 'Alternative tourism: tourism and sustainable resource management', in V.L. Smith and W.R. Eadington (eds) *Tourism Alternatives: Potentials and Problems in the Development of Tourism*, Chichester: John Wiley, 76–87.
- Porritt J. (1995) 'Talk on environmental issues', *Managing Tourism: Education and Regulation for Sustainability Symposium*, 16 November, Commonwealth Institute, London.
- Prince Charles (1996) 'How tourism destroys the world's beauty', *Green Hotelier*, International Hotels Environment Initiative (IHEI), London. Cited in N. Schoon (1996) 'Is there such a thing as a green holiday?', *The Independent* 14 November, p. 3.
- Proctor P. (1988) 'House members call for tighter regulations of reservations systems', *Aviation Week and Space Technology* 19 September: 123.
- Rambo A.T., Gillogly K. and Hutterer K.L. (eds) (1988) *Ethnic Diversity and the Control of Natural Resources in Southeast Asia* (Michigan Papers on South and Southeast Asia, no. 32), Center for South and Southeast Asian Studies, University of Michigan, Ann Arbor, MI.
- Romeril M. (1994) 'Alternative tourism: the real tourism alternative?', in C.P. Cooper and A. Lockwood (eds) *Progress in Tourism, Recreation and Hospitality Management*, vol. 6, Chichester: John Wiley, pp. 22–9.
- Savignac A. (1992) Address by the Secretary General of the World Tourism Organisation to the United Nation Conference on Environment and Development, 4 June, Rio de Janeiro, Brazil.
- Shaw G. and Williams A. (1992) 'Tourism, development and the environment: the eternal triangle', in C.P. Cooper and A. Lockwood (eds) *Progress in Tourism, Recreation and Hospitality Management*, vol. 4, London: Belhaven Press, pp. 47–59.
- Sussmann S. (1992) 'Destination management systems: the challenge for the 1990s' in C. Cooper and A. Lockwood (eds) *Progress in Tourism Recreation and Hospitality Management*, vol. 4, London: Belhaven Press.
- Truitt J.L., Teye V.B. and Farris M.T. (1991) 'The role of computer reservations systems', *Tourism Management* March: 21–36.
- Twist W. (1996) *Environmental Management for Hotels: The Industry Guide to Best Practice*, 2nd edn, London: Macmillan.

- Vyarkarnam S. (1992) 'Social responsibility: what do leading companies do?', *Long Range Planning* 25(5): 59–67.
- Wardell D. (1987) 'Airline reservations systems in the USA', *Travel and Tourism Analyst* January: 45–56.
- Wheeler B. (1994) 'Ecotourism: a ruse by another name', in C.P. Cooper and A. Lockwood (eds) *Progress in Tourism, Recreation and Hospitality Management*, vol. 6, Chichester: John Wiley, pp. 3–11.
- Wild C. (1994) 'Issues in ecotourism', in C.P. Cooper and A. Lockwood (eds) *Progress in Tourism, Recreation and Hospitality Management*, vol. 6, Chichester: John Wiley, pp. 12–21.
- Wood D. (1991) 'Corporate social performance revisited', *Academy of Management Review* 16(4): 691–718.
- WTO (1992a) 'Tourism and environment', *WTO News* 6 (June): 2.
- WTO (1992b) 'Environment-friendly tourism products: a WTO survey of members of the Association of British Travel Agents (ABTA)', *WTO News* 6 (June): 6–7.
- WTO (1995) *Sustainable Tourism Development*, background paper by WTO Secretariat, WTO Asian Tourism Conference, Technical Session, 13 January, Islamabad, Pakistan.

Index